MEDIEVAL V

'Skoda's overview of the medieval theory and norms with regard to aggression and its punishment, on the one hand, and the concrete violations of these customs and the penalties imposed upon the perpetrators, on the other, is one of the most complete summaries of the use of violence in medieval France available. It rightly stresses the fact that the vengeful acts of citizens were not meaningless or aberrant irregularities, but phenomena at the heart of urban life.'

Jelle Haemers, *The American Historical Review*

'Skoda must be applauded for the strength and coverage of her analysis of gender and medieval violence and her successful approach to integrating archival and literary sources.'

Zrinka Stahuljak, *French Studies*

'Skoda not only fills an important lacuna but also articulates, in a highly nuanced manner, how violence functioned as a popular form of communication and was integral to premodern communities' sense of self. Interdisciplinarity was a prerequisite for this book, and Skoda's is an accomplished one. She has gone where earlier social and criminal historians were reluctant to venture . . . The result is a thought-provoking cultural history of premodern and mainly urban violence that will be read with great profit, especially by social and urban historians, and by students of violence in general.'

Guy Geltner, *Tijdschrift voor Geschiedenis*

Hannah Skoda is Tutorial Fellow in History at St John's College, Oxford. She has published on the subject of concepts of the law in medieval France, co-editing an interdisciplinary volume on legalism with the anthropologist, Paul Dresch, and she is currently embarking on research into the misbehaviour of students in fifteenth-century Oxford, Paris and Heidelberg. Other publications have ranged from Dante to the experience of disability in the Middle Ages. She is particularly interested in the relationship between constructions of deviance, and the ways in which those thus labelled react to these stereotypes.

OXFORD HISTORICAL MONOGRAPHS

Medieval Violence

Physical Brutality in Northern France, 1270–1330

HANNAH SKODA

OXFORD
UNIVERSITY PRESS

OXFORD
UNIVERSITY PRESS

Great Clarendon Street, Oxford, OX2 6DP,
United Kingdom

Oxford University Press is a department of the University of Oxford.
It furthers the University's objective of excellence in research, scholarship,
and education by publishing worldwide. Oxford is a registered trade mark of
Oxford University Press in the UK and in certain other countries

First published 2013
First published in paperback 2015

Published in the United States of America by Oxford University Press
198 Madison Avenue, New York, NY 10016, United States of America

British Library Cataloguing in Publication Data
Data available

Library of Congress Cataloging in Publication Data
Data available

ISBN 978–0–19–967083–3 (Hbk.)
ISBN 978–0–19–873787–2 (Pbk.)

For all victims of violence and for those who grow up believing violence to be acceptable or inevitable.

Contents

Preface

This book aims to explore the meanings, functions, and place of violence in northern French society before the outbreak of the Hundred Years' War. It begins from the premise that the very presence of violence is socially contingent, and explores the ways in which it was used and the responses it provoked. A number of methodological approaches are used, in part suggested by the nature of the surviving evidence: from legal material, legislative documents, letters, and sermons, to the literary offerings of poets and early vernacular playwrights. Historiographical interest in violence has risen dramatically in recent years, and is often focused upon the relationship between violence and the development of states. This book focuses not upon military or judicial violence, but upon the quotidian brawls and brutality which, in many ways, made up the fabric of everyday life. It aims to show just how 'normal' violence could become, whilst at the same time provoking horror and outrage. And it aims not to lose sight of the very real suffering engendered by these actions. Studying violence is an important counterpoint to an often romanticized view of the period, but equally a closer look reveals that a gloomy portrait of a brutal and incessantly cruel Middle Ages is also misleading: violence provoked ambivalent and troubled reactions, and was never passed over in silence.

The book aims at a broad readership. It is hoped that those interested in the France of the later Middle Ages will find something of interest or at least provocation here, but it is also hoped that those studying constructions of deviance from an interdisciplinary perspective will respond to some of the ideas and that their relevance may extend beyond northern France 1270–1330.

Many people have been more than generous with their time and comments on this work. Unfortunately I cannot name them all here, but none have been forgotten. In particular though, I would like to acknowledge the ever-kind support and inspirational guidance of my D.Phil. supervisors, Dr Malcolm Vale and Dr Gervase Rosser, and of Dr Matthew Kempshall. My D.Phil. examiners Professor David D'Avray and Dr Jean Dunbabin provided crucial criticism and comment. Thanks to Sara Gordon for invaluable help with indexing, and to my friends and colleagues for such generous-spirited reading of drafts. More widely, members of the History Faculty at Oxford have been always ready to offer ideas and encouragement, notably Professor Chris Wickham and Dr Patrick

Lantschner. Versions of chapters of this book have been presented at numerous seminars, and the comments received there have all helped to develop lines of research: I would particularly like to thank those who commented at the Oxford Medieval History Seminar, the Oxford Late Medieval History Seminar, the Oxford Medieval French Seminar, the Seminar in Medieval History at the Institute of Historical Research, the Oxford Medieval Church and Culture Seminar, and all who attended my presentations at various conferences. Very special thanks go to Dr John Watts for his infinite patience, very careful reading, and wonderfully insightful comments: his intellectual generosity has been very inspiring.

Much of the material here is bound to be provocative, and I am afraid that there must remain many mistakes: these are clearly all my own!

The book has been made possible by generous support during my D.Phil. from the AHRC, Wadham College, Oxford History Faculty, and Zaharoff Research Fund. Subsequently, a Junior Research Fellowship at Merton College, Oxford, and research support at my current college, St John's, have provided stimulating opportunities to continue work on this.

Finally, I would like to thank my lovely husband, son, parents, grandmother, brother, wider family (particularly Richard, Nick and Malcolm), and friends, without all of whom my life would be immeasurably poorer. You are all a constant inspiration.

List of Illustrations

Abbreviations

ADPC	Archives départementales du Pas-de-Calais, Arras
ADN	Archives départementales du Nord, Lille
AMA	Archives Municipales d'Abbeville
AN	Archives Nationales, Paris
Beaumanoir	Philippe de Beaumanoir, *Coutumes du Beauvaisis*, ed. A. Salmon, 3 vols. (Paris, 1899, repr. 1970)
BL	British Library
BN	Bibliothèque Nationale
Boutaric, *Actes*	E. Boutaric (ed.), *Actes du Parlement de Paris, 1254–1328*, 2 vols. (Paris, 1863–7)
CUP	H. Denifle and E. Châtelain (eds.), *Chartularium Universitatis Parisiensis*, 4 vols. (Paris, 1889–97)
Delmaire	B. Delmaire, *Le Compte Général d'Artois pour 1303–1304* (Brussels, 1977)
Etablissements	P. Viollet (ed.), *Les Etablissements de Saint Louis*, 4 vols. (Paris, 1881–6)
Furgeot and Dillay, *Actes*	H. Furgeot and Dillay, M. (eds.), *Actes du Parlement de Paris: Deuxième série de l'an 1328 à l'an 1350. Jugés (lettres, arrêts, jugés)*, 3 vols. (Paris, 1920–75)
NRCF	N. van den Boogaard and W. Noomen (eds.), *Nouveau recueil complet des fabliaux*, 10 vols. (Assen, 1983–96)
Olim	A. Beugnot (ed.), *Les Olim, ou Registres des arrêts rendus par la cour du roi*, 3 vols. (Paris, 1839–48)
Ordonnances	E. de Laurières (ed.), *Ordonnances des Rois de France*, 22 vols. (Paris, 1849)
RHGF	*Recueil des historiens des Gaules et de la France*, 24 vols (Paris, 1738–1904)
RR	A. Strubel (ed.), *Le Roman de Renart* (Paris, 1999)
Tanon	L. Tanon, *Histoire des justices des anciennes églises et communautés monastiques de Paris* (Paris, 1883)

THEMA *Thesaurus Exemplorum Medii Aevii* at http://gahom.ehess.fr/thema/index.php

Names are cited in the form and language in which they appear in the documents (though the 's' for *cas sujet* has been removed in the interests of clarity, except in cases where such an 's' survives in the modern form of the name—e.g. Gilles).

Introduction

> Je ne suis pas marry que nous remerquons l'horreur barbaresque qu'il y a en une telle action, mais ouy bien dequoy jugeans à point de leurs fautes, nous soyons si aveugles aux nostres.[1]

Our vision of the Middle Ages is haunted by the spectre of extreme violence, and there is a smugly self-congratulatory tinge to modern characterizations of this brutal and cruel period.[2] But the image needs revisiting. Partly because violence continues, in multiple ways, to be common. And partly because it is a label applied to the medieval period often thoughtlessly. Attitudes towards violence in the Middle Ages were, in fact, sophisticated, and interacted in complex ways with the actual perpetration of violence which forms the subject of this book: I aim to uncover the multiple levels of meaning behind such gestures and yet the disapproval and even shock which they engendered.

Physical brutality and the instrumentalization of its threat, still mesmerize collective mentalities. Moreover, the frightening connotations of cruelty are often also insidiously used to label and marginalize unwanted groups.[3] It is all too easy to dismiss violence as a merely dysfunctional product of deviant behaviour, wilfully turning a blind eye to its centrality in power structures and even in quotidian social relations. Paradoxically at once arresting and fascinating, and yet elusive in meaning and significance, violence is not culturally aberrant, but embedded in the very frameworks of meaning promoted by society itself. This is not to claim

[1] 'I am not averse to us noticing the barbaric horror of such an action, but rather to us judging their faults so harshly whilst blind to our own': Michel de Montaigne, 'Des Cannibales', from *Les Essais*, I. xxx. 216, ed. J. Balsamo, M. Magnien, and C. Magnien-Simonin (Paris, 2007).

[2] e.g. E. Gibbon, *The Decline and Fall of the Roman Empire*, 5 vols. (London, new edn. 1994), iii. 1068: 'I have described the triumph of barbarism and religion'.

[3] Tennenhouse distinguishes two kinds of violence 'that which is "out there" in the world, as opposed to that which is exercised through words upon things in the world, often by attributing violence to them': N. Armstrong and L. Tennenhouse (eds.), *The Violence of Representation: Literature and the History of Violence* (London, 1989), 9.

that it is unchanging, but contingent upon the structures of everyday life and the shifting norms of societies. We need to ask ourselves why violence provokes such enduring fascination alongside such persistent eagerness by society to abnegate responsibility for it.

At first sight, fourteenth-century sources seem to confirm the brutality of the Middle Ages. For example, in Dante Alighieri's masterly exposition of this life and the afterlife in the *Inferno*, violence is omnipresent and a structuring principle: he shows physical brutality to be systemic, complex, and adaptive.[4] Dante stands above his time, but was also rooted in its historical realities and attitudes, underlining the centrality of violence in thirteenth- and fourteenth-century society. It both formed an integral part of social relations and provoked broader discussion. But Dante, while placing violence at centre-stage, also expressed heartfelt condemnation of its excesses and cruelty. And in this respect, he was perhaps even more typical of his time. Violence was not accepted as inevitable or its presence straightforwardly condoned. Rather, the period is characterized by extremely nuanced attitudes towards violence, and by a deep-rooted ambivalence concerning its role. This ambivalence questioned the functions of violence and the relationship between violence and the law; challenged its social centrality and hesitated regarding the interpersonal or collective implications of physical brutality. This was an age where people thought carefully and problematically about violence and its implications. The aim of this book, then, is to consider the complexity of those attitudes, as revealed in discussions about, and representations of, physical violence, as well as to examine the perpetration of violent acts in late thirteenth- and early fourteenth-century Paris and Artois.

1. WHAT WAS VIOLENCE?

The term 'violence' encompasses an enormous range of phenomena, from subtle structural exclusion or moulding of particular groups, to verbal manipulation, to physical damage done by one human being to another. It is this latter sense which is the subject of study here, with particular focus on violence by the populace, or 'popular violence', violence which was widely characterized as illegitimate, and is still often considered to represent merely the irrational, excessive display of physical force.[5] This is

[4] Dante Alighieri, *Inferno*, in *Commedia*, ed. and tr. J. Sinclair, 3 vols. (Oxford, new edn. 1981), i.

[5] On definitions of 'popular', see A. Gurevich, *Medieval Popular Culture* (Cambridge, 1990), 1–35, 224.

indeed the sense of the Old French term 'violence': physical gestures lacking officially instituted systematic frameworks of authority and meaning, condemned by legal processes and the rhetoric of authorities.[6] Chivalric violence, military exploits, judicial punishment, and religious persecution, perpetrated as they were by hegemonic groups, will not be explicitly discussed. Yet although these phenomena were not encompassed by the medieval French 'violence', they were part of a common phenomenon of physical brutality and contributed to the same discursive framework: the borrowing of such gestures by perpetrators of illicit violence and the deliberate resonances evoked by popular brawlers or urban rebels was a powerful way of gaining attention. And whilst nobles also carried out illicit brutality of staggering cruelty, it is the blows struck by the ordinary townsmen and women and subaltern rural dwellers (and their rich parallels with noble violence) which capture our attention here.

This book examines the functions and motivations of the supposedly ubiquitous interpersonal violence of the late thirteenth and early fourteenth centuries. Violence was both a means of spectacular communication, and a way of achieving concrete goals: both performing and performative. Its mechanisms were rooted in cultural paradigms which shaped its perpetration, and its motivations were deeply embedded in socio-cultural context, even when overlaid with economic needs. This is not to deny that physical brutality could be perpetrated by psychopathic individuals without further motivation, but it *is* to claim that even when enraged, or drunk, or over-excited, the perpetrators of interpersonal violence were, even at an unconscious level, influenced by the norms of their society. The relationship between the functions of violence, and attitudes towards it, was, of course, reciprocal: contemporary responses to violence, as expressed in sermons, popular literature, oral accounts, moral treatises, and legal discourse were shaped by the practice of violence, but also influenced its perpetration, and demand study in their own right if we wish to understand the role of violence in this society. Indeed, the more fundamental question of definition lies at the heart of medieval ambivalence about physical violence: the term 'violentia' referred to disordering brutality, and the term 'vis' tended to indicate the physical force deemed to reinforce social order. However the distinction was not only unclear, but the subject of repeated debate, rendering this a particularly fruitful period for exploring the multiple overlapping roles of violence, its multifaceted appearances in society, and its persistence.

[6] *Le Robert Dictionnaire historique de la langue française*, 2 vols. (Paris, 1992), ii. 2261. NB: This book will not, therefore, focus upon military or judicial violence, though motifs drawn from these spheres are shown to have influenced other manifestations of violence.

This book considers a hitherto understudied period of interpersonal violence in northern France, and examines, one by one, a range of kinds of popular violence rarely studied together despite their overlaps and resonances: street violence; violence in the tavern; student violence; urban rebellions; and domestic violence. Street violence comprised interpersonal brawls, vengeance killings and public humiliation, whereas violence in the tavern was more self-consciously frivolous. Students were notoriously brutal, but their deviance was as much a label applied to them as it was a reality, and one of which they were acutely aware. The laughter which often accompanied tavern brawls and student fights was, perhaps surprisingly, still evident in the playfulness of many urban uprisings, although the political goal of this type of violence was much more clearly articulated. And whilst the ordering function of violence may have been most prominent in the perpetration of violence against one's wife, it was here in the home that ambivalence about the justifiability of violence seems to have caused the most anxiety. Setting these forms of violence side-by-side deepens our interpretive insights into the complexities and self-referentiality of the medieval use of physical brutality. These types are visibly distinguished and shaped by considerations of space, from the intimate setting of the home to the public and politically loaded arena of the town square. But they also indicate the wide range of contemporary thinking and ambivalence surrounding the subject and evoke provocative issues of communication, publicity, identity, stereotypes and expectations, and moral, political, and legal justifiability.[7] It is by uncovering the many layers of medieval ambivalence concerning interpersonal violence—its interpersonal or collective implications; its ordering or disordering effects; its fluid relationship with the law—that we can hope to rectify both stereotypical demonizations of the Middle Ages, and determinist claims about the inescapable rootedness of violence in human nature.

2. SCHOLARLY APPROACHES TO VIOLENCE

Discussion of violence can hardly be confined to a single paradigm: rather the subject invites a multiplicity of perspectives. Fundamentally, scholars from various different disciplines have been fascinated by the question of why mankind is so prone to physical violence: whether it is an intrinsic

[7] 'Space' here is used in the sense elaborated by H. Lefèbvre, *Writings on Cities*, tr. and ed. E. Kofman and E. Lebas (Oxford, 1996), 100–3: space both creates and is created by social interchange; it is not a vacuum waiting to be filled, but a meaningful concept actively constructed and produced by the societies who inhabit it.

element of life, a defining feature of our humanity, the remnants of the attempt to establish human society in the face of the divine, or an integral feature of power.[8] But, whilst violence is clearly not just a social construct, nor is it merely an instinctive and innate human characteristic. Studying violence requires a close reading of the gestures used and awareness that violence is a kind of exchange or transaction between perpetrator, victim, and spectator; more fundamentally, violence itself is a subjective concept, readily used as a derogatory label in the exercise of power.[9] Violence has interested philosophers, social scientists, and historians alike, and the insights afforded by a range of disciplines have profoundly nuanced understandings of the role of violence in society as integral to fluid social relationships.[10]

Physical force is certainly an ever-present building block of social and political structures, and provides a visible or more insidious embodiment of hierarchies and exclusions; most notably, violence has been posited as a defining feature of the emergent state.[11] Echoing medieval ambivalence about violence, scholars searching for the function of violence have repeatedly encountered the problem of the tension between violence as ordering and disordering, used to reinforce hierarchies, but equally capable of subverting them.[12] And violence can be expressive or instrumental, symbolic or practical, emotional or strategic, or more often, but more problematically, all at once.[13] Violent gestures are driven by individual emotion and social concern, and by the confluence of the two.[14]

[8] K. Lorenz, *On Aggression* (London, 1967); R. Girard, *La Violence et le sacré* (Paris, 1972); W. Burkert, *Homo Necans*, tr. P. Bing (Berkeley, Calif., 1983); W. Sofsky, *Violence: Terrorism, Genocide, War*, tr. A. Bell (London, 2003).

[9] D. Riches, 'The Phenomenon of Violence', in D. Riches (ed.), *The Anthropology of Violence* (Oxford, 1986), 8, 11.

[10] One of the most important texts in this respect is Y. Castan on 18th-cent. Languedoc: *Honnêté et relations sociales en Languedoc* (Paris, 1974). Such has been the basis of anthropological attempts to typologize violence: e.g. J. Black-Michaud, *Cohesive Force: Feud in the Mediterranean and the Middle East* (Oxford, 1975), particularly 1–32.

[11] e.g. M. Weber, *Economy and Society*, tr. G. Roth and C. Wittich (New York, 1968); P. Ricoeur, *État et violence: Troisième conference annuelle du foyer John Knox* (Geneva, 1957). Hannah Arendt, though, famously questioned the assumption that violence straightforwardly produces power: *On Violence* (New York, 1970). The relationship between violence and the law was explored by Walter Benjamin ('Zur Kritik der Gewalt', *Archiv für Sozialwissenschaft und Sozialpolitik*, 47 (1920/1), 809–32), and the notion that law could ever disassociate itself from the practice of violence, controversially, by Jacques Derrida (*Force de loi*, Paris, 1994).

[12] e.g. P. Stewart and A. Strathern, *Violence: Theory and Ethnography* (London, 2002), 1.

[13] Ibid. 6–7, 12; B. Schmidt and I. Schröder (eds.), *Anthropology of Violence and Conflict* (London, 2001), 8–10.

[14] Stewart and Strathern, *Violence*, 108–12.

The value and mechanisms of symbolic action are highlighted in the explorations of cultural anthropology, with attention paid to a careful balance of function and dysfunction.[15] Such models can have misleadingly static implications, and the post-structuralist emphasis on 'process' is salutary. In particular, Pierre Bourdieu's notion of 'habitus' shifts attention to the processual, adaptive quality of interpretative frameworks of violent social action in practice.[16] Violence as process is as much about representation and mediation as it is about the actual gestures involved, and the representation of violence depends most strikingly upon its definition by those with the power to delineate it.[17]

Although violence is notoriously difficult to historicize (principally because of the shifting nature of the source material), attempts to demonstrate its contingent nature have been obliged to try.[18] The most straightforward response to this question has been to seek long-term trends in the decline of violence; more subtly, some historians have focused on its changing features and societal functions, and repression or instrumentalization either by nascent states, or through subtler shifting psychological structures.[19] Medievalists have been amongst the first to critique these teleological accounts, sometimes via the careful use of statistical evidence, sometimes via close attention to the complex cultural resonances of

[15] e.g. V. Turner, *Dramas, Fields and Metaphors: Symbolic Action in Human Society* (Ithaca, NY, 1974); C. Geertz, *The Interpretation of Cultures* (New York, 1973).

[16] P. Bourdieu, *Language and Symbolic Power*, tr. G. Raymond (Cambridge, 1991), 50–3.

[17] See F. Brookman, *Understanding Homicide* (London, 2005), 2.

[18] See e.g. M. Braun and C. Herbereichs, 'Einleitung' in Braun and Herbereichs (eds.), *Gewalt im Mittelalter: Realitäten—Imaginationen* (Munich, 2005), 7–39; M. Kintzinger and J. Rogge, 'Einleitung', in Kintzinger and Rogge (eds.), *Königliche Gewalt—Gewalt gegen Könige* (Berlin, 2004), 1–8.

[19] N. Elias, *The Civilising Process*, tr. E. Jephcott (Oxford, new edn. 2000); latterly, nuancing but fundamentally agreeing with the position of Elias, P. Spierenburg, 'Faces of Violence: Homicide Trends and Cultural Meanings: Amsterdam, 1431–1816', *Journal of Social History*, 27/4 (1994), 701–16. Such statistical analysis is summarised by T. Gurr, 'Historical Trends in Violent Crime: A Critical Review of the Evidence', *Crime and Justice: an Annual Review of Research*, 3 (1981), 295–350; M. Eisner, 'Long-Term Historical Trends in Violent Crime', *Crime and Justice*, 30 (2003), 83–142. It has led to virulent debates: see e.g. the articles of Monkkonen and Graff (respectively, 'Systematic Criminal Justice History: Some Suggestions', *Journal of Interdisciplinary History*, 9/3 (1979), 451–64; 'A Reply', *Journal of Interdisciplinary History*, 9/3 (1979), 465–71; and E. Johnson and E. Monkkonen, *The Civilization of Crime: Violence in Town and Country since the Middle Ages* (Urbana, Ill., 1996)); and the debate about the English case in *Past and Present*: L. Stone, 'Interpersonal Violence in English Society, 1300–1980', *Past and Present,* 101 (1983), 22–33; J. Cockburn, 'Patterns of Violence in English Society: Homicide in Kent', 1560–1986', *Past and Present,* 130 (1991), 70–106; J. Sharpe, 'Debate: The History of Violence in England: Some Observations', *Past and Present,* 108 (1985), 206–15; L. Stone, 'The History of Violence in England: Some Observations—A Rejoinder', *Past and Present,* 108 (1985), 216–24.

medieval violence.[20] In recent years, the historiography of medieval violence has undergone rapid expansion, though thirteenth-century French popular violence remains a lacuna, with attention focused on early medieval, and late medieval or early modern, crime and violence.[21] For the central Middle Ages, attention has been attracted primarily to chivalric violence in France, or to popular violence in England where the legal sources are much denser.[22] Historians have been concerned to indicate the groups most affected by popular violence and to explore its timing and socially integral role.[23] Drawing upon sociological models, the pervasiveness of violence in medieval culture has tended to be explained by its crucial role as an accepted mechanism for regulating and adjusting social structures and relations.[24] More recently, Claude Gauvard has focused upon the socio-economic contingency of particular forms of violence, concomitantly exploring the relationship between the development of proscriptive

[20] G. Schwerhoff, 'Zivilisationsprozess und Geschichtswissenschaft: Norbert Elias' Forschungsparadigma in historisches Sicht', *Historische Zeitschrift*, 266 (1998), 561–607; H. Duerr, *Nacktheit und Scham: Der Mythos vom Zivilisationprozess* (Frankfurt, 1988); see also the discussion in S. Carroll, 'Introduction', in Carroll (ed.), *Cultures of Violence* (London, 2007), 16; M. Schussler, 'German Crime in the Later Middle Ages: A Statistical Analysis of the Nuremberg Outlawry Books, 1285–1400', *Criminal Justice History*, 13 (1992), 11–60; V. Groebner, *Defaced: The Visual Culture of Violence in the Middle Ages*, tr. P. Selwyn (New York, 2004); H. Boockmann, 'Das grausame Mittelalter: Über ein Stereotyp in Geschichte', *Wissenschaft und Unterricht*, 38 (1987), 1–9; G. Althoff, 'Schranken der Gewalt: Wie gewalttätig war das "fristere Mittelalter"?', in H. Brunner (ed.), *Der Krieg im Mittelalter und in der frühen Neuzeit* (Wiesbaden, 1999), 1–23.

[21] e.g. M. Greenshields, *An Economy of Violence in Early Modern France* (Pennsylvania, 1994); R. Muchembled, *Violence et société: Comportements et mentalités populaires en Artois (1400–1660)* (Paris, 1985); J. Ruff, *Violence in Early Modern Europe* (Cambridge, 1996); G. Halsall, *Violence and Society in the Early Medieval West* (Woodbridge, 1998). The most recent synoptic study of medieval violence leaves popular violence in the late 13th and early 14th cents. largely undiscussed: W. Brown, *Violence in Medieval Europe* (Harlow, 2011).

[22] e.g. A. Cowell, *The Medieval Warrior Aristocracy: Gifts, Violence, Performance and the Sacred* (Woodbridge, 2007); R. Kaeuper, *Chivalry and Society in Medieval Europe* (Oxford, 1999); B. Hanawalt, *Crime and Conflict in English Communities, 1300–1348* (Cambridge, Mass., 1979); J. Given, *Society and Homicide in Thirteenth-Century England* (Stanford, Calif., 1977); E. Cohen, 'Patterns of Crime in Late Fourteenth-Century Paris', *French Historical Studies*, 11/3 (1980), 307–27; and J. Misraki, 'Criminalité et pauvreté', in M. Mollatt (ed.), *Études sur l'histoire de la pauvreté*, 2 vols. (Paris, 1974), i. 535–76; an exception is A. Finch, 'The Nature of Violence in the Middle Ages: An Alternative Perspective', *Historical Research* 70/173 (1997), 249–68, which focuses on early 14th-cent. violence as prosecuted in the ecclesiastical court of Cérisy in Normandy.

[23] e.g. B. Geremek, *The Margins of Society in Late Medieval Paris*, tr. J. Birrell (Cambridge, 1987); P. Maddern, *Violence and Social Order: East Anglia, 1422–1442* (Oxford, 1992); T. Dean, *Crime in Medieval Europe* (London, 2001); M. Meyerson, D. Thiery, and O. Falk (eds.), *'A Great Effusion of Blood?' Interpreting Medieval Violence* (Toronto, 2004), particularly 4–9.

[24] e.g. D. Kagay and L. Villalon, *The Final Argument: The Imprint of Violence on Society in Medieval and Early Modern Europe* (Woodbridge, 1998), pp. xv–xx.

attitudes towards violence and developing state structures.[25] Indeed, legalistic attitudes towards interpersonal violence have proved an ideal way to explore and to problematize the development of the implementation of state power through legal mechanisms.[26]

The cultural implications of violence have drawn historians of an anthropological persuasion to study its ritual elements, at once affirming, dynamic, and oppositional.[27] Honour is a central motif and has been rendered key to many explanatory frameworks of patterns and economies of violence;[28] further work has stressed the sensitive, dialogic, and adaptive qualities of medieval aggression.[29] Most effectively, historians have returned to the question of what constituted 'violence' as such in particular historical circumstances, a question which invites reflection upon political attempts to wrest the perpetration of legitimate force from private individuals into the hands of the law, where the term 'violence' was no longer considered apposite.[30] The study of the law in relation to interpersonal violence has exponentially increased our understanding of the role of, and attitudes towards, brutality in later medieval France.[31] Legal discourse and the practice of violence are no longer studied in isolation, as both are seen to be central to the conflicts which shaped everyday life in the Middle Ages.[32]

[25] 'Au quatorzième et quinzième siècles, en France, le discours sur la violence devient un élément de la construction de l'État': C. Gauvard, *Violence et ordre public au Moyen Age* (Paris, 2005), 11. See also N. Gonthier, *Cris de haine et rites d'unité: La Violence dans les villes, XIIIe–XVIe siècle* (Turnhout, 1992), particularly 215–17.

[26] See, most recently, J. Firnhaber-Baker, 'From God's Peace to the King's Order: Late Medieval Limitations on Non-Royal Warfare', *Essays in Medieval Studies,* 23 (2006), 19–30, and T. Bisson, *The Crisis of the Twelfth-Century: Power, Lordship and the Origins of European Government* (Princeton, 2008).

[27] e.g. E. Le Roy Ladurie, *Le Carnaval de Romans* (Paris, 1979); Y. Bercé, *Fête et révolte: Des mentalités populaires du XVIe au XVIIIe siècles* (Paris, 1976).

[28] e.g. W. Miller, *Bloodtaking and Peacemaking: Feud, Law and Society in Saga Iceland* (Chicago, 1990). In medieval France, the notion of 'renommée' was key: see Gauvard, *Violence,* 13–16.

[29] e.g. B. Rosenwein (ed.), *Anger's Past: The Social Uses of an Emotion in the Middle Ages* (Ithaca, NY, 1998).

[30] Such studies focus principally on the struggle to contain noble violence and private wars. See particularly J. Firnhaber-Baker, 'Seigneurial War and Royal Power in Later Medieval Southern France', *Past and Present,* 208 (2010), 37–76. The demonization of particular groups has been linked to this rise of central power: e.g. F. Rexroth, *Das Milieu der Nacht* (Göttingen, 1999), 333–47.

[31] C. Gauvard, *De grace especial: Crime, état et société en France à la fin du Moyen Age* (Paris, 1991); L. de Carbonnières, *La Procédure devant la chambre criminelle du parlement de Paris au XIVe siècle* (Paris, 2004).

[32] See notably, D. Smail, 'Hatred as a Social Institution in Late Medieval Society', *Speculum,* 76/1 (2001), 90–126.

3. THE REGION AND THE PERIOD

This book turns to hitherto understudied regions in this respect, tempted by the richness of the source material and the intrinsic interest of areas of rapidly changing social structures and developing civic ideologies: Paris and Artois (see Figure 1).[33] Artois was enjoying a period of economic prosperity and mercantile expansion: it was a centre notably of cloth production and banking, as well as an important trading centre for wool and even wine.[34] Paris likewise was prosperous, with a thriving commercial scene and a busy and skilled artisanate, as attested to by the Parisian Provost, Étienne Boileau in his *Livre des métiers*.[35] The town was self-important as the centre of an increasingly powerful monarchy and administration, and the seat of an internationally renowned university.[36] An anonymous writer, with evident exaggeration, but resonant pride, punned on Paris and Paradisus, and Jehan de Jandun praised its people, moderate in all things.[37] The images of everyday life in Paris, placed under the bridges of scenes from the *Vie de Saint Denis* from the early fourteenth century, evoke a Paris of social diversity with lepers sounding their clappers, physicians examining urine, and young people fishing and swimming in the Seine: in this portrayal, it is a hive of bustling activity, of learning and leisure, commerce and religious devotion.[38] However romanticized this vision, much recent scholarship has clearly illustrated that medieval cities were not subject to rigorous social zoning, and rich

[33] R. Muchembled, *La Violence au village: Sociabilité et comportements populaire en Artois du XVe au XVIIe siècle* (Turnhout, 1989).

[34] Cf. R. Fossier, *La Terre et les hommes en Picardie*, 2 vols. (Paris, 1968), ii. 570–98; R. Berlow, 'The Development of Business Techniques Used at the Fairs of Champagne from the End of the Twelfth Century to the Middle of the Thirteenth Century', *Studies in Medieval and Renaissance History*, 8 (1971), 28–35; J. Lestocquoy, *Patriciens du Moyen Age: Les Dynasties bourgeoises d'Arras du XIe au XVe siècle* (Arras, 1945).

[35] Étienne Boileau, *Les Métiers et corporations de la ville de Paris*, ed. R. de Lespinasse and F. Bonnardot (Paris, 1879).

[36] Cf. R. Cazelles, *Nouvelle Histoire de Paris: De la fin du règne de Philippe Auguste à la mort de Charles V, 1223–1380* (Paris, 1982).

[37] Anon., *Recommendatio Civitatis Parisiensis*, in Le Roux de Lincy and L. Tisserand (eds.), *Paris et ses historiens au XIVe et XVe siècles* (Paris, 1867), 22–9; Jehan de Jandun, *Tractatus de laudibus Parisius*, ibid. 54.

[38] The *Vie de Saint Denis* was presented to Philip V in 1317 by his chaplain Gilles, Abbot of Saint Denis: see W. Egbert, *On the Bridges of Medieval Paris: A Record of Early Fourteenth-Century Life* (Princeton, 1974), 3–23. The manuscript is BN Ms fr. 2090–2092, and a presumed third part is Ms lat. 13836; there is also a mid-14th-cent. copy, Ms lat. 5286. For the money changer, goldsmith, beggar, fishermen, lepers, singing clerics, and physicians, see respectively Ms fr. 2091, fos. 105^v^, 111^r^, 97^r^, 129^r^, 99^r^, 125^r^; for musicians, swimmers, and livestock sellers from the surrounding countryside, see respectively Ms fr. 2092, fos. 8^v^, 10^v^, 18^v^.

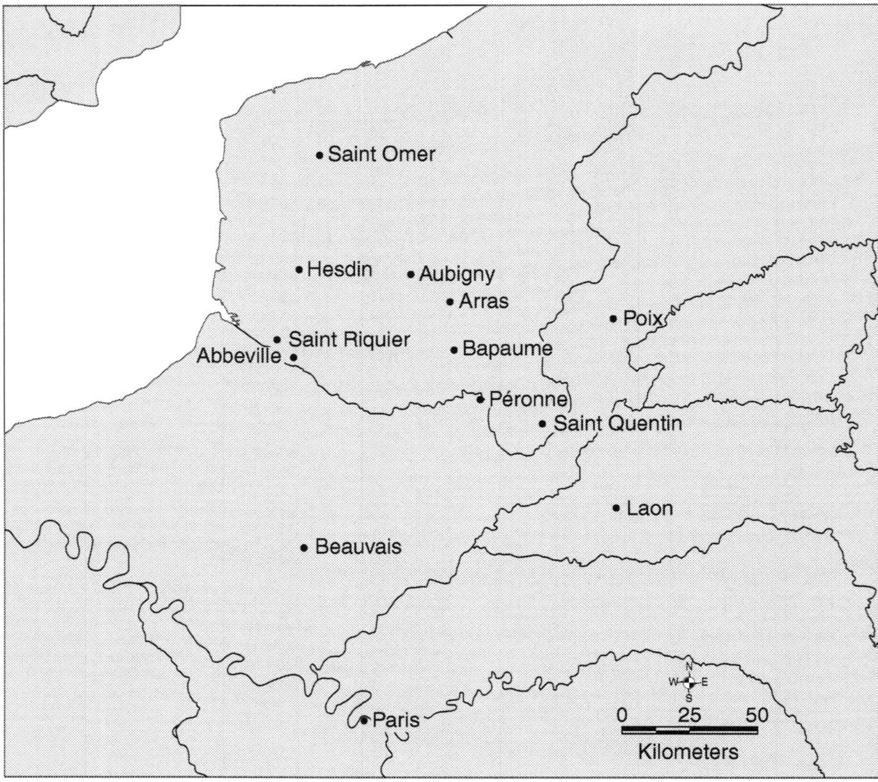

Fig. 1. Map showing north-eastern French towns under consideration

and poor encountered each other regularly, providing opportunities for a rich variety of social interactions.

Both regions were, by contemporary standards, highly urbanized. Nevertheless, Artois still had a large rural population, and the kind of social and geographic mobility which we tend to associate with urbanized areas was not yet a regular characteristic. Paris was obviously much larger, and formed by a constant influx of immigrants who swelled its population enormously in the latter part of the thirteenth century.[39] Yet it also retained close ties with the surrounding countryside, with many inhabitants moving between the two, and social networks spanning the divide.[40]

[39] S. Roux, *Paris in the Middle Ages*, tr. J. McNamara (Pennsylvania, 2009).

[40] G. Fourquin, *Les Campagnes de la région parisienne à la fin du Moyen Age* (Paris, 1964), 219–20. Cf. D. Nicholas, *The Growth of the Medieval City: From Late Antiquity to*

Fig. 2. Model of Arras, 1716, by the engineer Ladevèze, now in the Musée des Beaux Arts in Arras. The layout of the town was largely unchanged from the thirteenth century. Author's photograph.

This book's study of Paris encompasses this more rural hinterland, following the remit of many of the sources, the nebulousness of the line between the city and its region, and the similar commercial patterns and social structures in both.

Despite their growth and the enthusiasm of a Jean de Jandun or the satirical poet who took as his premise that a downbeat God would choose to come to Arras to cheer himself up,[41] both Paris and Artois were beset with tension: rapid growth was accompanied by intensified economic, social, and political grievances.[42] The sting in the tail of Guillaume de Breton's early thirteenth-century eulogy of Arras, the principal town in Artois, is telling: 'Atrebatum potens, urbs antiquissima, plena/Divitiis,

the Early Fourteenth Century (London, 1997), 179, 210; D. Nicholas, *The Later Medieval City, 1300–1500* (London, 1997), 72.

[41] R. Berger, *Littérature et société arrageoise: Les Chansons et dits artésiens* (Arras, 1982), no. 1.

[42] Cf. Nicholas, *Growth*, 273–81, 287; Nicholas, *Later Medieval City*, 14–24.

inhians lucris et foenore gaudens.'[43] Wealth brought with it questionable morality and grasping behaviour. And the dire warning sounded by Bernard of Clairvaux to potential students in the late twelfth century presented Paris not as the heavenly city, Jandun's paradise, but as the earthly Babylon, den of vice and pride.[44] By the end of the century, both areas were undergoing processes of profound upheaval. As Paris grew in size and political and commercial importance, life became increasingly precarious for many, and the wealth of the few was offset against the poverty and marginalization of the many, excluded because of economic disadvantage, physical difference, or as the result of an accident.[45] In Artois, the ascendancy of commerce was marked by obsessive references to the wheel of fortune and the precariousness of economic success.[46] Structures of power were debated, as guilds came to share power with older oligarchies, both competing against a monarchy anxious to expand control.[47] Textile production created its own tensions, and was no longer adequate to deal with the demographic saturation of many of the towns in this area, engendering an edgy dependence upon international trade.[48] Moreover, the geographical position of Artois as a frontier region laid it open to damage from war in neighbouring Flanders: local inhabitants were obliged to offer service under the count of Artois, himself killed at the battle of Courtrai in 1302, and the records refer again and again to the 'dégastement' ('laying waste') of the region caused by war.[49] Quite apart

[43] 'Powerful Arras, very ancient city, filled with wealth, grasping for profit and rejoicing in reward': *Œuvres de Rigord et Guillaume le Breton*, ed. H.-F. Delaborde (Paris, 1882), ll. 97 and 94–5.

[44] See particularly S. Ferruolo, *The Origins of the University: The Schools of Paris and their Critics, 1120–1215* (Stanford, Calif., 1985). In many ways, the paradigm is that of Augustine's 'two cities': see Augustine, *De Civitate Dei*, ed. M. Dods (London, Modern Library Edition, 2000).

[45] See particularly the number of accidents in Guillaume de Saint Pathus, *Les Miracles de Saint Louis*, ed. P. Fay (Paris, 1931); Geremek, *Margins*, particularly 167–209; S. Farmer, *Surviving Poverty in Medieval Paris* (Ithaca, NY, 2005), particularly 74–104 and 136–64.

[46] See notably, Jacquemart Giélée, *Renart le nouvel*, ed. H. Roussel (Paris, 1961), ll. 7731–2, 312; Adam de la Halle, *Le Jeu de la Feuillée*, ed. J. Dufournet (Ghent, 1977), l. 860. J. Ribard, 'A propos de l'epilogue de "Renart le nouvel"; Quelques réflexions sur l'allégorie de fortune', in H. Roussel and F. Suard (eds.), *Alain de Lille, Gautier de Châtillon, Jakemart Giélée et leur temps* (Lille, 1978), 307–20.

[47] Nicholas, *Growth*, 275–87.

[48] Ibid. 279; moreover, severe weather-based shortages offset the apparent prosperity of these towns from the 1290s: Nicholas, *Later Medieval City*, 14.

[49] Cf. A. Derville, *Les Villes de Flandre et Artois, 900–1500* (Villeneuve d'Ascq, 2002), 109–24; G. Sivery, *L'Économie du royaume de France au siècle de Saint Louis (vers 1180–vers 1315)* (Lille, 1984), 151–98, particularly 164–75. On the effect of war in the later Middle Ages, see Muchembled, *La Violence au village*, 55–107. Artois has suffered repeatedly in this way over the centuries, and it is for this reason that a thriving hub of medieval Europe bears now remarkably little trace of this history.

from these hostilities, a period of rapid demographic growth was coming to an end in the countryside, with near saturation of the available resources, and what has been labelled 'stagflation' even prior to the appalling famine of 1315.[50] Paris and its hinterland were not immune to these rising tensions, suffering from both the precarious nature of commercial relations and from the increasing sluggishness of production. The situation was not improved by debasement of the coinage ordered by the monarchy.[51] After rapid growth in the thirteenth century, the influx of population began to tail off in the fourteenth. And although this study largely stops before the outbreak of the Hundred Years' War in 1337, rising hostilities meant mounting tension and discomfort in the city. Interaction between the two regions was continuous, promoted by commercial relations, the University, immigration, and cultural production: the vernacular literature famously emanating from Artois, and most particularly Arras, in this period reached a broad audience in the Parisian milieu.[52] This, then, was a period of social ferment, and it is perhaps the fertile combination of prosperity and the growing awareness of its fragility which accounts for the rich crop of vernacular literature emanating from Paris and Artois. These were centres of cultural innovation and subversive literary commentary, and violence was one of the preferred subjects for such performances.

This wealth of imaginative literature provides some of the most evocative insights into the role of interpersonal violence in these societies. Never straightforward mirrors of society, these texts (for it is in this form that we can access them today) engaged with social and cultural norms, problematized them, and embodied the dialogue between those norms, the composers and the audiences who read, listened to, and watched them. Artois, and, at its centre, Arras, was the birthplace of secular vernacular theatre; of the comic and extremely violent *fabliaux*; of the stories of cunning Renard the fox; and of a profusion of vernacular lyric poetry.[53] The *Puy* and *Confrérie de Notre Dame des Ardents*, the poetic society at the heart of the cultural scene in Arras, of which more anon, provided an internationally

50 Guy Bois, *The Crisis of Feudalism: Economy and Society in Eastern Normandy, c.1300–1500* (Cambridge, 1984), 265–73; W. C. Jordan, *The Great Famine: Northern Europe in the Early Fourteenth Century* (Princeton, 1996), particularly 24–39.

51 R. Cazelles, 'Quelques réflexions à propos des mutations de la monnaie royale française', *Le Moyen Age*, 72 (1966), 83–105, 251–78.

52 e.g. P. Bougard, *Histoire d'Arras* (Paris, 1988), 63–7, 73–5; A. Derville, 'Arras au 13e siècle: à propos de la thèse de Roger Berger', *Revue du Nord*, 64 (1982), 193–200; Berger, *Littérature*; M. Ungureanu, *La Bourgeoisie naissante: Société et littérature bourgeoises d'Arras au XIIe et XIIIe siècle* (Arras, 1955), 97–264.

53 The most recent and stimulating study is C. Symes, *A Common Stage: Theater and Public Life in Medieval Arras* (Ithaca, NY, 2007).

renowned platform for the prowess of Arras in the arts, and was the origin of an extraordinary series of debate poems, as well as a set of twenty-four surviving satirical verses.[54] These texts stand out for their rich and complex treatment of the themes not of epic or of romance, but of everyday life, or at least the rhetorical trope of everyday life in all its absurdities and ludicrous losses of dignity: violence is, of course, a common thread. Many of these texts, notably the *fabliaux*, also circulated in Paris, and the regularly documented minstrels in Paris added their own compositions, famously the surprisingly engaging 'dits' which consist of rhyming lists on a given subject, or the cleverly constructed polemical poems of Rutebeuf and a few anonymous students.[55] In the fourteenth century, vernacular theatre developed rapidly in the capital with the composition of a set of forty mystery plays celebrating the miraculous action of the Virgin Mary, often borrowing their plots from earlier Marian miracle tales such as those of Gautier de Coinci.[56] And closely related to these performances were the performances of preachers, ensuring the propagation of moral theology amongst wide audiences whom they attracted with their powerful rhetoric and appeals to quotidian concerns. Yet again, interpersonal brutality and brawls are an ever-present, sometimes comic, sometimes disturbing, element in these texts.

4. THE SOURCES

The complexity of these cultural artefacts comes into sharp focus when they are juxtaposed with the surviving legal material. This was a period of major legal transition, marked by the growth of increasingly stridently expressed legal norms and further attempts to wrest the control of jurisdiction by ever more powerful authorities: it was a time marked by an emergent self-consciousness regarding crime and justice. Whilst rising tensions in Paris and Artois tended to exacerbate interpersonal violence, legal shifts increased ambivalence towards the phenomenon.

[54] For the poems, respectively A. Långfors, A. Jeanroy, and L. Brandin (eds.), *Recueil général des jeux-partis français* (Paris, 1926); R. Berger, *Littérature*. The two institutions seem to have been the same thing, although this has been the subject of much debate: Symes, *Common Stage*, 218. See also A. Butterworth, *Poetry and Music in Medieval France: From Jean Renart to Guillaume de Machaut* (Cambridge, 2002), 133–50.

[55] Online edns. of the *Dits* at http://tapor.mcmaster.ca/~hyperliste/home.htm, accessed Aug. 2011; Rutebeuf, *Œuvres complètes*, ed. M. Zink, 2 vols. (Paris, 1989).

[56] *Les Miracles de Nostre Dame par personnages*, ed. Gaston Paris and Ulysse Robert, 7 vols. (Paris, 1876–93); Gautier de Coinci, *Miracles de Nostre Dame*, ed. F. Koenig, 4 vols. (Geneva, 1955).

Paris was subjected to a host of often competing jurisdictions. The Châtelet was the court of the *prévôt* of Paris, and derived its powers from royal authority: it was the court of first instance for the city. Furthermore, the bishop exercised jurisdictional authority, as did the chapter of Notre Dame, and a series of surviving seigneurial jurisdictions, often of an ecclesiastical nature. Only the records of these latter survive in any quantity, in registers compiled to deal with conflicts of jurisdiction.[57] The problems with using such sources for quantitative study are manifold: they do not represent the accurate documentation of every crime which took place or even every crime which was prosecuted, as they were selected to illustrate particular purposes. For the late thirteenth and early fourteenth centuries, the registers of Saint-Germain-des-Près, Saint-Maur-des-Fossés, Sainte-Geneviève, and Saint-Martin-des-Champs have been used. Each set of records has its own agenda. Moreover, the registers include details not only of the areas within the city walls, but also of the parishes owned by these powers outside Paris, though all within a twenty-mile radius and within the socio-economic remit of the capital. As Gauvard has pointed out, many brawlers preferred to fight at the gates of the city, believing flight thus to be easier, and social networks maintained through violence tended to bridge the divide between town and hinterland.[58] Not only do such records provide evidence of outbreaks of violence, but they also give insight into constructions and manipulations of deviancy. The royal *Trésor des Chartes* provides a collection of early letters of remission, which afford unique insight into hermeneutic frameworks of violence as understood both by the perpetrators and by the authorities.[59]

Arras and the surrounding region of Artois can be glimpsed via the Trésor des Chartes des Comtes d'Artois, representing one of the numerous jurisdictions attempting to regulate criminal behaviour in this period.[60]

[57] Such registers survive for this period for the jurisdictions of Saint-Maur-des-Fossés (AN, LL112); Saint-Germain-des-Pres (AN, LL1077); Saint-Martin-des-Champs (AN, Musée, no. 356); and Sainte-Genevieve (Bibliothèque Sainte-Geneviève, FH 23): they have been edited by F. Tanon, *Histoire des justices des anciennes églises et communautés monastiques de Paris* (Paris, 1883), part II: 'Les hautes justices qui étaient entre les mains du clergé régulier ou séculier ... ne différaient nullement de celles qui appartenaient ailleurs aux seigneurs laïques et qu'elles n'avaient rien de commun avec les justices ecclésiastiques proprement dites, ou officialités', 3–4. These sources are generally in French.

[58] C. Gauvard, 'Violence citadine et réseaux de solidarité: L'exemple français aux XIVe et XVe siècles', *Annales ESC* 48/5 (1993), 1117–18.

[59] e.g. AN, JJ42, JJ49 etc.: see bibliography. These have been copied onto large parchment rolls. At this stage, these sources are generally still in French.

[60] Series A in ADPC. The seigneurial jurisdiction in Artois competed with municipal jurisdictions, and a multitude of smaller jurisdictions of ecclesiastical bodies. See also A. Laurence, 'Les Comptes du Bailli d'Arras au XIVe siècle: Source de droit criminel et pénal' (unpubl. thesis, École des Chartes, 1967): summary in *Positions des thèses soutenues*

These archives include conflicts of jurisdiction, wherein scores of witnesses were asked to describe all the criminal cases from a given place over the previous decades, as well as responses to complaints about the corrupt behaviour of certain *baillis* responsible for comital jurisdiction.[61] The bulk of the *trésor* is constituted by the financial accounts of the local *baillis*, detailing the crimes for which fines were incurred or compositions agreed:[62] the Artois *baillis* were indeed rather less exalted than royal or seigneurial *baillis* in other parts of France, for they amounted to fifteen in Artois, each responsible for only a small area, and acting as executive officers for both the municipal and the comital courts.[63] The general accounts of the overall *bailli* of Artois, and those of his successor, the *receveur*, include the annual accounts of all the local *bailliages* within the larger administrative district: these complete accounts survive only for the period *c.*1285 to 1315.[64] The local *bailli* would have tried cases of

par les élèves de la promotion de 1968 pour obtenir le diplôme d'archiviste paléographe (Paris, 1967), 57–64. This interesting thesis focuses only on Arras, and discusses all kinds of crime and the process of prosecution, rather than inviting reflections specifically on interpersonal violence; sometimes the author assumes greater reliability and coverage for her source material than is justified.

[61] e.g. A904, A929, A930 etc.: see bibliography. These are large parchment rolls, and are mostly in French, with the exception of a few, e.g. A18/2 for Buscoi, in Latin.

[62] Accounts of individual *bailliages* in ADPC, A123, A124, A126, etc: see bibliography. These accounts are contained in packages of loose documents. It has been noted that peace was made with the friends of the victim, and a composition paid to the comital authority very frequently, perhaps because the financial incentive for the legal authority was much more enticing than an expensive punishment. Cf. C. Small, 'The Costs of Urban Justice: The Example of Arras, 1300–1329', in M. Miglio and G. Lombardi (eds.), *Simbolo e realtà della vita urbana nel tardo medioevo* (Rome, 1988), 255–68, 268. All these accounts were divided into 'Esplois', 'Rechoites', and 'Despens': most information about justice is in the 'Esplois', though occasionally details of expenses for carrying out corporal punishment, or the ongoing financial benefits of confiscated land are accounted for in the 'Despens' and 'Rechoites' respectively: where the same crime is mentioned in all three types of accounts, the terminology remains constant, suggesting that we can reliably comment upon lexical choices. Every effort has been made to ensure that, as far as statistics are concerned, each event is only counted once, though variable spellings sometimes render this challenging! In compiling figures for crimes, I have first added all crimes mentioned in the accounts, and then compiled separate tables using only the slightly smaller figure of crimes accounted for only in the 'Esplois'—reassuringly, the proportions remain constant whichever method one uses. Where a case involving, say, three aggressors, was accounted for as three separate cases, I count it as such, given that accounting does not always take that form, and the choice therefore represents a particular perception of the event. However, if, in a fight, the two opposing parties are tried separately, I count the event as a single act, as it clearly constitutes one event and is only accounted for as two cases since aggressors on opposing sides could, logically, not be tried together.

[63] Ibid. 266.

[64] Complete accounts in ADPC, A815/1, A815/2, A123/1, A123/2, A124, A126/1, A126/2, A127/1, A128/1, A128/2; ADN, B13595, B13596, B13597. NB: fos. 1–56 of ADN, B13596, refer to 1303–4, and have been edited in B. Delmaire, *Le Compte Général d'Artois pour 1303–1304* (Brussels, 1977): references given here to this document will refer

high justice on behalf of the count which were then to be handed over to the municipal *échevinage*: sadly, all the registers of the *échevinage* have been lost in Arras, most notably in a catastrophic fire during the bombardment of 1917.[65] The town of Abbeville, near Arras, however, rather miraculously has been able to preserve its Livre Rouge de l'Echevinage.[66] *Les Olim*, records of the Paris Parlement, contain records of cases involving either protagonists too socially elevated to be tried locally, or appeals against unfair jurisdictions: use of the *Olim* is, of course, problematic, as only cases with very significant perceived repercussions reached this forum.[67] This is naturally also a valuable source for Parisian violence in this period.

The nature of these sources does not permit any synchronic conclusions about patterns of crime over the period 1270 to 1330.[68] Moreover, being restricted by what survives, the historian is unable to compare like for like in the Artois region and in Paris, either in terms of precise dates, or in the mechanisms of prosecution and recording. However, with these caveats in mind, and with close attention to the processes by which crimes were recorded in the archives, it is possible to uncover a picture of violence as contingent, embedded in social relations both instrumentally and symbolically, and beset by layers of hesitation and ambivalence. Medieval people resorted readily to violence, but they were upset and concerned about its consequences.

The approach adopted here will be multivalent. Its aim is to acknowledge the communicative qualities of violence, to illuminate its mechanisms and its impact, and to engage with medieval ambivalence concerning physical force. Social introspection aside, systemic violence provokes discomforting but not insurmountable reflections upon the operations and mechanisms of social networks.

> Violence is an extrapolation
> Of the cutting edge
> Into the orbit of the smile.[69]

to Delmaire's numbering. These accounts are contained in large parchment rolls, apart from B13595 and B13596 which have been bound into large volumes.

[65] On the relationship between the *échevins* and the comital *bailli* in Arras, see C. Small, 'Prisoners in the Castellany of Artois in the Early Fourteenth Century', *Social History/Histoire sociale*, 26/52 (1993), 345–72.

[66] AMA, MS 115.

[67] A. Beugnot (ed.), *Les Olim*, 4 vols. (Paris, 1839–48); also E. Boutaric (ed.), *Actes du Parlement de Paris*, 2 vols. (Paris, 1863–7), and H. Furgeot and M. Dillay (eds.), *Actes du Parlement de Paris: Deuxième série de l'an 1328 à l'an 1350*, 3 vols. (Paris, 1920–75).

[68] Such an approach has been attempted by Cohen, although it has been remarked that the changing nature of her sources for the early and late 14th cent. undermine her conclusions: E. Cohen, 'Patterns of Crime in Fourteenth-Century Paris', *French Historical Studies* (1980), 307–27.

[69] T. Hughes, *Tales from Ovid* (London, 1997), 11: this is the age of iron.

1

Grammars of Violence

Brutality was an integral part of the social experience of the men and women of thirteenth- and fourteenth-century Paris and Artois, who recognized that violence could communicate powerfully, both to victims and to observers: both punitive judicial violence and extra-judicial interpersonal brutality could convey messages about social relationships. Physical violence was a kind of language. But no communication can be meaningful in the absence of shared norms and conventions: grammars. Grammars shaped the complex ways people engaged in, and responded to, violent gestures, and provided interpretative frameworks: they circumscribed the meanings of certain physical gestures and specified the relationship between different violent enunciations, their contexts, and their speakers. And these grammars were expressed in a variety of discursive contexts: moral, legal, literary.

While students and clerics were usually aware of theological, medical, and political concern with the meanings of physical brutality, the merchants, craftsmen, and labourers of rural and urban areas were confronted with such issues in sermons, popular miracle tales, performed literature, and the practice of law. Examination of these grammars will reveal them to have been diverse, sometimes overlapping, sometimes conflicting. Many provided paradigms for reading physical damage to, or marks upon, the body itself. Even the notion of law was not a monolithic framework, but a series of attempts to engage with other normative discourses in order to circumscribe how violence was to be perpetrated and interpreted; and law and morality were not synonymous.[1] These grammars were not only top–down processes, but grew organically and in reciprocity with communities: in fact, they were also shaped by the same gestures they purported to regulate. Indeed all these discursive strands, from imaginative literature to sermons to proverbs to legal discourse and procedure, were dependent

[1] 'It seems that human law does not set up an obligation in the court of conscience. An inferior power has no jurisdiction in a superior court': Thomas Aquinas, *Summa Theologica*, Prima Secundae, q. 96, art. 4.6: quoted in D. Coquillette, 'Equity', in J. Strayer (ed.), *Dictionary of the Middle Ages*, 13 vols. (New York, 1982–9), iv. 501.

upon being performed and upon the reaction of their audiences.[2] Gossip and rumour drew their material and their logic from this variety of discourses on physical gestures and violence: the chatter of the community illustrated the overlaps, contradictions, and corroborations in these multiple approaches to understanding violence.[3]

Notions and practices of violence centre, of course, on wounding and marking the physical body: accordingly, this chapter will trace the development of frameworks for understanding these physical marks, the ways in which such frameworks were problematized, and the use of such a logic to assess physical violence in a legal context. But in examining this legal context, it will become clear that the violence of the law was equally dependent on such frameworks, and equally problematic and contested. The aim is to build up a holistic picture of how communities thought about violence, introducing the various types of source material available—from sermons, hagiography, and popular literature, to legal custumals, prosecutions, and remissions. Violence was increasingly understood as meaningful, but this brought with it multiple problems and layers of ambivalence.

1. FRAMEWORKS OF MEANING

1.1. Religious-didactic frameworks

Physically violent actions were made meaningful through an increasingly explicit semiology of marks on bodies. These were not necessarily discussions about brutality, but provided ways of thinking about and interpreting the visible effects of violence. A starting point was developed in a spiritual context, wherein bodies were popularly depicted as legible. The growth of interest in the Eucharist in this period rendered the reading of bodies fundamental to the practice of the Christian faith, and placed the physical body as mediator between heaven and earth: renewed focus upon Christ's body intensified the somatic quality of the piety of ordinary Christians.[4] The resurrection of the human body was firmly established by the Church at the Fourth Lateran Council, and again at the Second

[2] Cf. H. Jauss, *Toward an Aesthetic of Reception*, tr. T. Bahti (Minneapolis, 1982), e.g. 19.

[3] C. Wickham, 'Gossip and Resistance among the Medieval Peasantry', *Past and Present*, 160/1 (1998), 3–24; C. Gauvard, *De Grace Especial: Crime, état et société en France à la fin du Moyen Age* (Paris, 1991), 126–8; D. Smail and T. Fenster, 'Introduction', in their *Fama: The Politics of Talk and Reputation in Medieval Europe* (Ithaca, NY, 2003), 1–14.

[4] Cf. M. Rubin, *Corpus Christi: The Eucharist in Late Medieval Culture* (Cambridge, 1993), 1–35, 98–107.

Council of Lyons in 1274, encouraging theological thinking to take place along bodily lines.[5] One's bodily appearance became intimately connected with one's spiritual state, both in this life and the next, and bodily expressions of piety were valorized, most dramatically with the Franciscan stigmata.[6] Saintly asceticism and self-mortification were not a flight from physicality, but an exploration of the potential of fleshliness to reveal one's faith and trust in God: St Christopher apparently 'bore Christ . . . in his body by mortification';[7] Conrad, the spiritual master of St Elizabeth of Hungary, flogged her 'so severely that the marks of the lashes were still visible three weeks later', for the benefit of her humility, obedience, and patience.[8] Such tales were famously committed to manuscript in the work of Jacques de Voragine, the Dominican archbishop of Genoa from 1292, and were widely disseminated throughout Europe.[9]

The interpretation of physical gestures in hagiographical collections like this reached wide audiences, as the texts were used by preachers in popular homiletic performances. Preaching underwent widespread development and expansion in the thirteenth century, and its intensification contributed significantly to the dissemination of a hermeneutics of signs on bodies. Short illustrative stories known as exempla, and inserted into a sermon in order to make a moral point, were fascinated by the physical body as the literal sign of the unseeable in the soul.[10] Étienne de Bourbon explained in his *Tractatus de diversis materiis praedicabilibus* that exempla had four functions: to enable people to seize the meaning more quickly; to understand more easily; to remember more thoroughly; and to put into practice more effectively.[11] Exempla survive in special collections, and were usually preserved in Latin for swift circulation amongst clerics. While some of these stories were taken from patristic or from oral tradition,

[5] Cf. C. W. Bynum, 'Material Continuity, Personal Survival and the Resurrection of the Body: A Scholastic Discussion in its Medieval and Modern Contexts', in Bynum, *Fragmentation and Redemption: Essays on Gender and the Human Body in Medieval Religion* (New York, 1991), 239–99.

[6] *Writings of the First Companions: Scripta Leonis, Rufini et Angeli Sociorum S. Francisci*, ed. and tr. R. Brooke (Oxford, 1970), 188. This is the first type of gesture outlined by J.-C. Schmitt, where bodily states indicate inner movements of the soul: *La Raison des gestes dans l'Occident médiéval* (Paris, 1990).

[7] Jacobus de Voragine, *The Golden Legend: Readings on the Saints*, tr. W. Granger Ryan, 2 vols. (Princeton, 1991), ii, no. 100, 10–14.

[8] Ibid. ii, no. 168, 302–18.

[9] Ibid. i, pp. v–x.

[10] Cf. C. Ho, 'Corpus Delicti: The Edifying Dead in the *Exempla* of Jacques de Vitry', in J. Hamesse *et al.* (eds.), *Medieval Sermons and Society: Cloister, City, University* (Louvain-la-Neuve, 1998), 203–18.

[11] Cf. Étienne de Bourbon, *Tractatus de diversis materiis praedicabilibus*, ed. J. Berlioz and J. L. Eichenlaub, 3 vols. (Turnhout, 2002–).

many claimed to be drawn from everyday life: in order to be powerful, they needed to key into a framework of shared logic with their audience, but also served to crystallize those frameworks. Both saints' lives and exempla required interpretative subtlety on the part of the audience and a distinction was drawn between *admiranda* and *imitanda*: listeners or readers were well aware that stories were often merely illustrative, using the signifying power of the body to demonstrate a spiritual point, but not encouraging listeners to 'try it at home'.[12]

In many exempla, the consequences of spiritual crimes were described as physically manifested upon the body through the action of an external force, whether by God, devils, or human beings. The physical sign could render visible an invisible sin, or function punitively and correctively. The visualization of sexual impurity was a favourite theme in the exempla of Ranulphe de la Houblonnière: witness the priest who apparently bore his impure hands before the altar, and was divinely struck with paralysis until his death.[13] The paralysis communicated the impure nature of his soul to others, providing an appropriate riposte to the priest's misuse of his own body, but it also prevented him from repeating the crime. Blasphemy meets with divinely sent physical punishment instantaneously, reiterating legal prescriptions for the removal of a blasphemer's tongue.[14] Physical damage to the body can be clearly read: 'saepe puniuntur aut semper, hic aut in futuro, in membro de quo peccant et contra quod peccant'.[15]

Much popular literature also described such signs on bodies, often also exploring the gestures which caused them. Exempla, saints' lives, and secular popular literature were not distinct genres and were often performed in similar contexts: the widespread bodily semiotics explored in much religious literature in this period played a fundamental structural role in many *fabliaux*. For instance, a sermon exemplum of Jacques de Vitry tells of a wife avenging herself on her abusive husband by telling the king that her husband is a doctor but needs to be beaten in order to perform his medical wizardry;[16] the same story found its way into an early

[12] Cf. R. Kieckhefer, *Unquiet Souls: Fourteenth-Century Saints and their Religious Milieu* (Chicago, 1984), 4–15.

[13] N. Beriou, *La Prédication de Ranulphe de la Houblonnière: Sermons aux clercs et aux simples gens à Paris au XIIIe siècle* (Paris, 1987), sermon 4, 53.

[14] e.g. *Chronique de Primat*, tr. Jean de Vignay, *RHGF* 23, 66. Jean de Joinville tells us that Louis had the lips of blasphemers branded: *Vie de Saint Louis*, tr. C. Smith (London, 2008), 318.

[15] 'They are often or always punished, in the present or the future, in the part of the body with which or against which they sin': Étienne de Bourbon, *Tractatus*, nos. 391 and 392.

[16] Jacques de Vitry, *Exempla*, ed. T. Crane (London, 1890), no. 237.

thirteenth-century *fabliau*.[17] Whilst entertaining their audiences, *jongleurs* exploited a widely acknowledged bodily semiotics in order, at least superficially, to strengthen their moral didacticism. In this case, the marks on the body of the 'médecin malgré lui' were polysemous: believed by the king to signify the man's expertise, the wife and audience are aware that they punitively indicate his own abusive behaviour.[18]

1.2. Medicine

It is telling that a reference to medical thought and physicians provides this point of contact between popular literature, sermons, and theology. The legibility of bodies in popular hagiography and sermon exempla was intertwined with concomitant medicalization of thinking about the body, given renewed impetus by the availability of Avicenna's *Liber canonicis medicinae*, and a variety of other texts transmitting learned medical traditions from Arabic cultures.[19]

The two contexts might seem to us completely distinct: the one reading marks on bodies as indicative of spiritual states, the other reading marks to understand physical conditions. But the distinction was not drawn so clearly in this period: body and soul were intertwined and these hermeneutic frameworks overlapped. Indeed, religious-didactic literature frequently used medical readings of symptoms analogously. Explicitly medical terminology coloured the theological quodlibets of thinkers such as John of Naples, and preachers metaphorically referred to sin as a wound and confession as blood-letting.[20]

In a medical context, it was of paramount importance not only to recognize the significance of bodily signs, but to be able to differentiate between them. Medical theory increasingly privileged the notion of symptoms as the visible manifestations of otherwise invisible diseases, and this paradigm gradually superseded a preoccupation with attempting to cure

[17] W. Noomen and N. Van Den Boogaard (eds.), *Nouveau recueil complet des fabliaux* (Assen, 1983–98), ii/9—these references indicate the volume and story number (henceforth *NRCF*).

[18] Molière's *Le Médecin Malgré Lui* (1666) is a later version of the same story.

[19] Cf. C. H. Haskins, *Studies in the History of Mediaeval Science* (Cambridge, Mass., 1927), 18.

[20] P. Biller, 'John of Naples: Quodlibets and Medieval Theological Concern with the Body', in P. Biller and A. Minnis (eds.), *Medieval Theology and the Natural Body* (York, 1997), 3–8. Preachers fond of such analogies included Ranulphe de la Houblonnière and William of Luxembourg: see Bériou, *Prédication*, 45–50; A. Sularik, 'The Preaching of William of Luxembourg at the Paris Schools between 1267 and 1285', in *Preaching and Society in the Middle Ages: Ethics, Values and Social Behaviour. Proceedings of the XII Medieval Sermon Studies Symposium* (Padua, 2002), 143–71.

the symptoms *per se*. Closely allied to this appeared a growing interest in anatomy, revealing a similar interest in the relationship between bodily signs and their meaning.[21] Not only physicians, but also surgeons, were swept along by this current, with a growing body of texts and the gradual professionalization of the discipline working out a new epistemology of surgery wherein external indicators such as abscesses were read as evidence of internal bodily problems.[22] More sophisticated theories of pain were developed, both in medical symptomatology, and in hagiographical readings of saintly suffering; and concomitant with understanding pain came a greater awareness of what constituted cruelty.[23]

Importantly for our purposes, such readings were becoming increasingly relevant in a legal context, where physicians were employed to testify to the gravity of wounds: the meaning of particular violent acts was to be read accordingly.[24] These physicians were to draw on moralizing and medical readings of violently inflicted marks on bodies.

2. VIOLENCE AS COMMUNICATION

2.1. Literature

Similar readings of violent gestures via their effects on bodies were prevalent in much of the popular literature of the period. This performed literature took it as a given that violence could have a communicative purpose, as both functional and punitive.[25] Such stories were intended as entertainment, and not only engaged with ways in which contemporaries thought about the effects of violence, but discursively shaped such attitudes, and, importantly, undercut and problematized them. The corpora of both the *fabliaux* and the *Roman de Renart* are cases in point: dating mainly from the early thirteenth century (though continuing to be per-

21 R. Mandressi, *Le Regard de l'anatomiste: Dissections et invention du corps en Occident* (Paris, 2003), 245–83.

22 M. McVaugh, *The Rational Surgery of the Middle Ages* (Florence, 2006).

23 E. Cohen, 'The Animated Pain of the Body', *American Historical Review*, 105/1 (2000), 36–68; D. Baraz, *Medieval Cruelty: Changing Perceptions: Late Antiquity to the Early Modern Period* (Ithaca, NY, 2003), 123–42.

24 e.g. L. Tanon, *Histoire des justices des anciennes églises et communautés monastiques de Paris* (Paris, 1883), 468, 484, 500.

25 Physical violence was also an important theme in courtly literature, but such texts tended to focus upon chivalric violence, and to address rather more restricted audiences. This is, of course, a generalization as the treatment of violence in courtly literature is extremely subtle and problematic, as are questions of reception: see e.g. R. H. Bloch, *Medieval Misogyny and the Invention of Western Romantic Love* (Chicago, 1991), 113–64.

formed orally throughout the period), they appealed to a broad social range.[26]

For example, the violence in the *fabliau Les Trois Aveugles de Compiegne* punishes three blind men for their inability to pay for their meal and lodging in the inn, and aims to force payment.[27] The inn-keeper explains that their damaged bodies testify to their misdemeanour: 'Chascuns aura de son cors honte'.[28] A threat to the economic order is suppressed and corrected by violence whose meaning is clear, but whose communicative function is undercut by the pleasure in suffering enjoyed by the clerk who artificially engineered the whole situation. Likewise the *Provost a l'aumuche* is unable to keep his piece of stolen lard because of protracted beatings, and the marks on his body are to discourage him from behaving in the same way in the future.[29] These are comic tales whose humour challenges expected paradigms of communication and marks on bodies by the sheer excess of the brutality. But the stories do defend what they see as a rightful use of violence. The base knight of *Berengier au lonc cul* tries to usurp a noble identity by means of sham knightly exploits, and is put in his place by the violence of his wife who masquerades as another knight.[30] He misuses the signs of violence to deceive, returning each day with 'ses escuz/ . . . troëz et despeciez' (ll. 142–3). To reinforce the wrongfulness of his position in the social hierarchy, there is a sexual dimension as well: his wife poses as a man, forcing him to confront his own lack of masculinity as symbolically 'Do poin li chiet l'espee nue'.[31] Order is restored here, but the complexity of the gender constructions and the humiliating nature of the violence provokes troubled laughter.

[26] Cf. 'Introduction', in *NRCF* i, pp. i–xx, for an account of the widespread survival of manuscripts from the late 13th cent. P. Nykrog considered the stories to be parodies for a courtly audience (*Les fabliaux: Étude littéraire et de stylistique medieval,* Copenhagen, 1957); this was in response to J. Bédier's argument that they addressed townspeople (*Les fabliaux: Études de littérature populaire et d'histoire littéraire du Moyen Age,* Paris, 1893); scholarly consensus now assumes a varied audience, including courts, peasants, townspeople, etc., e.g. C. Muscatine, *The Old French Fabliaux* (New Haven, 1986), N. Lacy, *Reading Fabliaux* (New York, 1993), S. Gaunt, *Gender and Genre in Medieval French Literature* (Cambridge, 1995). The Renart stories were rewritten in various forms at the turn of the 13th and 14th cents., famously by Jacquemart Giélée (*Renart le nouvel,* ed. H. Roussel, Paris, 1961), this latter being more overtly didactic and allegorical. The focus here is on the more complex earlier versions: see H. Roussel, 'La Structure narrative de *Renart le nouvel*', ibid., and F. Suard, *Alain de Lille, Gautier de Châtillon, Jakemart Giélée et leur temps* (Lille, 1978), 321–32.

[27] *NRCF* ii/9.

[28] 'Each one will be ashamed because of his body': l. 187.

[29] *NRCF* iv/24.

[30] *NRCF* iv/34.

[31] 'The naked sword fell from his fist': l. 206.

But the anxious undercurrents in the *fabliaux* that violence might over-signify or deceive were taken to another level in the *Roman de Renart* where violence does not communicate or marks on bodies signify at all: these are stories about the disintegration of meaning. The *fabliaux*'s non-noble human beings are replaced by the brutal aristocratic animals of the *Roman de Renart*. In the *Renart*, the function of a given violent act is confused and often non-existent, and no order is restored by violence, simply disorder and nightmarish scenarios of degenerating cycles of ever increasing cruelty.

The non-signification of violence is effectively encapsulated in the game of 'plantées' played by the animals in *La mort de Renart*.[32] This game involved standing on one leg, and trying to keep one's balance when charged at by another animal: the cat knocks over the wolf, the bull then joins the fray, but is knocked over by the cricket, who is then knocked over by the wild boar; problems occur when no one can shift Tardif, the snail. This game is brutally violent, but it remains ludic: the suffering bodies have no meaning other than the fun of the blows. Even in those scenes where a certain rationality of vengeance is discernible, straightforward vengeance swiftly gives way to sadistic play; witness Renart's vicious treatment of his friend, Tibert the cat.[33]

In the *fabliaux*, violence is superficially functional, and the forms chosen by its perpetrators are depicted as tailored to re-establish hierarchies: it is the degree of brutality which subverts straightforward interpretative paradigms. In contrast, the forms of violence are openly dysfunctional in the *Renart*. The juxtaposition of rape scenes from the two sets of texts highlights this fundamental divergence. In the *fabliau Constant du Hamel*, the rapist explicitly rapes his female victims in order to punish those of whom they are, according to the *fabliau*, the sexual property.[34] The rapes are described abruptly: the victims, irrelevant to the meaning of the violence, do not even display reactions, and only their bodies signify the humiliation of their partners. In contrast, Renart's rape of the female wolf, Hersent, is described in great detail, because here there is no function other than sexual desire and cruelty. Hersent's personal reaction is made explicit, and the narrator repeatedly dwells on Renart's desire and pleasure, and on Hersent's sense of utter humiliation: 'Ne volt lessier en nule guise/Que il n'alast a lui gesir/Et faire de lui son plesir'.[35]

[32] *Le Roman de Renart* (henceforth *RR*), ed. A. Strubel (Paris, 1999), XVIII—the number refers to the 'branch' of the tale.

[33] *RR* VI.

[34] *NRCF* i/2.

[35] 'He was determined not to leave without sleeping with her, and taking his pleasure from her': II, ll. 542–4.

But the focus of the description is not on any ulterior motive or layer of reason, simply upon the violence itself. This dysfunction is embedded in the very structure of the *Renart* which consists of a number of interdependent branches, each forming an episode in the life of the eponymous hero.[36] The stories are non-linear and their open-ended branches are arranged in different orders in the various manuscripts. Indeed, they can be rearranged ad infinitum. Where the *fabliaux* tend to close with a neat epilogue highlighting the communicative quality of the violence (however troubling), the *Renart* constantly challenges the very notion of closure. Even death, the ultimate violent sign, means nothing here: the fox pretends to die again and again, whether as part of a plan to eat the cockerel or the crow, or because he really is very ill, but he always springs back into life with a flourish.[37]

Grammars of violence become irrelevant, as the very meaning of a given act is challenged in the *Renart* via the technique of 'réécriture': many of the branches reinterpret earlier episodes, so that even the hermeneutics of violence are never stable but always in flux, open to renegotiation. Rewriting or retelling attains its apogee in *La Mort de Renart* where, in the process of going back over the dying fox's life, the animals produce a host of different accounts of the rape of Hersent. In his confession, Renart rewrites the rape as an act of charity; the donkey archpriest, Bernart, reinterprets rape and all sexual acts as acts of praiseworthy virtue and relegates all chaste people to hell; and then Ferrant, the packhorse, reinterprets the act yet again as a simple case of adultery: the initial scene of rape is constantly evolving, being reinterpreted and rewritten. Whereas the *fabliaux* engage with anxiety about the acceptability of violent communications, the Renart stories go further in troubling the fundamental paradigm that violence enjoys any agreed or stable meaning.

2.2. Legal Discussions

These contrasting assessments of the way in which violence communicated engendered a need for legal frameworks to provide a way of distinguishing between ordering and disordering violence. The meanings of particular gestures were not just assessed by degree of physical harm, but by careful distinctions; nevertheless different legal discourses, revealed in custumals, municipal charters, and royal law, did not always agree with one another straightforwardly. Although the fourteenth century saw a decline in the tarification of crimes, this was less the case in areas of

[36] J. Scheidegger, *Le Roman de Renart, ou, le texte de la dérision* (Geneva, 1989), 3.
[37] *RR* XVIII.

customary law, and legal paradigms continued to promote publicly shared ways of reading particular acts.[38] Tarification of penalties reveals cultural hierarchies of physical gestures, but these various frameworks or grammars for interpreting violence were engaged in a task subtler than mere classification and codification.[39]

Legal mechanisms

This is the moment to elucidate how these legal frameworks functioned. The later thirteenth and early fourteenth centuries was a period of multiple overlapping jurisdictions and legal frameworks, and of increasingly explicit discussions of the role of law. It marked a shift towards 'a conscious, verbalized system of norms that people in a society are supposed to observe and that is followed in authoritative settlement of conflicts', without eliminating the bewildering judicial variety characteristic of many medieval societies.[40]

At a macrocosmic level, canon law coexisted with lay law: the two usually engaged with different spheres of people's lives, the spiritual and the temporal respectively, but there were significant areas of overlap and potential conflict, notably regarding marriage. Canon law was established by the precepts of the ecclesiastical hierarchy, and yet often drew upon the insights of Roman law.[41] Study in the expanding universities focused upon either canon or Roman law, or upon the complex intertwining of the two achieved in Bartolo da Sassoferrato's (1314–57) *ius commune*.[42] Lay law was constituted by a complex mixture of customary law and Roman law, the latter's influence often remaining indirect and unacknowledged. Customary law was tempered by growing levels of royal legislation, and more significantly, by the fragmentary nature of the differing customs of diverse times and places.

The legitimacy of a custom depended upon habit or *consuetudo*: it had to be demonstrated that it had been in use for a significant length of time within a particular community.[43] The conceptual problem for the historian of assessing whether customs arose from judgments or vice versa is left

[38] Gauvard, *Grace*, 128.

[39] 'Nous envisageons la "peine" en tant que forme culturelle qui participe dans les jeux des pouvoirs et dans la reproduction des rapports sociaux': H. Benveniste, 'Le Système des amendes pénales en France au Moyen Age: Une première mise en perspective', *Revue d'histoire du droit français et étranger*, 70 (1992), 1.

[40] F. Cheyette, 'Suum cuique tribuere', *French Historical Studies*, 6 (1969), 288.

[41] J. Brundage, *Medieval Canon Law* (London, 1995), 59.

[42] See C. Donahue, jun., 'Law, Civil', in *Dictionary of the Middle Ages*, vii. 418–25.

[43] Philippe de Beaumanoir, *Les Coutumes de Beauvaisis*, ed. A. Salmon, 2 vols. (Paris, 1999), i, no. 683, 346–7; C. Allen, *Law in the Making* (Oxford, new edn. 1964), 80–115.

hanging by this criterion.[44] The impulse to write down customary law grew rapidly over the course of the thirteenth and fourteenth centuries, and not just in the context of communal charters: unlike the charters, usually composed in Latin, the compilations were often in the vernacular and tended to be far more detailed.[45] Compilers gave a variety of reasons for their decision, primarily citing the need to impose a degree of fixity and stability on the eternally fluid: they wrote 'si qu'eles soient maintenues sans changier des ore en avant'.[46] The role of these texts was to render explicit the diverse customs of their respective regions, without eliding their differences, and to underline, rather than to undermine, the intensity of the relationship between customary laws and local communities.

[44] Allen, *Law,* 120–8.

[45] The most famous customary law compilation dates from *c.*1283, and was by Philippe de Beaumanoir, a comital, and then a royal *bailli*, or legal representative: see Philippe de Beaumanoir, *Les Coutumes*, ed. Salmon (to which footnotes here refer) and *The Coutumes of Philippe of Beaumanoir*, ed. F. Akehurst (Philadelphia, 1992). These purport to be no more than the customs of just one region, and cannot be used as a source of law for other regions, but do serve to reveal a broader discursive shift towards exposition and clarification of customary law, and its rootedness in local communities. Thirteen manuscript copies survive: although focused on the Vermandois region, the *Coutumes* were disseminated a little more widely, and two copies in Picard dialect survive: BN 11557 (13th cent.); BN fr. 4516 (14th cent.). See also E. Lyon, 'Un manuscript inédit de Beaumanoir', in *Mélanges Paul Fournier* (Paris, 1929), 479–86. Another custumal was produced by an anonymous lawyer from Orléans between 1272 and 1273, and includes customary compilations from Touraine Anjou and the Orléanais: *Etablissements de Saint Louis*, ed. and tr. F. Akehurst (Philadelphia, 1996); when quoting from this text, I use the edition by P. Viollet, 2 vols (Paris, 1881–1886). Louis IX himself had nothing to do with the production or promulgation of this text, but it remains significant given its central appearance in two MSS of the *Ordonnances* of St Louis, in a custumal of the Touraine-Anjou region, and in a custumal from Orléans: *Etablissements*, i, p. i. A counterpoint is provided by *Li livres de jostice et de plet*, ed. P. Rapetti and F. Chabaille (Paris, 1850), where customary law from west-central France is more explicitly juxtaposed with Roman law, and formality underscored more referentially by the scholar author from the university of Orléans. The influence of Roman law was also stronger in the *Coutumier d'Artois*, ed. A Tardif (Paris, 1883), a set of customs apparently written between 1283 and 1302: see pp. xiv–xv. The author was a lawyer from Arras, who drew on Roman law, the decretals, customs, and personal experience in order to present a picture of customary law as exercised in Artois. The *Coutumiers* of Picardy and Ponthieu were less skilfully compiled, but date to the same period, with a particular focus on procedure and precedent: M. Marnier (ed.), *Ancien coutumier inédit de Picardie (1300–1323) contenant les coutumes notoires, arrêts et ordonnances des cours, assises et autres jurisdictions de Picardie au commencement du quatorzième siècle* (Paris, 1840). Beside this, we can place some of the customs confirmed in early charters granted to communes in the region of Artois, published in R. Fossier, *Chartes de Coutume en Picardie (XIe–XIIIe siècle)* (Paris, 1974): I cite Fossier, followed by document number and name of the relevant commune. I also refer to G. Espinas, *Recueil de documents relatives à l'histoire du droit municipal en France des origines à la révolution: Artois*, 3 vols. (Paris, 1934–43): I cite Espinas, followed by page number and the name of the relevant commune.

[46] 'So that they should be maintained, without change, from now on': Beaumanoir, i, no. 7, 4.

Defining violence

Customary law suggested shifting interpretations of specific kinds of violence by using different terms for violence in a very precise way. Where uncertainty remained, investigation focused precisely upon such lexical niceties, as in an instruction of 1293 to the *bailli* of Amiens to carry out an investigation into the differences between 'latrocinium' (brigandage) and 'melleia' (armed struggles): in an era of competing jurisdictions, such nuances had powerful repercussions.[47]

The concept of giving blows was circumscribed and refined in the custumals via the careful nuancing of different terms for this action. 'Ferir' designated the specific action of striking somebody, often with a single blow: Beaumanoir used it to evoke the idea of a poor man striking his lord.[48] 'Battre', on the other hand, was used in the context of a struggle, suggesting blows being struck often indiscriminately: an alternative expression was 'une colée donner' (to give a volley of blows).[49] Other words from the same semantic field carried more specific implications concerning the effect on the victim. 'Navrer' indicated a blood wound, and often occurred in the context of a murder or a mêlée.[50] 'Mehaignier' referred to beating up causing near death,[51] whereas 'afoler' implied damage necessitating the presence of a doctor.[52]

Nuances between the various methods of designating rape were clearly articulated. 'Forcer' (and other signifiers from the same root: 'esforcier', 'faire force', and so on) indicated non-consensual sexual relations.[53] This also implied taking something which belonged to somebody else and was often synonymous with 'rat', reflecting the notion of the woman as her husband or guardian's property:[54] 'forcer' was also used in conjunction with the term 'despuceler', again evoking the idea of material loss, because a woman without her virginity was of less value on the marriage market. The *Etablissements* were careful to distinguish 'despuceler' from 'forcer' however: the former referred to illicit sexual intercourse, even if both parties were consenting, whereas 'forcer' necessarily evoked resistance on

47 E. Boutaric (ed.), *Actes du Parlement de Paris*, 2 vols. (Paris, 1863–7), i, no. 2827, 278 (1293)—this reference in turn provides the reference for the relevant part of the *Olim* (Parlement registers).

48 Beaumanoir, i, no. 842, 434.

49 *Etablissements*, ii, part II, no. 24, 416.

50 Ibid., part I, no. 30, 45; Beaumanoir, ii, no. 1946, 482.

51 Beaumanoir, i, no. 841, 433; ii, no. 1702, 371; ii, no. 1947, 482.

52 Ibid., i, no. 841, 433.

53 e.g. ibid. i, no. 829, 430.

54 *Coutumier d'Artois*, XI.14, 45.

the part of the victim.[55] While 'forcer' engendered two victims, namely the woman and her husband or guardian, 'despuceler' victimized only the husband or guardian.[56] Customary law, in its various redactions, thus formalized the violence itself and defined what exactly constituted an illicit act: extra-marital sexual intercourse was defined as an act of public violence, rather than an activity affecting only the individuals directly involved. These lexical distinctions were reiterated in the context of imaginative literature: with the realism necessary to render their stories credible to urban audiences, the later *fabliaux* drew upon the legalistic lexical distinctions between different forms of violence and distinguished between different degrees of violence.[57] The three seduction episodes of *Le Prestre et le chevalier* are distinguished as 'despucelement' of the first victim (evoking themes of loss of material property for the priest, her guardian), 'séduire' for the mistress of the priest (connoting her sexual willingness), and 'sodomie' for the priest himself.[58]

Custumals evoked a wide spectrum of words to designate the action of taking life: 'tuer', 'ocir', 'murtrir' (and its derivatives), 'mourir' (and 'mettre a mort'), 'traison', and 'homicide'. 'Tuer' could be used in contexts as diverse as infanticide,[59] premeditated murder,[60] battle,[61] and manslaughter.[62] It implied that the murder was a by-product of a much broader set of circumstances. 'Ocir' and 'tuer' never appeared in the same clause, suggesting that there was a slight distinction in their meaning. In contrast with 'tuer', 'ocir' suggested that the act of murder *was* the totality of the event: both its outcome and its meaning. It was used either where there was an element of premeditation on the part of the aggressor, or where the killing apparently fulfilled a specific purpose.[63]

'Mourir' and 'mettre à mort' were subtly distinguished. The former was most often used to suggest a situation where loss of life was the *unplanned* outcome: it was used for accidental infanticide, unintentional killing in self-defence, and manslaughter.[64] Manslaughter was not designated as

55 *Etablissements*, ii, part I, no. 55, 79.

56 *Coutumier d'Artois*, XV.2, p. 48, XVI.2, 49.

57 H. Wheeler, 'Les Représentations de la violence dans les fabliaux et le *Roman de Renart*' (DEA thesis, Paris III Nouvelle Sorbonne, 2003), appendix B.

58 *NRCF* ix/103.

59 *Etablissements*, ii, part I, no. 39, p. 55.

60 Ibid., no. 40, 56. Here, the text discusses what to do if someone is caught with the intention of murdering somebody, but before the act: the conclusion is that he or she should not be corporally punished.

61 Beaumanoir, ii, no. 1669, 355.

62 e.g. ibid., no. 1942, 479; no. 1957, 487.

63 Ibid. i, no. 932, 472; i, no. 933, 472; i, no. 934, 473.

64 e.g. ibid. ii, no. 1943, 480.

such, and leniency accorded owing to the accidental nature of the murder was at the discretion of the judge. However, by such subtle shadings of language, the compilers contributed to an early sense of the implications of lack of intention.[65] The phrase 'mettre à mort' suggested a greater degree of intention, and is found in the context of war and vengeance.[66] 'Traison' frequently occurred in juxtaposition with the terms 'murtre' and 'homicide'.[67] Beaumanoir clarified that 'traison' did not always involve murder, whereas 'murtre' always involved 'traison'.[68] In contrast to murder, which was always premeditated,[69] homicide could designate a sudden death in a *rixe* or *mêlée*.[70] Some types of violence remained conceptually indistinct: there was no clear differentiation between infanticide, abortion, and 'encis', beating a pregnant woman so that she lost her baby.[71]

Custumals explored the mechanisms of interpersonal messages and the relationship between the perpetrator and interlocutor of an act of violence. The *Etablissements* stipulated that if an *homme costumier* struck the *prévôt* of his lord, he would be fined 60 sous, and that if he struck the lord himself, he would lose his fist: no such fines were mentioned for the lord himself.[72] Sometimes, however, the law codes eliminated distinctions in terms of enunciators of violence; the *Etablissements* specified that if a *gentil homme* were to challenge a *villain*, the ensuing battle should take place on equal terms.[73] In cases of rape, the law made it clear that the principal interlocutor against whom the violent message was directed was the woman's husband or guardian, as it was to him that damages were to be paid.[74]

The legal compilations of the thirteenth century elucidated the relative acceptability of violent acts, though often providing only ambivalent

[65] For comparative purposes, cf. T. Green, 'Societal Concepts of Criminal Liability for Homicide in Mediaeval England', *Speculum*, 47/4 (1972), 669–94: Anglo-Saxon English law made a distinction between intentional and unintentional murder, but this was withdrawn by Henry II's lawyers.

[66] Beaumanoir, i, no. 887, 449; no. 889, 450.

[67] *Etablissements,* ii, part I, no. 87, 143; Beaumanoir, i, no. 824, 429.

[68] Beaumanoir, i, no. 827, 430.

[69] Gauvard, *Grace*, 800–1; J.-M. Carbasse, *Histoire du droit pénal et de la justice criminelle* (Paris, 2000), 319–20. Beaumanoir, i, no. 827, 430.

[70] Carbasse, *Histoire du droit*, 319–20. Beaumanoir, i, no. 828, 430. The *Coutumier d'Artois* states that 'murdres' signifies any wrongful killing apart from spontaneous killing in a *mêlée*: XI.14, 45.

[71] Carbasse, *Histoire du droit*, 323–4. See the *Coutumier d'Artois*, XI.14, 45.

[72] *Etablissements,* ii, part I, no. 156, 292; no. 157, 293. See also *Coutumier d'Artois,* XV.1, 48.

[73] *Etablissements,* ii, part I, no. 87, 144.

[74] Beaumanoir, i, no. 926, 467.

criteria or disagreeing amongst themselves. Some violent acts, such as arson, were unequivocally condemned,[75] but more often elucidation nuanced boundaries of permissibility: for instance, robbery with the threat of violence was said to be actionable only if the victim responded with a suitable defence.[76] Violent self-defence was perceived as legitimate, but its acceptability was mitigated by the proviso that an armed defence could not legitimately oppose an unarmed attack.[77] Legal discussion grammatically specified how particular acts of violence could legitimately or illegimately be realized. Many custumals informed people that punching was, by and large, acceptable, whereas beatings with a stick or other weapon were not.[78] According to the *Etablissements*, a beating which did not lead to loss of blood should be tolerated, whereas one which shed blood was a much more serious matter: if limbs were lost, the severity of the incident was said to be even greater.[79] An act of killing was defined as murder when its context was one of dishonesty, lacking the crucial challenge which would place the act within a framework of vengeance.[80] Legal developments did not simply ban violence, but tried to direct and mould acceptable forms, as well as suggest how physical gestures should be interpreted. It was in this context that medical expertise was called upon to help apply these distinctions in practice to visible wounds.

The compilations bear witness to a growing concern with analysing how particular temporal moments might affect the meaning of a given violent communication and its collective implications. Beaumanoir concluded that fines for beatings on market days should be increased in relation to fines for beatings on non-market days: 60 sous for a poor man and 60 livres for a *gentilhomme* as opposed to 5 deniers for a poor man and 10 sous for a *gentilhomme*.[81] Crimes committed at night were deemed to be more nefarious, indicative of the criminal intention of the perpetrator.[82] Space was also important. Physical violence was deemed more threatening if it took place in church, in the market, or at a mill.[83]

Beaumanoir explored how the criminality and communicative meaning of a violent event was dependent upon intention, and the concept of

75 Ibid., no. 996, 504. Carbasse, *Histoire du droit*, 340–1.

76 Beaumanoir, i, no. 994, 503–4.

77 Ibid., no. 889, 450. Also e.g. Espinas, i. 143, Marck, and 95, Langle.

78 Espinas, i. 141–3, Marck.

79 *Etablissements*, ii, part II, no. 24, 415–17. The part of the body targeted was also significant: Espinas, i. 142–3, Marck. See also Fossier, no. 26, Ham.

80 *Etablissements*, ii, part I, no. 27, 37–8.

81 Beaumanoir, i, no. 839, 432; no. 840, 433. According to the customs of Marck, beatings on market days were also more serious: Espinas, i. 141–2.

82 e.g. Espinas, i, 140, Marck; 93, Langle.

83 Carbasse, *Histoire du droit*, 326–8; e.g. Espinas, i. 142, Marck.

reasonable precaution. To this end, he mentioned that an accidental death without nefarious intention did not constitute a violent communication. Games in this period were extremely risky, potentially causing painful physical damage. Beaumanoir cited the example of archery, demonstrating that, if proven to be an accident, the lack of evil intent robbed the event of any more sinister meaning.[84] Premeditated violence was perceived as more nefarious, even whilst its communicative value might be clearer.[85]

Emotion was an important factor, and violence inspired by 'mautalent' or 'ire' was to be heavily punished.[86] But whilst spontaneous anger was a deadly sin and condemned both in religious discourse and in customary law, the lingering anger which was often equated with hatred was seen as still more problematic. In the context of moral philosophy Thomas Aquinas, pondering the relative sinfulness of hatred and anger, concluded by citing Aristotle and Augustine to say that hatred is the more dangerous as it is both a habit and a passion.[87] Roman law nuanced this position by suggesting that anger could be indicative of a loss of control and hence of full responsibility.[88] In letters of remission, anger was often used as an excuse to mitigate responsibility, but it was socially differentiated as it was more often used by those of higher social status.[89] For those of lower social status, inebriation was a more frequently cited excuse.[90] Of course, as a distinction, anger could also serve to denigrate certain perpetrators, and to undermine their own agency, notably in the case of women who were frequently stereotyped as more fragile prey to uncontrollable anger.[91] It functioned somewhat differently as a distinction depending upon the age of the perpetrator, with young people more likely to cite diabolical temptation.[92]

The role of communities

Local communities were involved in the production and reception of all these frameworks for interpreting violence: people consented to legal norms; provided tales for exempla; called for doctors' opinions; told stories

84 Beaumanoir, ii, no. 1941, 479: in this case, the culprit was to pay the victim if he survived and needed costly medical attention.

85 T. Green, 'The Jury and the English Law of Homicide, 1200–1600', *Michigan Law Review*, 74/6 (1976), 416. Beaumanoir, ii, no. 1575, 297 states madness as a mitigating factor, but explains that this can also be feigned to disguise premeditation.

86 e.g. Espinas, i. 143, Marck; 727, Wavans.

87 *Summa Theologica*, Prima Secundae, q. 46, all quoted in Gauvard, *Grace*, 686–7.

88 Ibid. 433. Gratian, c. 15, qu.1.

89 Gauvard, *Grace*, 453–4.

90 Ibid. 449.

91 Carbasse, *Histoire du droit*, 241.

92 Gauvard, *Grace*, 439.

and listened to sermons. Uncertain customs depended on the consent of the community and the perceived reasonableness and utility of the custom in question.[93] Although regulations purported to be fixed, customs were constantly changing and the 'grammars' of violence described above were open to debate.

Customs were intimately bound up with collective identities, even local pride; but they could respond flexibly to changing local needs, and were adapted and developed organically according to shared notions of reasonableness and usefulness. If the legitimacy of a particular custom was deemed insufficiently *notoire*, the procedure of *enquête par turbe* involving ten or more qualified people was used to establish its status, or of *enquête ordinaire* involving non-specialist witnesses heard one by one: the local community participated in establishing its own norms.[94] And individual cases were procedurally rooted in communities. Cases were often initiated because of a *fama*, the reporting of which was shaped by legal norms, but which also arose from the whole nexus of other normative discourses.[95] In many cases, bringing a legal case only represented the culmination of a series of irritations.[96] The *enquête publique* was based upon denunciation, and relied upon the accused to agree to submit to an investigation on pain of banishment. The *aprise* was a formal investigation without any need for consent, instigated by a *fama*: this was a preliminary to an arrest, at which point specific accusers would be invited.[97] In the towns of Artois, the municipal *échevins* applied customary law on behalf of the count, and responded increasingly to widespread rumours.[98] Likewise, seigneurial

[93] Beaumanoir, i, no. 683, 346–7.

[94] In J. Gilissen, *La coutume* (Turnhout, 1982), 65–6 and 68–9. See Ordonnance *Inquiretur de consuetudinibus in hunc modum* (1270), in Boutaric, *Actes*, i, no. 2547.

[95] T. Fenster and D. Smail, 'Introduction', in their *Fama: The Politics of Talk and Reputation in Medieval Europe* (Ithaca, NY, 2003), 3. *Fama* was discussed in the ordinances of St Louis, as well as in custumals: *Ordonnances des Rois de France*, ed. E. de Laurières (22 vols. Paris, 1849), i. 50 (1228), 79, no. 10 (1256); *Très ancien coutumier de Normandie*, ed. E. Tardif (1881–1903), 191, 202: quoted in A. Porteau-Bitker and A. Talazac-Laurent, 'La Renommée dans le droit pénal laïque du treizième au quinzième siècle', *Médiévales*, 24 (1993), 76–7.

[96] A. Soman, 'Deviance and Criminal Justice in Western Europe, 1300–1800: An Essay in Structure', *Criminal Justice History*, 1 (1980), 10. Gauvard, *Grace*, 141.

[97] G. Ducoudray, *Les Origines du Parlement de Paris et la justice aux treizième et quatorzième siècles* (Paris, 1902), 471–89; F. Akehurst, 'Good Name, Reputation and Notoriety in French Customary Law', in Fenster and Smail, *Fama*, 83.

[98] R. Grand, 'Justice criminelle, procédure et peines dans les villes aux treizième et quatorzième siècles', *Bibliothèque de l'École des Chartes*, 101 (1941), 67; F. Monier, 'L'Administration et la condition juridique des habitants de la ville d'Arras au douzième siècle', in *Mélanges Paul Fournier* (Paris, 1929), 551–64. Also useful is S. Hamel, *La Justice dans une ville du nord de la royaume de France au Moyen Age: Étude sur la pratique judiciaire à Saint Quentin (fin XIe-début XVe siècle)* (Turnhout, 2012).

jurisdictions in Paris (the records only survive for those belonging to ecclesiastical lordships) responded to community rumours by instigating cases, even those judged by customary law, and often allowed reputation within the community as a form of evidence. Many of the procedural developments traditionally seen as indicative of a more top-down approach to controlling violence (the demise of judicial duels in favour of legal process; growing royal legislation) were dependent on *fama*, and continued to root the practice of law in communities.[99]

Most importantly, this period marked a conceptual shift, albeit an ambivalent one, as top-down developments were explicitly motivated by the idea of 'commun pourfit', and violence was seen to be no longer merely interpersonal in its implications, but increasingly to affect the community. Beaumanoir refers to the common good in his customary compilation, but it was most fully worked out in royal law under the impact of Roman law and neo-Aristotelian notions of the bonum commune.[100] The gradual shift from an accusatorial to an inquisitorial system highlighted the way in which the common good was placed centre stage: it also continued to rely on local communities, by enhancing further the role of *fama*.[101] More formalized investigative procedures were developed, and large numbers of investigations now took place before the Parlement of Paris, and were based upon collected witness statements.[102] This shift and growing royal judicial power can be neatly framed by two popular versions of the well-known miracle story of *Guibour*: the mid-thirteenth-century narrative by Gautier de Coinci[103] and the 1368 play known as *Un Miracle*

[99] *Etablissements,* ii, Part 1, no. 3, 8–10; R. Bartlett, *Trial by Fire and Water: The Medieval Judicial Ordeal* (Oxford, 1986), 81. *Coutumier d'Artois,* XLIII.1, 10. Duels did not disappear and many cases are attested, e.g. in Abbeville, AMA, MS. 115, fo. 32^{v} (1274); G. Langmuir, 'Community and Legal Change in Capetian France', *French Historical Studies,* 6 (1969), 284.

[100] See M. Kempshall, *The Common Good in Late Medieval Political Thought* (Oxford, 1999), particularly 1–25.

[101] Grand, 'Justice criminelle', 70–3; B. Geremek, *The Margins of Society in Late Medieval Paris,* tr. J. Birrell (Cambridge, 1987), 13.

[102] L. De Carbonnières, *La Procédure devant la chambre criminelle du Parlement de Paris au quatorzième siècle* (Champion, 2004), 415–33. Also Porteau-Bitker and Talazac-Laurent, 'La Renommée', 67–81.

[103] Gautier himself was not the creator of the story, and based his own text upon a Latin original. The story seems to have originated in a real incident occurring in 1096 and recounted in the *Chronique d'Hélinand*: the twelve extant Latin versions from the early 12th cent. (including a version by Sigebert de Gembloux and a version by the monk Hermann de Laon: the latter will be referred to here) all seem to share a common origin and constitute the version which was then reused by Gautier de Coinci in the early 13th cent. Cf. V. Väänänen, *D'une fame de Laon qui estoit jugie a ardoir que Nostre Dame delivra: Miracle versifié par Gautier de Coinci* (Helsinki, 1951), 9–11: Väänänen provides edns. of the text of Gautier de Coinci, and that of the monk Hermann.

de Nostre Dame: Coment elle garda une femme d'estre arse produced for the Parisian Guild of Goldsmiths as part of their annual festivities.[104] This was socially embedded literature, engaging with the multiple discursive frameworks of hagiography, imaginative literature, legal proceedings, and even preaching.[105] In this story of a woman who has her son-in-law strangled, the two texts give significantly different emphasis to the legal procedure.[106] In the earlier version, a local episcopal official (the *vidame*) responds to a private accusation by the brother of the deceased, and the investigation is swiftly dismissed in only eight lines. In the later theatrical version, the royal *bailli* undertakes an extensive investigation (over 200 lines) responding to a *fama* in the community.[107] An interpersonal accusatorial system has been replaced by an inquisitorial system which claims to respond to community concerns and to protect the common good. Whilst these developments continued to root the reading and interpretation of violence in the community, they also represented a substantive shift in suggesting that the community as a whole, rather than just networks of individuals, was affected by, and should respond to, physical violence.

Concomitantly, appeals became more frequent, though the progress of an appellate system was halting: many tried to prevent appeals by violent intimidation, and there was no appeal against capital cases in customary law.[108] Remissions were fixed from the reign of Philip VI of Valois, but were not systematically registered so the evidence is only fragmentary for this early period. On the one hand, appellate jurisdictions served the cause of central authority, whilst drawing on ideas of rigour and pity:[109] the Paris Parlement was the court of first instance for parts of the kingdom possessed directly by the king, or for any trials of royal officers, or people and communities placed under royal protection; for everyone else, it was a

[104] All the plays in the collection were edited as *Miracles de Nostre Dame par personnages*, ed. G. Paris and U. Robert, 6 vols. (Paris, 1876–93). *Une Femme que Nostre Dame garda d'estre arse* is in vol. iv.

[105] J-C. Payen, 'Théâtre médiéval et culture urbaine', *Revue d'Histoire du Théâtre*, 35 (1983), 233–50.

[106] The portrayal of the legal system in this *Miracle* has already been observed by G. Guyon in 'La Justice pénale dans le théâtre religieux du XIVe siècle: Les *Miracles de Nostre Dame par personnages*', *Revue historique de droit français et étranger* (1991), 465–86. However his remarks are limited to observations on the inquisitorial system, and he does not attempt to compare the different versions of the story, focusing instead on the play itself.

[107] 'By the oath I have made to the king!': l. 669.

[108] Ducoudray, *Les Origines*, 530–5.

[109] P. Texier, 'La Rémission au quatorzième siècle: Significations et fonctions', in *La Rémission des crimes: Communications présentées par l'Institut Anthropologique et Juridique de Limoges* (Limoges, 1984).

court of appeal, though one in practice restricted to those with personal connections or of higher social status.[110] On the other hand, appeal and remission do suggest growing conceptual anxiety about who was principally affected both by interpersonal violent gestures and their effects on whole communities. Moreover, customary law continued to be important: du Breuil's *Stilus Curie Parlamenti* indicates the continuing reliance of the Parlement of Paris on custom, citing the style and custom of the *Châtelet* of Paris, the *Coutume générale de France*, royal ordinances, and the ordinary style of the Parlement.[111] Reform of the Parlement in this period under the Philips testified to a growing interest in rendering explicit the purpose of law and its hermeneutics of violence, as well as a sense that the whole community was affected by interpersonal violence.[112]

Interest in defining types of violence, and the suggestion that interpersonal gestures affected the community as a whole, naturally shaped punitive responses. Attempts to reconceptualize the implications of communicative violence by reducing compositions between individuals and imposing public punishments in a sense mirrored a shift in conceptions of chivalry whereby the quest for personal glory was eclipsed by the importance of the public good.[113] But a variety of interpretations of both judicial and illicit violence persisted. In 1267, Louis IX abolished a custom of Tournai which allowed private peace in cases of homicide, but customary law continued to promote compositions.[114] On the one hand, canon law framed punishment as penance, stressing its purifying role.[115] On the other hand, its customary role was often described as being primarily preventative and deterrent.[116] In conflict with this, the rise of arbitrary penalties in royal law undermined the deterrent role of punishment (there was no guaranteed level), and suggested that its primary role was exemplary.[117] Growing emphasis on personal responsibility in the framing of letters of remission was subverted in the ongoing, though increasingly

[110] F. Aubert, *Le parlement de Paris, 1314–1422* (Paris, 1890), 2–3. De Carbonnières, *La procédure*, 1–3.

[111] F. Aubert, 'Introduction', in G. Du Breuil, *Stilus Curie Parlamenti*, ed. Aubert (Paris, 1909), p. x.

[112] Ducoudray, *Les Origines*, 39.

[113] M. Keen, *The Laws of War in the Later Middle Ages* (London, 1965), 24.

[114] Ord. XI, p. 340, quoted in J.-M. Carbasse, 'Ne homines interficiantur: Quelques remarques sur la sanction médiévale de l'homicide', in S. Dauchy, J. Monballyu, and A. Wijffels (eds.), *Auctoritates: Xenia RC van Caenegem Oblata* (Brussels, 1997), 184.

[115] J. Brundage, *Medieval Canon Law* (Harlow, 1995), e.g. 152.

[116] Benveniste, 'Le Système des amendes', 6.

[117] Ibid. 14. *Coutumier d'Artois*, XLVIII.4, 111; Carbasse, *Histoire du droit*, 244.

debated, practice of punishing animals, where the purpose was spectacular exemplarity and purification.[118]

3. THE VIOLENCE OF THE LAW

Not only was the function of punishment unclear, but its separateness from illicit violence was not always obvious. If interpretations of physical violence were shaped in various ways, punishments should have been one of those shaping discourses: yet, punishment was itself violent and itself depended upon those frameworks for meaning. Punitive measures did not represent a straightforward political monopoly of physical force, but used violence in ways which were not always conceptually distinct from the types of increasingly illegitimate interpersonal violence which they purported to control. This was why executioners continued to ask for forgiveness from their victims: their actions were still read as interpersonal messages which could provoke vengeance.[119] In 1304 in Lens, the hangman was indeed vengefully murdered by one Jakemon Platel.[120] The acceptability of punitive violence was increasingly problematic, even when its communicative value was recognized. Moral philosophers spoke anxiously of the anger of judges, evoking notions of pity and equity, and the sense that violence was not always the appropriate response. Thomas Aquinas drew on both the Roman law impulse to transcend positive law through the exercise of discretion, and the Aristotelian idea that equity was a corrective for error.[121] Such discussions were mainly limited in this period to the sphere of moral philosophy, but the growth of royal remissions demonstrates their wider application.[122] Explicit discussions of punishment stressed that it must remain distinct from *saevitia*, while still preserving honour and peace, and although most 'unhangings' were the result of conflicts of jurisdiction, a few arose from a growing ambivalence about the appropriateness of brutal punitive violence.[123]

[118] e.g. the burning of a pig who killed a child in Fontenay-sur-Seine in 1278: Tanon, 378. Such a practice was increasingly controversial: in 1334, the mayor and *échevins* of Amiens were pursued for an abuse of justice after they hanged a horse which had killed a child: H. Furgeot and M. Dillay (eds.), *Actes du Parlement de Paris: Deuxième série de l'an 1328 à l'an 1350. Jugés (lettres, arrêts, jugés)*, 3 vols. (Paris, 1920–75), i, no. 988, 102–3.

[119] Gauvard, *Violence et ordre public au Moyen Age* (Paris, 2005), 68–9.

[120] ADN, B13596, edited in B. Delmaire, *Le Compte General d'Artois pour 1303–1304* (Brussels, 1977), no. 2614.

[121] *Summa Theologica*, Prima Secundae, q. 96, art. 6.

[122] Gauvard, *Violence*, 60.

[123] Ibid. 65, 75.

Much of this hesitation arose from uncertainty regarding the effects of illicit physical violence on the community as a whole. In other words, this was ambivalence about whether the common good needed to be defended at all costs from interpersonal violence, or whether such violence remained just that—interpersonal. In fact, the embeddedness of punitive violence in communities meant that capital punishment could be staved off at the last minute by an offer of marriage from one of the onlookers.[124] Such was the case in 1300 in Aire, when a woman claimed the right to marry a condemned man: the *bailli* was unwilling to admit this interpersonal reading of the implications of illicit violence and its violent punishment, but was overruled. The case degenerated into further violence, as irate members of the community rushed to save a man whose guilt they did not deny, but whose violent punishment they refused to disassociate from paradigms of extra-judicial conflict, and from which they were prepared to rescue him by their own violent agency, shouting, 'Kemugne, ce sera grans doleure se vous en leissies ansi mener le fil de vos bourgois'.[125] The would-be wife, Jehane li candelliere, was admonished by one compatriot, 'se tu as aucune cose commenchie se le parfai', and by another, 'Hastes vous, ales avant, si rescoues vo catel'.[126] In the enquiry afterwards, the *bailli* assumed that the mayor and *échevins* were complicit in the rescue attempt, since they were related to the condemned man: law and interpersonal relations were interconnected in everybody's minds, but the immediate assumption was that personal and familial concerns trumped any notion of the common good.

Punishment drew on the same frameworks of meaning as interpersonal violence, and legal practice itself was profoundly conflictual and often an adjunct to physical violence. The rooting of legal customs in communities meant that law itself (particularly civil actions) could be used for conflict and personal enmities by litigants, judicial authorities, and enforcers.[127]

[124] Ibid. 66–7. P. Lemercier, 'Une curiosité judiciaire au Moyen Age: La Grâce par mariage subséquent', *Revue d'histoire du droit français et étranger* (1955), 464–74.

[125] 'Commons: it would be awful if you allowed a son of one of your people to be thus disposed of'.

[126] 'Since you've started something, finish it; hurry up, go ahead and save your chattel': ADPC, A909.

[127] P. Bourdieu, 'La Force du droit: Éléments pour une sociologie du champ juridique', *Actes de la Recherche en Sciences Sociales,* 64 (1986), 3–19; W. Brown and P. Górecki, 'What Conflict Means: The Making of Medieval Conflict Studies in the United States, 1970–2000', in their *Conflict in Medieval Europe: Changing Perspectives on Society and Culture* (Aldershot, 2003), 6–7. Also S. Roberts, 'The Study of Dispute: Anthropological Perspectives', in J. Bossy (ed.), *Disputes and Settlements: Law and Human Relations in the West* (Cambridge, 1983), 1–24. Smail's work on 14th-cent. Marseille has illustrated this particularly clearly: 'Hatred as a Social Institution in Late Medieval Society', *Speculum,* 76/1 (2001), 90–126.

One Marote Maugarde in the parish of Saint-Martin-des-Champs in Paris was heard to boast that she knew the names of those who had murdered Guillaume Joli, and, presumably in an attempt at blackmail, that she would reveal those names should she be caught.[128] One man in Artois even earned himself the sobriquet 'litigator'.[129] Moreover, this was clearly perceived as a problem. The *Coutumier d'Artois* includes a lengthy description of a case involving the murderer of another man's valet which illustrated how to avoid false accusations. The writer tells us that the careful weighing of evidence was crucial in order to establish the truth, and most particularly, in order to avoid 'soupechon de haine', the enmity which could exploit the legal process.[130]

Even criminal prosecutions *ex officio* could operate in furtherance rather than resolution of local conflicts: many cases illustrate malicious use of legal mechanisms, and growing anxiety about malicious gossip and slanderous *fama* indicate this conflictual bias. Jehan Cabos, who spoke out against the corruption of the *échevinage* in Arras in the 1290s, and was then falsely accused of murder as a way of silencing him, is a case in point.[131] There was a variety of ways, including physical violence, of resolving conflicts, and law was one of the options used by the community when it was perceived to be the best strategy.[132] Moreover, physical violence often continued to accompany the legal process, as in 1317 when Alix de Cancupite, a woman acting on behalf of her sick husband, was mortally wounded by her legal opponents,[133] or in a case of 1281 in Saint Germain des Près, when one man pledged himself in court for a woman accusing another man of rape, and the hostility between the two pledges degenerated into physical blows.[134]

The enforcers of the law were often, in our terms, extremely corrupt, exploiting legal mechanisms in pursuance of personal gain, or in furtherance of their own hostilities. Yet many were not corrupt by their own logic, but operating in a context where the role of law and local feuds and conflicts were not clearly segregated. They blurred distinctions between grammars of violence and violence itself by enforcing the law brutally. Royal *sergents* were notorious in this regard: a famous complaint recalls the

128 Tanon, 467.

129 ADPC, A18/2.

130 *Coutumier d'Artois*, XLVII.13–18, 108–10.

131 ADPC, A1009.

132 T. Dean, *Crime in Medieval Europe* (Harlow, 2001), 41–3. B. Hanawalt and D. Wallace, 'Introduction', in their *Medieval Crime and Social Control* (Minneapolis, 1999), p. x.

133 Boutaric, *Actes*, ii, no. 5011, 199.

134 Tanon, 426.

violent seizure of a valet and a clerk of Geoffroy de Briançon, the royal treasurer in the rue Michel-le-Comte, by the *sergents* of the watch of Paris.[135] Some *sergents* were accused of the worst crimes, including rape.[136] St Louis's ordinance of 1254 tried to address such brutality and conflict within the legal system, but really only succeeded in highlighting the frequency of these practices, and in demonstrating that in many communities they played an accepted role.[137] Louis's attempt to stipulate that royal officials should be without local ties, and should move from post to post on a regular basis, was another grudging acknowledgement of this integral relationship between law and local conflicts.[138] A particularly cruel case from Merck in 1288 involved the wife and child of a man who had apparently committed suicide (and thus forfeited all his possessions) accusing the local *bailli* of having in fact murdered the man by drowning, so that he could enact a personal enmity and gain his enemy's chattels.[139]

Jurisdictional authority was itself a source of conflict. The apparently normalizing frameworks of law were the subject and cause of violent controversy which broke down distinctions between legal mechanisms and the violence which they purported to regulate. Jurisdictional rights were one of the most consistently disputed of noble prerogatives defended against crown encroachments, witness the case of Enguerrand de Coucy, fined 12,000 livres by Louis IX for the unjust hanging of three young squires caught poaching in his forest.[140] Messengers or judicial officers were frequently the targets of such tension, with several compelled to swallow the jurisdictional documents they were carrying, and others, like the officer of Thierry d'Hireçon, *bailli* of Arras, beaten, stripped, and put in the stocks by rival jurisdictional authorities willing to defend their prerogative at any cost.[141] Noblemen such as the lord of Wuillancourt

[135] A. Beugnot (ed.), *Les Olim*, 4 vols. (Paris, 1839–48), iii. 747, no. 25 (1312).

[136] e.g. Boutaric, *Actes*, ii. 293, no. 5868.

[137] L. Carolus-Barré, 'La Grande Ordonnance de 1254 sur la réforme de l'administration et la police du royaume', in *Septième centenaire de la mort de Saint Louis: Actes des colloques de Royaumont et de Paris (21–27 mai 1970)* (Paris, 1976), 85–96; see also G. Sivéry, 'Le Mécontentement dans le royaume de France et les enquêtes de Saint Louis', *Revue Historique*, 269/1 (1983), 3–24.

[138] *Ordonnances*, i. 65–75 (1254).

[139] The case was evoked in a series of complaints against the behaviour of the *bailli* of Merck, Henri du Mont: ADPC, A903/3.

[140] The trial is described in Guillaume de Saint Pathus, *La Vie de Saint Louis*, ed. H.-F. Delaborde (Paris, 1899), 36–40. Coucy was responsible for many other encroachments. In 1264, he was accused of injuries done to the abbey of Saint-Vincent of Laon which was under royal protection (Boutaric, *Actes*, i, no. 914, 83).

[141] e.g. ADPC, A54/15 (a messenger made to swallow letters in 1308); ADPC, A52/6 (a *sergent* beaten in 1306).

were particularly ready to brutalize representatives of the comital jurisdiction: an investigation into his behaviour found that he had beaten, wounded, and imprisoned a comital *sergent*, threatened one Jehan de la Sotière acting on behalf of the countess, 'k'il le comperroit de son chars et autres paroles laides et vilainnes', and then sent his brother and an armed group to break into de la Sotière's house.[142] Similar cases arose in the neighbouring Ponthieu, with the knight Jehan de Betencourt obliged to make amends to the King of England as count of Ponthieu, for threats and beatings administered to Edward's hapless official.[143] Within towns, competing jurisdictional authorities frequently came into tension with one another and the case could reach the Parlement, as in the 1250s, when the bishop of Arras complained that the *échevins* of the town had encroached into his jurisdictional territory in order to investigate a murder.[144] Things could become much more violent: in 1266, the *sous-bailli* of Arras hit the sacristan's *sergent*, injured a chaplain, calling him a ribald priest, and punched another cleric in the eye, most probably because of an ongoing jurisdictional dispute.[145] In Amiens in 1273, it was partly the thrill of the chase which led to jurisdictional and violent conflict, when the royal provost chased a criminal into the church, and then hit a cleric there, who had presumably tried to stop the pursuit in this place of sanctuary: the boundary between legal grammars and the violence they apparently regulated was fragmented, and the provost and his *sergent* were ordered to process penitentially barefoot to the Cathedral.[146] And sometimes it was not so much the cause of conflict as the manifestation: as we shall see in the chapter on urban uprisings, protest about fiscal impositions or infractions on local identities would often focus on jurisdictional boundaries, contesting their embodiment of divisions of power.

If, despite law's claims to regulate violence, it was itself intensely violent, violence also created its own communicative norms. Sociolinguistic studies teach us that language normalizes itself to some extent, creating its own conventions and shared meanings.[147] Such rules grew organically alongside other normalizing discourses, and, of course, often in conflict with them. Beatings to opponents' faces gained meaning through repetition, engaging at the same time with popular literary or hagiographical

[142] 'That he would pay for it with his own flesh, and other ugly and villainous words': ADPC, A956/1.

[143] AMA, MS 217, fo. 362r.

[144] Boutaric, *Actes*, i, no. 204, 17.

[145] Ibid., no. 1083, 100.

[146] Ibid., no. 1912, 175.

[147] J. Holmes, *An Introduction to Sociolinguistics* (Harlow, 1992), 12.

imaginings of the significance of defacement, and legally prescriptive interpretations of such gestures.[148] The many mutilations which took place during the period drew upon precedent for their connotations, cumulatively constructing frameworks of meaning. Several cases involving wounding the victim's arm suggested, through repetition of this motif, that it represented a specific form of punishment.[149] Sometimes, interpersonal violence could draw on the explicit meanings of judicial violence, reproducing motifs which were rendered intelligible through practice. So, for example, the cutting off of the nose was an ancient judicial punishment for adultery: whilst rarely used in judicial practice in thirteenth-century France, this was suggestive for many perpetrators of illicit violence, such as the brothers Robin and Jean de Fontaine, and Fourtin 'Le Blons' who cut the nose off Jean 'André', a royal valet; or Jehan 'de Sorel', and the brothers Guillaume and Simon 'de Laignicourt' who cut the nose off the squire known as 'Le Moine de Haplaincourt'.[150] Slicing an ear was a punishment for theft, and was a motif replicated in several cases of interpersonal violence.[151] It is striking that the majority of the more extreme mutilations which survive in the records were perpetrated by those of noble or gentle status. While it might be tempting to assume that the violence carried out by such figures may have provided models to be followed by those of humbler background, there is limited evidence for such an assumption: still, the profound cruelty of the brutality performed by thirteenth-century noblemen contributes to the suggestiveness of medieval violence more broadly. Furthermore, many of the definitions of particular acts imposed through law were contested by the meanings implicitly assigned to them by the perpetrators of violence. For example, university statutes and legal proscriptions condemned cutting the hair of prostitutes as an act of illegitimate brutality, but the students who engaged in this practice defined it, through repetition, as a form of moral policing.

[148] V. Groebner, *Defaced: The Visual Culture of Violence* (New York, 2004), particularly 34–5, 71, 87.

[149] e.g. the mutilation of the arm of Jean 'Le Conte' de Wailly by Jean 'le Picart de Chacemi' in 1316 (Boutaric, *Actes*, ii, no. 4994, 197); the mutilation of the arm of Pierre Dodun by the brothers Gobert, Jean and Colin 'Craques' in 1316 (Boutaric, *Actes*, ii, no. 5008, 199); the wounding of the arm of Mathieu de Donneville, a sergeant of the *bailli* at Amiens, by Bauduoin 'de Lumbres' in 1317 (Boutaric, *Actes*, ii, no. 5176, 217); the amputation of the fist of Durand, a cleric from Montdidier, by the brothers Jacques and Raoul de Roye in 1317 (Boutaric, *Actes*, ii, no. 5559, 257).

[150] The first incident is recounted in Boutaric, *Actes*, ii, no. 5636, 265 (1318); the second is no. 6256, 342 (1320), and no. 6580, 405 (1321).

[151] e.g. the victimization of a valet of Raoul de Nesle in 1309: Boutaric, *Actes*, ii, no. 3641, 61 (1309).

4. WHO WAS TO READ VIOLENCE?

Even where a clear distinction could be drawn between public punishment and interpersonal violence, the very justifiability of violent public punishment remained dubious: it was not clear that illicit acts of violence did affect the community as a whole or that representatives of 'the common good' should read violent communications as anything more than interpersonal. The relevance of interpersonal violence to social networks was widely acknowledged, but its impact on the wider community beyond these networks was still doubtful. This is one reason why the seigneurial records of Paris and Artois actually detail so few corporal punishments. The vast majority of the Artois accounts detail a composition made between the perpetrator and the victim (or the family of the victim in the event of the latter's demise), usually with a cut to the count, essentially as mediator. So, for example, in a typical case in 1288, one Wautier de Fierieves murdered a man in Hesdin, but was spared banishment on paying a composition of 4 livres to the friends of the victim and making public peace with them;[152] in Bapaume in 1301, one Flamenk le Vakier struck Simon Rikier, and was able to get away with a public demonstration of peace to the victim, and a payment to the count of 20 livres.[153] In some cases, composition was replaced by a fine, wholly payable to the count, thus elevating the case above the merely interpersonal, but avoiding the unambiguous statement of communal implications which corporal punishment represented: Masuel de Biailer and Huet au Piet, after murdering Fourdanide Sapegnies, got off with a series of fines, the last of 28 livres.[154] In a sense, the financial function of these records accounts for the emphasis on fines and compositions, rather than on corporal punishments; but this does not explain away the reluctance to punish physically, as where capital punishment was carried out (or where the culprit was banished on pain of capital punishment), the count acquired the forfeited possessions, and so the case was still noted: in any case, the expenses section of the accounts details precisely how much money was spent on hangman's rope and payments for executioners.[155] The same can be said of the cases in Paris. Here the nature of the records as proof of jurisdiction might lead us to anticipate accounts of spectacular

[152] ADPC, A126/1.

[153] ADPC, A166/8. [154] ADPC, A176/2.

[155] e.g. respectively, ADN, B13597, fo. 5^r; ADN, B13596, fo. 93^r accounts for purchase of more rope when the first batch broke after the criminal had been hanging for two days, and for the payment to some 'ribauds' for their involvement in the execution.

corporal punishment, but, aside from a handful of hangings, this is not the case. The majority of crimes were punished by confiscations and banishment: indeed, many perpetrators fled before they could be banished.[156] In many cases, peace between the victim or his or her family and the perpetrator was the principal consequence, as in 1266, when one Pierre Fillon murdered Almary de Maumont, but was subsequently able to make peace with the man's relatives.[157]

Communities were not so static in this period, nor legal mechanisms so well established, as to eliminate any ambivalence concerning the role of violence in society. Readings of the violent communications affecting the community as whole were not straightforward or undisputed. While Beaumanoir might comment that 'C'est li communs pourfis que chascuns soit serjans et ait pouoir de prendre et d'arester les maufeteurs',[158] it was not universally accepted that violence on the street should be read as a threat to the community, rather than indicative of personal concerns and merely interpersonal solidarities.

Such ambivalence emerges with particular clarity at points of disjuncture in the normal functioning of legal mechanisms. Complaints about dysfunctional and unfair legal treatment remove the apparently univocal gloss of the records to reveal more complex shadings of interpretation. In 1296, the count of Artois had received so many complaints from the inhabitants, the abbey, and the city councillors of Arras about the bizarre and corrupt behaviour of his *bailli*, Jehan de Beauquesne, that he instigated an investigation into all criminal proceedings directed by Beauquesne during his tenure of the office of *bailli*. He commissioned Raoul de Houtencourt, canon of Arras, Robert de Plaissiet, *bailli* of Hesdin, Henri Le Poivre of Senlis, and Jakemon Louchart called Barbe Dorée, to interview witnesses concerning all prosecuted crimes over the last few years and to inquire about the outcomes of all such prosecutions as well as notorious crimes which were never prosecuted.[159] Altogether, fifty cases were discussed, an enormous number of instances of questionable justice. Beauquesne was eventually deprived of his post, but only to reappear as *bailli* of Saint Omer three years later.[160] The majority of the incidents investigated concerned cases which had been promptly dropped after the arrest of the supposed culprit. A few evoked enormous fines levied by

[156] e.g. respectively: Registre criminel de Saint-Maur-des-Fossés, Tanon, 335; Registre criminel de Saint-Germain-des-Près, Tanon, 454.

[157] Registre criminel de Sainte-Geneviève, Tanon, 358.

[158] 'It is for the common good that each man should be a *sergent* with the power to take and arrest criminals': Beaumanoir, i, no. 950, 482.

[159] ADPC, A48/11. Again, this roll is unfortunately not subdivided.

[160] ADPC, A149/3; A155/4; A156/5.

Beauquesne and not noted in the records. The investigation revealed the impressively large-scale corruption of Beauquesne, but the very notion of corruption is problematic. On the one hand, Beauquesne's role as the count's legal representative was not clearly distinct from his role as an individual with his own personal hostilities; on the other hand, even as a public functionary, he was hesitant about how to read the implications of the various acts of violence with which he was confronted. The fact that such corruption was possible, the ways in which it was perpetrated, and the mixed reactions of the witnesses hint at the ambivalent frameworks within which violence was understood in this period.

The first case investigated concerned the murder of Jehan Feuchi by Robert des Cans in 1294. This was apparently the result of an intense street fight, watched by eight witnesses. After initially responding to the general report that there was a dead body in the street, the *bailli* decided not to press charges, and accepted a small monetary payment from the accused. The list of witnesses of the fight, and the equally long list of witnesses ready to testify that the supposed crime never took place, reveals the presence of tight interpersonal solidarities with which the *bailli* was unwilling to interfere; the witnesses interpreted the violence as socially significant, but its communal implications were evidently uncertain. This incurred the wrath of the municipal *échevins* who complained to the count; nevertheless, the fact that Beauquesne could get away with such inaction for several years suggests a widespread uncertainty amongst the inhabitants of Arras about the acceptability and reading of such violence. The violent events had operated at the intersection of the individual and the community, but Beauquesne's response was one of hesitancy: he recognized such public violence to be a threat to public order, but was equally aware that it negotiated relations still perceived in individual rather than communal terms.

Another case tells of an arson attack on the house of Karon de Bairy by the local tavern-keeper: the tavern-keeper stood in the street and threw lighted wood into the house. In this case, the *bailli* imprisoned the culprit, but the latter was subsequently released following the intervention of the local priest, mayor, and several friends. Again, it was not merely corruption which was at stake, but also Beauquesne's fundamental uncertainty about the need to discipline violence which was at once interpersonal, and disruptive to the practical well-being of the community: ultimately, he chose to accept that this was a violent message directed at individuals, not at the community as a whole. The interconnectedness of the various cases is particularly striking. The arson case was witnessed by Pierre de Savie, mentioned in the next case as rumoured to have killed his wife.

A number of rapes were read along similarly hesitant lines. Wauteron li Buriers and Sausse Soumillons were cited as guilty of the rape of a woman just outside the city walls on the road to Douai. While they apparently committed the crime in public and in daylight, Beauquesne ceased to prosecute the case upon receiving a bribe from friends of the accused, and effectively accepted that the violence was to be interpreted only in the context of bands of young men. Several cases of drunkenness or extreme anger leading to violence on the street were read and interpreted with uncertainty: on the one hand, they were seen to be disruptive to the community; on the other hand, they sprang from the dysfunction of the individual and the breakdown of interpersonal social relations. The wounding of a man by a drunken assailant in 1294 was not punished when a group of neighbours gathered together to offer a payment in kind—wine as it happened—to Beauquesne in return for dropping the case. Beauquesne was notoriously corrupt, but more complex issues were at stake given the willingness of the community to rally round the perpetrator, and Beauquesne's acceptance of this kind of payment, when by pressing charges he could have elicited a much larger fine. Likewise, Beauquesne was reticent when confronted with crime by young people arising from uncontrolled emotion: a beating by the children of Jehan Louchart and Gilles Wyons in 1294 was greeted with a degree of apathy by Beauquesne. He received no financial incentive not to prosecute, and there is no evidence of corrupt solidarities on his part: the threat to the community was not yet perceived in black and white terms.

The lack of single jurisdiction meant that the implications of a given act of violence were necessarily multivalent; society in Arras was negotiated by the jurisdictional authorities of the municipality, of the count, the cathedral chapter, and the abbey of Saint Vaast. When several authorities attempted to prosecute given crimes, they moved to protect their own communities, suggesting that violence posed a multiple threat. This multivalence was indeed exploited by many perpetrators of violence, and the connotations of the act for a given collectivity were thus clouded. One perpetrator evoked in the Beauquesne investigation apparently dragged his victim from the streets of the town of Arras into the jurisdictional territory of the abbey of Saint Vaast, further securing his immunity by bribing Beauquesne. It was unclear whether this crime should be read as an assault upon the common good of the municipality, as an assault upon comital authority, a threat to Saint Vaast, or as an essentially interpersonal crime. Moreover, the *bailli* could find himself caught up in interpersonal rivalries, as his role as legal protector and his private persona overlapped. In 1293, Jakes de Courteres murdered Maroie des Lices in front of eight witnesses; the complainant was the daughter of the dead woman, but she agreed to drop complaints upon the condition that her father should be released from prison where he had been placed owing to a suspicion of murdering a member of the Courteres family.[161] The *bailli* here was drawn into the vengeful relations between these two families as an agent in their feuding: he was the one who had dishonoured the des Lices father by imprisoning him, and he was the one who could avenge the des Lices by effectively legitimizing the murder of a Courteres. In this case, perpetrators of violence deliberately manipulated the dichotomy of communal versus interpersonal relations, profiting from the *bailli*'s hesitancy regarding the collective implications of violence.

5. CONCLUSION

Physical violence, whether executed by legitimate authority in the form of corporal punishment, or by individuals or groups in the context of quotidian interpersonal relations, had an acknowledged communicative function. It was a function made possible by shared frameworks of meaning, established through the very public discourses of hagiography, sermons, medical thinking, literature, customary law, and not least, through the practice of violence itself. These normalizing frameworks appealed respectively to different groups in society and, if we want to achieve a holistic sense of patterns and representations of, as well as responses to, violence, it is important to consider them all. And these frameworks were profoundly rooted in the needs of communities, symbiotic with their concerns and procedurally dependent upon their cooperation and involvement. The period was also one of top-down legal change, notably witnessing the growth of royal jurisdiction, but even these shifts served to reinforce community involvement in the establishment, interpretation, and implementation of 'grammars' to deal with violence.

These paradigms showed physically violent gestures to be highly differentiated, drawing upon shared meanings and communicating via shared understandings of the effects of painful marks on bodies. These models were also constantly challenged, notably in subversive popular literature, which pointed to the excessive signification of much violence, or even the breakdown of meaning altogether. The *Renart* texts showed that violence could exist for its own sake alone. And even the law itself in its multifarious forms was often a source or a means of conflict. This is a picture of

[161] ADPC, A41/28: this was in a subsequent complaint about Beauquesne.

multiple and fluid interpretive frameworks of violence, rooted in communities. It is a picture of rules and conventions which were themselves a cause of conflict, and of violent conflict which was making up its own rules and conventions.

New questions were being raised concerning the impact of interpersonal violence on communities, rather than just upon the individuals directly involved, but the assumption that violence effectively addressed the community as a whole continued to be doubted. Nevertheless, communities established the norms for reading and reacting to violence, and much interpersonal violence claimed a place in negotiating and contesting social relations. The effects of these attitudes on the representation and perpetration of violence in a quintessentially public and social space, the street, will be the subject of the next chapter.

2

Violence on the Street in Paris and Artois

Sometime in the 1290s, several unknown men were mutilated, their noses and tongues cut out in the 'orde ruele' before the house of Thomas Bourriane in Arras.[1] Overhanging houses blocked out the light, and the stench of sewage and filth filled the still, cold air.[2] This town street, typical of late thirteenth-century Paris or Artois, was a grotesquely appropriate scene for numerous acts of interpersonal violence, of physical brutality and damage. Admittedly, we have no way of identifying absolute levels of violence. The surviving records provide evidence for only a few jurisdictions amongst many—municipal, ecclesiastical, royal, and seigneurial—and therefore represent only a small fraction of prosecuted criminal behaviour; in any case, much prosecuted violence was never recorded. Given this caveat, and the possibility of undetected violence, known to criminologists as the 'dark figure', the numbers illustrated in Figures 3, 4, and 5 suggest that violence was fairly common.[3] The street was a place of everyday transactions, and amongst them, brawls, beatings with fists and knives, and vengeful attacks.

But, as we shall see, street violence nevertheless provoked shocked responses: interpersonal violence was not so normal as to be unworthy of comment. Whilst violence rates were high, they were not overwhelmingly so. Nor was violence so socially integral as to be deemed acceptable. Moreover, its public connotations and social centrality meant that legal authorities perceived the potential threat of such acts and intervened more regularly than in any other sphere: in many cases the street was specified as the location of the crime, but most often the records indicated the street implicitly by situating the crime outdoors but within the town walls. Every case reported is a case which was deemed, at least by some, to be damaging to the community, even if, as we have seen, the relationship between interpersonal and communal implications remained controversial. Most

1 ADPC, A48/11.

2 See J.-P. Leguay, *La Rue au Moyen Age* (Rennes, 1984), 53–63.

3 pp. 76 and 82 respectively. See C. Coleman and J. Moynihan, *Understanding Crime Data: Haunted by the Dark Figure* (Buckingham, 1996).

importantly, every case reported is a case which provoked discussion and, to a certain extent, ambivalence.

Ambivalence on various levels is illustrated by an investigation of 1307 into the contested jurisdictional rights of a small village outside Arras called Beaurain.[4] Several witnesses were summoned and described the wounding of a certain Hanot de Pumiers in a fight, the attack of one Robert Bretel 'droit en la rue' by Robert Vakier, and the frequent sight of groups of youths drawing swords in the street in front of the church and beside the fountain.[5] These eye-witness accounts of violence indicate the publicity of the street, the way in which certain details were remembered, and actions interpreted and read by innocent passers-by. This violence was motivated by a desire to communicate and, as we shall see, was interpreted as such by its spectators. Importantly, however, this violence evidently met with disapproval and shock. The case frames the main questions addressed in this chapter: what was the perceived role of violence on the street? Who were the main perpetrators and what gestures did they use? How was violence represented and remembered?

1. THE SPACE OF THE STREET

The street was a characteristically urban space: within the town walls, providing a way for densely packed inhabitants to move from place to place and to communicate, it was distinct from the roads and ways of the countryside.[6] In a sense then, it was a place of safety from the brigands who continued to plague the open highways, the private noble wars which ravaged the countryside, or even the pirates who corrupted the nearby sea.[7] Municipal rhetoric dwelt upon the security offered by the town, and

[4] ADPC, A929/2.

[5] 'Right in the street'. This trope is an intriguing replay of the popular motif in romances of a mythical fight taking place beside a chapel and a fountain, e.g. Chrétien de Troyes, *Le Chevalier au Lion*, ed. D. Hult (Paris, 1994), ll. 365–550.

[6] On the public nature of the urban street, see N. Gonthier, *Cris de haine et rites d'unité: La Violence dans les villes, XIIIe–XVIe siècle* (Turnhout, 1992), 91–7; D. Nicholas, *Urban Europe, 1100–1700* (London, 2003), 154–88.

[7] e.g. respectively, Jean de Monceaux and his accomplices were investigated in 1313 for ambushing a valet of Pierre Louis, bourgeois of Saint Quentin, on the public highway (Boutaric, *Actes*, ii, no. 4172, 113); the lord of Pinon rode with armed men and banner unfurled against Jehan de Monceaus in 1313 (Boutaric, *Actes*, ii, no. 4183, 114). Of course, in practice, towns were not entirely safe from brigands, and were frequently attacked by such bands, but this served to increase fearfulness and further to heighten the desirability of the town as place of protection and refuge: e.g. in 1313, Jean du Plessis, knight, and five squire accomplices were fined for violently attacking the inhabitants of Saint Quentin (Boutaric, *Actes*, ii, no. 4242, 119). Piracy around the small town of Neuport was

upon the brutality of the nobles of the region who reputedly 'Tenoient grans bastons et lons,/Dont il froient sour les crepons/Et par mi testes et par bras/Les vilains, les bourgois d'Arras'.[8] Yet, paradoxically, the street also embodied all that was seen to be sinful and hostile and excessive in towns, in contrast to a growing nostalgia for a pastoral idyll.[9]

Whether vice-ridden or well-controlled, this was a liminal space, a place between places, and thus a space in which social relations in these ever-shifting communities could be most effectively negotiated. As the late thirteenth-century townsman stepped out into the street, he articulated his role within urban society, and his actions were read accordingly.[10] In the thirteenth-century Parisian *Dit des rues de Paris*, what seems at first glance to be little more than a rhyming list of street names presents a vivid and necessarily recognizable picture of the street as a place of noisy, muddy, and rat-infested social interaction (ll. 114, 423, 535): prostitutes solicited customers (ll. 54–5, 503–5); women gossiped (l. 125); acquaintances chatted (ll. 317, 368–9); artisans and sellers plied their trades (ll. 28, 488, 513); and, of course, inhabitants argued and fought (ll. 82–4, 533–5).[11] Iconographically too, violence was a vivid motif in depictions of street life. In an image from the 1317 *Vie de Saint Denis*, alongside the trading, begging, and entertainment depicted on the bridges, two men are shown brawling in the middle of the street; one tears at the other's ear, raising his other arm to strike him on the head; the other grabs his hair, pushes his chin, and gives him a sharp kick in the shin.[12]

And the street was rich in symbolic resonances. It was an important topos in theological discourse, and a central metaphor and metonym in

particularly notorious: in 1288, the men of Neuport were accused before the *bailli* of Merck of decapitating eleven fishermen, and throwing their heads into the sea (ADPC, A903/3); in another case before the Paris Parlement in 1322, the merchants of Neuport and Dunkerque were accused of killing the father of one Jean 'de Castembier' and stealing his ship, the *Saint Michel*, and its cargo of wine (Boutaric, *Actes*, ii, no. 6927, 476). See also Gonthier, *Cris*, 10–12.

[8] 'Wielded great long batons, with which they struck the villains and burghers of Arras on the backs, on their heads and arms': R. Berger, *Littérature et société arrageoise: Les Chansons et dits artésiens* (Arras, 1982), no. XVI, ll. 167–70.

[9] The pastourelle tradition is typical: e.g. Jean Bodel, *Le Jeu de Robin et Marion*, ed. J. Dufournet (Paris, 1989) arises out of the urban Arras context.

[10] These are the implications of the German term, *Öffentlichkeit*: cf. G. Jaritz (ed.), *Die Straße: Zur Funktion und Perzeption öffentlichen Raums im Späten Mittelalter* (Vienna, 2001), 5.

[11] Ms. Paris, BN MS fr. 24432, fos. 257^v–260^v. On the notorious noisiness of the medieval street, see 'Le dit des crieries de Paris' by Guillaume de Villeneuve, BN MS fr. 837, fos. 246^r–7^v. Eds. of these texts can be found on http://tapor.mcmaster.ca/~hyperliste/home.htm (accessed Aug. 2011).

[12] BN, MS fr. 2092, fo. 20^v. See V. Egbert, *On the Bridges of Medieval Paris* (Princeton, 1974), 65.

political thought, a sophisticated trope for consideration of the relation between individual and community. These connotations, combined with the publicity of such a space, rendered the street an ideal arena for the negotiation of social relations. According to Isidore of Seville, the street was one of the key components of the city, and its communal implications were its defining feature.[13]

The street is first and foremost a space to facilitate movement. In theological discourse, the image of the 'via' more generally became ubiquitous for the visualization of the journey of the individual soul, with Dante's journey in the *Commedia* being paradigmatic.[14] The idea of a journey of life along a particular road is, of course, at least classical in origin, most famously embodied in the choice of Hercules. The choice between the rocky and steep path of virtue, and the flat, broad, and welcoming path of vice, was one reiterated by scriptures.[15] It was exploited by medieval theologians, most notably Thomas Aquinas who described the spiritually healthy choosing the 'via spiritualis', and the sick having to walk on the easier ground.[16] The trope was often aesthetically elaborated through reiteration of the importance of a well-constructed and straight path: Hugh of Saint Victor evoked the measurers who ensured the regular construction of urban streets, as he explained in his *Didascalion* that 'the taut cord shows the path of the true faith'.[17] However, the street was also a metaphor for the broader circumstances in which that individual operated. This was the sense of the ideal street, the heavenly Jerusalem, depicted so often in contemporary ecclesiastical iconography, most notably at Chartres Cathedral, as the representation of a virtuous and rightly ordered collectivity.[18] But as well as representing both the spiritual journey of the individual and the spiritual health of the whole world, the metaphor of the street evoked the intersection of the two. Christ declared that 'I am the way, the truth and the life', and in Aquinas's exegesis, the Church itself became the 'via', the collective path to salvation; it was the path through spiritual life chosen by the individual, while mapping his or her journey

[13] Isidore of Seville, *Etymologiae*, ed. W. Lindsay (Oxford, 1911): 'Plateae perpetuae ac latiores civitatum viae sunt': 15.2.23; and 'strata dicta quasi vulgi pedibus trita': 15.16.6.

[14] Cf. P. Boglioni, '*Via*: La Rue et la route dans les sources religieuses du Moyen Age', in Jaritz, *Die Straße*, 31–45; H. Hundsbichler, '*Via sive vita*: Strasse und Weg in der Christlichen Metaphorik', ibid. 9–30.

[15] Matt. 7: 14.

[16] *Summa Theologica*, Secunda Secundae, q. 43, art. 1 c.

[17] Hugh of Saint Victor, *The Didascalion*, tr. J. Taylor (New York, 1961), 141.

[18] See L. Hull Stookey, 'The Gothic Cathedral as the Heavenly Jerusalem: Liturgical and Theological Sources', *Gesta*, 8 (1969), 35–41. Revelation 21: 21.

through societies and collective temptations and struggles.[19] A similar conceptualization of the street coloured political discourse. In popular organological metaphors for human society, the individual body was evoked as an organism with a proper way of functioning comparable to that of a rightly ordered city, with the veins, like streets, transporting the energizing blood from place to place and ensuring the health of the whole.[20] And vice versa, the city was described as a potentially healthy body, with the streets ensuring rightful communication between its different parts.[21]

This theological and political conceptualization of the street as the place of intersection of the individual and the collectivity found expression in a more practical way as cities were developed and remodelled in this period. Late thirteenth-century urban development peaked in the geographical areas of northern Italy, Flanders, and north-east France: great efforts were made to ensure the straightness of the streets, with accompanying discourse stressing the straight street 'to enhance decorum' as a metaphor for the virtue of the individual, for the ideal society, and as the link between the two.[22] Increasingly town councils employed *mensores* or measurers to ensure the geometrical layout of streets and town defences. In Arras in the 1290s, a measurer was killed by a gang of youths;[23] a case of unintentional murder in 1304 involved a measurer who became embroiled in an angry dispute with his father;[24] and again in 1311, another measurer killed a man by night.[25] Moreover, the cleanliness of the street was increasingly attended to: the surviving records of Douai, for example, refer repeatedly to the well-kept street as central to the practical and moral well-being of

[19] John 14: 6; Boglioni, '*Via*', 37; *Summa Theologica,* Partis Tertiae Supplementum, q. 71, art. 1 c.

[20] From the 12th cent., the re-reading of the commentary of Calcidius on Plato's *Timaeus* contributed to the popularity of the organological metaphor for human society, i.e. the comparison between the human body, the city state, and the cosmos: William of Conches is usually cited as the precipitator of such studies, which famously included John of Salisbury's *Policraticus.* See P. Dutton, 'Illustre Civitatis et Populi Exemplum: Plato's *Timaeus* and the Transmission from Calcidius to the End of the Twelfth Century of a Tripartite Scheme of Society', *Mediaeval Studies,* 45 (1983), 108–12; T. Struve, *Die Entwicklung der Organologischen Staatsaufassung im Mittelalter* (Stuttgart, 1978).

[21] Alain de Lille, *The Plaint of Nature,* tr. J. Sheridan (Toronto, 1980), 67–221.

[22] J. Friedman, *Florentine New Towns: Urban Design in the Late Middle Ages* (Cambridge, Mass., 1988), 207.

[23] ADPC, A48/11. Likewise, an account of the laying out of town defences and roads at Ardres *c.*1200 records Simon the Dyker, 'so learned in geometrical work, pacing with rod in hand': quoted in K. Lilley, *City and Cosmos: The Medieval World in Urban Form* (London, 2009), 65.

[24] ADN, B13596, edited in B. Delmaire, *Le Compte General d'Artois pour 1303–1304* (Brussels, 1977), no. 2279.

[25] ADPC, A282/2.

the community.[26] Attention became focused on the street as a space with an ideal form, a form which embodied representations of the spiritual life of the individual and of society striving to emulate a heavenly model.

Such concepts were crystallized during religious and civic processions, which served to marry the implications for the individual with the social and collective religious connotations of such spaces: the street was dramatized as the space where individual and collective responsibility, both spiritual and civic, met.[27] Collective processions were a frequent feature of the towns of north-east France and Paris: for example, Arras was the scene for a lavish annual procession from the cathedral to the town square, when individuals took their place in the collectivity to process the miraculous candle which embodied civic identity from the chapel in the town square to the Cathedral and back. While such spectacles explored the connotations of the street on special days, violence on the street exploited its social connotations on a quotidian basis.

Legal discourse concerning violence on the street was correspondingly alive to such associations. Interpersonal violence was perceived as primarily the concern of the implicated individuals and their social networks, but, as the notion of the common good was increasingly expounded, legal responses referred to the effects of interpersonal violence on the community as a whole.[28] This shift in emphasis was given particular potency by the renewed influence of Roman law: violence which was carried out in public was particularly condemned in view of its disruptive social implications. It is no coincidence that such legal considerations flourished most particularly in the same period as the emergence of the 'chemin publique' ruled directly by the king.[29] Most practically, such texts banned the carrying of weapons on the street.[30] Violence on the street was understood as the point at which individual action attempted to shape and to threaten broader social networks: punitive action was necessitated by a concern for

[26] G. Espinas, *La Vie urbaine de Douai au Moyen Age*, 3 vols. (Paris, 1913), iii, nos. 72, 1245, 52; no. 212, 143 (1250); nos. 513, 387 (1268): 'Ban échevinal interdisant de jeter des détritus sur la voie publique'.

[27] Lilley, *City*, 304.

[28] On the notion of the common good, see M. Kempshall, *The Common Good in Late Medieval Political Thought* (Oxford, 1999), 1–25; E. Lecuppre-Desjardin and A.-L. Van Bruaene (eds.), *De Bono communi: The Discourse and Practice of the Common Good in the European City (13th to 16th Centuries)* (Turnhout, 2010).

[29] C. Gauvard, *Violence et ordre publique au Moyen Age* (Paris, 2005), 271: 'Remarquons que leur genèse est concomitante de la notion de chemin publique dont le tracé irrigue le royaume et dont le roi est le maître, à charge pour lui d'y faire régner la paix.'

[30] e.g. in 1331 in Issy (near Paris), Jehan le Roy was arrested for carrying a dagger attached to his belt: this was in contravention of the provost's explicit ban: L. Tanon, *Histoire des justices des anciennes églises et communautés monastiques de Paris* (Paris, 1883), 440.

the well-being of the community. Nevertheless, as we have seen, an unwillingness persisted to accept unequivocally the collective implications of essentially interpersonal violence. And while the *raison d'être* of law was apparently to establish the rightful ordering of society, the violence which legal mechanisms attempted to stem claimed to fulfil a very similar function.

2. THE ROLE OF STREET VIOLENCE

The medieval street has been stereotypically characterized as a place of irrational, unpredictable outbreaks of violence, dismissed by Chesnais as 'violence archaïque, instinctive, pulsionelle'.[31] The reality was subtler: violence on the street was an integral part of social relations, with a deeply rooted rationale (though rarely consciously articulated), to manipulate self-image, and one's place within the community. And it was a phenomenon which contemporaries thought carefully about, and responded to in nuanced and ambivalent ways. Focus on self-image and one's place within the community broadly corresponded to the notion of honour:[32] street violence protected the 'psychic property' of the individual, his or her sense of self and place within social networks.[33] This type of apparently petty but socially integral violence bears immediate comparison with several other historiographically well-worked forms of violence on the street. The North Italian and particularly the Florentine case is well-known for its ubiquitous political and factional violence which tended to profit from the audience which the street provided:[34] in contrast, interpersonal street violence in northern France was not so overtly political, but more intimately connected to the day-to-day functioning of social relations. At the other end of the spectrum from the North Italian political violence is the 'carnivalesque' violence famously described by Bercé:[35] such mocking but apparently ultimately conservative exuberance stands in contrast to the

[31] J. Chesnais, *Histoire de la violence* (Paris, 1981), 20.

[32] Gauvard locates honour as the crucial factor in outbreaks of illicit violence in this period and later: 'La violence suit partout les mêmes lois, celles de l'honneur, dont les effets sont gradués selon les sources envisagées'. *Violence*, 218.

[33] The term 'psychic property' was coined by M. Greenshields, *An Economy of Violence in Early Modern France: Crime and Justice in the Haute Auvergne, 1587–1664* (Philadelphia, 1994) to evoke notions of 'honour, property, dignity and worth' (p. 232).

[34] See C. Lansing, *The Florentine Magnates: Lineage and Faction in a Medieval Commune* (Princeton, 1991), 164–91.

[35] Y.-M. Bercé, *Fête et révolte: Des mentalités populaires du XVIe au XVIIIe siècle* (Paris, 1976), 13–16; see M. Bakhtin, *L'Œuvre de François Rabelais et la culture populaire au Moyen Age et sous la Renaissance*, tr. A. Robel (Paris, 1970), 13–21.

quotidian but largely unhumourous nature of the interpersonal violence taking place on the streets in northern France at the turn of the thirteenth and fourteenth centuries.

Acts of violence on the street could help to shape the identity of the assailant, and were empowered to do so by the presence of spectators, and by the interpretations of these observers: these were highly public events. Indeed, these spectators also often faced arrest for their complicity in the violent spectacle: in 1268 in Saint-Maur-des-Fossés, three men were arrested for watching a triple murder and failing to intervene in any way.[36] The murder of Jehan de Feuchi by Robert des Champs in 1294 was witnessed by at least eight people, most of them women.[37] When Renard de Hangrest stabbed and killed Jehanet Biautayon d'Espagne in 1303, the various elements of the event made a deep impact on other members of the community: Witt du Rivage recalled how he saw the blow of the dagger, and then played Good Samaritan to the fleeing victim; Maiheus Trabaillars saw only the blow with a palm, and then a heated chase; another witness claimed to have seen a sword; another heard Renard cry out 'tu le comparras'; several saw the perpetrator fleeing and noted his bloody hands; and a couple watched Renard go down to the river to wash his dagger.[38] Although night is frequently associated with the perpetration of violent crime, relatively few of the prosecuted crimes took place after sunset—only 5 per cent in Artois, and 15 per cent in Paris.[39] The night offered secrecy and security for professional criminals, but eliminated the audience required by the more common acts of violence which were integral to social relations. A few cases apparently took place at dusk, when work was over, and the night was yet to begin: this was a moment when there was still sufficient light for the violence to be observed by passers-by.[40]

The records illustrate the perceived potential of vengeful violence on the street to defend and negotiate social identities. In 1301 in Saint Omer, a certain Clais Skelle murdered his father's killer: thus, the record implies, he not only satisfied his anger, but defended his place and honour in society.[41] The street provided him with a public arena where he could act

36 Tanon, 329. 37 ADPC, A41/28. 38 AMA, MS 115, fo. 56v.

39 R. Muchembled observes that in 15th-cent. Artois, most crimes took place at dusk: *La Violence au village: Sociabilité et comportements populaires en Artois du XV au XVIII siècle* (Turnhout, 1989), 31, and at night, ibid. 119. When a crime took place at night, the record explicitly refers to this, suggesting that it was an exceptional detail. Otherwise, the timing of a given crime is rarely mentioned.

40 e.g. ADPC, A930/4: 'en l'eure d'entre soleil encousant et jour falant', when Jehanes de Dienart murdered Haniaus de Boiele, and was seen to do so by several townspeople of Arras; in 1337, Gillet de Saint Quentin and Adam Crestien fought each other in the street in Saint-Martin-des-Champs: Tanon, 494.

41 ADPC, A169/1.

not only as an individual against his enemy, but also place himself in an honourable position with regard to the local community. A man who burnt down a barn in Hesdin was hated so much that he was murdered in 1290.[42] In Abbeville much of the prosecuted violence occurred during an enforced truce between the two parties, and this timing was remarked upon not only for its legal implications (the fine would be higher), but because it indicated the presence of a long-standing feud. Such was the case with Jehan du Bellais and Wylars Baalart in 1320,[43] and with Colin, son of Robert le Potier, and Jehan Petit as Roses, the former borrowing a sword and *pourpoint* from his friends to attack the man with whom he was supposed to be, at least temporarily, publicly reconciled:[44] the ubiquity of faction and rivalry in this society was self-perpetuating.

The prevalence of honour and feuding practices does not mean that these were societies held back in an anachronistic pre-commercial culture; nor does it indicate straightforwardly that urban groups sought aspirationally to emulate the mores of chivalry. In these towns, honour and pride were already embedded in commercial practices. When a bourgeois of Amiens, Grignard de Bailleul, attacked Tassart 'li Borgnes', a burgher of Amiens, his explicit motivation was revenge for Tassart's humiliating pursuance of him for debt: the episode was placed in a feuding context by the legal evocation of the truce which had been formally sworn between the parties.[45] Making peace was also a very public event, watched in similar ways to the acts of violence which it apparently resolved. In the 1320s in Saint Omer, a peace made between Michel Odoulph and his friends and Stassiot Roussiel and his friends, following the murder of Stassiot's son, was so poorly adhered to that the *bailli* of Saint Omer gathered about twenty witnesses to attest that they had seen the peace being secured some sixteen years previously.[46]

Most such premeditated violence was associated with groups of assailants, and issues of honour or vengeance were revealed by the family connections between the perpetrators. About 11 per cent of the recorded cases in Artois explicitly described the collective assailants as related to each other, indicating a common and familial interest in the perpetration of the crime reminiscent of feuding societies:[47] for example in Bapaume in 1290, the three sons of Jehan de Coges lay in wait for a neighbour in a planned attack from which the neighbour eventually died.[48] Such cases

42 Respectively: ADPC, A123/2; A128/1.

43 AMA, MS 115, fo. 49ʳ.

44 Ibid., fo. 40ᵛ.

45 Boutaric, *Actes*, ii. 194, no. 4962 (1316).

46 ADPC, A958/1.

47 Cf. J. Given's similar observation concerning English homicide in the same period: *Society and Homicide in Thirteenth-Century England* (Stanford, Calif., 1977), 44–8.

48 ADPC, A128/2.

were common: in 1303, the two Cokerel brothers killed a common enemy, and in the same year two brothers together with their tutor killed Maiheu de Cossy.[49] The evidence is too scanty to draw definitive conclusions about vengeance, but the familial connections certainly hint at the socially strategic nature of such acts and their inescapably social role. Several cases involved a father acting with his sons: for example in 1274, near Lens, Daniel du Maisnil, his brothers and his father conspired together to kill the son of Martin de Goy, apparently a vengeance killing provoked by an issue of family honour.[50] Members of the Latre family in Saint Omer were victims of beatings in 1304 and 1307, but were prosecuted for violent retaliations in 1306 and 1307.[51] Some families could be excluded from a community through repeated violent victimization, as suffered by the Panons in Bapaume.[52] Whilst neighbours often turned on one another, neighbourly ties could equally provide tight-knit solidarities, poignantly illustrated in the case of a neighbour of Jehan du Markais in Hacicourt near Arras who tried to prevent a group of young men from stealing the cherries from Jehan's orchard, and who was murdered for his pains.[53]

Although legal records provide only oblique evidence of how street violence was conceived by its perpetrators, the legal filter itself illuminates the ways in which violence was interpreted by legal authorities and by the members of the community who reported and helped to prosecute cases: the choices made by those recording violent crime—which details to include, terminology used, description of consequences—reveal deep-rooted interpretative habits, illuminating how violence was read by those who sought to limit its occurrence. Records of legal prosecutions demonstrate a clear perception that identity was a central issue in the perpetration of violence on the street. Those who witnessed and reported crime, and those who recorded it, stressed that the identities of the perpetrators and of the victims were crucial indicators of the meaningfulness of a given act of violence. Though the records are abrupt and lack detail, they always identify male perpetrators by name and, where appropriate, by profession: likewise, male victims, where possible, are identified by name. Where the identity of the perpetrator remained unknown, the record explicitly said so, indicating the significance attached to the specific person involved. Of

49 AMA, MS 115, fo. 56^{v}.
50 ADN, B13597, fo. 114^{r}.
51 Respectively: ADN, B13596, fo. 60^{r}; B13597, fo. 55^{v}; B13597, fo. 35^{v}; ADPC, A221/6; ADPC, A225/4. For a similar case with the Cugnie family, see ADPC, A166/8 and A249/2.
52 e.g. 1304: ADN, B13596, fo. 58^{r} (two separate incidents); 1311: ADPC, A276/1.
53 1279: ADPC, A929/1.

course, this was often a pragmatic detail since the perpetrator was to be punished or fined, though in the case of the Paris records which were not compiled to fulfil the procedural function of identifying criminals to be tried, but merely to record jurisdiction in a particular matter, the inclusion of identity suggests that it was seen as intrinsic to the meaning of the act. This was particularly the case with repeat offenders, such as Colart Bacon in Hesdin, found guilty of murder in 1286, and taking the goods of a suicide in 1312; Gillon Fins in Bapaume who violently robbed his mother-in-law in 1304, beat up an enemy in 1307, and was himself beaten in 1311; or Enguerran des Trois Marchés in Saint Omer, guilty of beatings, murders, and carrying weapons.[54] The types of violence carried out on the street were shown to be contingent on the identity of the perpetrator, but the process was also perceived as a reciprocal one, as the records reveal contemporary observers' perception that street violence could in turn shape the position of the individual within social networks.

That these naming practices represented a conscious choice is indicated by the stark contrast with recorded cases involving women, who participated in street violence more often than one might expect.[55] Revealingly, women were rarely named personally, but most often designated simply by locality: for example, 'une femme de Buscoi'.[56] Observers thus indicated their place in a communal network, but minimized their individuality. In many cases, women were identified by mention of their relationship to a man, for example 'la femme de Simon de Polinchove' or 'la soeur de Ansel Clipart'.[57] Again, while acknowledging the place of a given woman in society, such designations implicitly obliterated their standing as individuals. A conflict of jurisdiction in Arras in 1258 between the cathedral chapter and the municipality, and eventually referred to the Parlement in Paris for mediation, gave lengthy details about the placing and nature of a particular murder which had happened on the street within the designated area of the *cité*, but referred to the victim at the centre of the discussions only as 'unam feminam occisam'.[58] Such abruptness was not only characteristic of legal reports of crimes, but also of the ways in which they were evoked by witnesses. An enquiry into

54 Respectively for Colart Bacon: ADPC, A123/1, A304/5. Respectively for Gillon Fins: ADN, B13596, fo. 85^{v}, and ADPC A205/2; ADN, B13597, fo. 76^{v}; ADPC, A282/2. Respectively for Enguerrand des Trois Marchés: BN, Coll. Flandre, 287, fo. 2^{r}; ADPC, A176/6; ADN, B13597, fo. 35^{v}, and ADPC, A221/6.

55 Given finds that 'Homicide in thirteenth-century England was an overwhelmingly male phenomenon': *Society and Homicide*, 135.

56 ADPC, A18/2.

57 ADPC, A156/5, A124/1.

58 *Olim*, i, no. XI, 46.

jurisdictional rights at Hesdin in the 1310s called upon thirty witnesses, twelve of whom independently described the murder of a woman by Vaastin de Beaurain: even though they claimed to have seen the corpse of the dead woman, they described her only as a woman from Hesdin.[59] Even in cases where women emerged from the passivity of victimhood, and were demonized as cruel perpetrators of violence, they were referred to only in relation to their male victims: in 1303 in Abbeville, a woman apparently murdered Fouket Roussel, and in another case in the same town, the precise timing of the crime and the victim's name were specified, but the woman remained an empty type.[60]

The gendered nature of the ways in which interpersonal violence was reported and understood as negotiation of one's place in the community is embodied in cases of violence to force lucrative marriages: a charge of corruption levelled against Jehan Biauparisis and Mahieu Li Anstier in Arras accused Biauparisis of having the reluctant brother of his intended daughter-in-law beaten, and Li Anstier of turning a blind eye to a murder by one Hanot Wauquetin in order to blackmail Hanot into allowing the marriage of his sister (with her dower of 400 livres) with one of his cousins.[61] Furthermore, marriages were contested through violence (even if not always on the street), as in the case of Jacquemon, who paid the jailor at Amiens to let his unwanted son-in-law die in prison. But there were many twists in this story, which illustrate the dangers in reading family loyalties in any straightforward way. Jacquemon tried to preserve family honour through the murder of a son-in-law, but Wiot, his contract killer, delegated the task to his own son-in-law, who was thus firmly implanted in Wiot's family network. However, the murdered man turned out to be Wiot's own brother, Gautier. Jacquemon's violent removal of his son-in-law from the family network was matched by his close solidarity with his son, with whom he perpetrated a brutal attack in 1305; yet the victim of this last attack was his own nephew, Colart Cordele, a poor man who died from his wounds: this nephew had tried to glean the wheat from behind him as he was harvesting and come too close, angering Jacquemon and his son who picked him up by his hood, hurled him to the ground, and spurred his horse to ride over the crumpled body.[62] Family honour was to be defended and enacted violently, but who was included in such a network was negotiable. Honour overlapped with more overtly financial

[59] ADPC, A955/1.

[60] AMA, MS 115, fo. 54^{v} (both cases).

[61] APDC, A931/2.

[62] ADPC, A208/2—the nephew died within eight days; Jacquemon was also accused of illegally selling wheat in his own home to avoid paying market dues; see also ADPC, A815/1.

concerns: quite possibly, Jacquemon was unhappy with a connection to the family of a convicted criminal and a jailor, and likewise, had little affinity with a man described as 'povre'. The communicative quality of violent gestures by individuals was acknowledged and the identities of these individuals were given centre stage; but these were also social identities, placing perpetrators and victims in broader networks, and assuming their acts of violence to have communal ramifications.

3. THE PERPETRATORS OF STREET VIOLENCE

Six principal, though overlapping, categories of perpetrators were implicitly delineated in the legal records. They illustrate a complex combination of the reality of criminal groups, alongside stereotypical constructions and the practicality of who was easiest to catch.

First, and most prominently, the records feature well-established male members of the community with named artisanal or mercantile professions, including some related to the documented ruling groups in these towns, notably the Crespins, Loucharts, and Quesnois in Arras.[63] Importantly, victims came from the same groups: these acts of brutality were not overtly driven by vertical tensions, but were means of regulating horizontal relationships within social groups.[64] Professions ranged from barbers, to bakers and butchers, to surveyors, weavers, tailors, and fullers, and even some doctors.[65] Strikingly, many perpetrators came from professions directly related to the rapid process of urbanization in this period: surveyors, masons, brick-makers, builders, tilers, plasterers, and weighers. A poem of the *Confrérie des jongleurs* in Arras describes the terror of a fictional mason 'qui estoit en faïde mortel', who only emerged from his house driven by hunger to do his work with one hand whilst, with the other, defending himself 'De ses anemis par deriere'.[66] In Paris, this

[63] e.g. Crespin; ADN, B13597, fo. 81^{r}; ADPC, A48/11, A41/28, A48/9; Louchart: A41/28, A48/11; ADN, B13597, fo. 165^{r}; Kesnois: ADPC, A289/1. A similar conclusion was reached by J. Misraki, 'Criminalité et pauvreté en France à l'époque de la guerre de cent ans', in M. Mollat (ed.), *Études sur la pauvreté* (Paris, 1974), 536. During this period, patronyms still tended to indicate the occupation of the subject and were not yet inherited. Hanawalt concludes that in England it was the main families in villages who led crime: B. Hanawalt, *Crime and Conflict in English Communities, 1300–1348* (Cambridge, Mass., 1979), 129.

[64] See Gonthier, *Cris*, 23.

[65] e.g. respectively: ADN, B13597, fos. 114^{v}, 106^{v}, and 81^{r}; ADPC, A282/1; Tanon, 321; AN, JJ66, fo. 79, no. 212.

[66] e.g. respectively: ADPC, A282/1; Tanon, 495; ADN, B13597, fo. 119^{r}; Tanon, 377, 433, 457; ADPC, A48/11. 'Who was in a mortal feud ... defending himself from his enemies behind him': Berger, *Littérature*, no. VIII, ll. 121, 131.

socio-economic group formed around 40 per cent of all known perpetrators. In Artois, professions were only expressly recorded in 15 per cent of cases, but many more perpetrators were implicitly placed in this same socio-economic group. The names and vocations of such perpetrators were juxtaposed, Sauwalon the dyer or Waleri the fisherman and Wailars the barrelmaker, for example.[67] Frequently, identity was established in the record by effective inclusion of the perpetrator's address; for example, Jehan du Goy, living in Yser (a tiny settlement on the outskirts of the village of Aubigny in Artois) apparently murdered on commission a neighbour named Robert d'Yser.[68] Such details had important implications, in a period of numerous competing jurisdictions.[69] Often, the nickname of the assailant was also given: Jean Grolet, dit Petit Pont—Little Bridge; Macciot, dit le Geolier—the Jailor; Perrard de Libera, dit le Batard—the Bastard.[70] A particularly pugnacious individual was nicknamed Jehan le Bateur.[71] Such nicknames had little jurisdictional relevance, but a great deal of relevance for the local community, placing the assailant clearly in networks of local solidarities. More specifically, such networks were perceived as so vital to the understanding of violence that in many cases the records detailed who commissioned a given act of violence: for example, Pierre Maiettiand and Herbert Roussiau apparently killed Robert, nicknamed Beghe, on behalf of Gautier dit le Betoutart, a relative of theirs.[72] The strategic nature of the violence, and its place within rivalrous familial and social networks, was acknowledged.

Overlapping with this category of assailants was that of young people, whose violence was stereotypically more likely to include a playful element, but which nevertheless was perceived as integral to the negotiation of social relations by the authorities, a perception revealed by the way in which they were identified.[73] Young people were described as 'fils de . . . ' or 'enfans de . . . ': these terms did not designate children in the modern sense, but the age-group of youths emerging from adolescence but not yet fully settled with their own families and occupations. In fact, out of 866 recorded cases in Artois, 135 were explicitly described as involving

[67] AMA, MS 115 fos. 33r 32v.

[68] ADN, B13597, fo. 84v.

[69] In this particular area, the seigneurial jurisdiction was engaged in an ongoing dispute with the local abbatial jurisdiction.

[70] Respectively: Tanon, 379, 433; AN, JJ66, fo. 163v, no. 408.

[71] ADN, B13597, fo. 97v.

[72] ADPC, A18/2.

[73] Muchembled finds 59 per cent of violent crime perpetrated by young men: *Violence*, 40. J. Ruff comes to the same conclusion in his study of early modern European violence: *Violence in Early Modern Europe, 1500–1800* (Cambridge, 2001), 125–6. Also Gonthier, *Cris*, 43–54.

someone's offspring. Such phraseology also connected the assailants immediately with a family network: when the children of Jakemon le Belle apparently murdered two men at Aubigny in the 1280s, their designation not by individual name but by shared father indicated the perceived familial interest in their act of violence.[74] In 1283, in Saint Omer, the children of Joel de la Fontaine, designated thus, insulted and assaulted the comital *bailli*; their misbehaviour was implicitly characterized as a familial trait.[75]

Women form a third category: the lack of any further detail in the records regarding these women rendered gender their defining characteristic rather than socio-economic status. But few were mentioned at all: these legal records placed clear emphasis on the social function of street violence and, in general terms, women were perceived as marginal to the public negotiation of social relations and therefore marginal to the perpetration of such violence. Where women did perpetrate violence, it was described as aberrant, diabolical, and often hidden from view: witness the case of a husband cruelly murdered in his bed in Abbeville on St Fuscien's night in 1303.[76] Unsurprisingly, the most common sphere of involvement of women in violent crime on the street was sexual crime, where women were most often the unhappy victims. In the rare cases where a woman's complaint was upheld, women were most often designated merely as sexual objects, albeit wronged ones: common terms were 'garce', indicating a young girl, or, with more derogatory connotations, 'basellete'.[77]

A fourth category involved temporary inhabitants of a given place, most notably students and other young men of clerical status. Such assailants formed only around 11 per cent of all prosecuted cases, a low figure as they were *de iure* subject only to ecclesiastical courts, because of their clerical immunity from temporal jurisdiction. Their identity was always thus categorized because they would then be handed over to an ecclesiastical court, but they were nevertheless treated by the authorities as a distinct group with their own distinctive forms of violence.

Strangers to a town formed a fifth category, and responses to violence perpetrated by strangers were exacerbated by nebulous fears of 'otherness'. Given that Artois was dangerously close to the conflict in Flanders, and suffered the consequences of soldiers passing through and not so infrequent raids, it is perhaps surprising that strangers or foreigners were rarely prosecuted. But if the focus was upon the community, protecting those outside it was largely irrelevant, and exclusion of transients was adequate. Travellers usually were depicted acting alone, thus drawing a contrast between their behaviour as marginal to day-to-day social relations, and

74 ADPC, A815/1.
75 ADN, B13595, fo. 1^{r}.
76 AMA, MS 115, fo. 54^{v}.
77 e.g. ADPC, A259/3.

group violence perceived as playing an integral role in local communities. Moreover, whereas groups of assailants, usually related, were depicted carrying out their violence by day and on the street as a public spectacle, the type of violence carried out by travellers was typically characterized as nocturnal, aberrant violence, associated with private houses or hostels and detached from everyday life.[78]

Anxieties about foreigners did exist, witness a typical decree of 1314 concerning the right to arrest criminous strangers in Lille, but such legislative concern did not translate in any straightforward way into prosecutions: whether this is because the numbers of strangers in these towns were limited by the hostility, because transients were harder to catch, or whether because of a preoccupation on the part of the authorities with local social networks is impossible to say.[79] Likewise, foreigners were rarely recorded as victims of violence, though this may reflect an unwillingness to protect those outside the immediate community.[80] It is striking that there is altogether very little evidence in these archives of interpersonal violence arising from the broader military conflict. Where it occurred amongst soldiers on campaign, the records retain their concern with the effect on local communities and their social networks, by simply transposing those same tensions into the context of the army camp. In 1297, for example, the three Copin brothers, Robert, Lambert, and Jehan, were accused of the murder of Guiot de Warwiler while serving in the army in Flanders; the count demanded that they be acquitted because Guiot had admitted to killing the father and brother of his assailants.[81] The case was seen as one of local import and, further, not even to affect the community as a whole, perceived instead as a semi-legitimate negotiation of relationship between individuals.

A spate of cases of paedophilia in Paris, where extremely young girls were apparently abducted and raped repeatedly, were all attributed to Lombards visiting Paris for commercial reasons.[82] The aberrancy of such

[78] e.g. Tanon, 471, 524.

[79] Boutaric, *Actes*, ii. 139, no. 4451 (1314). Fear of foreigners was ongoing in this frontier region: see Muchembled, *Violence*, 55, 86.

[80] A rare case in Artois recounts the wounding of an Englishman: ADPC, A48/9.

[81] ADPC, A2, fo. 4^{r}.

[82] e.g. Tanon, 471, 492, 537. A further case of paedophilia in 1321 recounted in the records of the Paris Parlement is of a rather different nature: here the assailant of the 9-year-old Jeannette was no transient figure, but the son of a well-to-do mercer, named Ivonet le Breton; although he was prosecuted for rape, he was acquitted on marrying the young girl, and a case was only later brought because his parents refused to support the young couple financially. This case was presented as distasteful, but not so aberrant that the perpetrator, an established member of the community, could not be re-absorbed back into that community and sense made of his actions (Boutaric, *Actes*, ii, no. 6637, 416). A case in Saint Omer also attributed the rape of a young girl to a Lombard merchant, ADPC, A176/6.

crimes was stressed; visitors to the town were not part of established social networks, and therefore their violence was conceived in radically different terms. Amongst these, the records distinguished between transient assailants, predominantly such Lombard merchants, and permanent immigrants who were accepted as fully fledged members of the community, although their geographical provenance was not forgotten. For example, a certain Richard the Englishman, living in the Paris region, murdered his Parisian-born mother-in-law; his integration into local networks was acknowledged, alongside a continuing awareness of his different origin.[83] In 1290, Berthelot le Camus was accused of murder in the parish of Sainte-Geneviève in Paris; he was identified as being of English origin, and the legal record drew attention to his continuing otherness by describing how nobody attempted to contact him for the year and a half during which he was imprisoned.[84] Immigrants were identified by their name, profession, and origin: the majority came from Brittany and Lorraine, though the accused also came from Burgundy, Normandy, and England.[85]

Interestingly, a sixth potential category, consisting of those excluded from society, the beggars, prostitutes, and vagabonds who are stereotypically associated with the world of violent crime, feature far less frequently in these records.[86] Perhaps marginals were simply less involved in violence and the social negotiations and conflicts which it tended to explore. Apprentices appear occasionally: they were marginalized by their subordination and their transience, but they were set apart from other marginal groups since their connection with their masters afforded them some slight integration.[87] Although these groups *were* repeatedly demonized by communities intent upon creating their own sense of cohesion, the general absence of marginal groups in the legal prosecutions of customary law highlights the preoccupation on the part of the authorities with the type of crime which was most obviously socially engaged. Strikingly, marginals also appear only relatively rarely as victims.

Thinking about the demonization of particular excluded groups raises the spectre of medieval anti-Semitism.[88] This is the period in which the

83 Tanon, 334.

84 Ibid. 349. Hanawalt also finds no 'criminal class' in the English case: *Crime and Conflict*, 221.

85 e.g. Tanon, 474, 487, 495, 347, 349.

86 This is in contrast to the findings of B. Geremek, *The Margins of Society in Late Medieval Paris*, tr. J. Birrell (Cambridge, 1987), 6–20.

87 e.g. the case of a 'ribaud', who murdered his master, a burgher of Amiens, and then fled to England in 1261(Boutaric, *Actes*, i, no. 645, 58).

88 This is such a major subject that it merits separate study, and is therefore not a focus of this book. It has received magisterial treatment in David Nirenberg, *Communities of Violence* (Princeton, 1996), particularly 43–68, and William Chester Jordan, *The French*

blood-libel took hold in France, the absurd idea that Jews were deliberating massacring the host; amidst mounting anti-Semitism, Jews were expelled from the realm. It is the period culminating in the conspiracy theory that lepers, under the orchestration of the Jews, were trying to poison the wells. Indeed, it is the period of conspiracy theories *par excellence*, where the notion of excluding a particular group by labelling their behaviour, real or imagined, as deviant and criminous, developed exponentially: witness the Jews, the Templars, lepers, even the papacy.[89] The Jews were labelled as deviant, and were simultaneously the victims of criminal behaviour. It is curious then that we find no examples of anti-Semitic violence or anti-Semitic constructions of violence by Jews in the seigneurial records of either Paris or Artois. Damaging attributions of deviant behaviour to Jews *did* happen: witness the various prosecutions undertaken by the Parlement. In 1317, for example, the royal *bailli* of Vermandois was ordered by the Parlement to pursue a Jewish surgeon named David who lived in Saint Quentin and was accused of poisoning several Christians.[90] Likewise, violence against Jews was certainly common—witness the daily cruelties attested to in Jewish literature, and the appalling brutality of the so-called Shepherds' Crusade in 1320, which even the crown attempted to stem.[91] But in the implementation of customary law in these communities of Artois and Paris, the focus was upon violence which was perceived as integral to the quotidian functions of communities, in which Jews were seen to be only marginal figures.[92]

This emphasis in the legal records on the identities of those involved in violence sprang from the ways in which crimes were reported by local communities. And this point is key: these were not hegemonic frameworks imposed upon communal reactions, but legal responses actively shaped by the community. Communal understandings of violence on the street were illustrated most strikingly in surviving records of conflicts of

Monarchy and the Jews: From Philip Augustus to the Last Capetians (Philadelphia, 1989), particularly 177–260.

89 Also of homosexuals: see M. Goodich, *The Unmentionable Vice: Homosexuality in the Later Medieval Period* (Santa Barbara, Calif., 1979), pp. xv, 71–88, though it would seem that persecution in fact was less draconian than in theory. On the 'creation' of marginals more generally, corresponding to a sense of crisis and growing central control in 14th-cent. England, see F. Rexroth, *Das Milieu der Nacht: Obrigkeit und Randgruppen in spätmittelalterlichen London* (Göttingen, 1999), 333–47; and in France, J. Watts, *The Making of Polities* (Cambridge, 2009), 146–7.

90 One of his apparent victims was a priest who had lent him 200 livres; his brother-in-law was also accused of complicity and altering coins in 1316 (Boutaric, *Actes*, ii, no. 5023, 201).

91 Jordan, *French Monarchy*, 248.

92 I have found no such cases in the comital archives, and occasional cases in the records of the Paris Parlement: e.g. Boutaric, *Actes*, ii, no. 5014, 200 (1316).

jurisdiction and indicate a similar focus on identity. In such cases, the testimonials of various witnesses concerning their experience of violent crime in a given area were diligently collected and transcribed. In 1270, the chaplain of the Count of Artois heard thirty-one witnesses describe all the cases of criminal violence which they could recall over the past forty years in the small village of Buscoi near Aubigny in Artois.[93] The purpose of the enquiry was to elucidate the boundaries of a series of competing jurisdictions. Altogether, forty-eight cases of violence (including multiple rapes) were described, revealing a striking level of violence over a forty-year period in a small village. The witnesses' statements were obviously shaped by the way in which they were interrogated, but demonstrate sufficient diversity to suggest that the hermeneutics of the acts of violence described were communally held and not just imposed by legal frameworks.

In all but two cases, the witnesses provided precise names for the perpetrators, who were identified as established members of the local community; the two exceptions concerned cases where a perpetrator explicitly avoided the publicity of the street, and was never found. A notorious murder and rape was described by identification of the perpetrators as Jean de Habire and his companion, while the woman was dismissed as 'a certain Marote'. Contemporaries thus indicated that it was the identities of the assailants which made this act of violence socially meaningful. In another murder, Gerard de Moncelat and four young companions murdered Robert le Plat: the crime took place in the street, and one of the witnesses explained that the location was just in front of his house. Family relationships were perceived as playing a crucial role. For example, Colard de Buscoi and his grandson murdered Jean Furnarimy after the latter insulted the grandfather: a case of vengeance was evoked via a description of the involvement of family members acting in concert. The spectacular nature of such cases was again noted in accounts of how Renerus, dit Petitdoit (comically mistranscribed in a copy of this record as Petitvit), struck Colard de Vimy, who then rushed to fetch his sword whilst shouting threats and insults at his assailant. Violence arising from an ongoing quarrel was connected to the neighbourly identities of the aggressors. One of the witnesses specifically recalled the verbal exchange between the violent participants, as Petitdoit shouted 'Veni foras multrator, et defende te'.[94] These witnesses not only observed violence, but interpreted it by selecting specific details which they felt were relevant.

[93] ADPC, A18/2. This roll has not been subdivided in any way.

[94] 'Come out into the street, murderer, and defend yourself': obviously the translation into Latin draws our attention to the legal process of filtering going on here.

4. TYPES OF VIOLENCE

In the Trésor des Chartes des Comtes d'Artois, murder is the most frequently prosecuted crime, with 351 cases arising in the region over a thirty-year period.[95] Adding a number of fights resulting in the death of one of the combatants, but not punished as murder, would increase this figure to 384: although legal distinctions between deliberate homicide and unintentional manslaughter had yet to be fully articulated in legislative terms, a *de facto* distinction was observed in the prosecution of violent crime, most obviously through the imposition of more lenient penalties on the guilty parties. In Artois, the next most frequently prosecuted type of violence is beating, wounding, or fighting: 251 such cases are recorded. The hierarchy is reversed in the case of Paris, where beatings are most heavily represented, with 176 cases, and only 129 murders.[96] Rape was comparatively common in both regions, with forty-one cases in the Artois records, and twenty-one in Paris. Acts of violence very often involved the use of weaponry, though this is not always specified in the records.[97] Proportionately, records of beatings referred most often to the use of weapons, particularly because this helped to indicate the degree of gravity of the beating: whereas a murder was clearly a murder, with or without the use of a sword, a beating entailed far more grievous consequences if it involved weapons. Nevertheless, the use and ready availability of weapons indicates a general preparedness for violence in a society where this was a ubiquitous tool of negotiation and contestation of social roles. Carrying weapons was a sign of status, particularly potent for groups of young men, like the children of Wautier le Grain, fined for strutting through the streets fully armed.[98]

Terminology is illuminating. Most frequently, weapons are only indicated by the generic 'armes', or the use of a verb such as 'navrer' which implies the presence of a sharp tool. Where the precise weapon is specified, knives, sticks, and clubs featured most prominently, presumably as the implements which came most readily to hand:[99] they are designated by

95 Cf. Figure 4. This was partly owing to the inadequacy of contemporary medicine: Muchembled, *Violence*, 38. The majority of these cases took place on the street, but not all explicitly so.

96 Cf. Figure 5.

97 In the English case, which benefits from more detailed documentation, Hanawalt finds the vast majority of cases to have involved weaponry: *Crime and Conflict*, 100.

98 BN, Coll. Fl. 287, fo. 1^r.

99 Gonthier notes the frequency of household objects used as weapons in 13th-cent. Lyons: *Cris*, 113.

the terms 'coutel a pointe', 'baston', and 'tison'.[100] More unusual weapons were also noted: whether aspirational, like bows and arrows, specialized, like a 'misericorde' dagger, or drawn from everyday life, such as ploughshare or a whip.[101] Jehan Faverel was acquitted by the Paris Parlement in 1258 from a charge of murdering Jehan Tanpiere with a dagger, when it was revealed that Tanpiere had produced the dagger first, provoking a struggle for control of the weapon.[102] This contrasts with the situation explored by Muchembled for the Artois region in the late fourteenth and fifteenth centuries where he notes that swords were the most common aggressive weapons:[103] the difference is most likely explained by the very different nature of legal records to which he refers, and which tended to highlight only the behaviour of the more prosperous levels of society who would have had easier access to such weaponry. Swords were nevertheless occasionally mentioned in the thirteenth-century records, and interestingly were not limited to the upper echelons of society. The sword was the centre of attention when Pierre d'Yser allegedly chased Antonin le Lavendier with a sword, apparently hurling the weapon at his adversary when he realized that he could not catch him.[104] An armed pursuit along the street was frequently recalled in the records: the street provided such memorable events with a space rich in public and communal connotations, and extended the meaning of violence beyond the merely personal. When in Aubigny during the 1290s, one burgher was seen to chase another down the street, finally catching him and administering a fatal beating, the violence was located in a public sphere with social implications.[105]

Criminal records seem to be most alive to the potential of violence to shape the identities of young men, with the street providing an arena where they could at once publicly explore their individual identities, and manipulate the place of these identities in broader social networks. Rapes which took place in the street were perceived as at least partially motivated by the desire of young men to prove their virility and hence earn themselves a 'macho' identity amongst their circle of friends, as in the attempted rape of a young woman by two clerics, Guillemet Mirse, and Mahieu Goiade in Abbeville. After abducting her from her house, they

[100] e.g. respectively: ADPC, A149/3; Tanon, 535; ADN, B13597, fo. 81^{r}.

[101] See respectively, ADPC, A176/6; ADN, B13596, fo. 113^{r}; B13597, fo. 108^{v}; B13596, fo. 116^{v}.

[102] *Olim*, i. 66 (1258).

[103] Muchembled notes 61% of the cases examined involving 'armes blanches', i.e. daggers, swords, etc.: *Violence*, 31.

[104] ADPC, A48/11.

[105] ADPC, A918/8.

raped her outdoors, but she escaped their grasp: the case was corroborated by witnesses. They later stole clothing from her mother, apparently because they were afraid of losing face.[106] The majority of rapes in Artois were carried out by young men in public, but the rapists chose the slightly remote roads outside the town rather than the street, demonstrating ambivalence between the intimacy of the act and their desire to make their actions known. A rape of 1268, recalled by witnesses during a conflict of jurisdiction in 1290, took place on the road near the wood;[107] in another conflict of 1278, witnesses recalled how a woman at Aubigny was raped just outside the village, beside the open land.[108] Likewise, in Paris, rapes tended to take place in public, but outside the city gates, at once aberrant and publicity-seeking. In 1287, Jehanot de Crespieres apparently raped an old lady outside the gate of Bourdeles, then kicked and abused her, and stole her chickens and her clothing: the incident was excessively cruel, but in humiliating his victim, the perpetrator sought to express his own identity.[109]

Rapes were most often thought to involve multiple aggressors. This is comparable to the English situation, where, despite the chronic under-reporting of the phenomenon of rape, it is clear that gang rapes were extremely common and that most often the woman was simply a pawn in a struggle over honour between men.[110] In 1286, the sons of Ansel le Hubert allegedly raped their own cousin on the street in Bapaume: she was an easy victim for them because of her young age, a mere 'meskine', and because, owing to the family connection, she initially trusted them.[111] The assailants were young men, described as 'enfans', evidently anxious to prove their macho identity and insert themselves visibly into the adult world of sexually active men. The terms used to describe their treatment of the girl were 'battre, ferir, faire force', suggesting a kind of holistic approach to rape as a general display of brutality and misplaced attempts to construct masculinity. The terminology of rape could also involve such vocabulary as 'efforcier' and 'contre son gré', as in the 1304 case of the rape of Agnès de Blaton by Jaquemon Horelore, Bertoul d'Origin, and Jehan Rajoine in Arras.[112] Agnès herself brought the complaint, and apparently described her attack on the street in these terms. However, owing to social

[106] AMA, MS 115, fo. 40v. Many charges of rape were brought in order to try to force a young man into marrying his victim: E. R. Yahil, 'A Rape Trial in Saint Eloi: Sex, Seductions and Justice in the Seigneurial Courts of Medieval Paris', in M. Goodich (ed.), *Voices from the Bench: The Narratives of Lesser Folk in Medieval Trials* (London, 2006), 251–71.

[107] ADN, B955.

[108] Described as 'campos': ADPC, A18/2.

[109] Tanon, 360.

[110] Hanawalt, *Crime and Conflict*, 108–9.

[111] ADPC, A123/1. See also ADPC, A140/1.

[112] ADN, B13596, fo. 65v.

pressure and the humiliation of proving that she had indeed been raped, she retracted the claim and replaced the phrase 'contre son gré' with 'avec son gré'. The crucial issue was not even so much her consent, as the degree of her resistance to the assault: in this case, the young men were relatively successful in asserting their sexual prowess without having to face severe penal consequences. Indeed, rapes often provoked ongoing violent disputes, demonstrating their integral position in social relationships: in 1281, the wife of Baudoin l'Ors accused Randoul the plasterer of raping her, provoking a fight between two other men, Thomas des Hales, his *sergent,* and Robin Lescot.[113]

Much violence was accompanied by extreme levels of verbal abuse, and often verbal abuse on its own was sufficiently offensive as to evoke charges. In Sotière near Arras in the 1310s, a certain Jehan was assailed with the violent threat 'k'il le comperroit de son chars', duly noted in the records and taken to reiterate the criminality of the subsequent violence by his aggressor.[114] Other insults were constructed in such a way as also to address the onlookers, witness the shouted 'Aler par la mort de Dieu, je l'ochirrai' in Merck in Artois in the 1290s:[115] this expletive successfully attracted the attention of passers-by and drew them into a network of those involved in the violent actions. Most often insults were not detailed in direct speech in this way, but evoked by terms such as 'laides paroles', 'laidengier', 'vilainer',[116] or the Latin 'multa verba contentiosa'.[117] Insults helped to locate the function of the violence, drawing attention to its communicative aspect and its perceived role in negotiating the relationship between the individual and the collectivity: shouting at one's adversary in public placed the violence of the individual in a network of interactions, and such shouts were remembered and recounted.[118] Verbal violence often served to blur the boundary between extra-legal conflict and its prosecution and regulation, as insults formed a regular part of court proceedings. For the historian, recorded insults render scenes of violence with vivid (and sometimes comic) immediacy, as in 1334 when one Thomas Boulart was punished by the ecclesiastical court at Cérisy in Normandy for calling his legal opponent, 'unum stercus in suo naso'.[119]

113 Tanon, 426.

114 'He would pay for his with his own flesh': ADPC, A956/1.

115 'By God's death, I will kill him': ADPC, A921.

116 e.g. ADN, B13597, fo. 86^v; B13597, fo. 87^v; B13597, fo. 15^r respectively.

117 AN, JJ49, fo. 27, no. 49.

118 'En insultant son adversaire, l'agresseur lui conteste un droit essentiel, le droit à exister au sein de la communauté': Gonthier, *Cris*, 137. Cf. also Leguay, *La Rue*, 157.

119 'A piece of muck in his nose': *Registre de l'officialité de l'abbaye de Cérisy*, ed. M. Dupont (Caen, 1880), 126.

While the sources rarely detailed the precise gestures involved in acts of violence and brutality, it is clear that brutality was often focused on the face of the victim, indicating a desire to humiliate and shame, as well as simply to damage physically.[120] The story of a disfigured priest in the *Miracles de Saint Louis* (subsequently cured by praying to the putative saint) demonstrates just how socially humiliating facial impairment could be, and the extent to which that sense of shame could be internalized.[121] In 1311 in Abbeville, Jehan Platine wounded a certain Wylardin Mourat in the face with a stick during a violent argument; the latter, disfigured, died of his wounds.[122] In cases involving a reciprocal struggle, such as that between a leather-worker and Jehannin Chapelain from Brittany in Paris in 1333, where both were at once victim and assailant, we can note a similar focus on the infliction of wounds to the head: this was both the most potentially damaging and the most humiliating area of the body.[123] Wounding in the head is most often designated by the simple 'navrer en la teste', suggesting a deliberate and strategic blood wound to the head. Eyes were very frequently targeted: blinding represented defeat, humiliation, and economic loss.[124] Such was the case, for example, in 1332 when a group of furriers targeted the face of their colleague in Saint-Martin-des-Champs: they gave him a 'si grant coup sus l'uelg, que il lui estoit estaint, et n'en veoit guoute', and by blinding their victim ensured his shame, whilst incapacitating him economically.[125] In a strategic and humiliating display in 1336, one Jehan Lenluminé, a furrier, was accused of cutting off two fingers of the right hand of his victim Thomas Lebreton, a leather-worker: the incident involved multiple participants, and was described as a 'riote'; moreover, it was probably part of a violent relationship, since Lebreton had been arrested the previous day for attacking Lenluminé with a sword, and was also accused of cutting off the legs of another (confusingly named) Thomas Lebreton, goldsmith.[126] Such acts of humiliation became public spectacles.

120 Muchembled notes a particular focus on the beard of the opponent: *Violence,* 167.

121 Guillaume de Saint Pathus, *Les Miracles de Saint Louis,* ed. P. Fay (Paris, 1931), no. 29, 88–90.

122 AMA, MS 115, fo. 51^{v}.

123 Tanon, p. 474.

124 e.g. the severe wounding and blinding of Rogier de Baigneux between Paris and Vanves in 1282: Tanon, 382. On attitudes to blindness, see M. O'Tool, 'The *Povres Avugles* of the Hôpital des Quinze-Vingts: Disability and Community in Medieval Paris', in J. Firnhaber-Baker and M. Cohen (eds.), *Difference and Identity in Francia and Medieval France* (Farnham, 2010), 157–75.

125 'Such a great blow to the eye, that they damaged it, and he could not see anything': Tanon, 467. See also e.g. a series of cases in Abbeville involving blows to the head: AMA, MS 115, fos. 32^{r}, 49^{r}.

126 Tanon, 483.

Much of the violence seems to have arisen from a spontaneous outburst of emotion, but it could still seen to be meaningful and shaped by common tropes. Groups of youths became dominated by anger and anger spilt over into violence.[127] In 1304, one Walon du Grant Fosse in Aire was explicitly accused of brandishing weapons 'par ire'.[128] Anger is indicated primarily by the large number of murders recognized as accidental: fights which arose without malice aforethought, and which had tragic consequences as tempers rose and weapons flew. In 1281, two brothers from the small village of Tolent took out their swords in playful spirit, but, as they became carried away, the scene ended in tragedy as one killed the other.[129] Such explosive angry violence was generally associated with bands of young men.[130] Individual grievances were redressed through violence, but it was the networks of social relations that were fundamentally at stake. Group violence was frequently associated with bands of youths behaving wildly but essentially playfully, their exuberance provoking outbursts of emotion with tragic consequences. Such was the case in 1286 at Arras of Wautier Feret and Jaquemart Vinart who teasingly attacked a rival youth, Mikiel du Hamel, in the street and, amidst the swiftly escalating violence, killed him.[131] In many such cases, emotions would run high until a serious wound occurred; the records then explicitly stated that the victim died of his wounds within forty days.[132]

5. THE CONTINGENCY OF STREET VIOLENCE

Interpersonal violence was socially engaged, using the street as a stage for physical gestures which challenged or corroborated social relationships, and its forms were contingent upon particular socio-economic contexts. Whereas some historians have suggested that levels of violent crime differed according to the demographic density of an area,[133] others have adopted a more qualitative approach indicating that different forms of urban development favoured particular forms of violence.[134] Claude

[127] See B. Rosenwein, *Anger's Past: The Social Uses of an Emotion in the Middle Ages* (Ithaca, NY, 1998), 1–6.

[128] ADN, B13596, fo. 76^{r}.

[129] ADPC, A938/3.

[130] Gonthier notes exactly the opposite in Lyons: most common was the 'rixe entre individus, comme la transposition roturière du duel aristocratique': *Cris*, 112.

[131] ADPC, A123/2.

[132] e.g. Tanon, 408.

[133] e.g. Given, *Homicide*, 177.

[134] e.g. Gonthier, *Cris*, 216, who suggests that urban social structures were particularly propitious to feuds. J. Chiffoleau has argued for 14th-cent. Avignon that the urban

Gauvard has even suggested that the fundamental structures and functions of violence did not shift with urbanization, but that increasingly densely populated areas did offer greater potential for existing forms of violence which could now become more meaningful through the developed sense of spectacle, and numerically increased audience.[135] Violence on the street was dependent on forms of social structure as it negotiated the position of the individual within that structure; while it certainly became a more potent tool with the publicity of the town, it was also an adaptive one as contemporaries struggled to cope with swiftly shifting socio-economic circumstances.

For the Artois region, the contrast between five, very different *bailliages* within the overall administrative region illustrates such variations: comparison of the proportions of different types of violence in these towns reveals slight correlations with distinctive social structures, suggesting that violence played an integral role in such structures.[136] Analysis is constrained by the small sample size, but parallel methods of prosecution and recording in the different areas renders cautious comparison possible. Saint Omer and Arras were the most urbanized towns in the region; flourishing and prosperous, they continued to grow throughout the thirteenth century, and by the early fourteenth century were increasingly engaged in international trade, most notably of cloth and wine.[137] Arras, as the official centre of the county of Artois, was not only rich, but a prestigious and burgeoning cultural centre, the home of vernacular theatre in France; poetry lay at the heart of civic life, as wealthy merchants increasingly rivalled the itinerant *jongleurs* for literary recognition in the annual poetry competitions.[138] Levels of prosecuted violence clearly rise in the larger *bailliages* of Saint Omer and Arras. Quite simply, these towns had larger populations, and, moreover, as municipal life became increasingly regulated over the course of the thirteenth century, acts of illicit

experience of rootlessness engendered a specifically urban form of interpersonal violence: *Les Justices du pape: Délinquance et criminalité dans la région d'Avignon au XIVe siècle* (Paris, 1984). Cities were also characterized by the large number of marginals, and the association of such groups with crime has been explored by Geremek, *Margins*, 6–12.

135 Gauvard, *Violence*, 216–17; and Gauvard, 'Violence citadine et réseaux de solidarité: L'Exemple français aux XIVe et XVe siècles', *Annales ESC* 48/5 (1993), 1113–25.

136 See Figure 2.

137 See A. Derville, *Les Villes de Flandre et Artois, 900–1500* (Villeneuve d'Ascq, 2002); P. Bougard, 'L'Apogée de la ville (1191–1340)' in Bougard (ed.), *Histoire d'Arras* (Paris, 1988), 53–76.

138 See Berger, *Littérature*; M. Ungureanu, *La Bourgeoisie naissante: Société et littérature bourgeoises d'Arras aux XIIe et XIIIe siècles* (Arras, 1955); C. Symes, *A Common Stage: Theater and Public Life in Medieval Arras* (Ithaca, NY, 2007), 217–26.

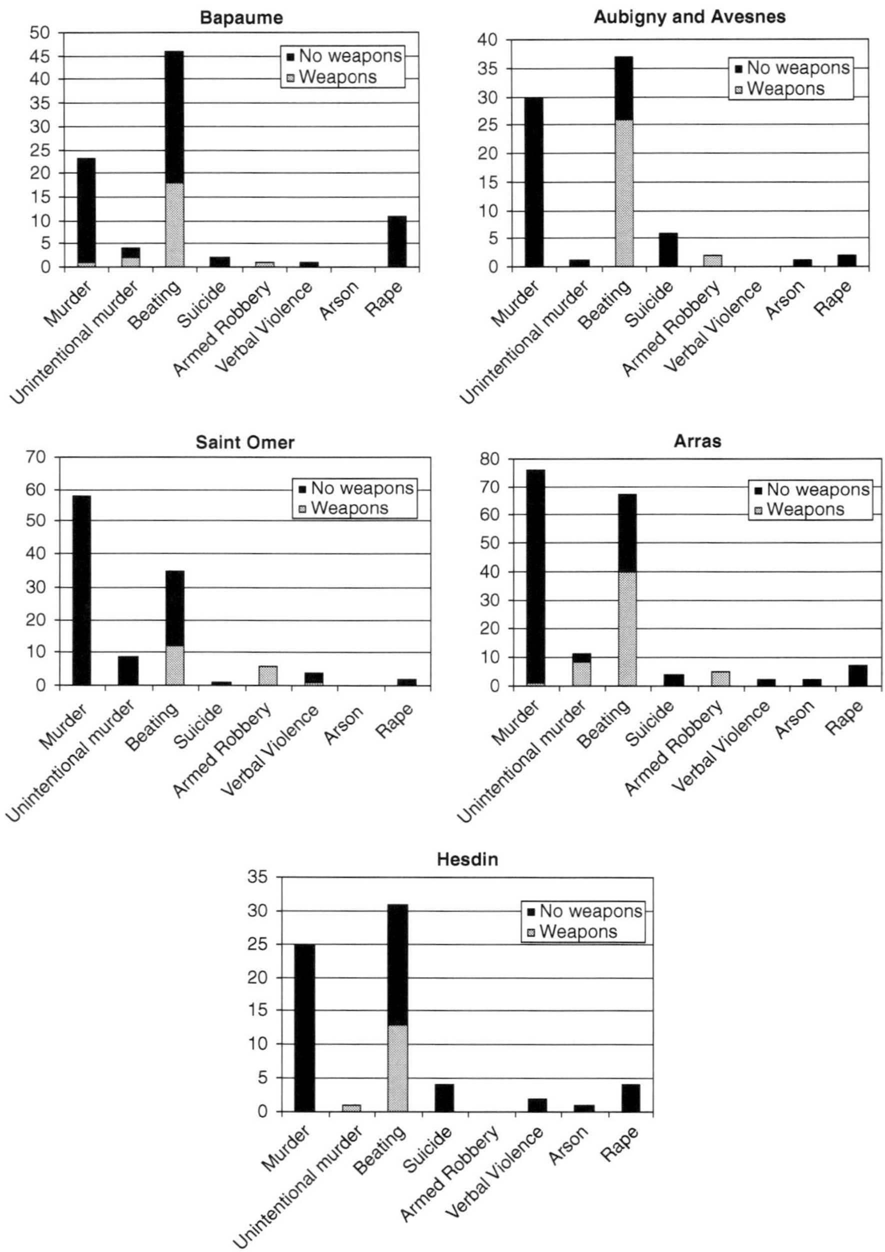

Fig. 3. These charts show the relative frequency of different types of violence in five Artois towns. 'Weapon' indicates that the source mentions use of arms; 'no weapons' indicates that no weapons are mentioned. Drawn from the accounts of the bailli of the comté of Artois from 1280 to 1314, ADN Series B, ADPC Series A.

violence were more likely to be prosecuted:[139] furthermore, Arras was a privileged town with its own jurisdictional rights, limiting the number of cases which the *bailli* could oversee and record in his financial accounts, so the number of crimes there is likely to have been higher than indicated by the records. Not only that, but the *bailli*, Jean de Beaukaisne, was prosecuted in the 1290s for flagrant corruption, and the failure to record a number of cases so that he could pocket the money. Nevertheless, the turn of the thirteenth and fourteenth centuries was a period of both economic and military disruption; as Philip IV struggled to subdue and retain control over the immensely rich Flanders region, so the neighbouring French areas suffered high taxation burdens, manpower obligations, and a deep sense of insecurity.[140] Saint Omer and Bapaume were particularly heavily affected by the Flemish war, afflicted by financial and human cost, as well as the disruption caused by transient soldiers, and the physical destruction of parts of the urban landscape.[141] In contrast, the counts of Artois continued to flourish and to boast extravagant demonstrations of their wealth and success: Hesdin was a town overshadowed by the building of an enormous comital castle and pleasure park in this period.[142] Although notable for its urban sophistication, Artois was still largely agriculturally based, and forms of social relations and, indeed, of violence, varied according to population density and social structures: the district of Aubigny and Avesnes, the most rural *bailliage* in Artois, places the more famous Arras in sharp relief.[143]

The ratio of murder to beating varied significantly from town to town. More commonly, prosecutions for beatings outnumbered prosecutions of murders, witness the cases of Bapaume, Hesdin, and Aubigny and Avesnes; but in the more densely urbanized areas of Arras and Saint Omer, the prosecutions for murders outnumbered those for beatings. It is unlikely that this is because more beatings were carried out with impunity in these areas, given that order was noticeably more tightly enforced in towns with a higher degree of urbanization. Rather this indicates that tempers and tensions were sufficiently intensified on the urban street to heighten the physical consequences of violence: inhibitions

139 On policing in towns, see Gonthier, *Cris*, 151–83.

140 See J. Strayer, *The Reign of Philip the Fair* (Princeton, 1980), 82, 324, 346.

141 See D. Nicholas, *Medieval Flanders* (London, 1992), chs. 7–8; F. Funck-Brentano, *Les Origines de la guerre de cent ans: Philippe le Bel en Flandre* (Paris, 1897), 673–81; M. Vale, *The Origins of the Hundred Years War* (Oxford, 1996), 199.

142 See M. Vale, *The Princely Court: Medieval Courts and Culture in Northern Europe, 1270–1380* (Oxford, 2001), 281–2.

143 See R. Fossier, *La Terre et les hommes en Picardie jusqu'à la fin du XIII*^e^ *siècle*, 2 vols. (Paris, 1968), i. 393; ii. 517.

upon displays of extreme feeling were apparently laxer in the larger towns. The proportions of murders explicitly described as unintentional—beatings from which the victim died within forty days—were also slightly higher in the urbanized areas (Arras, Saint Omer), again suggesting that fights and beatings were more intense in towns and engendered graver physical consequences. For example, in 1304, Pierot Ruet d'Esperleques wounded Jehan de la Tour after an angry fight; Pierot claimed that he had acted in self-defence, after a verbal dispute got out of control.[144] More murders in the urbanized areas were characterized by spontaneity, and their gravest consequences lacked malice aforethought: the density of population in the town seemed to favour outbursts of spontaneous violence and the physical expression of extreme emotion. In Saint Omer, in 1304, one Robert de le Pare killed his brother in just such an unintentional outburst; he was acquitted after pleading that he was overcome by anger, not acting rationally, and, moreover, disadvantaged by his young age.[145] In contrast, in the less urban areas, Aubigny and Avesnes most notably, murders were carefully planned affairs: the slower pace in rural areas allowed for the premeditation of violence in public. The relative use of weapons was not noticeably different from town to town, but Arras and Saint Omer recorded a slightly higher level of prosecution solely for carrying weapons on the street, indicating a greater level of policing.

Recorded cases of rape were clustered in certain areas. In Bapaume, cases of rape constituted 11 per cent of all prosecutions, compared to only around 2 per cent in the other towns. Bapaume's proximity to the Flemish border suggested that women in Bapaume were particularly endangered because of the presence of transient soldiers. Such causes are conjectural, but implicitly evoked by the emphases in the contemporary records, and the medieval observers who provided such accounts. Even rape, apparently driven by individual sexual desire, could be favoured by certain social conditions, and public rapes were perceived as fulfilling a social function, albeit an unacceptable one.

The recorded motivation of violent crimes varied from town to town. Hesdin stands out as a town in which a high proportion, 20 per cent, of prosecutions involved street violence against figures of authority: these were not collective rebellions, but beatings of comital *sergents* on the streets or of messengers sent from the count often bearing unpopular summonses. In 1305, one Jehan le Fournier, an inhabitant of Hesdin, disrespectfully insulted the mayor of a neighbouring village who was bearing a

[144] ADN, B13597, fo. 92^{r}. [145] ADN, B13597, fo. 87^{v}.

message from the count, and then beat him.[146] Similarly, in 1308, Craissin de Vaus engaged with this tradition of contesting authority by striking a burgher from a neighbouring town who tried to dictate how he might dispose of his inheritance.[147] Evidently, the building of the comital castle engendered a great deal of disaffectedness and tension, which manifested itself in a culture of individual acts of insubmission. The street provided an ideal forum for such acts of contestation, as it represented, both metaphorically and concretely, a place where the individual confronted the collectivity and could publicly contest or negotiate his place within it.

Acts of violence involving family members acting concertedly had different strategic value in different areas. They were rarest in Hesdin, presumably because the focus of tension here was diverted by the castle-building and by the large presence of foreign workers. In Aubigny and Avesnes, 30 per cent of prosecutions involved cases where family interests and honour were evidently at stake, demonstrating the importance of networks of familial solidarity and the role of violence within such solidarities: feud is an ongoing collective relationship, and in such a primarily rural community, its social value was prominent.[148] Typical were the Cointe family, who gathered together to murder Colart Gascon in 1303, and his relative, Mikelet Gascon in 1305 (as well as being accused of further breaking the peace in 1305).[149] The proportion of such cases slowly decreased as towns became more urbanized: they formed 28 per cent of prosecutions in Bapaume, a slightly more developed town, 20 per cent in Arras and Saint Omer. As towns developed, town-dwellers became typically more remote from family members, and networks of solidarities shifted: violence was used by groups other than the family and in the service of different solidarities and communities.[150]

In this respect, the most dramatic contrasts are revealed when the Artois region is compared with the thriving Parisian metropolis.[151] The records here are of a slightly different nature, compiled mainly to illustrate jurisdictional boundaries, but it unlikely that this procedural difference alone can account for the distinctions discernible between the two regions. Paris was beset by two main categories of violent crime on the street in this

146 Ibid., fo. 108ʳ. 147 Ibid., fo. 95ᵛ.

148 See J. Black-Michaud, *Feuding Societies* (Oxford, 1975).

149 Respectively: ADN, B13596, fo. 11ᵛ; ADPC, A208/2; ADN, B13596, fo. 114ᵛ; see also: ADPC, A205/1; A208/2; A259/2; ADN, B13596, fos. 43ʳ, 94ᵛ; B13597, fo. 83ʳ.

150 These figures of course can only lead to impressionistic conclusions. Violence in towns often continued to be motivated by familial feuds: Gauvard, 'Violence citadine', 1119–21; G. Espinas, 'Les Guerres familiales dans la commune de Douai aux XI et XIIIᵉ siècles: Les Trêves et les paix', *Nouvelle Revue Historique de Droit Français et Étranger*, 23 (1899), 415–73.

151 See figures 4 and 5, p. 82.

period.[152] The first, a type of violence specific to Paris and rarely found in the Artois region, might be termed ludic violence and was carried out principally by clerics (17 per cent of the assailants prosecuted by these courts for all types of crimes pleaded clerical status), concentrated in Paris because of the university: this kind of violence had no obvious social function, but formed part of a student culture of mockery and exuberance. Within this group, prosecutions for rape and beatings were proportionately high. Around 16 per cent of prosecutions were for acts of violence perpetrated at night—this kind of playful violence did not require the social publicity of daylight.[153] Perhaps because of this social disruption, clerics themselves were frequently victims of violence, witness the 1257 murder of a cleric by an exasperated Parisian barber.[154]

The second main type of street violence in Paris was again the type of violence carried out by young men, mainly from the middle rungs of society, in daylight and in public as an integral part of social relations. However, the exact positions of the participants and their motivations correlate to the very different nature of Parisian society as compared to Artois. Many more women were involved in crime in Paris. Around 13 per cent of all prosecuted assailants were female (though admittedly, often acting in concert with men), corresponding to the more active role women were expected to play in this metropolitan urban society. Moreover, the legal authorities, and the observers from whose accounts the records were constructed, were more alive to the possibility of women becoming involved in violence on the street in Paris, for it was more commonplace to consider women occupying an active social function.[155]

Provenance is another telling category, and indicates the importance of shifting solidarities in determining the nature of violence carried out on the street and its relationship to the role of individuals within social structures.[156] Of all named perpetrators and victims in Paris, 14 per cent were recorded as first-generation immigrants to Paris. This percentage should be compared to the mere 6 per cent of crimes perpetrated by family members acting in concert.[157] This is a dramatic difference from

152 I have found little evidence for this period of the bands of professional criminals often associated with towns: Gauvard, 'Violence citadine', 1125.

153 A caveat to this statistic: sometimes, the designation of night may have referred to the time at which the criminal was caught.

154 *Olim*, i. 31.

155 See S. Farmer, *Surviving Poverty in Medieval Paris: Gender, Ideology, and the Daily Lives of the Poor* (Ithaca, NY, 2001), 117.

156 Cf. Gauvard, *Violence*, 219–25.

157 This corresponds to Given's findings concerning the different nature of homicides in more urbanized English areas: *Homicide*, 177, although he suggests that women were *more* involved in areas of weak lordship, owing to more tightly knit families, 172.

the Artois region, where, apart from the special case of Hesdin, no cases were recorded involving immigrants or non-locals. Paris was a burgeoning city in this period, with a rapidly increasing population owing to the large numbers of immigrants; the *Miracles de Saint Louis* from the 1270s refers to a whole host of miracle-seekers living in Paris on their own after emigrating from the countryside, and forming new networks of support and solidarity with fellow immigrants: many of these miracles describe the support given by those from a similar background to an immigrant upon discovering his or her disability.[158] As a very large city with a mobile population, family networks were bound to become overshadowed by new networks of solidarity, particularly between those who had emigrated, often without their family. The types of social networks and solidarities in which violence played a communicative and negotiating role had dramatically shifted in the Parisian context. In 1268 in the parish of Vanves, under the jurisdiction of Sainte-Geneviève, two immigrants from Picardy became embroiled in violent altercation with a certain Bertaut le Grand, wounding him and gouging out his eye.[159] The perpetrators were not related, but geographical provenance revealed new networks of support in which violence was a central element.

6. SOCIAL MEMORY

Street violence was endemic in social networks and relationships, and its ready use as an instrument of public social communication was certainly evident to contemporaries, as revealed by the preoccupations and emphases of the records. However, its ubiquity and socially engaged character were not so anodyne that contemporaries were largely inured or indifferent to it. Clearly, violence was too important as a tool of social relations to engender apathy. It was shocking and memorable, and street violence was, by its very nature, a public occurrence which engendered very natural feelings of disgust. Finding a body was an event in itself: the gruesome details were remembered years later by an old man who had found the head and body of a murdered cleric on different sides of the street as a young boy.[160]

[158] Saint Pathus, *Les Miracles de Saint Louis*: e.g. the women in miracle 60, 118–25; the paralysed 28-year-old in miracle 2, 7–12.

[159] Tanon, 383.

[160] ADPC, A166/9. There are multiple accounts of finding bodies, e.g. ADN, B13596, fo. 33r, ed. Delmaire, no. 2550.

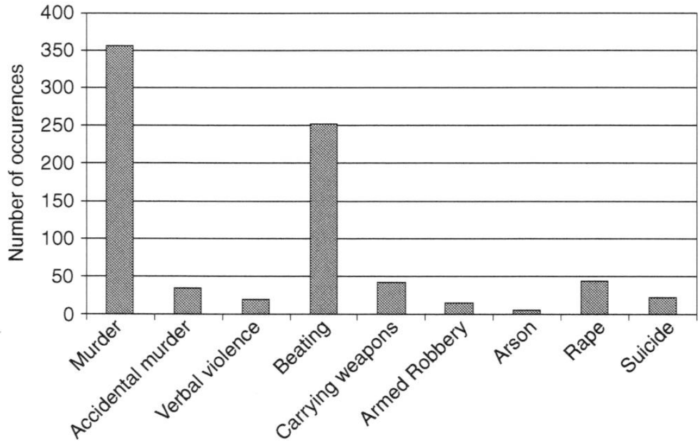

Fig. 4. Chart demonstrating types of violence in Artois, drawn on the *bailli* of the comté of Artois' accounts from 1280 to 1314: ADN Series B, ADPC Series A.

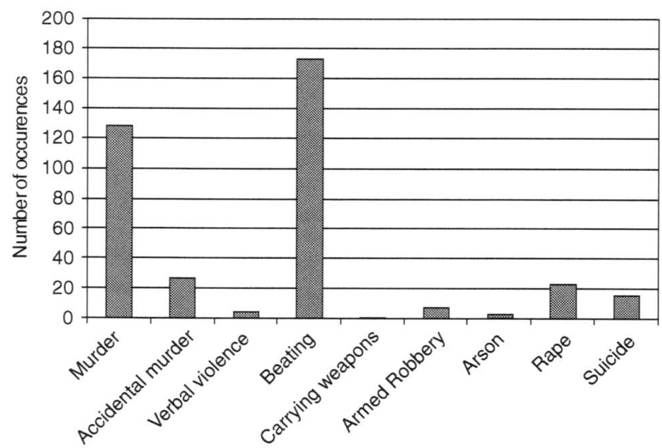

Fig. 5. Chart demonstrating types of violence in the Paris region, based on the registers of the seigneurial jurisdictions of Saint-Martin-des-Champs, Sainte-Geneviève, Saint-Maur-des-Fossés and Saint-Germain-des-Prés: F. Tanon, *Histoire des justices des anciennes églises et communautés monastiques de Paris* (Paris, 1883).

While the regular legal records filtered witnesses' interpretations of events, the numerous surviving records of conflicts of jurisdiction throw into particularly sharp relief the effect of acts of street violence on contemporary inhabitants over an extended time-span.[161] On 13 August 1303, an enquiry took place concerning the high justice of the abbey of Ham in Artois: Ham-en-Artois was a tiny village, and the enquiry details the reaction of the inhabitants to acts of violence over a forty-year period in the final years of the thirteenth century.[162] In order to prove their effective jurisdiction over criminal cases in this region, the abbey gathered thirteen witnesses to rack their memories and describe all the criminal prosecutions and their outcomes which they could recall as having taken place in the area. The thirteen witnesses described ten cases of violent crime occurring since about 1263. Five of the thirteen were described as 'chevaliers', and the others were ordinary parishioners. Apart from Jehan du Fail, knight, aged 32, all the witnesses were in their mid-forties or above, the oldest being 65: older members of the community were chosen as witnesses because of their supposed greater sense of moral responsibility, and also simply because of the longer period on which their memories could draw. The enquiry provides a real sense of the place of violence not just in individual memories, but in social memories of this community: memories of outbreaks of violence recalled up to forty years later clearly depended upon oral transmission and were filtered through numerous local discussions over the years.[163] Memory is a constructed phenomenon, not an automatic recall of past events.[164] As an essentially collective process, the configuring of social memories about violence underlines once again the communal implications of interpersonal brutality. Incidences of street violence were remembered as acts by individuals, but with communal

[161] e.g. ADPC, A18/1, A18/2, A35/2, A49/24, A904, A906/1, A/929, A930/4, A933/4, A938/3, A955/1, A956/1, A958/1; ADN, B955. These records of conflicts of jurisdiction are parchment rolls: they begin with a description of the precise nature of the conflict of jurisdiction, and then record the crimes remembered by each witness in turn. The numbers of witnesses called vary from five to twenty-five. The record was kept by the official of the count who was responsible for resolving quarrels of jurisdiction, though frequently also involved in them.

[162] A49/24: unfortunately, there are no subdivisions. I would like to thank Jean-Marc Dissaux, archivist at the Archives Départementales du Pas-de-Calais for alerting me to this document.

[163] The witness statements were quite formulaic, and point to the desire for homogeneity to which Smail has drawn attention, but the speakers were not simply aping each other or the expectations of the authorities, but engaging in a dialogue between individual memory, collective experience, and the structure of the procedure. See D. Lord Smail, 'Witness Programs in Medieval Marseille', in Goodich, *Voices*, 227–50.

[164] J. Fentress and C. Wickham, 'Foreword', in their *Social Memory* (Oxford, 1992), pp. ix–xii.

connotations; these witness statements interpreted acts which were taken to be at once messages about individual bodies, messages about the social body, and messages about the relationship between the two.

Given that Ham-en-Artois was a small village, with an estimated population of between 100 and 200 in this period, ten cases of violent crime falling within the remit of a single jurisdiction is high. The cases include seven victims of homicide, five assailants condemned to death, four banishments, three houses burnt down, a rape, a violent robbery, and one unknown crime for which the perpetrator was hanged, his house burnt, and all his possessions confiscated. Nevertheless each crime was remembered by an average of six witnesses, and each witness remembered an average of seven crimes. Evidently, violence was not so ubiquitous that it failed to leave an impression on the spectator or fellow inhabitant, an impression so deep that, forty years later, the details of the crime could still be recalled. Some of the witnesses would have been very young when they experienced the scene of violence recalled in this text: Jehan de le Bare, the first witness, a parishioner from Ham, described how he saw the dead body of Ansel Bredaine when he was just 10 years old; Warin Galiot believed that he was about 13 when he saw the same body. As children, these boys were clearly profoundly affected by the sight of violence, but their recollection of events also indicates communal tellings and re-tellings of the incident.[165] It was not only children who were affected by the sight of violence: other cases, such as the murder of Jakemin Blasmé by Martin Vassière and his brother, were recalled by witnesses who would have seen them while in their thirties. Violence may have been a frequent method of contesting social relations, but it was still shocking and impressive.

The witnesses were asked to specify when the act of violence occurred. This was the only point upon which they differed, with date ranges for a given act of violence sometimes spanning as much as a thirteen-year period. This implied a complex interaction between social and individual memory: although violence clearly had a profound impact on the whole community and many incidents passed into collective mythology, individuals still recalled personalized accounts of events and were not merely being prompted to give identical answers. The differences in dating the crimes demonstrate that individuals remembered them in terms of their place in their own lives, and not merely according to a socially structured

[165] Maurice Halbwachs's seminal work, *On Collective Memory*, ed. and tr. L. Coser (Chicago, 1992) suggests the inseparability of individual and collective memory: 170–3, 182–9. While witnessing brutality is bound to traumatize the individual, such memories are conditioned and made meaningful by collective processes.

chronology. Mimicking the interaction between the individual and the collective in events on the street, memories of street violence functioned at once in an individual and in the context of social networks.

Often, the witnesses described the sight of the violence itself. Such are the cases of Jehan de le Bare, Warin Galiot, and Eustasse Frankelin, all parishioners of Ham, who described seeing the murdered body of Ansel Bredaine fifty years earlier. As all three witnesses were at the time of the enquiry in their mid-sixties, we can imagine the three children probably stumbling across the body together. Likewise, Willaume de Carloi, another parishioner from Ham, 60 years of age, recalled seeing, twenty-two years earlier, the dead body of Renele Duponchel, killed by Nicaise Lelong, Pierre Lelong, Willaume Mantel, and Hue Durdenier. This man obviously had the knack of being in the wrong place at the wrong time, as he went on to describe seeing another dead body sixteen years previously. These men were not so accustomed or hardened to the sight of violence that they failed to pick out these incidents many years later, and these cases were sufficiently notorious and discussed in the community for details of the names of assailants and victims to be well-known. Details such as the placing of the violence—especially important in a conflict of jurisdiction—were recalled with precision: the body of Ansel Bredaine, for example, was found in the street in the village of Ham. The rape of a woman was specified as taking place outside the mill on the road outside Ham. Moreover, witnesses were quite clear on the time of day of an act of violence: this was one of the features which gave the act its specific character, and so it was clearly stated by all seven witnesses that Renele Duponchel was killed at night.

In many cases, the witnesses did not actually see the dead body, but experienced the violence in other ways. Some attested to seeing and hearing the hue and cry taking place afterwards, for instance four witnesses described the communal reaction and hue and cry following a rape. This expression of collective outrage at the crime was evidently memorable, and not simply an everyday event. However, the justice of Ham merely condemned the culprit to a fine for hitting the male companion of the victim, a typical response to rape in this period. Even when no dramatic hue and cry took place, witnesses still recalled the spreading of rumour about violent crime. Many witnesses remembered everyone talking about the perpetration of a certain crime and who might be responsible. Such local discussions were not merely idle gossip, quickly forgotten, but ones with which people engaged on a serious and long-lasting level. Eustasse Frankelin described how news spread of the murder of a woman named Susane on the road outside Ham, and how local suspicions alighted on

Marghe Crassemollie who was later arrested. Similarly, Hue de Tonnai, a 52-year-old knight recalled the rumours which spread six years previously concerning the murder of a certain Colin Cardel, accused of killing a valet called Fournier.

More subtly, memories persisted of the meaning or sense of certain acts: they were not merely remembered for their gruesomeness. Some time between 1283 and 1287, Martin Vassière and his brother murdered a certain Jakemin Blasmé. Shortly afterwards, one Willaume Blasmé, together with Warin Dufour and Jehan Julien carried out another murder: the recurrence of the Blasmé family name in a community this size suggest that an issue of family honour, perhaps a vengeance killing, was at stake. Five witnesses mentioned both these crimes and, though they did not explicitly describe their motivation, they chose to describe them consecutively, placing the second one year after the first (though they differed in the absolute date): moreover, both events were given as one item in each statement. This decision by witnesses to link the incidents implicitly evoked shared memories of the significance of the violence.

While these societies were saturated with violence on the street, violence was nevertheless a shocking and memorable occurrence. It played a central role in social relations, and was contingent upon a number of socio-economic factors, most notably degree of urbanization, but it also made a deep impression on individuals qua individuals and as part of a collective social memory. It remained impressed on the minds of a community as the point at which an individual, publicly and spectacularly, communicated violent messages about the bodies of himself and his victim and enacted events with collective repercussions.

Perhaps the greatest impression was left by the punishments suffered by the guilty party, problematizing the picture of a society completely hardened to the sight of violence. Very detailed descriptions were provided by nine witnesses of the complex punishment of Jehan de Cuham. He was first hanged by the officials of the count of Artois. The abbot of Ham complained that this was a contravention of his jurisdictional rights; the *bailli* of Aire, for the count of Artois, had the body cut down and dragged across the fields to Ham; and the abbot had the body dragged and hanged on his own land. Likewise, witnesses described in detail the hanging of stuffed cloth effigies of Willaume Blasmé, Warin Dufour, and Jehan Julien, since the count of Artois's men had already hanged the real men. It was not only extraordinary corporal punishments which were remembered, but also banishments, burnings of houses, even the original arrests.

7. CONCLUSION

Violence on the street was an integral function of social relations in this period, and the emphasis on its geographical, economic, and social contingency in the contemporary legal records demonstrates a profound contemporary awareness of this. The street was a unique forum for violence, as both in metaphorical and legal discourse it provided the junction between the individual and society: here the inhabitant stepped out of his house into the public sphere, and attempted to negotiate the relationship between his role as an individual and that as a member of social networks.[166] This characterization of the street was explored and elucidated by contemporary thinkers, and it filtered into their understandings of the perpetration of violence on the street. While violence was clearly common, it nevertheless provoked sufficient impact and awareness of its significance amongst contemporaries for a murder to be vividly remembered fifty years later: they remembered its role in mediating the juncture between the personal and the social, and while horrified, were unwilling entirely to dismiss such a widespread social strategy.

[166] See, of course (and for a later period), J. Habermas, *The Structural Transformation of the Public Sphere: An Inquiry into a Category of Bourgeois Society* (Cambridge, Mass., 1991), particularly 176.

3

'Oés comme il fierent grans caus!'

Tavern Violence in Thirteenth- and Early Fourteenth-Century Paris and Artois

Follow me now off the ill-lit street into the dingy but jocular environs of the urban tavern. On the street, readings of violence were coloured by a degree of ambivalence, but the fundamental paradigm of violence as communication remained a structuring principle, both in motivating, and in dictating attitudes towards, violence. But as we move into the noisy and dark medieval tavern, existing paradigms of violent communication are subverted and disrupted. Economic and social flux merited comment, and taverns were ideal spaces for this: violence in the tavern became not engagement in society, but commentary upon it.[1]

'Oés comme il fierent grans caus': thus the inn-keeper and audience are alerted to the fight taking place between the tavern customers in Jean Bodel's *Jeu de Saint Nicholas* of 1200.[2] The inn-keeper immediately intervenes to stop the fight, rhetorically demanding if the protagonist is 'faus', and connecting the concept of irrationality and violence by rhyming it with 'caus'. No audience would have been surprised by such a scene in contemporary literature. Taverns were notoriously the scene of riotous violence, both concretely and in the multiplying discourses surrounding such places and their associated practices of drinking, gambling, and arguing: Jonin memorably described the topos as 'A barrel, three prostitutes, and a ribald eating tripe in a smoke-filled atmosphere'.[3] Violent behaviour in this arena was often self-consciously characterized by a sense

[1] In many ways, this echoes claims regarding the later development of the 'public sphere', although the tavern remains particular because of its liminality: J. Habermas and S. and F. Lennox, 'The Public Sphere: an Encyclopedia Article', *New German Critique*, 3 (1974), 49–55.

[2] 'Listen to how they beat each other up!': Jean Bodel, *Le Jeu de Saint Nicholas,* ed. J. Dufournet (Paris, 2005), l.1162.

[3] Quoted in N. Coulet, 'Inns and Taverns', in J. Strayer (ed.), *Dictionary of the Middle Ages*, 13 vols. (New York, 1982–9), vi. 475.

of superfluity: in terms of causation, of form and gestures used, and outcome, this violence had no distinct function and that was, paradoxically, the point. By challenging and subverting the usual paradigms of violent communication, perpetrators and interpreters of violence in the tavern were able engage in a broader social critique. Of course, this was violence often fuelled by alcohol. *Violentia/vinolentia* was a well-used pun.[4] It is often suggested that this means we should take it less seriously, because drunken people do not stop to reflect upon their actions. But the premise of this book is precisely that all violence is socially contingent, driven by deep-rooted cultural prerogatives and profoundly expressive, even where these frameworks are operating at a subconscious level. Contemporaries were well aware of this, and whilst inebriation might have been seen to mitigate the deliberate threat to the community, wine did not eradicate meaning but rather twisted it.[5] Since classical times, wine has been seen to loosen the tongue, to stimulate the creativity of poets, playwrights, and performers, violent or otherwise.[6] Not all violence in the tavern was only commentary. In 1341, one Agnes la Payenne destroyed the hemp crop of her enemy, Guérin le Pioner, who had insulted her in the tavern by shouting that she was lying 'through her rotten teeth, like an old whore': the part of the conflict which took place in the tavern was very much socially engaged, but this was an unusual case.[7] More often, violence in the tavern was not restorative or corrective, but commented upon the nature of violence itself, and upon the society in which it operated, by drawing attention to its own futility.[8] This, as we shall see, was commentary which took subtly different forms in Artois and Paris respectively.

[4] Honorius Augustunensis, *Speculum ecclesiae: Sermo in conventu fratrum*, ed. J. Migne (PL 172), Sp. 1087–1194: quoted in R. Kaiser, *Trunkenheit und Gewalt im Mittelalter* (Vienna, 2002), 204.

[5] In fact, secular legal codes described alcohol as a mitigating factor which demonstrated the lack of premeditated intentionality in an act, and diminished the threat to the social body. In practice, the accused seem to have been well-aware of this view of inebriation: Gauvard found that alcohol was often used an as excuse by French petitioners for pardon in late 14th-cent. Paris, though in the final analysis, only 15% of homicides were attributed to drunkenness: *De grace especial* (Paris, 1991), 449.

[6] R. Dragonetti suggests that the tavern functioned as an image of the poet's workshop: 'Le *Jeu de Saint Nicholas de Jean Bodel*', in L. Arrathoon (ed.), *The Craft of Fiction: Essays in Medieval Poetics* (Rochester, Mich., 1984), 369–91.

[7] Boutaric, *Actes*, ii, no. 3675, 369.

[8] S. Rau and G. Schwerhoff, 'Introduction', in their *Zwischen Gotteshaus und Taverne: Öffentliche Räume in Spätmittelalter und Früher Neuzeit* (Vienna, 2004), 13–27. The work of Beat Kümin has been particularly effective in stressing the tavern as place of sociability: 'Friede, Gewalt und öffentliche Räume: Grenzziehungen im alteuropäischen Wirtshaus', in C. Ulbrich et al. (eds.), *Gewalt in der Frühen Neuzeit* (Berlin, 2005), 130–9; B. Kümin and B. A. Tlusty (eds.), *The World of the Tavern: Public Houses in Early Modern Europe* (Aldershot, 2002).

Given the paucity of legal documentation, we are more than ever reliant on the insights and comments of imaginative literature; but this is appropriate, for tavern violence was presented, as its literature claimed to be, as fuelled by wine, creative and critiquing, inspiring and drawing inspiration from the representations of tavern brawls and the social critiques in performed literature. The reciprocity between representation and behaviour was tight-knit.[9] Indeed, the distinction between legal documents and imaginative literature was particularly hazy in this context, with legal records, notably those of Abbeville, providing colourful narratives emotively constructed with direct speech.[10] Much of the commentary here must necessarily restrict itself to perceptions, often idealized, of the role of the tavern, but the imaginative roles of the space inevitably shaped the reality.

The exterior appearance of a tavern often resembled a normal house, but was marked out by distinctive signs displayed above the entrance.[11] The position of the taverns was full of potential in these 'moralised townscapes':[12] visible and often centrally located, opening onto the street, but with much of the activity focusing on underground chambers, they were at once a part of, and a comment upon, the rest of society.[13] While taverns were distinct from the old French 'auberges', their history is a shared one. Hostelries began to reappear as charitable institutions catering for the rising popularity of pilgrimage from the twelfth century. By the thirteenth century, with a generalized rise in trade, a growing demand manifested itself from merchants for accommodation for which they were willing to pay.[14] The concomitant growth of taverns is largely a thirteenth-century phenomenon, and one which reached its highest proportions in the fourteenth century.[15] A tavern was often simultaneously a place of

9 Following Jauss, D. Raybin comments on the tavern plays that 'it is the conjunction of production and reception that matters. Without the original intellect, innovation will not arise. Without a responsive audience, the intellect will pass unnoticed': 'The Court and the Tavern: Bourgeois Discourse in *Li Jeu de Saint Nicolai*', *Viator*, 19 (1988), 177–92.

10 Cf. AMA, MS 115.

11 Cf. H. C. Peyer, 'Schlusswort', in Peyer (ed.), *Gastfreundschaft, Taverne und Gasthaus im Mittelalter* (Munich, 1983), 259.

12 K. Lilley, *Urban Life in the Middle Ages: 1000–1450* (London, 2002), 242.

13 J. Dufournet, 'Variations sur un motif: La Taverne dans le théâtre arrageoise du XIIIe siècle', in *Farai chansoneta novele: Hommage à Jean-Charles Payen* (Caen, 1989), 161–75.

14 J. van Houtte, 'Herbergswesen und Gastlichkeit im mittelalterlichen Brügge', in Peyer, *Gastfreundschaft*, 177; Strayer, 'Inns and Taverns', 469–70.

15 N. Coulet, 'Propriétaires et exploitants d'auberges dans la France du Midi au bas Moyen Age', in Peyer, *Gastfreundschaft*, 119. On the gradually growing demand for inns from princely households, see M. Vale, *The Princely Court: Medieval Courts and Culture in Northern Europe, 1270–1380* (Oxford, 2001), 153–4, 161.

commerce, with wine being sold at retail on the premises.[16] As commercial enterprises, taverns appeared to belong to a new economic order. Moreover, as 'merchant's time'—where time itself was a commodity, to be controlled, manipulated, and exploited—increasingly competed with ecclesiastical time, where the passing of time was the prerogative of an omnipotent God, tavern-keepers essentially demanded payment for time spent in the taverns, and were seen to appropriate God's role of distributing time.[17] Usury, the financial exploitation of time, was associated with the growth of trade and of taverns, both in contemporary literature and in the juxtaposition of prohibitions against usury, alcohol, and night-time violence in many royal ordinances.[18]

But taverns were also temporally differentiated from quotidian commercial life. A widespread sense prevailed that time spent in taverns was somehow distinct from time in the outside world—that one could spend hours there without realizing it, or emerge only five minutes later, feeling that one had been away for days. Preachers characterized taverns as places in which religious worship was forgotten and time wasted away.[19] A dramatic poem from the *Confrérie des Jongleurs* of Arras lauds 'Saint Oison', the patron saint of the time-wasting which takes place, at great expense, in the taverns of contemporary Arras. The almost mystical slowing of time, and blurring of boundaries between night and day, is elaborated in the late thirteenth-century Artesian *Jeu de la Feuillée* of Adam de la Halle, when fairies enter the scene and institute a paradoxical period of timelessness (ll. 566–7).[20] Here in the tavern, fortunes are made and lost in an instant, and time is made to speed up and slow down at the will of the participants; when the monk falls asleep for an instant, his companions claim that one of them played at dice on his behalf during the hours he was asleep, and lost spectacularly (ll. 969–75).

[16] Coulet, 'Inns', 475.

[17] B. Ribémont, 'Arras, le vin, la taverne et le "capitalisme": Le Théâtre profane du XIIIe siècle et la question d'argent', *Moyen Age*, 111 (2005), 61; J. Le Goff, 'Le Temps du travail dans la "crise" du XIVe siècle: Du temps médiéval au temps moderne', in *Pour un autre Moyen Age* (Paris, 1977), 46–7.

[18] *Le Jeu de Saint Nicholas*, ll. 284–90; *Ordonnances des Rois de France*, ed. E. de Laurières, 22 vols. (Paris, 1849), i. 67.

[19] e.g. Anon., *Ci nous dit: Recueil d'exemples moraux*, ed. G. Blangez, 2 vols. (Paris, 1979–86), 455, 1–8, cited in http://gahom.ehess.fr/thema (accessed Feb. 2012), henceforth THEMA.

[20] Adam de la Halle, *Le Jeu de la Feuillée*, ed. J. Dufournet (Ghent, 1977).

1. TAVERN VIOLENCE AND THE AUTHORITIES

Since tavern violence was often highly self-conscious, and conducted in dialogue with social comment on the world of the tavern, we shall need to pay even closer attention than usual to the *representations* of the tavern and what went on there. In the next section, therefore, we turn to the discussion of taverns in a range of sources—sermons, legal materials, poems, songs, and plays—before exploring the patterns of tavern violence as apparently experienced in Artois and Paris.

The distinctiveness of the tavern made it the perfect space from which to observe and to pass scathing comment on the phenomenon of violence itself and on social change and economic excess more generally. Violence in the tavern was most often of a non-fatal nature, arising spontaneously, and stopping just as abruptly. As long as the brutality remained within the tavern, it was seen as violence amongst individuals who provisionally occupied a space detached from the rest of the social body: society as a whole did not feel itself to be endangered.[21] For this reason, taverns and their associated behaviours were grudgingly tolerated by the legal authorities. Unsurprisingly though, even violence which took place inside the tavern was condemned by moralists. Of course, preachers railed against the moral dangers of the tavern, and were concerned by the moral implications for the individual tavern-goer.[22] When drunkards were portrayed suffocating on their own vomit, or an inveterate gambler shown on his way to the gallows and afterwards to eternal damnation, the preachers exhorted their audiences to avoid such behaviour by focusing on the moral fate of the individual.[23] The equation of the tavern with criminality is one which recurs with monotonous regularity in the exempla: one tells how a cleric was tempted to frequent a tavern, and was consequently mistakenly arrested and hanged along with the murderers who were entertaining themselves there.[24] And it was not only earthly perdition which the taverns were said to represent. The *Liber Exemplorum* establishes them

[21] Cf. the similar observations in B. Hanawalt, 'The Host, the Law and the Ambiguous Space of Medieval London Taverns', in *'Of Good and Ill Repute': Gender and Social Control in Medieval England* (Oxford, 1998), 104–23.

[22] e.g. the rector of a local church was warned by the ecclesiastical court in Cérisy in Normandy to cease frequenting taverns in 1314: *Registre de l'officialité de l'abbaye de Cérisy*, ed. M. Dupont (Caen, 1880), 294–5.

[23] e.g. respectively F. Tubach, *Index exemplorum: A Handbook of Medieval Religious Tales* (Helsinki, 1969), no. 1806; *Dits de Jean de Saint Quentin*, ed. B. Munk Olsen (Paris, 1978), 77–85, cited in THEMA.

[24] Étienne de Bourbon, *Tractatus de diversis materiis praedicabilibus*, ed. J. Berlioz and J. L. Eichenlaub, 3 vols. (Turnhout, 2002–), 404, cited in THEMA.

as clear designators of moral evil and eternal damnation as it exhorted the avoidance of sinful thoughts by comparing them to the stench of the tavern which should serve as a warning to pass by without entering.[25] Alcohol was repeatedly demonized. In a story about a thief who used alcohol in order to make his victims fall asleep so that he could steal from them, alcohol has unambiguously catastrophic consequences.[26] Preachers reserved their strongest criticism for clerics who frequented taverns. Various church councils reiterated these fulminations against the frequent loss of clothing and loose sexual mores associated with taverns, their theatrical extravagances, and the brawls and violent quarrels which demonstrated the perdition and immorality of the participants.[27]

However, the condemnation was not so straightforward. The preachers hinted that what really concerned them was not the fate of the individual in the tavern (aside from clerics), who was generally a complete reprobate anyway, but the potential effect of such violence on society. These preachers were not speaking to audiences of tavern-goers or of inveterate drunkards and gamblers: it is unlikely that such people bothered to turn up to the sermons, knowing that they would simply be roundly condemned. The preachers were addressing large audiences of God-fearing citizens, who hoped thus to be given an entertaining public spectacle and to learn more about their role in society. As such, the preachers warned them of the dangers of the tavern, of its potential risks to the rest of society, and suggested how these risks might be avoided.[28]

In a political context, the very presence of taverns was perceived as pernicious, and express attempts were made to ban them altogether as places of entertainment. In 1254, a royal ordinance forbade taverns to accept custom from any residents of the town: they were merely to serve the utilitarian function of offering refreshment to travellers.[29] Nevertheless, in the context of growing notions of the welfare of the community, or the 'common good' as the essential goal of government and law, the primary concern of the authorities was for the effect of taverns on the surrounding community, rather than for what happened within the

25 Anon., *Liber exemplorum ad usum praedicantium*, ed. A. Little (Farnborough, 1966), no. 91.

26 Ibid., no. 157.

27 Respectively: Innocent IV's 1245 *Apparatus super Decretalibus [Gregorii IX]*; 1291, Council of Salzburg: in G. Mansi *et al.* (eds.), *Sacrorum conciliorum nova et amplissima collectio*, 29 vols. (Florence, 1960–1), xxiv. 1077–8, all quoted in H. Waddell, *The Wandering Scholars* (London, 1927), 278; Kaiser, *Trunkenheit*, 198.

28 *Liber exemplorum*, no. 91.

29 *Ordonnances*, i. 67. See W. C. Jordan, 'Anti-Corruption Campaigns in Thirteenth-Century Europe', *Journal of Medieval History*, 35/2 (2009), 204–19.

taverns.[30] Ordinances were entitled 'for the utility of the kingdom', and it was explicitly stated that 'we wholeheartedly wish for the peace and tranquillity of our subjects, in whose comfort we take solace; and we are angry against those who do them harm and who envy their peace and tranquillity'.[31] Gambling with dice was condemned because of its communal implications: it was those who played dice 'communement', or 'par commune renommée', who were principally castigated.[32] It was clearly civic society which was to be protected when it was ordained that prostitutes were to be chased from the towns, and sent outside the town walls.[33] There was no concern for the prostitutes themselves, or for their own reform. The same kinds of concern were demonstrated in some local ordinances about taverns promulgated in Paris. The principal anxiety here was that the kind of company found in taverns might corrupt 'good' society, and tavern-keepers were forbidden from supplying drink to people of known bad character, and from providing a refuge for criminals who could then emerge to disturb the public peace.[34] But the tavern-goers themselves were largely to be left alone, their behaviour in the tavern seen as critiques which were, at least, contained.

In legal practice, intervention inside taverns was constrained by ambivalence about interfering in interpersonal conflicts which lacked obvious wider ramifications. Cases were only prosecuted when they resulted in an incident which affected the social environment or threatened the common good.[35] When violence within the tavern became fatal in its consequences, the legal *sergents* stepped in, on the basis that this was no longer detached from society, but something with more far-reaching and tangible implications. In 1246, a murder in one of the taverns of a parish of Saint-

[30] Cf. J. Dunbabin, *Captivity and Imprisonment in Medieval Europe* (Basingstoke, 2002), 7.

[31] 'We sincerely wish for the peace and repose of our subjects, in whose repose we can rest, and we are very indignant against those who do them injury, and who envy their peace and tranquillity': *Ordonnances*, i. 67.

[32] Ibid. 67. See a rare case of prosecution for dice gambling in Eperlecques: ADN, B13597, fo. 116^{v}.

[33] See the expulsion of prostitutes and brothel-keepers in Sainte-Geneviève: L. Tanon, *Histoire des justices des anciennes églises et communautés monastiques de Paris* (Paris, 1883), 348–9. Keiko Nowacka reminds us of the difference between theory and practice in this respect in 'Persecution, Marginalization, or Tolerance: Prostitutes in Thirteenth-Century Parisian Society', in M. Cohen and J. Firnhaber Baker (eds.), *Difference and Identity in Francia and Medieval France* (Farnham, 2010), 175–96.

[34] e.g. Tanon, 366 (1291); 436 (1281).

[35] In contrast, R. Muchembled found that 55% of homicides in Artois took place in the tavern; he uses letters of remission (not available for the earlier period) which give more detail on the location of violence, but he is writing about a later period when the tavern appears to have been more stridently demonized: *La Violence au village: Sociabilité et comportements populaires en Artois du XV au XVIII siècle* (Turnhout, 1989), 31.

Germain-des-Près attracted the attention of the authorities, even though the action did not emerge from the building—a man quarrelled with his companion and, in the heat of the moment, drew a knife and stabbed him—the gravity of the incident being such that this could not be dismissed as mere commentary, for it threatened the stability of society.[36]

Secondly, the authorities intervened when the spatial limitations of tavern violence were violated. When violence began in the tavern, but emerged onto the street, the law would not ignore it. The space of the tavern was a space apart from everyday social interactions, whereas violence in the street was violence engaged with social realities, with more far-reaching implications for the common good. The sources present enormous interpretative problems: if minor brawls within the tavern were not reported, was this because they did not take place, or because the law was not too worried about them? Literary evidence would suggest a legal tendency to ignore violence within the tavern, since the drama and poetry associated with this context clearly place so much violence within the tavern building: a fight could be resolved 'K'ainc nel seut maires n'eskevins'.[37] Of course, much of this evidence is coloured by poetic exaggeration, but these texts relied on a certain degree of familiarity and realism for their comic effect. Of the various crimes originating in the tavern milieu noted by the *baillis* of Artois, the majority culminated in brutality on the street, with all its associations of publicity and spectacle: some even involved a chase down the street in front of a fascinated audience.[38] The tavern crimes which were actively prosecuted in Paris likewise reached a climax on the street.[39] Often, the notion of transition from interior to exterior was evoked in the records, demonstrating an awareness of this as a cardinal moment when society in general became endangered: a stabbing in the 1270s was reported as taking place as the victim stepped out of the door of the tavern.[40] Alternatively, violence could result in the intrusion of the outside world into the tavern and thus attract the attention of the authorities. In 1279, an officer of the Paris *prévôt* entered a tavern to attempt to arrest, on unconnected charges, two men drinking there: one of the men was killed in the resulting brawl.[41] The legal officials intervened because of the gravity of the offence, but also embodied a legislative perception that the intermingling of the outside world and that of the

36 Tanon, 446.

37 'Without the mayor or *échevins* knowing anything about it': R. Berger: *Littérature et société arrageoise: Les Chansons et dits artésiens* (Arras, 1982), no. V, 141–52, l. 113.

38 e.g. ADPC, A938/3.

39 e.g. Tanon, 495, 498 (a case of theft).

40 Ibid. 330.

41 Boutaric, *Actes*, i, no. 2222^E, 210.

tavern was itself problematic; criminals could seek shelter and encouragement in the tavern milieu.[42]

2. TAVERN VIOLENCE IN NORTH-EAST FRANCE

The city of Arras embodied many of the socio-economic and cultural changes of which taverns were in a sense the symptom. An extremely successful cloth-making industry in Arras brought the citizens wealth and, increasingly, international trade and banking contributed to this prosperity: significantly, much of this trade was in the commerce of wine.[43] Local taverns rose to prominence with these processes of economic growth: increasing numbers of transient international merchants required accommodation, and the inhabitants of the town could afford the leisure time and financial expense involved in frequenting a tavern. Drawing energy and vibrancy from prosperity, Arras was also an exciting literary centre, with no fewer than five of the earliest vernacular plays composed and performed there; and the rich cultural scene was enlivened by the presence of the 'Puy', a prestigious poetic society which organized an annual competition and which generated a wealth of satirical poetry and songs on its fringes.[44] Much of this literary entertainment centred on taverns, feasting, and drinking. Other towns in the region experienced similar growth: Abbeville for instance, for which an important judicial register survives, was wealthy and enjoyed a growing commerce in wine.[45] Taverns provided a space in which to comment upon the instability of commercial growth, increased fluctuations in employment and financial prosperity, as well as the growing need for credit.[46]

The view of tavern violence revealed by the financial accounts of the *bailli* of the count of Artois or by the register of Abbeville is oblique and should be treated with caution: most tavern violence was simply not

[42] Tanon, 366–7.

[43] G. Paoli, 'Taverne et théâtre au Moyen Age', in *Théâtre et spectacles hier et aujourd'hui: Moyen Age et Renaissance* (Paris, 1991), 75–6. Cf. M. Ungureanu, *La Bourgeoisie naissante: Société et littérature d'Arras* (Arras, 1955), 28; R. Fossier, *La Terre et les hommes en Picardie: Jusqu'à la fin du XIIIe siècle*, 2 vols. (Paris, 1968), ii. 570–98; A. Derville, *Les Villes de Flandre et d'Artois (900–1500)* (Villeneuve d'Ascq, 2002); P. Spufford, *Power and Profit: The Merchant in Medieval Europe* (London, 2002), 191, 212.

[44] C. Symes, *A Common Stage: Theatre and Public Life in Medieval Arras* (Ithaca, NY, 2007), 216–27; Berger, *Littérature*.

[45] F.-C. Louandre, *Histoire d'Abbeville* (Paris, 1845), 262.

[46] For a full discussion of contemporary anxiety about socio-economic change, cf. A. Murray, *Reason and Society in the Middle Ages* (Oxford, 1978), 188, 210; L. Little, *Religious Poverty and the Profit Economy in Medieval Europe* (London, 1978), 1–57.

reported, and so the records give the misleading impression that all acts of violence culminated in murder. The sources only rarely indicate whether violence originated in the tavern environment; often only the description of the nature of the brawl indicates that the violence originated there. Yet tavern violence must have been commonplace. In Abbeville, a non-dated incident in the register of the *échevinage* (probably from the 1280s) recalled how a man died of natural causes in the tavern as he sat down to enjoy his drink, and described the uproar and immediate imprisonment of the other revellers: the spontaneous assumption that violence had been committed (later corrected when the body was investigated and no marks were found upon it) hints at the frequency of physical violence in such a setting.[47]

Such violence was not limited to social outcasts, the marginals of society who are often associated with the tavern milieu:[48] rather, it involved a variety of social groups with sufficient experience of the new commercial order to feel in a position to comment upon it. The Arras tavern plays, which effectively span the course of the thirteenth century, draw attention to what has been rather crudely termed 'l'embourgeoisement de la taverne', but what might more properly be described as the social diversification of the tavern.[49] At the beginning of the century, the tavern topos, at least in literature, did tend to evoke the marginal, dysfunctional member of society—witness Bodel's *Jeu de Saint Nicholas* where the principal figures in the tavern are those of the two thieves who attempt to make a living from casual crime. Likewise, *Le Courtois d'Arras*, from just a little later, retells the story of the prodigal son in a tavern with cunning prostitutes, though now accompanied by a variety of other silent, but less marginal, drinkers.[50] By the latter half of the century, represented by Adam de la Halle's *Jeu de la Feuillée*, a surreal comic review, the tavern is frequented by all kinds of social groups: a monk, young servants, apprentices, Adam himself, his father, and three friends. This development is supported by the legal evidence. The aristocracy do not appear to have frequented taverns in this period: mention of their presence in legal records does not occur until the letters of remission of the late fourteenth and fifteenth centuries. Likewise, the billeting of soldiers in inns and their riotous behaviour in taverns was not yet a regular feature. In Artois tavern brawls, we find, for example, sons of successful artisans,[51] cloth-makers,[52]

[47] AMA, MS 115, fo. 29v.

[48] e.g. B. Geremek, *The Margins of Society in Late Medieval Paris*, tr. J. Birrell (Cambridge, 1987), 109.

[49] Paoli, 'Taverne', 73–83.

[50] Anon, *Le Courtois d'Arras*, ed. E. Faral (Paris, 1958).

[51] e.g. ADPC, A267/1. [52] e.g. ADPC, A18/2.

butchers,[53] as well as specified burghers of the towns,[54] and even sons of the local provost.[55] Often, the source details that the perpetrator was a 'valet', most probably indicating a position of apprenticeship, and suggesting a younger age band involved in these incidents with fewer family responsibilities.[56]

This was self-consciously excessive violence, which, by challenging the equilibrium between violent gestures and their meaning or motivations, evoked a world of imbalance and superfluity. Accordingly, the motifs which punctuated tavern violence in Artois embodied rapid economic growth, unreliable signs, and misleading meanings. Or at least this is the spin they were implicitly given in legal and literary evocations. Performed literature often exploited the tavern setting to critique and engage with the implications of broader changes, specifically through the ways in which violence was presented. The relationship of plays to the practice of violence is a complex one: they help us to interpret violent practice, but they also provide interpretative models for real outbreaks of brutality, whilst drawing on those episodes for inspiration. The plays were performed to broad audiences, engaging with mundane concerns, and they problematized the very issues which preoccupied their spectators: indeed, many were performed in the tavern and invited audience participation.[57] As Andrew Cowell has convincingly argued, the popular plays and *fabliaux* from Arras and its surrounding region in this period revealed the contemporary world to be lacking in balance, where the return expected of a word, or of a coin, was one that exceeded what should have been its original signifying value.[58] Furthermore, they placed violence centre-stage, demonstrating how brutality can mimic, and thus draw attention to, this pervasive disequilibrium. Through their often humorous scenarios, they subverted the paradigm whereby violence was taken to be meaningful because its signifying gestures matched their signified meaning, whether in vengeance strategies or punitive violence. Popular literature interpreted tavern violence as deliberately subverting this careful sense of balance, and parodying the excess which, as Cowell shows, the playwrights detected in society at large.

53 e.g. ADPC, A308/1.
54 e.g. ADPC, A918/8.
55 e.g. ADPC, A267/1; A18/2; A308/1; A918/8; A126/2.
56 e.g. APDC, A163/2.
57 A. Hindley '*L'Escole au deable*: Tavern Scenes in the Old French Moralité', *Comparative Drama*, 33 (2000), 468.
58 See A. Cowell, *At Play in the Tavern: Signs, Coins, and Bodies in the Middle Ages* (Ann Arbor, 1999), particularly 1–13, 243–9; notions of excess and disequilibrium in this chapter owe much to Cowell's excellent book.

Semiotic overload is initiated by the very titles of the plays. Bodel's *Jeu de Saint Nicholas* plays on the pun of 'jeu' meaning a game, and 'jus' meaning wine (the two were homophones in this period): the tavern is immediately highlighted as a context in which the immediate signifier (here the name of the play) is destabilized, lacking in balance with regard to its signified(s). The effect is more extreme in Adam de la Halle's *Jeu de la Feuillée*, for here, as well as the word play on 'jeu', understanding 'feuillée' involves a quadruple word play: a homophone for 'folie', 'feuillée' also evoked in courtly literature the notion of a leafy bower offering a haven from the rush of civilization;[59] it was the name of the ornate building in the centre of Arras's main square where the reliquary of the town's miraculous candle was kept; and it could refer to the bunches of leaves suspended from the taverns' exteriors in order to identify them.

Such implicit critique of social disequilibrium was further developed via literary exploitation of the disjunction between appearance and reality.[60] Signifiers most often exaggerated with catastrophic and violent consequences. The relationship of that violence to the reality to which it responded was similarly shown to be excessive. The fabliau *Les Trois Aveugles de Compiègne* most straightforwardly thematized the appearance/reality motif by placing the notion of blindness at the centre of the plot.[61] The clerk pretends to give a *besant* to the blind men, and 'Chascuns cuide ses compains l'ait'.[62] After enjoying a magnificent feast in a tavern on what they believe to be their wealth, they are, of course, unable to pay, and beaten up by the irate tavern-owner, who is convinced that they are mocking him. The recurrence of words of belief associated with the blind men, and words of the senses with the clerk emphasize the disruption of a straightforward semiotic system: the clerk's words exaggerate reality, and the meal of the blind men represents the apparent creation of wealth from nothing, while the result is total loss. The ensuing violence as a response to a misperceived reality both destroys the paradigm of violence as a balanced and meaningful response, and comments on the untrustworthiness of appearance in a changing socio-economic context. The violent gestures of the tavern-keeper exaggerate the reality of the situation: 'L'un va doner

[59] The first occurrence of this word which I have been able to find is in the 12th-cent. Béroul, *Tristan et Iseut*, ed. A. Ewert (Oxford, 1939), l. 1840, 55, where it describes the leafy bower constructed by the fugitive couple in the woods. See also Cowell, *At Play*, 228.

[60] Ibid. 133.

[61] *NRCF* ii/9. The commentary of Noomen and Boogard, ii. 154–5, indicates that the provenance of this *fabliau* is most likely Picard. See also Cowell, *At Play*, 164–9.

[62] 'Each one thinks that his companion has it': l. 34.

une grant buffe,/Puis fet aporter deus lingnas' in response to his perception that they have deliberately tricked him.[63]

Literature drew attention to the potential of certain motifs and to their broader implications: the perpetration of, and legal responses to, 'real-life' violence tended to focus on the same topoi. The untrustworthiness and excess of words spoken, coins given, blows struck in tavern literature, echoed the disintegration of meaning in the reported legal cases. Tavern violence, though drunken, challenged legal attempts to codify the interpretation of violence and to construct a valid semiotic system of physical gestures, thus underlining the disequilibrium of the rest of society. It is certainly given such a spin in recorded legal cases. The disjuncture between such violence and any straightforward extraction of meaning is indicated by the frequent unresolved mystery surrounding such incidents. A report of an episode in Abbeville, for instance, failed to question why the victim had been killed: it was assumed that this was a chaotic atmosphere where violence did not respond to straightforward processes of causation, in contrast to other forms of violence considered in this book.[64] Two other tavern incidents in the same town were characterized by the same enigmatic quality: in one a drinker was found drowned in the pond of the count of Ponthieu and neither the cause nor the murderer ever discovered;[65] in another a drinker was chased until he could no longer be seen, and his body was found seven days later with no explanation.[66] Unlike violence in other spheres of life in this period, it was unclear as to what wrong brutal gestures were responding. Nevertheless, the social memory of such cases survived for a long time, perhaps all the more so because they remained mysterious and therefore more fascinating: in the small town of Bonnières near Arras, an inquiry in a jurisdictional conflict of 1311 heard how a body had been found after a tavern incident in 1266 and the case never solved;[67] another case, supposed to have taken place about twenty-five years previously, remained unsolved even though the two perpetrators were widely known.[68]

If the legal records underlined the fragmentation of appearance and reality, its connection to the excess of tavern violence continued to be rendered explicit in much performed poetry. The dramatic encomium to 'Saint Tortu', the personification of wine, was written between 1240 and

[63] 'He gives one a great blow, and then makes someone fetch two clubs': ll. 174–5.

[64] This is in contrast to other forms of violence, where the motivation of recorded crime *was* implied. AMA MS 115, fo. 29^{v}.

[65] Ibid.

[66] Ibid., fo. 30^{r}.

[67] ADPC, A955/1.

[68] Ibid.

1249 for the *confrérie des jongleurs* of Arras, and would have been recited at their annual festivities.[69] Evoking the 'miracle' of false courage worked by wine, the theme of multiplication is introduced when for the drunken person 'une cose li sanle trois', and both fear and unnecessary violence are induced by imagined or exaggerated insults. A full-blown brawl breaks out when one of the drunkards throws his wine into the fire, for no reason, and another draws his sword, 'Qu'il cuide amender cel outrage': 'amender' evokes ideas of financial balance and retributive justice, but the signified purpose of this violence, which was to restore order in the tavern, is totally overwhelmed by the extent of the signifier, which 'desfait tout le parage'.[70] As such, violence in the tavern itself achieved no concrete function and was self-consciously exaggerated: literary portrayals and perhaps even brawlers themselves used violence to comment upon the increasingly unbalanced nature of the extremely commercialized society in which they lived.

Violence in the tavern most commonly led to exclusion from this milieu, indicating that excessive contestations of one's place within a given society led to exclusion, and so were not socially functional but self-destructive. In the imagined scenarios of *Courtois* and the *Jeu de la Feuillée*, those who made a nuisance of themselves are simply thrown out. Most such cases do not attain the legal records since these were minor disturbances in which the law was not interested. However, we do learn something of exclusion in those extreme cases where the excess of behaviour within the tavern ultimately engendered the suicide of the perpetrator. This would seem to be the most likely explanation for the mysterious drownings of the brawlers in Abbeville: drowning was, in any case, the most frequent form of suicide, as it could be construed as an accident, and was therefore not punished so severely.[71] A case in Aubigny involved accidental fratricide in the tavern:[72] excessive actions led to the self-inflicted death of the killer, and might be taken as a symbol for the tragic cycle of excessive violence responding to circumstances of disequilibrium and unequal exchange, followed by self-destruction.

The critique of contemporary commercial modes was most sharply focused when tavern violence broke out over questions of credit and trickery. The long debate in *Le Jeu de Saint Nicholas* between the tavern-keeper and the character Auberon about the payment for the

[69] Berger, *Littérature*, no. V.

[70] 'One thing seems as three': l. 38; 'He wants to avenge this wrong': l. 87; 'They mess up all their surroundings': l. 88.

[71] Cf. A. Murray, *Suicide in the Middle Ages*, 2 vols. (Oxford, 1998), i. 28–9, 181.

[72] ADN, B13596, edited in B. Delmaire, *Le Compte General d'Artois pour 1303–1304* (Brussels, 1977), no. 2511.

wine foregrounds the notion of credit, the lack of balance in transactions, and resulting violence (ll. 272–89).[73] This is immediately linked to critique of contemporary Arras through the very structure of the play, which frames the Artesian tavern scenes with scenes in the exotic palace of the Saracen King: whereas the palace represents fixed wealth by its inclusion of the king's treasure, a static capital sum, the tavern is a synecdoche for the now familiar world of financial circulation and unexpected growth and loss.[74] In contrast to the explicit announcement of the royal fortune (ll. 485–7), the tavern presents a long dispute between client and tavern-keeper over the immediate payment for wine which will be consumed later (ll. 272–89). Gambling is indeed the most usual outcome of such situations, and thirteenth-century literature exploits the topos with virtuosity.[75] These scenes invariably end in violence, with the ludic quality of the whole proceedings emphasized, and the risk element and wastage of contemporary commercial relations mimicked. Dice are presented as a violation of balanced systems of representation as beliefs are swiftly reversed by the treachery of the dice: 'J'ai quaernes, le plus mal gieu!' complains Auberon.[76] Later on, the interpretation of the value of the dice themselves becomes disputed, and their status as signs further complicated: Cliquet furiously asserts that he has a two-point lead, while Pincedé doggedly demands his winnings, and as Cliquet angrily shouts 'Mauhedé ait qui che me roeve,/Puisc'on voit que seur les dés vient!' the scene erupts into violence.[77]

In practice, the most common form of provocation of tavern brawls was also financial, rendering their perceived commentary on new economic and commercial orders all the more direct. Many cases refer to the contested payment of the 'escot', a term whose polysemy serves to marry many of the comments on social excess which were implicit in violence in the tavern. Originally, 'escot' indicated a valuable piece of gold, an object of intrinsic economic value: in violently contesting its payment, tavern-goers implicitly commented on the untrustworthiness of coins, and such a connotation was accepted by legal records in choosing this term. Over time, 'escot' came to refer to payment for food, and tavern-goers who

[73] For precision on the economic sense of this scene, see L. Foulet and C. Foulon, 'Les Scènes de taverne et les comptes du tavernier dans le *Jeu de Saint Nicholas* de Jean Bodel', *Romania,* 68 (1944), 422–44; N. Wilkins, 'Yet More about the Tavern Bills', *Zeitschrift für romanische Philologie*, 82 (1966), 339–44.

[74] Cf. Ribémont, 'Arras', 59–70.

[75] Dufournet, 'Variations', 164.

[76] 'I've got a double four, the worst throw!': l. 308.

[77] 'Curse him who demands this, because you can see the dice are doing well for me!': ll. 909–10.

refused to pay it blamed excessive prices. Through a process of slippage, 'escot' came to indicate either the payment, or the food itself, specifically a meal convivially shared. And, by extension, the word implied an expense shared amongst friends: 'Voila pour mon escot puisqu'il vous a pleu moy inviter a vostre feste'.[78] So when the 'escot' was not paid, a friend was refusing to play his part: equilibrium was disrupted, prices were challenged, sociability was thrown into disarray. A series of expressions involving the risk associated with shared payment arose, some literal, some figurative: 'conter escot' (to make someone else pay for you), 'mettre à grant escot' (to mistreat someone), 'aller à perilleux escot' (to be in great danger), and so on. When the companions of an Abbeville tavern pursued their former friend through the town shouting out 'prendes le, prendes le, k'il en porte sen escot!', they were evoking financial disarray and the failure of friendship; the slippage from 'sen' to 'nostre' in their somewhat disingenuous claim, 'nous ne le demandons pour nul mal, mais il en porte nostre escot', reiterated the instability of companionship, ownership, and the degeneration into excessive violence.[79]

Just as audiences witnessed the tavern-keeper and customer arguing at length over the payment and credit for a glass of wine in the *Jeu de Saint Nicholas*, so in Abbeville the issue of credit and trickery was hinted at when one witness described how a gambler had lost all his clothes at dice, and then returned to the tavern to pay back a part of his debt.[80] Likewise, another victim, distraught that 'il ne pooit paier', fled from the tavern, and was retrieved some days later as a corpse 'sans caup et sans plaie'.[81] Such cases recurred in the Artois records, and payments were shown to be no straightforward exchange of one item representing the value of another, but full of trickery and disequilibrium. This violence undid straightforward paradigms whereby the gestures revealed the financial motive, for that motivation was confused and shifting. A particularly interesting case from the small town of Buscoi near Arras intriguingly replayed incidents from Bodel's *Jeu de Saint Nicholas,* as three thieves disputed the possession of some stolen treasure, their dispute culminating in physical violence and murder when one of the thieves became particularly angry at the refusal of the other two to tell him where they had hidden the booty.[82] The presentation of the story in what is presumably a simplified form, and certainly a stereotypical one corresponding to clichés propounded by

[78] All these meanings are attested to in F. Godefroy, *Dictionnaire de l'ancien langue française* (Paris, 1881).
[79] AMA, MS 115, fo. 30^{r}.
[80] Ibid., fo. 29^{v}.
[81] Ibid., fo. 30^{r}.
[82] ADPC, A18/2.

literature such as the *Jeu de Saint Nicholas,* demonstrates the common perception that monetary matters caused violence in the tavern, and that money was problematic because characterized by deception. Dice and gambling could be seen as the ultimate symbol of a society of unreasonable return and sudden loss, of semiotic disequilibrium where one single throw of the dice could change everything. The legal records demonstrate that there was a clear, and most probably justified, perception that dice represented a major cause of violence in everyday tavern brawls. The cluster of accounts of such violence in the Abbeville register focused on the theme of dice: one player lost so dramatically that he knocked over the candles and fled from the tavern.[83]

Companionship was equally fragile in this rapidly evolving commercial context. Failed friendships could provoke violence which through its own excess commented upon the breakdown of balance and order: this excess was visible both in the extreme profusion of gestures and in the undermining of networks of companionship which were generally assumed to sustain violence. Typical provocations for such acts of violence reiterated the topoi explored in the dramatic literature. The hypocrisy of the other revellers in *Le Courtois d'Arras* was replayed in the Abbeville incidents. In the first, the victim left the tavern to fetch extra money to pay his debts, and the apparent friend who stepped out with him was later detained as his murderer (though subsequently released owing to lack of evidence).[84] It would seem that the hypocrisy foregrounded by the plays characterized the real-life tavern, where, perhaps subconsciously, drinkers commented upon the hypocrisy of the commercial world around them. Likewise, in another incident, some companions were playing together, explicitly described as 'compaignons', before one of them attempted to trick the others by escaping and was, in turn, chased to his death by them: the legal records described a world where no one could be trusted, and the participants themselves were implicitly commenting on the grasping character of the world around them.[85] In contrast to the thesis expounded by Muchembled that violence responded primarily to the intrusion of the stranger into Picardy, and thus represented a tool of self-definition, most violence in the tavern explicitly occurred between so-called companions, people who knew each other already, who assumed friendship, or even relations.[86] Many such cases highlighted the accidental nature of the

[83] AMA, MS 115, fo. 30^{r}.

[84] Ibid., fo. 29^{v}.

[85] Ibid., fo. 30^{r}.

[86] Muchembled, *Violence*, 86–94. A. Finch also finds that violence was between locals: 'The Nature of Violence in the Middle Ages: An Alternative Perspective', *Historical Research,* 70/173 (1997), 266.

violence. In Artois, only 11 per cent of brawls related to the tavern milieu involved strangers: the rest mostly involved so-called friends or family, with four cases resulting in the accidental death of the brother of the perpetrator.[87] One particularly tragic incident resulted in patricide when a son drunkenly quarrelled with his father.[88] The notion of friends or family who could turn on you so suddenly with such catastrophic results was an indictment of society at large, and suggested that a seemingly trustworthy system of signs—whereby indications of friendship suggested true loyalty and support—hid other more sinister implications. A couple of cases recounted the murder of an inn-keeper by the guests at the inn, and once again could be interpreted as a damning commentary on commercial relations where friendship disguised greed and self-interest.[89]

In the taverns, anger was construed as excessive, spontaneous, uncontrolled, and unbalanced: Rosenwein has argued that, while aristocratic anger was perceived as a righteous display of power and authority, amongst less elevated social groups it was deemed sinful, and even comic.[90] In a case of 1278, the *Olim* show how a tavern-goer killed his brother by mistake when an attempt was made to arrest them in the tavern for other misdemeanours: panic reigned, and regret came too late.[91] In the early stages, there were typically a large number of witnesses, enhancing the theatrical atmosphere of the occasion and its potential as social commentary. The record of an incident in Abbeville described the 'grant plente de gens' who witnessed the death.[92] The theme of foolish anger reaches a climax in *Le Jeu de la Feuillée*, where it is personified in the figure of the *dervé*, a comic figure, whose anger springs from no rational cause: he gratuitously insults his father's kindness (ll. 1083–4), excessively responds with violence (l. 1089), and provokes yet more, as his father is sadly obliged to beat him to calm him down (l. 1091).[93]

The Artois taverns were described as characterized by rapid and emotional accumulations of gestures. This crescendo effect drew attention to the semiotic excess of the climactic physical gesture as its degree of brutality was so distinctly underlined. The most common terms in the Artois accounts to describe such brawls are 'mêlée' and 'bataille': the

[87] ADPC, A128/2, A149/3; ADN, B13596, Delmaire, no. 2511; Boutaric, *Actes*, i, no. 2222^{E}, 210.

[88] ADN, B13596, Delmaire, no. 2279. In Roman law, the mentally ill were not to be held responsible for patricide.

[89] ADN, B13596, fo. 111^{v}, Delmaire, no. 693.

[90] Cf. B. Rosenwein, 'Introduction', in Rosenwein (ed.), *Anger's Past: The Social Uses of an Emotion in the Middle Ages* (Ithaca, NY, 1998), 5.

[91] Boutaric, *Actes*, i, no. 2222^{E}, 210.

[92] AMA, MS. 115, fo. 29^{v}.

[93] On madness, see Cowell, *At Play*, 190–223.

former drew attention to the sense of muddle, of accumulation of gestures on all sides, while 'bataille' underlined the lack of a single defining action. The majority of acts of violence associated with the tavern milieu in the Artois records involved multiple aggressors: such incidents were chaotic spectacles, and the scene of carnage must have been memorable. The records of a dozen of these events specifically draw attention to their spectacular nature, and the presence of an audience: many of the accused in the records were tried for their colluding presence at the brawl, encouraging the perpetrators by providing an audience.[94] Such anarchic spectacles could be seen as providing their audiences with a visual representation of the unbalanced nature of society. The swift pace of these incidents lacked the careful foresight and planning characteristic of feuds, and the spontaneity of such affairs meant that weapons tended to involve whatever came to hand most easily. Hence, the Artois accounts recorded a proliferation of knives, which people would have carried for practical, non-violent purposes. Sticks and other tools of medieval everyday life also played an important role. The usual signification of a particular object was diverted, invested with new meaning. Likewise, in the few cases involving swords, the records implied commentary on the distorted use of what should be a chivalrous weapon of war. The case of tavern fratricide recounted in the records of the Paris Parlement juxtaposes knives and swords in a chaotic mixture, as tragic consequences ensue from misdirected actions.[95] Most frequently, however, there was not even time to reach for the most rudimentary weapon, and hands, feet, and nails were used in undignified struggles. In the reported cases, many incidents did end in death, but this is, of course, deeply misleading since these were the cases which attracted the attention of the law, particularly when there was the possibility of financial gain for the *bailli*. However, it is clear that the vast majority of such cases were accidental. These incidents were reported using the semantic field of accident: 'mescheance' or 'jeu', followed by a fatal outcome. Tiny fines, the sudden flight of the perpetrator having unexpectedly compromised his position in society, or the hiding of an unplanned corpse in a field, all point to the frequency of what we would now label manslaughter.[96]

The excess of tavern violence was embodied in the clothing motif. The garment is at once a sign in itself, and a sort of meta-sign whose function-

[94] ADN, B13597, fo. 19^{v}.

[95] Boutaric, *Actes*, i, no. 2222^{E}, 210.

[96] e.g. the 1270 case in Buscoi where the corpse was hidden in a field: ADPC, A18/2.

ing can shed light on other semiotic systems.[97] The motif of torn clothing in the tavern reflected on excess and disequilibrium, for as the gamblers bet their clothes, the attempted multiplication of funds resulted in the damage of this most fundamental sign of wealth. As a sign in itself, the significance of clothing was very familiar in the Middle Ages: the shedding of clothing was often linked to rites of passage, and evoked the topos of nature versus civilization, suggesting an engagement with the tension between the two.[98] The eponymous hero of *Courtois d'Arras* wrecks his luxurious clothing after his credulous acceptance of the values of the city ultimately proves self-destructive and leads to his exclusion from the town, to work, in filthy clothes, in a pig-sty: his over-investment of belief in the signs of the city has resulted in the degradation of the primary sign of this (ll. 367–79).[99] In *Le Jeu de Saint Nicholas* the clothing of the perpetrators is ripped in a display of futility. The clothes here have been completely reduced to objects of economic value (as the customers must pay with them), but even this signifying power is destroyed when they are carelessly torn by the protagonists engaging in violence which responds to, but fails to balance, the overplay of the game of dice: Caignet, the servant of the tavern, panics when he realizes that 'nos wage empirent/Car cist ribaut tout se descirent,/Et si n'ont drap qui gaires vaille'.[100]

The hermeneutics of clothing in the tavern plays provides insights into the ripping and tearing of clothing in legal reports of the practice of tavern violence: significance was accorded to the motif, since trouble was taken to record it. One of the Abbeville drinkers lost all the clothes from his back before drowning.[101] As a valuable economic commodity, indeed, in many cases, the only valuable possession, clothing was frequently lost in episodes of gambling. To lose clothing was to lose dignity, but to tear frantically at someone else's clothing was not very dignified either; nor was grabbing the hair of one's opponent, as is attested to in a tavern in Avesnes in 1306.[102]

[97] R. Howard Bloch, *Medieval Misogyny and the Invention of Western Romantic Love* (Chicago, 1991), 40–6; Roland Barthes has demonstrated the multiple social significations of clothing, and its semiotic potential, as, based on Saussurian models, he describes how 'le langage, comme le costume, est à la fois, système et histoire, acte individuel et institution collective': quoted in O. Blanc, 'Historiographie du vêtement: Un bilan', in *Le Vêtement: Histoire, archéologie et symbolique vestimentaires au Moyen Age* (Paris, 1989), 8; R. Barthes, 'Histoire et sociologie du vêtement', *Annales ESC* 12/3 (1957), 430–41.

[98] J. Le Goff, *A la recherche du Moyen Age* (Paris, 2006), 160.

[99] *Courtois d'Arras* is loosely based upon the story of the prodigal son.

[100] 'They are lessening our payments: these louts are tearing everything up, and they don't have any cloth which is worth much anyway': ll. 920–2.

[101] AMA, MS. 115, fo. 29^{v}.

[102] ADN, B13597, fo. 43^{v}; ADPC, A221/1.

But throwing caution, dignity, and honour to the winds was part of the point.

Despite their brutality, often these scenes were humorous and were certainly intended as such in their literary incarnations whose *raison d'être* was to make the audience laugh. Jokes are usually provoked by a consciously introduced gap or disequilibrium between signifier and signified: the signifier ostensibly represents a single notion, but contains a destabilizing multiplication of meaning. And such jokes played an integral role in society. Plays and poems in this period were not detached cultural artefacts, nor passive observers of social change: they were fully engaged in social issues, enjoying a complex relationship with the society of which they formed a part. The slips of parchment, or 'rôles', with which the actors were supplied, allowed room for extemporization and spontaneous response to the audience's interventions.[103] Stages varied in form, but were often not raised and allowed for a much more intimate relationship between audience and actors.[104] The distinction between reality and representation was thus blurred, as audience and actors became intermingled in a common engagement with the issues raised by the drama.[105] As a result, these plays did not merely comment upon the tavern milieu, but they helped to construct ways of seeing tavern brutality in Artois as deliberately failing to respond rationally or in a balanced way to perceived wrongs, and more broadly as comment upon the excess and lack of balance in society as a whole.

3. TAVERN VIOLENCE IN PARIS AND THE ILE-DE-FRANCE

As we travel from Artois towards Paris, the representation of tavern violence shifts. Legal evidence remains sparse, but literary testimony continues to provide us with ways of reading and interpreting what remains. Much of the imaginative literature emanating from Paris and the Ile-de-France situated itself in a rather different tradition, that of medieval Latin satirical poetry, often labelled as goliardic or the poetry of 'wine,

[103] G. Runnalls, 'An Actor's Rôle in a French Morality Play', *French Studies,* 42 (1988), 398–407.

[104] H. Rey-Flaud, *Le Cercle magique: Essai sur le théâtre en rond à la fin du Moyen Age* (Paris, 1973), 44–52, 78–86.

[105] 'A theatrical event was simultaneously real, ritualised and representational . . . the reality of early dramatic realism is that it regularly staged its capacity to be any or all of those three things at once': J. Enders, *Death by Drama and Other Medieval Urban Legends* (Chicago, 2002), 19.

women and song'.[106] This poetry came from across Europe, much of it from Germany, but it particularly inspired vernacular poets in the Paris area, most famously Rutebeuf. Summarizing the trope, and juxtaposing Latin and French, an anonymous thirteenth-century poet sang that 'Femes, dez et taverne trop *libenter colo*'.[107]

An anonymous debate poem, entitled 'Le Desputaison du Vin et de l'Iaue', continues in a tradition dating back to Horace and popular in Latin poetry.[108] The French version takes a common trope, the question of whether water or wine is more inspirational and useful, and turns it into a full-blown battle between not only water and alcohol, but between various different types of wine, vying with each other for first place and resorting, bizarrely, to physical violence. The wine from Auxerre (regularly cited in vernacular theatre as the most popular type of wine in taverns) shows its hand as the most likely to incite brawls amongst its drinkers, boasting that 'Je faiz gent triper et saillir/Et guerroier et assaillir'.[109] This violence is anarchic, just as the violence between the wines themselves is labelled as counterproductive by Cupid, the one holding the feast;[110] the profusion of terms for violence juxtaposed with one another adds to this sense of accumulation. But unlike tavern violence as portrayed in the literature from Artois, this violence is not just excessive, but completely aimless: the Auxerre wine smugly concludes that 'Je les fais ensemble combatre,/Et puis les abas .iiii. à .iiii.'.[111] In this rendition, men may be made bold and violent by wine, but it is wine which has the last laugh: 'il n'est chief en homme/Que tout à terre je n'estonne'.[112] When water is

106 The 'goliards' have long been assumed to be a brotherhood of satirical poets, romantically labelled, 'wandering scholars': J. Symonds, *Wine, Women and Song: Medieval Latin Students' Songs* (London, 1884), 17–25; H. Waddell, *Wandering Scholars*, particularly 192–208. See also G. Whicher, *The Goliard Poets: Medieval Latin Songs and Satires* (Westport, Conn., 1949). In fact there is little or no evidence that 'goliard' denoted anything more specific than theatricality: J. Szövérffy, *Secular Latin Lyrics and Minor Poetic Forms of the Middle Ages: A Historical Survey and Literary Repertory from the Tenth to the Late Fifteenth Century*, 4 vols. (London, 1992–5), ii. 444–60; G. Rigg, 'Golias and Other Pseudonyms', *Studi Medievali*, 18 (1977), 65–109; B. Gillingham, 'Turtles, Helmets, Parasites and Goliards', *Music Review*, 95 (1994), 249–74.

107 'I gladly cherish women, dice and taverns': Anon., *Des fames, des dez et de la taverne*, ed. V. Väänänen, *Neuphilologische Mitteilungen*, 47 (1946), 104–13, l. 5.

108 Edited in T. Wright, *Latin Poems commonly attributed to Walter Mapes* (London, 1841), 299–306. On the motif, J. Hanford, 'The Medieval Debate between Wine and Water', *Proceedings of the Modern Language Association*, 28/3 (1913), 315–67; N. Crowther, 'Water and Wine as Symbols of Inspiration', *Mnemosyne*, 32/4 (1979), 1–11.

109 'I make people jump about and agitate, and battle and assault each other', ll. 73–4; See *Jeu de Saint Nicholas*, ll. 591–3; *Courtois d'Arras*, ll. 206–7.

110 ll. 435–7.

111 'I make them fight together, and then I knock them down several at a time', ll. 75–6.

112 'There is no man's head that I can't knock to the ground', ll. 83–4.

finally able to riposte, he repeatedly stresses the futile violence caused by wine, 'noisses et contens/Omecides et roberies;/Et assés de ribauderies'.[113] Yet the poem ends inconclusively, and it remains unclear whether water or wine brings more inspiration. If wine inspires creativity in Artois, and excessively so, the futility of wine's battles and indeed of the whole tavern milieu is depicted in this poem from Paris. The gratuitousness of actions here draws attention, not to the imbalance of socio-economic developments, but to their perceived emptiness.[114]

One reason for such a difference lies in the very different nature of the two cities. The taverns of Artois were shaped by commercial prosperity and populated principally by tradesmen and artisans, whereas the Paris taverns, or at least those which we meet in the records, were frequented often by clerics (often students), and those on the margins of society.[115] Arras's taverns catered for those engaged in everyday socio-economic realities, whereas Paris's taverns catered for those who entertained a somewhat tangential relationship to such realities. Students were set apart by their age, their provisional residence in Paris, their distinctive legal status, and their sense of being 'intellectuals', already detached by their profession from more mundane realities. They met prostitutes, thieves, and social outcasts in the taverns, who were similarly ready to dismiss the contemporary world as empty show.

The dichotomy must not be drawn too sharply. Arras had its own marginals, and Paris taverns were not unknown to successful tradespeople. In 1320, a case in Paris recapitulated many of the themes more common to tavern brawls in Artois. The tavern-keeper, Oudard 'Godmele', called a Parisian burgher Robert d'Acy a ribald, a cheat, and a thief, and threatened him with a knife; upon further investigation, it transpired that Robert had publicly called Oudard a money-launderer, and had hit him. The dispute was part of an economic conflict but, in its excessiveness, subverted paradigms of the meaningful functionality of violence, as well as critiquing the disequilibrium of a commercialized society: as if to make the point explicitly, the two participants placed self-consciously excessive price tags on their injuries, with Robert claiming that he would rather have lost 200 silver marks than be so wounded, and Oudard riposting that he would

113 'Arguments and debates, homicides and plunderings, and lots of ribaldry', ll. 270–2.

114 Dufournet describes what is, in many ways, a similar contrast, but he sees this as a chronological rather than a geographical contrast: 'Variations', particularly 172–3.

115 This is extrapolated from the anecdotal evidence surviving for this period, and is also suggested by the later 14th-cent. evidence gathered and analysed by E. Cohen in 'Patterns of Crime in Fourteenth-Century Paris', *French Historical Studies,* 11/3 (1980), 307–27; cf. E. Châtelain, 'Notes sur quelques taverns fréquentées par l'université de Paris aux XIVe et XVe siècles', *Bulletin de la société de l'histoire de Paris et de l'Ile de France,* 25 (1898), 87–109.

rather have lost 400 silver marks than have been so insulted.[116] But these two were not typical participants in Paris tavern brawls: they were successful merchants and fully accepted members of society, more like the customers of the Artois taverns. More common in Paris were the marginal, the socially excluded, and the transient. For these groups, tavern violence was a way not of commenting upon the commercial excess of society, but a method of dismissing it altogether. In place of the Artesian mimicry and exaggeration of processes of social representation (friendship, economic exchange, violence), the violence of Parisian taverns, and the discourse surrounding such violence, was characterized as destructively opposed to surrounding society. The Parisian streets were studded with taverns.[117] In the 'Dit des rues de Paris', the speaker regularly stops off in taverns for a refreshing drink on his peregrinations through the rhyming streets of the city.[118] These taverns are liminal spaces, opening onto and readily accessible from the street, but set apart, retreats of a sort. Their presence was nevertheless highly public, as tavern-keepers sent out criers into the streets to advertise the good price and quality of their wine: in the 'Dit des Crieries de Paris', the cries of tradesmen intermingle with the seductive invitations to drink. Drinking was a sociable activity and taverns were places where one could meet friends and have a chat, but they were also characterized as places of changeability, of bad luck and of loss; the speaker in the 'Dit des Crieries' loses his clothing because he spends too much on food and drink and laments the unkindness of fortune's wheel.[119]

The legal presentation of tavern violence in Paris drew attention to its futility, but was, in many ways, quite similar to the types of cases we find in Artois. In legal accounts, Parisian violence was frequently linked to failed gestures of masculinity, revealed as empty and futile. Taverns were associated with more or less ritualized actions of rivalrous masculinity, but the embodiment of this in obscene gestures usually degenerated into pointless brawling. Individual gestures are impossible to reconstruct given the nature of the legal sources, but it is clear that sexuality was central to these situations, given the large number of cases involving prostitutes: while prostitutes themselves were increasingly condemned by legal restrictions, abusive behaviour towards them continued to pro-

[116] Boutaric, *Actes*, ii, no. 6246, 341.

[117] Châtelain, 'Notes', 1–23; P. Champion, 'Liste des tavernes de Paris, d'après les documents du XVe siecle', *Bulletin de la Société de Histoire de Paris*, 39 (1912), 259–67.

[118] *Dit des Rues de Paris*, BN MS fr. 24432, fo. 257^{v}–260^{v}, ll. 132, 267–70, 448–50, 499–500.

[119] Ll. 123–6 and 187–92 respectively: Guillaume de Villeneuve, *Les Crieries de Paris*, BN MS fr. 837, fo. 246, publ. at http://www.humanities.mcmaster.ca/~hyperlist/crierie.htm (accessed Aug. 2011).

voke a legal response.[120] Sometimes such violence arose out of quarrels between the pimp and his potential customers. For instance, an enormous fight in 1288 in Sainte-Geneviève involved a quarrel between a pimp and a drinker and culminated in a brawl involving a multitude of drinking companions: this dispute degenerated into a joyous and anarchical spectacle of brutality, where there was no point, no significance, apart from the fun of the fight.[121]

According to the registers, most such cases began with a single blow, which then led to a thorough beating:[122] verbal threats are rarely mentioned in these sources, indicating a sense of violence for fun, emptied of any significance.[123] Many cases amongst those reported had fatal consequences, but none of those noted in the registers were described as intentional murder, merely beatings which went too far, or which culminated in the drawing of weapons.[124] Most frequently, knives were drawn, the most spontaneous weapons as they came easily to hand, and which, unlike swords, had no representative mock chivalric value, or judicial implications. Knives were drawn from quick-tempered emotion, and fulfilled only the purpose of prolonging and intensifying the quarrel. Moreover, in some cases, the victim was stabbed in the back, as he attempted to leave the tavern.[125] Medieval violence which was intended as semiotically loaded communication struck at the face, or at least at the front of the victim: by striking at the back, the perpetrator demonstrated a lack of interest in the victim's understanding of the message of the violence, and carried out a gesture full of fury, but with no further signification.

The literature produced in connection with this setting took this sense of futility a stage further and celebrated the meaninglessness of gestures in the tavern. The goliardic poetry of the twelfth century had situated itself in the tavern to cast this milieu as a sort of perverted *locus amoenus*, and the poets of Paris and the Ile-de-France exploited a number of these motifs to similar effect, and provided a hermeneutics of violence which paradoxically emptied it of meaning. A favourite goliard theme was the injunction

[120] e.g. one Perrenele was banned from Sainte-Geneviève in 1300 for keeping a brothel: Tanon, 350.

[121] Ibid. 361. This incident is not explicitly situated in the tavern, but the presence of a pimp associates it with this milieu.

[122] e.g. ibid. 432–3—this case involved the robbery and then gratuitous abuse of a drunken man who had presumably emerged from the tavern and was found lying in a field.

[123] It is significant that verbal threats are not mentioned here, because they are mentioned in other contexts, e.g. in incidents of violence on the street.

[124] e.g. ibid. 546—although in this case, the tavern-keeper appears to have planned the murder.

[125] Ibid. 330.

'carpe diem', an ethics whereby one should never stop to consider the significance of actions, to prevaricate or reflect, but merely to enjoy oneself as much as possible. This ethos was located in a proposed alternative university—that of the goliardic renunciation of the search for meaning.[126] Mimicking the vocabulary of the university, learning was now to be nourished with the food and drink of the tavern: it was no longer to be a search for the exegesis of texts or of moral experience, but the quest for immediate enjoyment. A comical little thirteenth-century poem from Provins (Seine-et-Marne) recapitulated this theme, describing the exclusiveness of 'nostre gent', and the requirements to 'entrer en l'ordre' (ll. 46 and 48): only those who give up all their time to dice and the joy of the tavern may join. 'Seize the moment' is the first message of the poem, for wine will take away anxieties.[127] In practice, the celebratory nature of much behaviour in Parisian taverns is striking: far from evincing shame at the implications of their gestures, tavern-goers were shown to engage in wild revelries with no ulterior motivation.[128] The officially accepted locus of the frequent student celebrations (to mark the arrival of a new student or a feast-day for example) was very often the tavern.[129] When violence occurred, it was marked by a sense of spontaneity: a 1307 case of murder in the Saint-Germain register recounted the flight of the over-excited killer of an ecclesiastical *sergent*; the incident took place in the street most notoriously lined with taverns, the rue de la Harpe.[130] Nothing in the record indicated that the violence was intended to demonstrate anything or to redress any grievances. The only significance was afforded by the official record of how long the victim took to die, as this defined the criminality of the act. The register of Saint-Martin-des-Champs tells us that, in 1337, a group of six companions went to the tavern 'de la Nasse' at dusk; their initial camaraderie swiftly descended into brawling as three of the friends, Roulant, Raulin, and Richart, beat their friend Guillaume, who responded by hitting Raulin on the head with his fist.[131] False companionship continued to characterize many of these incidents, as in 1246 at the beginning of Lent, when a man was killed in the tavern beside his companion.[132]

[126] 'Gaudeamus igitur', in Symonds, *Wine*, 165–7.

[127] 'La Patenostre du vin', in A. Jubinal, *Jongleurs et trouvères ou choix de saluts, épitres, rêveries et autre pièces légères des XIIIe et XIVe siècles.*

[128] There were, however, many reported cases of thieving in the tavern, e.g. Tanon, 350 (where a man was accused of drugging his victims in the tavern), 447, 498, 536.

[129] Cf. Châtelain, 'Notes', 1–23.

[130] Tanon, 421. [131] Ibid. 499. [132] Ibid. 446.

Yet unlike the earlier poetry of the Goliards, thirteenth-century French poetry emphasized that the emptiness of gestures in the tavern was, in the final reckoning, neither joyous nor carefree. 'Carpe diem' is ultimately a hopeless message. The poetry of the thirteenth-century Rutebeuf comments on the futility of life, as embodied in the pointless gestures of the Parisian tavern.[133] The 'Dit de la Griesche d'Hiver' and the 'Dit de la Griesche d'Ete' explore the misery of life, poverty, coldness, reversal of fortune, and locate the epitome of such experiences within the tavern. Drinking in the tavern is portrayed as a futile gesture, only allowing escape from any sense of meaning in oblivion:

> Ne s'en vont pas longue chargent:
> Por ce que li argens art gent,
> N'en ont que faire,
> Ainz entendent a autre afaire:
> Au tavernier font dou vin traire.[134]

These punning lines follow on from the speaker's assertion that money is devoid of any significance at all: he describes how the money will disappear in any case, and can never enhance his situation. Wine is the only use for it, and wine, according to the speaker, itself lacks even the significance of taste, since the revellers do not even drink it, but pour it down their throats: 'Ne boivent pas, chacuns le coule'.[135] Likewise, dice are not even portrayed as deceptive or excessive; rather, according to the nihilistic Rutebeuf, they will always lead to total loss.[136] The total loss they cause is described in a series of oppositions, which serve to denude terms altogether of meaning. The lines 'Contre le sout me rent la livre' seem to evoke the semiotic disequilibrium and excess which we encountered in Arras, with the idea that dice and their milieu can create unbalanced return;[137] however, the next line counters, with black humour, 'de grand povreté', and the semiotic content of 'livre' is nullified as it is found to mean its very opposite. Again, the common saying 'De mon avoir ne sai la soume' is repeated, leading us to expect such excessive riches that they cannot be counted, but this optimism and semiotic excess is quickly shattered as we learn that the reason he cannot count his riches is

133 M. Zink (ed.), *Œuvres completes de Rutebeuf*, 2 vols. (Paris, 1989).
134 'They're not burdened with money for long, because it burns their fingers, they don't have anything else to do, so they get on with other matters, and make the tavern-keeper pour wine': 'La Griesche d'Este', i. 190–7, ll. 73–7.
135 'They don't drink it, but pour it': ibid., l.79.
136 Ibid., l. 62.
137 'For a penny, it gives me a pound': 'La Griesche d'Yver', i. 184–9, l. 20.

that 'il n'i at point'.[138] Rutebeuf is well aware of the festive nature of much tavern behaviour, but evacuates any meaning from the notion of a festival, merely noting its transitory nature and its lack of any further significance: 'Lor faut la feste,/Lors remaignent chansons de geste'.[139] Nothing but empty fiction remains.

Although apparently driven by the inspiration of wine, Rutebeuf's poems on the subject are ultimately about oblivion, a theme pursued by other poets from the area. In an allegorical poem by the Clerc de Vaudoy (from Seine-et-Marne near Paris), the speaker describes his travels through Niceroles (a pun on 'nice' ('stupid')) and his attempts to warm himself by going into a tavern: yet he is kicked out of each tavern, insulted by the other drinkers, and told that, unless he spends money, he is unwelcome (ll. 41–40).[140] The only outcome is further travels to the lands of 'Trambloi', 'Froidure', 'Doleur', and so on. This nihilism is taken a stage further, with bizarrely comical consequences in Watriquet de Couvins's 'Les trois dames de Paris', a bawdy tale of three women who spend an entire evening in high spirits drinking in the tavern, leave all their clothes behind in payment, and shamefully fall into a drunken stupor in the mud.[141] The carefree attitude of these women leads to utter shame and social reversal (ll. 285–7), and as they lie there, their husbands and other passers-by assume that they have been murdered (ll. 196–7). The tavern has led not just to oblivion, not even to death, but something less meaningful, more uncertain: the women are horrifically buried alive (ll. 223–5). But they scramble out of their graves, inevitably return to the tavern, and collapse from the cold. When their bodies are found a second time, witnesses are alarmed, believing that they must be possessed by the devil to have risen from the dead, and when the women groggily call out for another drink, everyone flees. Signs are misread, their true meaning ignored or invented, and the most fundamental states of life and death rendered meaningless. The violence in this tavern is not excessive but pointless, for it was not even real: the women were not murdered, but only covered in mud and filth because of their own behaviour.

This is a theme echoed in the legal presentations. In Arras, tavern-keepers were frequently perceived as peace-makers.[142] In contrast, in

[138] 'I don't know the sum of my riches'; 'I don't have any': ibid., ll. 29–30.

[139] 'Then the party ends, and only stories remain': 'La Griesche d'Este', ll. 87–8.

[140] Pierre Ruelle, *Les Dits du Clerc de Vaudoy* (Brussels, 1969): 'Le dit de Nicerole', 72–4. The poem dates from the mid-13th cent.

[141] BN, Arsenal, 3525, fos. 88ra–94ra; ed. in *NRCF* x. 122. The gendered denigration of women who drink is also striking: L. Martin, *Alcohol, Sex and Gender* (Basingstoke, 2001), 95. See also Cowell, *At Play*, 173–8.

[142] e.g. *Le Jeu de Saint Nicholas*, ll. 1163–8.

Paris, the opposite was the case: a case of 1336 in Saint-Martin-des-Champs presented a tavern-keeper actually arrested for encouraging acts of violence in his tavern presumably for their entertainment value.[143] Witnesses explained that the host had encouraged the drinking of a group of inebriated men, and allowed them to quarrel and strike one another; the fight then emerged onto the street. This tavern-keeper from Saint-Martin-des-Champs drew attention to the way this violence was intended to be merely amusing: it formed part of a world where gestures were evacuated of representational value.

The literature of Paris taverns picks up on the theme of clothing, which was so prevalent amongst the Arras dramatists. However, it would seem that, while in Arras clothes were torn or ripped, here they were more frequently entirely destroyed or lost. The tearing and ripping of clothing in Arras permitted clothes to exercise a continued semiotic role, but one where there was a sense of excess and disequilibrium in a critique on contemporary socio-economic growth. The motif of lost clothing, popularized in goliardic poetry, contested this notion, by destroying the signifier altogether, and thus evacuating all meaning from the situation. The 'Trois dames de Paris' lose all their clothing and wander around stark naked (ll. 152–64), and the narrator of the 'Dit de Niceroles' comments that one 'perdra ses drapiaus' (l. 48).[144]

Much of the literature of Paris taverns, again drawing upon earlier Latin poetry, was concerned with religious parody, partly owing to this literature's origins amongst young and disrespectful clerics. Likewise, the Arras plays located religious parody in the tavern context. There are a host of implications in this choice, but one would seem to be directly linked to their critique of signifying frameworks in the societies in which they operated.[145] Medieval theology frequently linked the need for signs to the Fall itself, arguing that since man had chosen to exercise free will and to open up the possibility of unrestrained evil, differentiation via signs was necessitated.[146] Whilst in classical literature, wine got the creative juices flowing, in Christian theology it was also the ultimate sign, the eucharistic

[143] Tanon, 488.

[144] 'Lost his clothing'.

[145] The situating of religious discourse in the tavern in the Arras plays has been a matter of debate with regard to the *Jeu de Saint Nicholas*, with T. Hunt arguing that the tavern here is characterized by the absence of religious concerns ('A Note on the Ideology of Bodel's *Jeu de Saint Nicolas*', *Studi Francesi*, 58 (1976), 69), and others arguing the opposite, e.g. Raybin, 'The Court', 178–81. In the later Arras tavern plays though, religious concerns are explicit.

[146] Cf. R. Markus, 'Signs, Communication and Communities in Augustine's *De Doctrina Christiana*', in *Augustine's De Doctrina Christiana*, ed. D. Arnold and P. Bright (Notre Dame, Ind., 1995), 97–108.

emblem which compensated the Fall and, through transubstantiation, became not just sign but reality. The *Jeu de la Feuillée* of Adam de la Halle drew attention to the overload of semiology in contemporary society by critiquing the Church's use of relics, and mockingly placing the monk in the tavern with his 'relics', whose signifying powers he milks excessively to great financial reward. The tavern itself then becomes the locus of a mock liturgy as the tavern-keeper exhorts Adam to 'fache grant sollempnité/De che saint c'on a abevré'.[147] By emphasizing unbalanced semiologies through a crude parody of the Church, the play locates itself in a Christian timeframe, and one which is not merely 'post-lapsarian' in its reliance on a system of signs, but really 'post-post-lapsarian', because even the signs of the Church itself have become excessive and replete with multiple meanings. Likewise, the signifying value of violence is exaggerated, as gestures exceed any communicative necessity. *Courtois d'Arras* makes a similar point as, after commenting in the tavern garden that, 'Souz ciel n'est irnes quë il i faille', Courtois finally realizes that this is actually a false Eden, not a pre-lapsarian one; it is an Eden where signs are deceptive because they have double or even triple meanings.[148] This is a world of the decadence of signs. In contrast, the religious satire of Parisian poetry draws attention, not to the excess of religious language, but to its apparent pointlessness. A thirteenth-century macaronic 'patenostre du vin' interpolates lines of the Lord's Prayer in a general panegyric of the tavern lifestyle.[149] The first line, '*Sanctificetur*, li bons vins' appears simply to rewrite the hallowed subject, but the grammatical structure breaks down with the verbal, 'Me mist au fond de mes greniers': not only is meaning changed, it is destroyed.[150] Likewise, the '*Debitoribus*; aprendez,/ *Nostris*; à manoier .iiij. dez' redefines debt not as sin but as economic loss, but grammatically fails to add up.[151] The effect is a series of blasphemous juxtapositions—'*Nomen tuum*; li taverniers'—which do not just reassign meaning, but which undermine it altogether.[152] In a famous Latin mimicry of Thomas Aquinas's hymn in praise of the Eucharist, wine has no meaning other than sheer hedonism.[153] This is then, apparently, a world where signs mean nothing, or even where there are no signs, just objects and pleasure: violence in Parisian taverns was imaginatively situated in a pre-lapsarian utopia.

147 'Act very solemnly for this saint, of whom we have drunk': ll. 1022–3.
148 'There is no other garden under heaven which rivals it': l. 281.
149 Jubinal, *Jongleurs et trouvères*, 68; this wine is apparently drunk in Provins (l. 2).
150 'Hallowed be, the good wine', 'put me down in the dumps', ll. 1, 3.
151 'For our debts, teach/To us, to handle 3 dice', ll. 43–4.
152 'Your name, the tavern-keeper', l. 4.
153 'Hymn to Wine', in Symonds, *Wine*, 135.

4. CONCLUSION

Taverns, and their associated violence, were not widely approved of in this period, and attracted much hostile comment and castigation from moralists and legalists alike. However, they provided a space of commentary which was widely celebrated in contemporary literature. Arras and other towns in the Artois region were burgeoning economic centres with associated socio-economic change, and taverns provided a space in which gestures could be tailored to comment upon these shifts and upon the functioning of violence itself. The perpetration of violent gestures in these taverns, and, more visibly to the historian, the discourse constructed around them in the famous Arras vernacular plays, engaged with the excess of new and changing social patterns, and the sense of disequilibrium in society. They critiqued these trends by reproducing the concept of lack of balance and of over-representation, over-signification, or excessive response in their own self-presentation: they created a depressing kind of post-post-lapsarian world where signs not merely existed, but were overloaded with multiple meanings particularly where violence was concerned. In contrast, in the thriving and more diverse university city of Paris, tavern violence was presented as engaging with change in a more carefree, escapist way, satirizing the semiotic overload of social patterns by rejecting signification altogether to produce violent gestures empty of meaning. This was taken further by literary discourses which explicitly drew attention to this meaninglessness in a kind of pre-lapsarian space where signs were unnecessary, understanding not called for, reflection outlawed, and where an ethos of 'carpe diem' reigned supreme.

As such, taverns were arenas of collective commentary rather than action, and society could not afford to make too much of a fuss about them. It was not until the later fourteenth century that taverns would be explicitly associated with the devil, particularly in literary discourse.[154] For the moment, they remained detached spaces where violent commentaries on social change could be engaged in with relative impunity, and where notions of violent communication could be playfully subverted.

[154] Cf. F. Rexroth, *Das Milieu der Nacht: Obrigkeit und Randgruppen in Spätmittelaltlichen London* (Göttingen, 1999), 333–50; Martin, *Alcohol*, 62.

4
Student Violence in Thirteenth- and Early Fourteenth-Century Paris

Students formed a distinct category of violent offenders: young, playful, and desperate to impress. Much as they might have liked to, students did not spend all their time in the noisy tavern: they stepped across its threshold into the world of the busy Parisian streets, the crowded student hostels, and the austere colleges. When inside the taverns, they responded to the fulminations of preachers by claiming that their violence was meaningless play: against the moralistic condemnations of their degenerate behaviour, they self-consciously emptied their gestures of signification. As they walked outside, they responded in more complex ways to these criticisms, even as they continued, mainly, to have fun. Students were at a transitional stage in their lives, and anxious to assert powerful identities.

In the late thirteenth-century *Jeu de la Feuillée* by Adam de la Halle, Adam's theatrical persona refuses to join in the raucous laughter and drinking of his friends, who promptly retaliate mockingly: 'Vois ke maistre Adans fait le sage/Pour chou k'il doit estre escoliers'.[1] The play was written for, and performed in, an Arras tavern: it was explicitly socially embedded, drawing the audience into its laughter and featuring contemporary characters whose existence is documented in administrative records.[2] The sharp sarcasm of Adam's remark is effective because it engages with two polarized stereotypes of student behaviour: on the one hand, students could be disparagingly characterized as too absorbed in study and religion to partake in macho pursuits of drinking, violent games, and sexual relations; on the other hand, they were repeatedly condemned as drunken and violent rapists. The comedy's exploitation of these two diametrically opposed models, an opposition that is a source of humour in itself, demonstrates their currency in the thirteenth century. Adam is

[1] 'Look how Master Adam is being a good boy/Because he's going to be a student': Adam de la Halle, *Le Jeu de la Feuillée*, ed. J. Dufournet (Ghent, 1977), ll. 949–50.

[2] R. Berger (ed.), *La Nécrologie de la confrérie des jongleurs et des bourgeois d'Arras*, 2 vols. (Arras, 1963), ii; e.g. the Crespins, mentioned p. 159 for the Feast of the Purification 1292.

mocked on two levels: for his stand-offishness, which hints at the tense relations between students and townspeople, and because his companions ironically suspect that he will in fact be yet another loud and drunken scholar. And it is this relationship between student behaviour and the ways in which it was labelled which forms the subject of this chapter.

Students were acutely aware of these conflicting stereotypes and knew that their behaviour was constantly observed and commented upon: inevitably, such models in turn shaped their behaviour. Although this kind of violence frequently provoked international repercussions and complex political manœuvrings between king, pope, religious orders, and the international community, here the focus will be on the role of violence in the everyday lives of these young men and those with whom they came into contact on a daily basis.[3] Students were often drunk, often joking, usually frivolous. Loud and ebullient, they could be carried away by the momentum of their own misbehaviour. But their brutality was never unmotivated, even when they were so drunk as to bury that meaning under layers of noisy exuberance. What was violence by students trying to achieve? How did attitudes to student violence coalesce, and how did they influence the perpetrators? Violence ranged from drunken beatings and fights, to abuse of prostitutes and rape, mocking brutalization of conscientious students, and large-scale battles between groups of different geographical provenance, or town and gown. Most students came from an urban background, though they were of diverse geographical and socio-economic origins, and remained acutely aware of such differences while students.[4] Of course, not all students were routinely involved in violence, and the corruption of the student body by a noisy and deviant minority is a frequent theme in university statutes, sermons, and letters.[5]

[3] This kind of everyday student violence, whilst a historiographical commonplace, has not been submitted to much detailed analysis in this period, with the notable exceptions of C. Hammer, 'Homicide in Fourteenth-Century Oxford', *Past and Present*, 78/1 (1978), 4–23; C. Gauvard, 'Les Jeunes à la fin du Moyen Age: Une classe d'âge', in *Les Entrées dans la vie: Initiations et apprentissages. XIIe congrès de la société des historiens médiévistes de l'enseignement supérieur public, Nancy, 1981* (Nancy, 1981), 225–44 (though principally about a later period).

[4] Around 15–20% of students were 'poor' and 'of social integration, lifting the university out of its environment and transforming it into an egalitarian community based on shared "academic activity", there was not a trace': R. Schwinges, 'Student Education, Student Life', in H. de Ridder-Symoens (ed.), *History of the University in Europe*, 2 vols. (Cambridge, 1992), i. *Universities in the Middle Ages*, 204–10; W. Courtenay, *Parisian Scholars in the Early Fourteenth Century: A Social Portrait* (Cambridge, 1999), 1ff.; J. Dunbabin, 'Meeting the Costs of University Education in Northern France, *c.*1240–1340', *History of Universities*, 10 (1991), 1–27.

[5] e.g. H. Denifle and E. Châtelain (eds.), *Chartularium Universitatis Parisiensis*, 4 vols. (Paris, 1889–97), i, no. 60, 116–17 (reformation of the house of poor scholars). Henceforth, *CUP*: references will be given indicating volume, document, and page numbers.

Time in Paris was a formative period for students, one in which they had to attempt both to fashion, and to understand, the nature of their place in society. Gilles li Muisis's *Lamentation* of *c.*1350, a nostalgic review by a blind 80 year old of his time as a student, is predicated on this recognition of studenthood as the moment in which one begins to forge one's social identity.[6] Students ranged from age 14 to 21 years old: the 'scholarii simplices' were aged between 14 and 16 and represented about 50 per cent of students; the 'baccalarii' aged between 16 and 19 formed about 30 per cent of students; finally, the master-students, aged 19 to 21, continued their studies in the higher faculties of medicine, theology, law, were often responsible for teaching younger students, and represented about 20 per cent of the student body.[7] There is no significant evidence to locate violent actions more particularly amongst one of these groups, though the involvement of masters in drunken brawls did provoke particular disapproval.[8]

The early years of the University of Paris provided a highly conflictual setting for student violence.[9] Though fired by intellectual idealism and royal pride, the University was coloured from the start by conflict and violent debate: the legal privileges embodied in the original 1215 statute arose from the jurisdictional tensions caused by a famous tavern brawl between a group of German students and townspeople in 1200.[10] Likewise, the 1215 statute immediately addressed the issue of student morality, demonstrating awareness of their marauding and provocative behaviour.[11] Conflict at an institutional level continued through the century, with tensions between the friars and the secular masters over control of the university reaching a dramatic peak in 1253.[12] The University was fiercely defensive of its privileges throughout the century,

6 'Li lamentations l'abbé Gillis Le Muisit', in J.-M. Kervyn de Lettenhove (ed.), *Poésies de Gilles li Muisis*, 2 vols. (Louvain, 1882), i. 8–22.

7 Schwinges, 'Student Education', 196. In 1528, the Venetian ambassador made a telling observation about the immaturity of the students when he stated that the students in Orléans were 'tutti uomini, e non come negli altri studii di Franza, garzoni': quoted in C. Vulliez, 'Une étape privilégiée de l'entrée dans la vie: Le Temps des études universitaires à travers l'exemple orléanais des derniers siècles du Moyen Age', in *Les Entrées dans la vie*, 162.

8 *CUP* i, no. 425, 479–81.

9 S. Ferruolo, *The Origins of the University: The Schools of Paris and their Critics* (Stanford, 1985), 4. See also G. Jehel and P. Racinet, *Education et cultures dans l'Occident chrétien du XIIe au XVe siècle* (Paris, 1998), 110–37.

10 Ibid. 281. Pride in the university is particularly evident in Jehan de Jandun, *Tractatus de laudibus Parisius,* in Le Roux de Lincy and L. Tisserand (eds.), *Paris et ses historiens au XIVe et XVe siècles* (Paris, 1867), 32–72, particularly 34–40.

11 *CUP* i, no. 20, pp. 78–9.

12 G. Leff, *Paris and Oxford Universities in the Thirteenth and Fourteenth Centuries: An Institutional and Intellectual History* (New York, 1962), 34–48. See also G. Geltner,

defending its jurisdictional immunities against perceived hostile interference by town authorities.[13] The atmosphere was one of uncertainty and struggle, and though the violence examined in this chapter functioned at a personal level, the dominant conflictual ambiance provided a fertile context.

It is largely thanks to these struggles that the historian is able to gain an insight into the everyday life of the student in the thirteenth century. Statutes produced by the University itself in order to defend its privileges, papal bulls attempting to regulate student morality and negotiate in the numerous disputes in which they became involved, and royal ordinances trying to preserve the prestige which the University brought to the crown, have been gathered by Heinrich Denifle and Emile Châtelain in the *Chartularium Universitatis Parisiensis*.[14] The legal material which should supplement these documents is minimal. Students, as clerics, enjoyed jurisdictional immunity: both *privilegium fori* (the right to be tried only by an ecclesiastical court) and *privilegium canonis* (that anyone laying a hand on a cleric risked excommunication).[15] These jurisdictional privileges were reiterated in papal bulls of 1194, 1208, and most stridently in Gregory IX's *parens scientiarum* of 1231.[16] It is unfortunate that the records of the bishop's court, where students *were* justiciable, do not survive. The University was reluctant to keep any evidence of student misdemeanours, and we can only turn to the scanty material of students mistakenly prosecuted by secular jurisdictions either in Paris or in their place of origin. Moreover, fights involving students and non-students were likely to be recorded in secular jurisdictions, affording an oblique view of the behaviour of the students themselves.[17]

The jurisdictional immunity of the student body was a major source of tension in town–gown relations, and fuelled stereotypes of anarchic students, apparently answerable to nobody. Much of the source material dealing with attitudes towards student misbehaviour springs from such tensions. Chronicles recorded major outbreaks of violence between towns-

'Mendicants as Victims: Scale, Scope, and the Idiom of Violence', *Journal of Medieval History*, 36/2 (2010), 126–41.

[13] See P. Kibre, *Scholarly Privileges in the Middle Ages: The Rights, Privileges, and Immunities of Scholars and Universities at Bologna, Padua, Paris and Oxford* (Cambridge, Mass., 1962), 85–131.

[14] *CUP*.

[15] M.-M. Davy, 'La Situation juridique des étudiants de l'Université de Paris au XIIIe siècle', *Revue d'Histoire de l'Église de France*, 17 (1931), 298.

[16] *CUP* i, no. 82, 140–1.

[17] See L. Tanon, *Histoire des justices des anciennes églises et communautés monastiques de Paris* (Paris, 1883). Also, a few letters of remission from the early 14th cent. survive in the AN, series JJ.

people and students, providing official historical accounts of the international repercussions of such events, and drawing on and shaping stereotypical representations of students.[18] Sermons and exempla contributed a more moralistic characterization of students, drawing on observed behaviour and accounts from the confessional, and combining comment and didacticism: many of the preachers had themselves been students at the University.[19] An overtly hortatory tone characterized the profusion of manuals of recommended behaviour, most famously those of Guillaume de Tournai, the Pseudo-Boethius, and Jean de Garlande in the thirteenth century; they juxtaposed the model of the studious, pious youth with the stereotype of the degenerate drunkard, and specified particular moments when one was most at risk from the temptation of sin. They were widely read and survive in numerous manuscripts.[20] The voices of the students themselves can be obliquely heard in the surviving letters; though mostly model letters begging parents for financial help, they occasionally detail specific incidents and demonstrate how students could manipulate descriptions of their own behaviour to fit acceptable models.[21] More creatively, student poetry, notably that of the highly sophisticated Rutebeuf, subversively engaged with stereotypes and explored how manipulations of identity could negotiate the polarized frameworks of student behaviour.[22]

[18] e.g. Matthew Paris, *Chronica Majora,* ed. H. Luard, 7 vols. (London, 1866), iii; *Annales Prioratus de Dunstaplia (AD 1–1297)* ed. H. Luard, Rolls Series, 26, 3 vols (London, 1866), iii; Ralph of Coggeshall, *Chronicon Anglicanum,* ed. J. Stevenson, Rolls Series, 66 (London 1875), 192; Roger of Hoveden, *Chronica,* ed. W. Stubbs, Rolls Series, 51, 4 vols. (London, 1871), iv; *Les Grandes Chroniques de France,* ed. J. Viard, 10 vols. (Paris, 1920–53); Guillaume de Nangis, *Chronique et continuation de sa chronique,* ed. H. Géraud, 2 vols. (Paris, 1843); *Chroniques de Saint Denis* in *RHGF,* 24 vols. (Paris, 1898), xx. 677; Girardus de Fracheto, *Chronique, RHGF* xxi. 23; Vincentius Bellovacensis, *Chronique,* xxi. 72; *Chronicon Girardi ab Arvernia,* xxi. 214; *E Chronico Alberici Monachi Trium Fontium,* xxi. 599; *Majus Chronicon Lemovicense a Petro Coral et Aliis conscriptum,* xxi. 764; *E floribus Chronicorum etc. auctore Bernardo Guidonis,* xxi. 695; *Chronique Anonyme,* xxi. 84; *Chronique anonyme,* xxi. 142; *Excerpta e Memoriali Historiarum Johannis a Sancto Victore,* xxi. 642.

[19] C.-V. Langlois, 'Sermons parisiens de la première moitié du XIIIe siècle, contenus dans le manuscrit 691 de la Bibliothèque d'Arras', *Journal des Savants* (1916), 488–98, 548–59.

[20] Pseudo-Boethius, *De Disciplina Scholarium,* ed. O. Weijers (Leiden, 1976); William of Tournai, *De instructione puerorum,* ed. J. Corbett (Notre Dame, Ind., 1955); L. Paetow (ed.), *Two Medieval Satires: La Bataille des xii de Henri d'Andieli and the Morale Scholarium of John of Garland* (Berkeley, Calif., 1914).

[21] C. H. Haskins, 'The Life of Mediaeval Students as Illustrated by their Letters', in *Studies in Mediaeval Culture* (Oxford, 1929), 1–36.

[22] Rutebeuf, *Œuvres complètes,* ed. M. Zink, 2 vols. (Paris, 1989).

1. STEREOTYPES

Stereotypes are typically distorting, but do not arise in a vacuum. The stereotypes by which student behaviour was described and explained were essentially reactions and attitudes to violence already performed. Moreover, they were largely constructed by those who had once been students themselves, and who looked upon university life with ambivalence. Stereotypes responded to observed behaviour, but equally, observable behaviour responded to stereotypes, and negotiated the models imposed on it by moralists, disciplining authorities, and parents.

Such reciprocity is underlined in criminological labelling theory: it is argued that deviance is created by societies which establish the rules defining it as such, and that the labelling of offenders provides the impulse for secondary deviance which would not have occurred had the label not been applied. Such a theory is concomitantly dependent on notions of identity formation, and the argument that self-concepts can only be formed as reflections of others' conceptions of us.[23] Labelling simply cannot be a neutral and objective process as opponents of the theory suggest, by arguing that deviant behaviour precedes labelling.[24] Rather, labels are used to manipulate observations in the interests of the labellers' preoccupations, most often with the purpose of excluding those deemed to represent a threat. Some even argue that labelling can be a positive process, providing the possibility of reinclusion into society, hence Braithwaite's model of 'reintegrative shaming': still it is a deliberate process with important consequences.[25] Whether labelling is reintegrative or exclusive, it is a process with historical agency. 'Deviant' behaviour is linked to identity which can only be constructed in relation to others' views of us; and the relationship between labels and behaviour is a mutually symbiotic one.

In some contexts, students found themselves confronted by the model of the virtuous and studious youth, whose spirituality was untrammelled by base materialistic concerns. Such stereotypes were given a positive and hortatory spin in the statutes accompanying the proliferating foundation

[23] A good summary is R. Akers, *Criminological Theory: Introduction and Evaluation* (Chicago, 1999), 151–76. Cf. F. Tannenbaum, *Crime and the Community* (New York, 1938), 19–20; H. Becker, *Outsiders* (New York, 1963), 9, 31.

[24] D. Bordua, 'Recent Trends: Deviant Behavior and Social Control', *Annals*, 369 (1967), 153. The theory is often also criticized for its determinism, but writers such as Becker went to great lengths to stress that labelling can produce many outcomes, and is the result of a process of interaction.

[25] J. Braithwaite, *Crime, Shame and Reintegration* (Cambridge, 1989), 54–68.

charters of colleges to house students in the thirteenth century. The 1274 regulations for the establishment of the college of Sorbonne evoked motifs of studiousness, spiritual and intellectual endeavour, material austerity, and rigid morality.[26] The regulations for the foundations of Guillaume de Saône in 1268, Raoul d'Harcourt in 1280, and Jean Lemoine in 1300 were of a similar nature.[27] Although such regulations had a primarily legislative and prescriptive purpose, they contributed to the construction of a model of studenthood which became widely acknowledged.

A series of interconnected characteristics emerge from such models. The first attribute of the 'true' student according to such statutes was humility, both intellectual and social, manifested in a quiet and submissive manner.[28] This humility in the genuine student would apparently be accompanied by a lack of interest in gathering material possessions, and the embracing of a rationally ascetic life. Material disinterestedness was to extend into the embracing of their clerical status in terms of sexuality: while depraved students might be frequenters of taverns and brothels, the true student would avoid the diabolical temptation of such places and would live a life of continence and chastity. Thus both the lifestyle and the intellectual endeavour of the true student would apparently be entirely focused on religious ends, and piety and godliness would be revealed at every turn. The true student was, according to such texts, acutely aware of the perils of sin: Gilles li Muisis, recalling his days as a student, described how as a true and honest student he was obliged to devote much effort to avoiding the 'moult de périeuls/Trop plus en jovènes k'en gens vieuls'.[29] Finally, the genuine student was characterized as conscientious and called by a love of intellectual pursuit in the interests of greater spiritual understanding.[30] The crucial distinction between the genuine and the false student is recurrent in these texts. In the foundation regulations of the College of the Treasurer, those who failed to conform to the prescribed model of student behaviour were to be categorized as both undeserving and impostors: 'the perverse and unstudious and ribald and gamesters or haunters of whores and taverns' are distinguished from the 'good and true scholars'.[31]

[26] Early statutes of the Sorbonne: *CUP* i, no. 448, 505–14.

[27] N. Gorochov, *Le Collège de Navarre de sa foundation (1305) au début du XVe siècle (1418)* (Paris, 1997), 129.

[28] e.g. Reformation of the House of Poor Scholars: *CUP* I, no. 60, 116–17; early statutes of the Sorbonne: *CUP* i, no. 448, 505–14.

[29] 'The many perils, which afflict young people so much more than the old': Gilles Li Muisis, *Poésies*, ed. J.-M. Kervyn de Lettenhove, 2 vols. (Louvain, 1882), 22.

[30] *CUP* i, no. 60, 116–17.

[31] Foundation and Regulation of the College of the Treasurer: ibid., no. 423, 476–8, and no. 499, 584–5.

An aspect of this positive characterization of the true student, not elaborated on in the statutes but clearly present in more general conceptions of the role of the cleric, was the concept of cosmopolitanism. As servants of the Church, students were ideally to rise above local interests, and join in the pursuit of spiritual understanding. When justifying his favourable treatment of students with regard to protection of their jurisdictional immunities, Philip IV evoked the conscientiousness of students, and their sacrifice of friends, family, and material wealth in the interests of the precious 'pearl of wisdom': emphasis was placed particularly on their departure from their native lands, their forsaking of regional loyalties, and their travels after their studies 'to flood the world with their knowledge'.[32]

Whilst this stereotype of the ideal student was constructed prescriptively, with a hortatory function, students and clerics more generally could find themselves mocked by means of precisely these models of clergyhood; the supposed studiousness, lack of regional loyalty, and unworldliness of clerical students was often evoked with critical intent. Perhaps most stingingly, derogatory portrayal of this stereotype tended to focus upon the issue of masculinity. Masculinity was not a unitary concept in the medieval university, but one open to widely differing constructions. While the statutes lauded a clerical masculinity of resistance to temptation and spiritual struggle, an alternative model suggested that male credibility was predicated upon sexual exploits. Biting remarks were made about the questionable masculinity of clerics apparently vowed to a life of chastity: students would have been all too familiar with the stories of literally emasculated clerics in the popular *Roman de Renart* or in the *fabliaux*.[33]

To some extent, a riposte to such mockery lay in underlining the macho nature of study itself, by selecting for study texts of an aggressively sexual nature, and by stressing the combative nature of academic disputations.[34] Students could present themselves as knights of the university: an anonymous educational treatise by a German student at Paris in *c.*1347

[32] Du Boulay, *Historia Universitatis Parisiensis*, 6 vols. (Paris, 1665–73), iv. 165.

[33] e.g. J. Dufournet, *Du Roman de Renart à Rutebeuf* (Caen, 1993); *Le Roman de Renart*, ed. A. Strubel (Paris, 1999): 'Le jugement de Renart', ll. 880–1; 'Le fabliau du prestre teint' and 'Le fabliau du prestre crucefie': *NRCF* respectively vii/81 and iii/20.

[34] Stephen of Tournai: 'There is public disputation which is against the sacred constitution, as to the incomprehensible deity, about the incarnation of the Word, verbose flesh and blood irreverently quarrels', quoted in R. Mazo-Karras, *From Boys to Men: Formations of Masculinity in Late Medieval Europe* (Philadelphia, 2003), 91. Debating students were also disparagingly compared to fighting cocks, with one preacher pointing out that this was ridiculous in the eyes of laypeople: BN MS, Mat 2516a, fo. 52, ed. in F. Lecoy de la Marche (ed.), *La Chaire française au Moyen Age* (Paris, 1886), 452. M. Curry Woods, 'Rape and the Pedagogical Rhetoric of Sexual Violence', in R. Copeland, (ed.), *Criticism and Dissent* (Cambridge, 1996), 58; J. Le Goff, 'Quelle conscience l'université médiévale a-t-elle eue d'elle-même?', in *Pour un autre Moyen Age* (Paris, 1999), 181–98.

asserted that scholars at the university 'milites fiunt', and were crowned as 'domini scientiarum'.[35] However, it was not enough simply to reinsert the language of chivalry and aggressive sexual exploits into a student context: stereotypes and models of masculinity were manipulated in more complex ways. They had to be, for, as well as finding themselves denigrated as emasculated, students were condemned as violent rapists, and this was not necessarily empowering.

Preachers decried the supposedly uncontrolled sexuality of students. Whilst actively constructing concepts of deviance, these preachers, as former students themselves, could draw upon direct observation: their purpose was not just to denigrate, but pastoral. Numerous didactic and illustrative sermon exempla presented the motif of the lecherous student and his concubine, together with an awareness that students could be provocatively mocked for their apparently chaste and emasculated state.[36] Conflicting paradigms of masculinity were evoked, and students were stereotyped as more likely to conform to a sexually charged and aggressive model of masculinity than to a chaste and spiritual construction of gender. Jacques de Vitry's fulminations against the perceived ubiquity of illicit and violent sexual activity amongst students proceeded from an explicit admission that students engaged in such gestures because of a misguided sense that therein lay the path to honour and self-esteem.[37] Preachers focused disgustedly upon the violent treatment prostitutes apparently suffered at the hands of their student clients; Prévostin in the mid-thirteenth century graphically elaborated the received stereotype of student behaviour by describing them running around at night, armed, breaking down doors of houses, and beating prostitutes, ripping up their clothes, and cutting their hair.[38]

The work of the preachers was essentially performative, and the public audiences who gathered to hear a sermon rendered the labelling process one of public shaming; while this was surely intended as 'reintegrative shaming' *avant la lettre*, the effect could be counterproductive. This oral stereotyping was supplemented by the textual impact of student manuals, often emanating from similar sources, and likewise produced by those who had formerly been students: manuals lacked the public humiliation of a sermon to focus more intently upon the student's individual conscience.

[35] 'They were made soldiers/knights' and 'lords of knowledge': quoted in A. Cobban, *The Medieval Universities: Their Development and Organization* (London, 1975), 232.

[36] e.g. J. Welter, *Tabula Exemplorum* (Paris, 1926), no. 155, 44.

[37] Jacques de Vitry, *The Historia Occidentalis of Jacques de Vitry*, ed. J. F. Hinnebusch (Fribourg, 1972), 278.

[38] Respectively BN, MS Lat. 16498, quoted in de la Marche, *La Chaire française*, 460; BN, MS Lat. 14804, fo. 102^{v}, and Arsenal 543, fo. 226^{r}, quoted in Ferruolo, *Origins*, 263.

Student manuals constructed an ideal student type against a foil of the 'typical student', with his associated attributes of drunkenness, uncontrolled sexuality, and brutality. The Pseudo-Boethius described the risks of sinfulness and violence inherent in student sexuality, taking the rape of Lucretia as the starting point for his didactic discussion.[39] University statutes were founded upon such assumptions in their condemnatory generalizations about student behaviour, attempting both to encourage students to reform their behaviour and to belie such stereotypes, but this also contributed to the labelling process. The regulations of 1251 placed student treatment of women, both prostitutes and non-prostitutes, second in a list of described and proscribed behaviour, including brawls, housebreaking, night-wandering, theft, and homicide.[40] The regulations of 1269 made the treatment of women even more prominent, whilst repeating many of the same formulae, and provided a much more detailed portrayal of apparent student behaviour in this respect: they were accused of raping women, oppressing virgins, and breaking into houses in order to disturb innocent women in their beds.[41]

When disciplining misbehaviour, university and royal responses depended upon such sweeping generalization, and again, although regulations aimed to ensure the good reputation of the university, their construction of deviance was their most salient feature. Where individual students were prosecuted by secular jurisdictions and therefore the cases documented, the records of their misdemeanours exploited common tropes to create an interpretative framework for understanding student violence. Although records of legal prosecutions were primarily to be informed by the facts of a case, the recurrence of certain terminologies and structural presentations of acts of violence suggest the engagement of these records in the labelling process. Different sources of labelling, the moral and the legalistic, drew on shared tropes, and were mutually influential. All were concerned about the wider ramifications and even European repercussions of petty student misbehaviour. The scenario evoked by Rutebeuf was seen to be typical:

> [il] boivent tant quë il s'entestent,
> Si font bien li troi ou li quatre
> Quatre cens escoliers combatre
> Et cesseir l'Universitei. (ll. 36–9)[42]

[39] Pseudo-Boethius, 101–3. [40] *CUP* i, no. 197, 222–4.

[41] Ibid., no. 426, 481–2.

[42] 'They drink so much that they begin to quarrel/Three or four do this/And then four hundred students are quarrelling, and the university has to shut down': Rutebeuf, 'Li diz de l'Universitei de Paris', in Rutebeuf, *Œuvres*, ii. 376–9.

Student brutality was further characterized as turbulent and disordering. Misbehaviour was frequently characterized by preachers with chaotic terms such as 'discolus', 'divisus', 'tumultus'.[43] The most common verb to describe violent gestures in the university and papal statutes which attempted to regulate student behaviour is 'turbare', evoking the disordering and confusing effect of such actions.[44] Similarly, the term 'discordia' is recurrent in such statutes, particularly in the context of the violent rivalry between the various 'nations' of the university, the formal solidarities based on the geographical provenance of the students.[45] Describing such discord in 1265, the legate used terminology directly lifted from post-Augustinian discussions of disordering and chaotic violence; another favourite term was 'disruptio', with evident chaotic implications.[46] The climax of edicts evoking student misdemeanours came in 1269, with a sentence from the official of the royal curia 'contra clericos et scholares, qui de nocte et die Parisiis cum armis incedunt and flagitia committunt'.[47] The spatial element added here to the trope of directionless violence was a recurrent feature of these characterizations of deviant student behaviour. Other statutes referred to the marauding nature of students, describing their wanderings across the town with the verb 'errare'.[48] The Pseudo-Boethius gave a specifically spatial spin to disruptive, disordering student behaviour, describing the wanderings of the bad student with an impressive accumulation of places: 'Discolus autem est qui discurrit per vicos et plateas, per tabernas, per meretricum cellulas, per publica spectacula, per pompas et coreas, per commensaciones et etiam per publicas cenas'.[49] Jacques de Vitry exasperatedly described student conflicts as arising from no other reason but 'occasione disputationum' and a love of contradiction.[50] According to Guiard de Laon, students committed more sins at Christmas than during all the other months of the year, and he dwelt at length on the bacchic and violent nature of such celebrations.[51] This was a theme reiterated in official regulations: in 1276, the papal legate, Simon de

[43] e.g. Robert de Sorbon, BN MS Lat. 15971, fo. 197.

[44] e.g. Innocent IV to the chancellor of the university in 1252: *CUP* i, no. 213, 238.

[45] NB: the 'nations' of the University did not correspond to straightforward political boundaries, nor did they have any of the connotations of the modern term 'nation'.

[46] *CUP* i, no. 406, 446.

[47] 'Against the clerics and scholars, who, night and day, march armed through Paris to commit scandals': ibid., no. 426, 481–2.

[48] e.g. ibid., no. 197, 222–4.

[49] 'The degenerate student is one who roams through the alleys and streets, through taverns, whores' dwellings, public shows, through processions and dances, banquets and public feasts': Pseudo-Boethius, 100.

[50] Jacques de Vitry, *Historia*, 278.

[51] BN, MS. Lat. 15959, fo. 132, quoted in C. Haskins, 'The University of Paris in the Sermons of the Thirteenth-Century' in *Studies in Mediaeval Culture* (Oxford, 1929), 69.

Brie, excommunicated the large numbers of students who, he claimed, used religious festivals as an opportunity to engage in armed violent behaviour, to play inappropriately and offensively, and moreover, 'alia nephanda exercere ludibria nichilominus presumentes'.[52] It was in this context that the university authorities worried particularly about the potential of festivals for inciting violence: many students were gathered in one place, and apparently more likely to engage in violent acts in order to try to impress one another.[53] Prescriptions for the oaths to be sworn upon inception into the arts faculty at the University engaged with such fears by including a clause that the student would not participate in any celebrations not explicitly sanctioned by the University authorities.[54] Likewise, the 'nations' were often characterized as a source of violent conflict between students.[55] University regulations were anxious about the solidarities and rivalries they promoted, and these anxieties contributed to the stereotyping of students as eager to band together in groups of geographical provenance.[56] The inception oath used biblical phraseology to oblige the student to inform upon any conspiracies to promote inter-nation violence, evoking the inevitability that 'insurge[t] natio[..] contra nationem, vel provincia[..] contra provinciam'.[57] Of course, the most popular location for placing such peer groups spatially was in the tavern. Preachers never tired of describing the tavern in their portrayals of student misbehaviour, characterizing it as a sort of perverted *locus amoenus*.

The links between the type of behaviour associated with students and the effects of their young age were a common trope. The immaturity and playfulness of youth was attributed to students by moralists, and also provided a framework for legal interpretations of student behaviour. According to such labels, students were easily led astray and enticed into sin because of their immaturity; a story in the thirteenth-century *Vie des Pères* suggested that youth's propensity for sin was partly inspired by a sense of moral impunity because death and divine retribution were still far off.[58] Charbonnier has noted that, in the letters of remission from the later

[52] 'Also daring to practice other wicked activities': *CUP* i, no. 470, 540–1. NB: the term 'ludunt' is specifically used.

[53] e.g. *CUP* i, no. 470, 540–1.

[54] Ibid., no. 501, pp. 586–7.

[55] e.g. see a Parisian sermon on the subject in manuscript Arras 691: C.-V. Langlois, 'Sermons parisiens', 554; P. Kibre, *The Nations in the Medieval Universities* (Cambridge, Mass., 1948), 20–1.

[56] e.g. *CUP* i, no. 409, 449–58, proscribing hand-to-hand fighting arising from rivalries between nations.

[57] 'Nation will rise against nation, province against province': ibid., no. 501, 586–7; cf. Luke 21: 5–19.

[58] F. Lecoy (ed.), *La Vie des Pères*, 3 vols. (Paris, 1987), iii, no. LXIII, ll. 27577–8.

fourteenth and fifteenth centuries, youth was frequently cited as a mitigating factor, suggesting an interpretative framework based upon a sense of diminished moral responsibility amongst young people.[59] A similar conclusion can be drawn from a much earlier letter of remission from 1330 for a murder and grievous bodily harm committed in the 1320s by an Orléans student: the student had apparently been led astray by his vengeful father, and corrupted by the weakness and natural propensity of youth to violence.[60] According to moral theorists, however, youth was not an excuse, but rather a weakness to be aware of, the better to combat it by means of physical discipline, witness the comments of the moralist Guillaume de Tournai.[61]

However, students were distinguished from other youths in several important respects in the process of stereotyping. First, it was suggested that students were characterized by arrogance, largely owing to their jurisdictional immunities. Of course, this was not a theme elaborated on by any statutes emanating from the University, for they, while critical of student behaviour, were anxious to preserve these privileges. In 1252, however, the Pope complained that common reports had reached him that students, aware of their immunities, were bearing arms, and gratuitously provoking and insulting their fellow townspeople.[62] Their special jurisdictional status is the principal reason why students were always defined as 'scolares' rather than the more generic 'iuvenes' in legal records, but this lexical choice also implies a sense that student violence was particular in form.[63] Second, students were characterized as *unrepentant* wrong-doers, and distinct in this respect from other categories of youthful offenders. Nicholas de Pressoir, a doctor of philosophy and canon of Paris, contrasted student behaviour with the Old Testament story of David's youthful sins with Bathsheba: in a sermon delivered in the 1280s on the day of the festival of St Nicholas, he described David's penitence for his youthful arrogance and sinfulness, and commented how students, instead of covering their heads in penitence like David, vainly and effeminately arranged their hair; instead of crying, they sang; instead of going to the Mount of Olives, they frequented taverns and brothels; and instead of sobbing and wailing, they sang to the accompaniment of tambourines and

59 P. Charbonnier, 'L'Entrée dans la vie au XVe siècle, d'après les lettres de rémission', in *Les Entrées dans la vie*, 72.

60 AN JJ 72, fo. 61, no. 71.

61 William of Tournai, *De Instructione*, 14; Cf. Augustine, *De Civitate Dei*, ed. M. Dods (London, 2000), ch. 12.

62 *CUP* i, no. 213, 238.

63 Cf. the observations made by Vulliez, 'Une étape', 178, though he is discussing primarily 15th-cent. material.

guitars.[64] The story of the prodigal son was popular in this period as a trope with which to mock the folly of youth, and to celebrate its redemption, yet Rutebeuf elaborated on how the common stereotyping of students excluded them from such a redemptive framework: he describes how the student comes to Paris to live an honest life, squanders his money, and engages in violence and illicit sexual relations, but subsequently enjoys no moment of conversion.[65]

Moralists and legalists could not allow student misbehaviour to be castigated only as innocent playfulness and, instead, discursively demonized student violence. An anonymous mendicant exempla collection from the late thirteenth century includes a fairground tale where the devil stands beside the student players in their games and breathes conflict and hatred into their relations until physical violence erupts.[66] Sermons warned that festive occasions were particularly inviting to demons, providing the devil with a superb opportunity to corrupt students and provoke them to violence.[67] Again, the stereotype was expressed in dichotomous terms, as students were described rejecting the celebration of Christ and the remembrance of his suffering in favour of devilish celebrations.[68] Legal sources readily engaged with this theme in order to label aberrant behaviour of students. In 1330, a letter of remission was granted to two students, brothers, who had apparently verbally abused, mutilated, and killed two other men several years earlier; they were granted a commutation of their sentence to one year's pilgrimage, but the matter was described as being of diabolical inspiration.[69] A similar remission was granted in 1331 to a certain Gilles des Biards, who had, with the help of a group of friends, apparently mutilated and murdered another man: again, his action was construed in diabolical terms.[70] The devil was not simply used allegorically or metaphorically, but students were portrayed as

[64] BN, MS Lat. 14589, fo. 1, partially edited in *Histoire Littéraire de la France,* xxvi (Paris, 1873), 457–8.

[65] Cf. e.g. the popular reworking of the story in *Le Courtois d'Arras*: Anon., *Le Courtois d'Arras*, ed. E. Faral (Paris, 1958). 'Dit de l'Universitei de Paris', ll. 21–56. Cf. also Guiard de Laon: 'Sic scolares abeunt in regionem longinquam cum veniunt Parisius et expendunt aliquando non solum portionem propriam sed paternam et maternam et fraternam necnon bona ecclesie', Arras, MS 329, fo. 58v.

[66] F. Tubach, *Index exemplorum: A Handbook of Medieval Religious Tales* (Helsinki, 1969), 88.

[67] Étienne de Bourbon, *Anecdotes historiques, légendes et apologues, tirés du recueil inédit d'Etienne de Bourbon dominicain du 13e siècle,* ed. E. Lecoy de la Marche (Paris, 1890), 161, 226.

[68] e.g. John Peckham, Library of Saint Mark's in Venice, Fondo Antico, MS 92, fo. 205, quoted in Haskins, 'Sermons', 70.

[69] AN JJ 66, fo. 56r, no. 146.

[70] Ibid., fo. 248r, no. 580.

literally acting 'diabolica instigatione'.[71] The trope was accompanied by an emphasis on the sheer cruelty of violence carried out by students. The term 'excessus' was used repeatedly, suggesting dysfunctionality and sadistic cruelty going beyond any strategic motivation.[72] Most revealing is the prevalence of adjectives and adverbs used to describe student behaviour in these usually dry and laconic legal records: crimes by students were described as 'horribiles'.[73] Students beat and mutilated their victims 'atrociter', 'crudeliter', 'letaliter', and 'inhumaniter', stressing their unnecessary cruelty and abnegation of behavioural restraints as civilized and rational human beings.[74] Such cruelty apparently drove its perpetrators outside a Christian framework of moral responsibility and redemption, suggested by the term 'damnabiliter'.[75]

Regulations emanating from the university or from the papacy concerning student behaviour reiterated this emphasis on excess and unnecessary cruelty. In 1261, the Pope referred to the 'gravibus excessibus' of the students of Paris.[76] Other terms included 'nefanda', with its connotations of moral depravity and religious damnation,[77] and 'flagitium', pointless but extreme acts of cruelty and abuse.[78] The sadistic stereotype was rendered more colourful by the frequent highlighting of verbal violence as an accompaniment to physical gestures of brutality. A letter of remission from 1331 for Adam Cadevake, accused of the murder some years previously of Jehan le Duc, described the original crime as a cruel mutilation and murder, accompanied by numerous and horrible insults.[79] Likewise, the stabbing of various people by Jehan de Rasi, evoked in a letter of remission of 1330, was described as accompanied by provocative verbal insults.[80] Repeated papal decrees referred to disruptive shouting by students, threats to their enemies, the friars, and insults gratuitously proferred.[81] The preacher and moralist Jacques de Vitry made explicit the connection between forms of exuberant student violence and their

[71] e.g. ibid., fo. 412^r, no. 988.
[72] e.g. ibid., fo. 317^r, no. 760.
[73] e.g. ibid., fo. 412^r, no. 988.
[74] e.g. ibid., fo. 163^v, no. 408. Ibid., fo. 161^v, no. 402, describes a homicide in the following way: 'crudeliter et inhumaniter verberavit, lesit, per vim et violencia, ense evaginato insultum fecit, vulneravit, letaliter percussit'.
[75] e.g. AN JJ78, fo. 9, no. 26.
[76] *CUP* i, no. 425, 479–81,
[77] 1276: ibid., no. 470, 540–1.
[78] 1269: ibid., no. 426, 481–2.
[79] AN JJ66, fo. 248^v, 581.
[80] Ibid., fo. 247^r, 570.
[81] e.g. respectively, sentence of Simon de Brie, papal legate, 1267: *CUP* i, no. 415, 463–7; papal decree to the archbishop of Paris, 1261: ibid., no. 425, 479–81; decree by Alexander IV to Reginald, bishop of Paris, 1256: ibid., no. 272, 308–9.

taunts and disruptive shouting: 'de verbis frequenter ad verbera procedebant'.[82]

Misplaced notions of honour and identity were also implicitly recognized in the prominent place assigned by commentators to peer-group pressure in stereotyping student behaviour. Students were portrayed as desperate to impress each other, and as easily swayed and led into violent behaviour by their contemporaries at the university;[83] the age-old fear of gangs of youths resurfaced in these discourses. At one level, the stereotypes engaged with the importance of friendship amongst students, which was sometimes even given a positive spin: the thirteenth-century *Vie des Pères* includes the story of a pair of students who were 'compaingnons'—'ensemblë a l'escole aloient/et de grant amor s'entramoient'[84]—and describes the virtuous one exhorting his companion to amend his ways, and to ignore the incitations to vice from their other friends.[85] However, more commonly, the emphasis was upon the malevolent influence of students upon each other, and their macho attempts to prove themselves. It was in this spirit that the famous observation of Philip Augustus in the early thirteenth century was evoked: that students were more doughty than knights in their readiness to engage in battle and to fight with each other in the interests of misplaced honour.[86] Records of legal prosecutions almost without exception attributed acts of student violence to groups or gangs of students. Although in this respect, the records were surely observing the historical reality that these acts of violence *did* tend to be perpetrated by multiple aggressors, the monotonous repetition of the phrase 'and his companions' suggests the presence of a trope and the pervasiveness of stereotypes.[87]

Yet students, by their very nature, were at the University in order to be taught, and the relationship between students and their masters was an all-important one, and an oft-repeated element of stereotypical characterizations of student behaviour. Students were repeatedly characterized as disrespectful, squandering the intellectual resources with which they were provided at the university, and even potentially violent towards their superiors. Here the process of stereotyping became more than ever

[82] 'They frequently proceed from words to blows': Jacques de Vitry, *Historia*, 278.

[83] e.g. Ibid.

[84] 'They went to school together, and loved each other dearly': *Vie des Pères*, iii, no. LXIII, ll. 27560–1.

[85] Ibid., ll. 27562–9.

[86] D. Cabanès, *Mœurs intimes du passé: La Vie d'étudiant* (Paris, 1949), 42. This comment was linked to the crown's recruitment in this period of trained clerics to fight the royal cause intellectually against papalists.

[87] e.g. AN JJ66, fo. 161^{v}, no. 402.

influenced by a basic fear of the inferior rising against his superior, perhaps even a more primitive and instinctive fear of patricide. The classic example of a student rising against his teacher in popular currency in the thirteenth century was Alexander the Great who killed his teacher Nectanébus, revealed to be his own father:

> Al fosse le trebuchet cum le mestre someille,
> Mortel coup ly done après en som l'oreille.
> La char ly ront, quasse l'os, les chevelz en peille.
> Dehé eit le clergon qui son mestre si veille![88]

The university regulations spoke of the necessity for respect towards the teachers, and papal decrees displayed anxiety about the threatening behaviour of students towards the masters.[89] Likewise manuals of behaviour assumed students to be particularly prone to violent behaviour towards their masters, warning of the propensity of students to suffer from a choleric temper, and that 'non est vero dignus scienciae qui sciencie insurgit preceptori'.[90] Thirteenth-century chroniclers demonstrated a particular interest in the motif, their interest in the burgeoning university of Paris leading them to resurrect older stories on this theme. For example, Matthew Paris repeated the tale of the brutal death of the ninth-century Scotus Erigena at the hands of his scholars, mistakenly conflating him with a priest and monk called John Scotus who was *almost* murdered by his students.[91]

It was this final motif which likewise captured the imagination of manuscript illuminators in the thirteenth century. There are surprisingly few surviving visual portrayals of scenes of university life, and even fewer depicting misbehaviour by students, with the striking exception of violence against the master. Many illustrations focused on Alexander the Great killing his teacher: they showed Alexander pushing him off a cliff, visually embodying the idea of a fall from a position of superiority to one of vulnerability.[92] Miracle stories, notably that of 'Robert le Diable',

[88] 'He precipitates him into the ditch while the master is sleeping, and gives him a mortal blow above the ear. He tears his skin, smashes his bone, rips his hair. Cursed be the student who treats his master thus!': Thomas de Kent, *Le Roman d'Alexandre*, ed. B. Foster and I. Short (Paris, 2003), ll. 484–7. Alexander kills his teacher because he believes he has nothing more to learn from him. Cf. also Alexandre de Paris, *Le Roman d'Alexandre*, ed. E. Armstrong *et al.* (Paris, 1994), ll. 367–8, where Alexander kills his teacher because he is so infuriated by rumours that he is his father.

[89] 1261: *CUP* i, no. 425, 479–81.

[90] 'He is not worthy of knowledge who knowingly rises against his master': Pseudo-Boethius, 100.

[91] D. Carabine, *John Scottus Eriugena* (Oxford, 2000).

[92] e.g. BL, Royal 20 B XX, fo. 11; The Hague, KB, 78 D 38 II, fo. 70^{r}; BN, MS fr. 24364, fo. 3^{v}.

engaged with the same trope, and it was the scene showing Robert killing his teacher in a fit of rage and disrespect which inspired artists to portray it visually.[93] Even Jacques de Voragine's *Golden Legend*, drawing on popular hagiographical tales, included references to students killing their teacher and again it was these scenes which particularly inspired artists: the Huntingdon *Golden Legend*, a richly decorated thirteenth-century Parisian copy, includes a vivid and grotesque portrayal of St Felix of Nola being martyred by his students.[94] The interest in this motif from illuminators suggests a more widespread fascination with it amongst viewers, and reveals anxiety about the potential of student power. Indeed, this motif perhaps serves to encapsulate all the other fears about student violence: it connected brutal gestures by students to the most basic fears about uprisings against authority, and evoked the potential for violence of a large number of people with common interests gathered in one place.

2. STUDENT MISBEHAVIOUR

Students were acutely aware of the ways in which they were being labelled, and this is evident from the mention of the stereotypes in the surviving letters sent home to parents, usually as appeals for further financial funds: these letters begin to indicate the range of possible reactions by students to the labelling process.

Such a reaction could be straightforwardly defensive. Most of these letters only survive in collections of model letters, templates which could be used by the individual student and adapted to fulfil his particular requirements.[95] They have been criticized as historical sources because of their evident perversion of the truth, and conscientious avoidance of any mention of bad behaviour; however, it is this very defensiveness which indicates their awareness of the pervasiveness of stereotypes, and their

[93] The story of Robert le Diable first appears in a late 12th-cent. version; a 13th-cent. prose rendition forms the opening chapters of the popular *Chroniques de Normandie*, the story also features in Étienne de Bourbon's *Tractatus de diversis materiis predicabilibus*; from the 14th cent., a *Dit* and a miracle play on the subject survive; there is a 15th-cent. French prose version. This fictional character is not to be confused with Robert le Diable, duke of Normandy, 1010–35. 'Le dit de Robert le diable', ed. K. Breul, in *Abhandlungen Herrn Prof. Dr. Adolf Tobler* (Halle, 1895), 464–509 (based on BN, MS fr. 24432); *Robert le diable, roman d'aventures*, ed. E. Löseth (Paris, 1903) (based on BN, MS fr. 25516); *Le* Miracle de Robert le dyable, ed. G. Paris and U. Robert, in *Les miracles de Nostre Dame par personnages*, 8 vols. (Paris, 1876–93), vi. 1–77 (based on BN, MS fr. 820). The *Chroniques de Normandie* have fine illustrations of the incident under discussion: BN, MS fr. 5388, fo. 10; BN, MS fr. 2623, fo. 1.

[94] San Marino, Huntingdon H.M. 3027, fo. 21^{v}.

[95] Cf. Haskins, 'Letters', 1–36.

desire to get their word in first with their parents. For example, the *Summa Dictaminis* of the travelling rhetorician Laurentius of Aquileia, composed at Paris in the thirteenth century and dedicated to Philip IV, contained a multitude of suggested letters to parents, drawing expertly on the rhetorical techniques in which Laurentius specialized, and explaining how the subject was most deserving as he had stayed away from taverns and other dens of vice, and abstained from engaging in the violent activities of the other students.[96] On occasion, students were even willing to sue for libel, as in the case of Master Arnaud de l'Hôpital, who claimed that he had been defamed by a series of ill-wishers, strikingly mostly female.[97] Misbehaviour was mentioned when it suited the letter-writer to manipulate the stereotype of the wicked student to place his own good behaviour in relief. A letter from the early thirteenth-century *Summa Dictaminis* of Rudolfus Turonensis begged the father for financial help because anarchic students had apparently threatened the writer and brutally abused him so that he was unable to continue his studies in his present state, and had been forced out of his room.[98] Likewise, another student claimed that he was robbed by four youths on his way to University, and was therefore in need of replenishment of his funds; a few even engaged with the idea of moral reform, explaining how the subject used to be badly behaved, but had now seen the light.[99] Some letters hinted at the propensity of students to mockingly subvert the labels placed upon them, and the role of ironic humour in their reactions. A late thirteenth-century letter from a Parisian student to a monk apparently holding custody of his possessions in his absence accused the monk of mismanagement; he effectively disabled any critical retaliation from the monk by characterizing himself as a wicked and depraved character before anyone else should have the chance to do so, and evacuating meaning from such labels by the humorous tone. The subject described himself as 'inutilis studens Parisius', and proclaimed the importance of 'bene comedendo, melius bibendo, optime dormiendo'.[100]

Stereotypes manipulate identities, subsuming individual traits in generalizations seeking to characterize whole groups. Student behaviour was primarily concerned with identity formation, and its engagement with the

96 e.g. The *Summa Dictaminis* of Laurentius of Aquileia, BL Harleian, MS 3593.

97 His claim against Agnes de Bossènes, wife of a money-changer, Pierre Bonami, a draper, and his wife, Agnès Saquerii, wife of a law professor, and Raymonde, wife of a Montpellier burgher, was rejected: Furgeot and Dillay, *Actes*, i, no. 95, 10.

98 Munich, Cod. Lat. 6911, fos. 54–5.

99 BL. MS. Royal 8 A. vi, fo. 25, quoted in Haskins, 'Letters', 7.

100 'A useless Parisian student'; 'Eating well, drinking better, and sleeping the best': *Codex Dunensis sive diplomatum et chartarum medii aevi*, ed. J. Baron Kervyn de Lettenhove (Brussels, 1875), no. 334, 482.

stereotypes imposed upon it was therefore inevitable at such a transitional stage in these young lives. Students were neither revolutionary nor passive, they were not concerned to overturn the established order (though this could be a side-effect of their actions), but nor did they simply do as they were told: 'The overriding student consideration was to become part of the established social pattern.'[101] But this was no simple task. The logic of student solidarities was multifarious: corporate, economic, gendered, or dictated by geographical provenance, socio-demographics, and age. They had a range of possible identities to negotiate and integrate into their sense of individuality and place in society.[102] The dichotomous stereotypes with which students were confronted, the conscientious and the violent, provided them with twin poles between which to explore their sense of selfhood and their relations to others. The expectations of intellectual and spiritual success and of moral superiority envisaged by the first model provided aspirations for students, but simultaneously provided a foil for them to act against if they wanted to avoid marginalization from mainstream society and narrow categorization as emasculated men of God. The denunciations of the second stereotype paradoxically proved empowering for students: by revealing what precisely people found frightening about students, they gave an insight into how these young men could turn that fear to their advantage and manipulate those around them. But this stereotype also labelled students as moral outcasts, and thus provided a model to react against, to defend their good name and their integrity to society. Neither stereotype corresponded precisely to identities and statuses sought by students, but both provided them with ways of behaving and interpreting gestures. And both sets of stereotypes provoked defensive and subversive responses.

The range of reactions to stereotypes were explored most explicitly by student poets who drew on their own experience as young men labelled 'deviant', and as perpetrators of violence.[103] They draw historical attention to the subtle negotiations of stereotypes carried out in physical behaviour. Rutebeuf was a former student of the University of Paris who apparently stayed in the city for the rest of his life, and produced satirical verse and comic tales with a distinctly personal bent. In his 'Dit de l'Universitei de Paris', he appears to condemn student misbehaviour, but invites more complex readerly reactions. The speaker engages with the first

[101] Cobban, *Medieval Universities*, 163.

[102] See J. Le Goff, *Les Intellectuels au Moyen Age* (Paris, 1985), 73.

[103] On reading student poets, see R. Copeland, 'Introduction', in Copeland (ed.), *Criticism and Dissent in the Middle Ages* (Cambridge, 1996), 1–24; and N. Zeeman, 'The Schools Give a License to Poets', ibid. 151–81.

stereotype of the conscientious student, evoking the potential it offered for gaining honour at Paris ('por pris et por honeur conquerre', l. 18), and lauding its suggestion of the international pursuit of learning (ll. 50–1).[104] However, he relocates this language of honour from the realm of pious learning, to the world of fighting and chivalry (l. 25), demonstrating how students could manipulate the honour-laden language of the first stereotype to dodge the categorization it implies, whilst accepting the status it provides. With regard to the second stereotype of the depraved student, the speaker subverts common denunciations by rhetorically accumulating examples of violent misbehaviour by students (ll. 26–36). The wider repercussions of student behaviour and the extent of student power generated by the fear inherent in the labelling process are evoked in a description of the widespread panic caused by a combat between three or four students (ll. 37–9). When he then claims that there is no life so good as that of the true student, readers are left wondering whether this figure is the conscientious one or recently described exuberant mischief-maker (l. 41). Conflicting models of honourable behaviour, and the potential for engaging with both of them, are cleverly invoked in the final lines:

> [il] c'en fait a ces amis honte—
> Mais il ne seivent qu'oneurs monte. (ll. 55–6)[105]

Stereotypes were both empowering and to be reacted against and subverted: students well knew this.

2.1. Peer groups

These young men were anxious to gain a place for themselves within their peer groups: central to identity formation, then, as now, this motivated much of their behaviour and misbehaviour. Existing labels gave them a choice between groups of drunken louts or pious intellectual communities, but the practice of student violence suggests a more subtle negotiation of these two poles. The prevalence in stereotypes of the notion of a group of youths made actual admittance to such a group all the more important as it promoted the idea that, if one was not part of a gang, there was something wrong. Since both sets of stereotypes served to exclude students from mainstream society, whether because of their intellectual

[104] 'To gain renown and honour', l. 18.

[105] 'He makes his friends ashamed,/But they don't know that honour is increased by this behaviour.' Zink's tr. ('Mais le mauvais étudiant ne sait ce qu'est l'honneur') takes a much more straightforward reading, but the plural form of 'seivent' must surely refer to the friends who have apparently condemned such a student.

calling, or because of their deviant behaviour, forming part of some form of solidarity became more pressing in order to avoid total marginalization. The scanty remaining evidence about student recreation points to the importance of camaraderie in all recreational activities, such as dinners, team games, or swimming and fishing from boats on the Seine.[106]

Violent posturing by students in front of their peers was common, both in an attempt to assure one's place within a group and to impress one's fellows. A formulary of Benedict XII focused upon marauding gangs, bearing weapons, playing sinful games together, and carrying out acts of brutality in front of one another.[107] Although regulations of the University itself and papal decrees recorded in the same cartularies contributed to the labelling process, they also often responded to specific incidents, providing a record of actual student behaviour beneath the interpretive superstructure. The excesses condemned by the Pope in 1261 were committed by groups of students, wandering armed around the town, and trying to impress one another.[108] The Pope noted their attempt to concretize their group identity, expressed through violence, and visualized by means of the banners, a motif evocative both of craft corporations and of knights advancing into battle. Again in 1269, the University had to deal with the problem of gangs of students, asserting their position within the group by the bearing of arms, a visual emblem of belonging; this time, the student gangs were using their numerical advantage to attack women on their own.[109] Stereotypes suggested to students that belonging to a group was a means of self-assertion; the misbehaving students could contest the model of a group of studious seekers of knowledge by selecting more active modes of behaviour.

Student violence revealed awareness of the potential of space; they explored ways in which their identities as part of a group could be mapped onto the city. The 'misbehaving' students occupied two particular spaces within the city of Paris and its suburbs. First, on a day-to-day basis, they were concentrated in the university quarter of the city, both for study and for accommodation: they neither anarchically and aimlessly roamed the city, nor remained studiously locked in their bedrooms. Student housing reached an extraordinary peak of density in the late thirteenth century,

[106] V. Egbert, *On the Bridges of Medieval Paris: A Record of Early Fourteenth-Century Life* (Princeton, 1974); A. Gabriel, *Student Life in Ave Maria College, Medieval Paris* (Notre Dame, Ind., 1955), 213–15.

[107] Vatican, MS. Ottoboni 333, fo. 72^{v}, quoted in Haskins, *Sermons*, n. 59. Such formularies were based upon material from the confessional, and produced for older sinners who needed to confess but had forgotten the sins they committed whilst students.

[108] *CUP* i, no. 425, 471–81.

[109] Ibid., no. 426, 481–2.

provoking bitter disputes over tiny scraps of land, and increasing numbers of houses with multiple floors.[110] The Rue du Fouarre was the most crowded of these streets, busy, tumultuous, and with both schools and accommodation.[111] The majority of taverns frequented by students lined either the neighbouring street, the Rue de la Harpe, or a group of coterminous streets a short distance away, including the Rue Saint Jacques, the Rue Saint Julien le Pauvre, and the Rue Saint Germain.[112] This suggests a deliberate geographical choice on the part of students engaging in violence in and around the tavern: they did not aimlessly wander until they came across a suitable place for a drink, nor did they simply go to the tavern underneath their lodging, but they followed a well-trodden path to a particular group of taverns at a short distance, and used their chosen routes and haunts violently to validate their adherence to a particular group. By frequenting the same spaces, they played on observers' fears of dense concentrations of students in a single place.

Nor were students swayed by moral proscriptions on wandering outside the town. By exploring spaces outside the city walls in groups, they asserted their identity as a powerful group within society, whilst refusing to be relegated to a marginal position, whether spatially or socially. For example, the university cessation of 1229 was provoked by brawls which began in a tavern in the Bourg Saint-Michel, a small village outside the city's walls on the Left Bank.[113] Festive moments in the year were popular occasions for students to break out of the narrow category imposed upon them as 'students of the University of Paris', and to give geographical meaning to this. The 1229 brawl took place during Carnival time, apparently making it harder for the Provost to identify who precisely had been involved in the violence. The Foire du Lendit likewise provided an opportunity to leave the city and gather in large numbers on the plain at Saint Denis, asserting a distinct and self-imposed group identity: an illustration of the Foire du Lendit from an early fourteenth-century

[110] S. Roux, 'Habitat urbain au Moyen Age: Le Quartier de l'université de Paris', *Annales ESC*, 24 (1969), 1196–1219.

[111] G. Boyce, *The English-German Nation in the University of Paris during the Middle Ages* (Bruges, 1927), 115.

[112] E. Châtelain, 'Notes sur quelques tavernes fréquentées par l'université de Paris aux XIVe et XVe siècles', *Bulletin de la Société de l'Histoire de Paris et de l'Ile-de-France*, 25 (1898), 1–23. Châtelain bases the majority of his conclusions about the locations and names of taverns upon the records of the English Nation in the 14th cent.: while these records post-date our period somewhat, there is no reason to suppose that these taverns were new from 1330 onwards.

[113] Matthew Paris, *Chronica Majora*, iii. 167; *Grandes Chroniques*, vii. 60. See S. Ferruolo, '*Parisius—Paradisus*: The City, its Schools and the Origins of the University of Paris', in T. Bender (ed.), *The University and the City: From Medieval Origins to the Present* (Oxford, 1988), 22–38, particularly 34.

Pontifical of Sens depicts a large, threatening gathering of students at the fair, some of them brandishing weapons.[114] Again, such wanderings feature in the penitentials for former students who needed to atone for youthful misconduct during festivals and fairs.[115]

The anxiety of preachers and legislators tended to associate misbehaviour with the Carnival and thus inadvertently to promote it, and festivities provided students with ideal opportunities to violently engage with their sense of identity: at the Carnival, ordinary boundaries and inhibitions were dropped, and group activities took place, rendered all the more potent by the guaranteed presence of an audience. Students were fond of donning masks, allowing them to engage with greater impunity in violence, but also concretizing questions of identity and transformation; this is commented upon in sermons, and is such a specific detail that it must be drawn from observed behaviour.[116] Repeated attempts by the University to ban festive occasions, only excepting the major religious festivals and the day of St Nicholas, patron saint of the scholars, indicate the frequency of student violence at such events.[117] According to the statute of 1276, students had taken to disrespectfully singing secular songs at religious festivals, engaging in illicit sexual acts, and bearing arms.[118] It is clear that, most of all, students were having fun: they demolished stereotypes of studious scholars with their sheer gregariousness and exuberance, but likewise subverted models of brutality by highlighting the element of playfulness. They demonstrated that, if violence was expected of them, they could live up to these labels, but also reaffirm their peer-group identities on their own terms.

Drunken students were clearly not in a position self-consciously to articulate complex motivations, but meanings were deeply culturally embedded. Much of this violence was stimulated by an excessive intake of alcohol. The consumption of alcohol was an important way of proving or earning one's adherence to a particular group, and this impression was only strengthened by the negative stereotype which suggested that being drunk was one way to form part of a student group. The famous tavern brawl of 1200 involving a group of German students was fuelled by alcohol, and was largely an exuberant commentary on the futility of life, but more than this, it evoked the importance of solidarity: when the servant of a German student was apparently struck, his master protected

[114] BN, MS Lat. 962, fo. 264, reproduced in the exhibition catalogue: *La Vie universitaire parisienne au XIIIe siècle* (Paris, 1974), 86.

[115] e.g. Vatican, MS. Ottoboni 333, fo. 72^v^, quoted in Haskins, 'Sermons', n. 59.

[116] e.g. *Histoire Littéraire*, xxvi. 76.

[117] e.g. *CUP* i, no. 470, 540–1.

[118] Ibid.

him and the other German students rushed to his defence ('factus est concursus').[119]

The effectiveness of belonging to a group is typically strengthened by acts of exclusion. Thus, the practice of disturbing the studies of more conscientious students was a potent one, which served to set the aggressor apart from his more studious counterpart, and mockingly to emphasize his adherence to a group while pointing out that the conscientious student was excluded from it. Moreover, it was a practice which responded to both models of student behaviour: engaging with the ideal of intellectual endeavour, but mocking it and asserting superior strength, it likewise absorbed the themes of disruption so often fulminated against. It was in response to genuine and repeated complaints in 1259 that the Pope vehemently condemned students disturbing the peace of their fellows; he acknowledged the solidarity of such disturbers, or 'turbatores', and pleaded for help from the secular arm of justice in enforcing discipline on such students.[120] Those who disturbed the study of others turned existing paradigms of student behaviour upside-down by carrying out a kind of rough justice themselves on those who chose to focus on their work: what moralists deemed praiseworthy was now deemed unacceptable and in need of an alternative discipline, and behaviour condemned by moralists was now presented as a norm and the requirement for social inclusion.

Student violence was both playful and sadistic, as peers engaged with each other, and vied to impress one another. A large number of cases involved an unfortunate ludic accident. For example, in 1304, Gerlach de Wetslaria, provost of a church in the diocese of Salzburg, admitted that, while a student, he had accidentally wounded a companion with a sword.[121] Such cases were bound to happen, given students' fondness for travelling around fully armed: a playful squabble could easily become far more serious. The notion of play initially was an expression of a desire for integration and solidarity, the disastrous outcome indicative of Gerlach's desire to prove his manliness to his companion. The propensity of students to choose swords demonstrates the issues of status at stake in their violent gestures. Such violence often arose out of a verbal dispute, playfully moving to blows and blood: two students in 1316 in Saint-Germain-des-Près argued until they were observed to 'se débatre jusqu'au sanc'.[122]

119 Roger of Hoveden, *Chronica*, iv. 120.

120 *CUP* i, no. 336, 387.

121 *CUP* ii, no. 641, 107.

122 'Fight until they drew blood': Tanon, 433—this case is not explicitly about students, but since the previous one *is* explicitly about clerics, this seems likely.

In 1311, the Paris Parlement reviewed a case involving two students (one of whose clerical status was debated), Gerard of Senlis and Gille le Charpentier: Gerard accused Gille of mutilating his hand.[123] Such students turned the idea of dysfunctional violence expressed in stereotypes of student behaviour to their advantage: they did not restrict themselves to overtly strategic violence, but twisted and perverted its forms to demonstrate the apparent superiority of the student who could afford to go beyond the merely functional in a boastful display of self-gratification. In 1315, a group of students, without obvious provocation, beat a carter in the parish of Saint-Germain-des-Près: the beating was self-perpetuating as each student probably strove to impress and to outdo his peers through a display of violence.[124] Many students strove to outdo the negative implications of the stereotypes imputed to them by the sheer horror of their actions. They subverted the first model of their intellectual prowess by diverting their supposed creativity to grotesque and highly visual ends, leaving distinctive visual traces on the bodies of their victims. Almost without exception, they acted in groups to assail their victims: a letter of remission of 1313 for the knight, Jehan d'Orbais, for actions committed when he was a student, indicates clearly that all his misdeeds were perpetrated as part of a group.[125] A horrible murder by this group of friends was deemed not to have been premeditated; instead, the record evokes the 'calor' and excitement inciting the band as a whole to violence.[126] Bond groups were not entirely dependent upon new acquaintances made at University, but could develop around a nucleus of family members and pre-existing friends.[127] All the cases mentioned culminated in murder, but the murder was never swift and straightforward: on the contrary, these acts of violence were notable for their long-drawn-out nature, their excessiveness, and the sadistic finishing touches. A remission from 1322 for the band of companions who murdered a series of victims notes that the beatings and mutilations of these victims lasted several hours, and that the victims then took several days to die:[128] this violence was not strategic, but expressive in its very dysfunctionality. A case remitted in 1330 again involved wounds in a number of different places on the body of the victim who endured several hours of stabbings and then took several days to die; these perpetrators used swords, as emblems of power, and

[123] *CUP* ii, no. 689, 148; *Olim*, iii. 637; Boutaric, *Actes*, ii, no. 3900, 86, and no. 3930, 89 (1310 and 1311 respectively).

[124] Tanon, 433.

[125] AN JJ49, fos. 3–3^{v}, no. 6.

[126] This was a mitigating factor.

[127] e.g. AN JJ66, fo. 33^{v}, no. 98.

[128] AN JJ61, fo. 127^{v}, no. 288.

assertions of a high status identity.[129] In one case, the master of a group of students was called upon to assert that they had not been in lessons at all that day, indicating the time period filled by their violence; these students again carried arms, and intensified the sadistic and excessive nature of their brutality by repeatedly insulting and mocking their victims.[130]

Such manipulations of polarized stereotypes of lonely students or marauding gangs, and negotiations of identity through adherence to a group with connotations of violent behaviour, were crystallized in the increasing tendency to create formalized gangs with given names and rules of conduct. Gangs of 'ribauds' and 'compagnons joyeux' are well-known from a slightly later period, but clues hint at their earlier presence.[131] In 1322 a letter of remission was granted to a cleric named Joffroi Boverout de Vignory, who had apparently formed part of a group of companions known in the document as the 'société ou conspiration et confédération de la bonne volonté'.[132] The case came to the attention of the courts initially because of public rumour: their exploits were apparently well-known, and no doubt stimulated by awareness that they formed a topic of conversation. The young men are not referred to in the document specifically as students, but the remission states that every member had clerical status: it is possible that, at the earlier period to which the document refers, they were students at the University, and it is equally possible that they were marginal to the university world, but shared many of the concerns and attitudes of students. Their victims were multiple, and were killed with sticks ('baculis'), clubs ('fustis'), and swords ('enses et aliis gladiis'); the companions struck their victims with their hands, then wounded them in multiple places, and insulted them repeatedly. And yet, they gained their letter of remission because witnesses were apparently willing to testify to their honourable nature. These young men were not interested in conforming to a model of spiritual vocation, but they *were* interested in demonstrating their belief in their superior intellectual status through mocking subversion of the language of religious confraternities (revealed in their name), and through their gruesomely creative violence. They

[129] AN JJ66, fo. 33^{v}, no. 98.

[130] Ibid., fo. 56^{r}, no. 146.

[131] The clerks of the 'Bazoche', 'une sorte d'école pratique à laquelle se formaient les jeunes gens qui se destinaient au barreau et à la magistrature', and their ludic rituals and parodic plays probably date from this period, though insufficient evidence survives to comment on their activities before the 15th cent.: A. Fabre, *Etudes historiques sur les clercs de la Bazoche* (Paris, 1856), p. xiii; H. Harvey, *Theatre of the Basoche: The Contribution of the Law Societies to French Mediaeval Comedy* (Cambridge, Mass., 1941).

[132] AN JJ61, fo. 127^{v}, no. 288.

perverted the stereotype of poorly behaved students by exceeding the tropes of violence suggested both by moralists and legalists, and by reclassifying a badge of sin as one of honour.

2.2. Masculinity

Students were confronted with conflicting models of masculinity: whilst many students were happy to adopt gendered identities characterized by spiritual valour and abstinence, some were unwilling to relinquish more secular constructions privileging aggressive sexuality, whether calqued upon chivalric models or drawn from broader social constituencies. Establishing a 'macho' image in front of one's peers was perceived to be crucial for these young men. They did not want to conform to the emasculated image of the chaste cleric, whether promoted as a positive model, or denigrated by mockers: they aimed to be respected both by their peers and by the wider public. At the same time, they were to some extent empowered by the prevalence of derogatory stereotypes, which labelled them as uncontrolled sexual prowlers: this both reflected and engendered fears and assumptions amongst society at large which could be gratifying for the young man in search of sexual status. As students explored and reinforced their own sense of masculinity, the notoriety of stereotypes of students frequenting prostitutes meant that their actions could readily be interpreted as those of laddish young men.

The frequent complaints about treatment of women by students and attempts to regulate this in the university legislation gained their subject matter, if not their manner of treating it, from observed behaviour and from real problems with which the university authorities were confronted. The statute of 1269 refers quite specifically to various forms of mistreatment of women.[133] The statute implicitly indicates how students used the tropes suggested to them by the stereotypes: non-consensual sexual relations, targeting of innocent parties, the juxtaposition of the innocent and naïve, and the guilty and too-knowing. Manipulating interpretative frameworks of such gestures could take the form of complete inversion, rewriting the boundaries between right and wrong, and the role of justice, in order to mould the implications of illicit sexual activity to the needs of the identity formation of the subjects. A famous relief on the south transept portal of the Cathedral of Notre Dame depicts a prostitute being pelted with muck and rotten eggs by students for swearing falsely in the Bishop's

[133] *CUP* i, no. 426, 481–2.

Court;[134] student violence becomes the representative of law and order, their association with the prostitute valorizing their masculinity, but their violence towards her indicating their sense of elevation above the baseness of her profession. Sexual status was, of course, also at stake in the students' treatment of prostitutes. Brothels were situated close to student residences and places of study, partly owing simply to the density of housing in this area of Paris, and partly owing to the vast profits to be made thereby by brothel-keepers.[135] Jacques de Vitry commented that many student dwellings hosted the students on the first floor, and a brothel on the ground floor: whilst deliberately drawing on and constructing a derogatory stereotype, the specificity of de Vitry suggests that he was also inspired by observation.[136] The frequentation of brothels was both spatially and behaviourally an integral part of student life, and often involved violence. Again, rather than merely sleep with a prostitute, many students used the opportunity to explore their sexuality, and to humiliate their sexual partners, cutting their hair for example.[137] Such examples indicate an awareness of the problematic juxtaposition of conflicting models of gender. While legal regulations increasingly tried to curb prostitution, the treatment of prostitutes did arouse concern. For example, in 1302, Adenot de Miaus apparently viciously beat a number of prostitutes, or 'fames foles' in the parish of Sainte-Geneviève, an area just a few streets away from the majority of student residences.[138]

Student writers often depicted themselves in literary form at the centre of romantic and sexual adventure. A whole genre of Middle High German texts surviving from the late thirteenth century, and written by former students, depict the departure of the hero to Paris to study; the texts focus on the relationships established between students and the girls they meet on their way to Paris and in the capital city itself (some of the students do not even reach Paris, as they become waylaid by a romantic adventure, and often get no further than Arras).[139] These fictional students discover that

[134] M. Camille, *Image on the Edge: The Margins of Medieval Art* (London, 1992), 139. Camille's reading of this image has been much debated, but the trope is sufficiently common for this particular example to provide a plausible and helpful visualization here.

[135] Roux, 'Habitat', 1196–1219; B. Geremek, *The Margins of Society in Late Medieval Paris*, tr. J. Birrell (Cambridge, 1987), 147.

[136] Jacques de Vitry, *Historia Occidentalis*, 91–2.

[137] Cf. The sermons of Prévostin in Haskins, 'Sermons', 58.

[138] Tanon, 355. This man, though close to the student milieu, may just have been a pimp.

[139] J. Schultz, *The Knowledge of Childhood in the German Middle Ages 1100–1300* (Philadelphia, 1995), 90. Edns. are available, e.g.: 'Studentenabenteuer A', in W. Stehmann (ed.), *Die Mittelhochdeutsche Novelle vom Studentenabenteuer* (Berlin, 1909), 198–216, ll. 114–15; 'Der Schüler von Paris', in H.-F. Rosenfeld, *Mittelhoch-*

their student status provides the perfect backdrop for successful courting: as students, they have spare time and are apparently not required to attend any lectures; they have considerable freedom to engage in illicit behaviour because of their jurisdictional privileges, and because their parents are far away; they enjoy a reputation for gallantry and masculinity; and they believe themselves to be particularly clever, and able to conduct complex sexual shenanigans.

Rapes by students were common, contesting the notion that sexuality should be transcended in the pursuit of learning. Most evaded detection, or at least were not recorded. Occasionally, a case provoked a conflict of jurisdiction, ensuring its written record for posterity. In one particularly extreme example, a rape of 'a certain woman' by a student named Jean le Fourbeur, engendered a debate over jurisdiction between the bishop and the University, with the Pope finally intervening in 1332 to resolve the matter.[140] Rapes by students stand out as having been particularly sadistic. In 1313, the cleric Fleuri de la Porte was accused of raping Ermine de Larbroye in Paris: rather than just seek sexual gratification, the defendant repeatedly insulted his victim, dragged her out of her house by the hair, and threw her violently to the ground before raping her repeatedly.[141] The exaggerated cruelty of this incident angrily contested models of young clerics as emasculated, but simultaneously perverted the model of merely lustful students, by rendering the violence excessive and spectacular. The desire of the perpetrator to promote his own aggressive construction of masculinity engendered a preoccupation with humiliating the victim, often by a particular focus on the woman's hair, as in this case. The presence of an audience could contribute to this sense of empowerment: Fleuri de la Porte explicitly dragged his victim from her house out into the street in order to rape her in front of her neighbours. Such students were proving their confrontational interpretation of gender not only by humiliating their female victims, but also by challenging the masculinity of the usual sexual partner of the woman in question. The husband of Ermine de Larbroye was accused of defending his wife with an iron bar: de la Porte, through engaging in violence first with the wife, and then with the husband, attempted to prove his superior sexual status set against that of two other parties.

deutsche Novellenstudien (Leipzig, 1927), 207–30, 270–93; Hugo von Trimberg, *Der Renner*, ed. G. Ehrismann, 4 vols. (Berlin, 1970), ii, ll. 13435–8.

140 AN L427, no. 65.

141 AN JJ49, fo. 27, no. 49. He may have been a student: in any case, as a young cleric, he shared many of the same concerns.

According to a number of incidents and university proclamations, students had a particular propensity for raping virgins. For example, in 1326 a remission was granted (owing to clerical status and a canonical oath of purgation) to Colard Burmet, accused of raping the daughter of a certain Roillet; Colard and his accomplices had apparently abducted his victim, imprisoned her against her will, and raped her.[142] Though the letters of remission usually address an individual, rapes very often involved bands of students acting together, the desire to explore sexuality intensified by the presence of a peer group. The 1269 university statute condemning student behaviour made the explicit point that students not only raped women, particularly virgins, but 'banded together for such ends'.[143] The suggestion of a semi-formal solidarity formed for the express purpose of carrying out sexual violence points to the profound implications of status and identity which it carried.

2.3. Geographical provenance

Where, in sexual relations, rivalries and rivalrous identities had to be consciously created and fostered, geographical provenance provided students with pre-existing frameworks for exploring their sense of identity in relational terms. The number of foreigners at the University of Paris continued to increase throughout this period, intensifying the importance of provenance in a student's sense of his place within the University. It was bound to remain central in a university context since a student's residence in Paris was only provisional: many students, particularly those from nearby Picardy, were able to return to their families during the summer, and the majority expected to return home following the end of their studies.[144] For example, the first Danish college was founded in 1275, followed by a stream of new colleges for students of particular geographical origin throughout the late thirteenth and into the fourteenth century.[145] Loyalties amongst students from the same locality were strong, to the extent that they offered each other financial and moral support: an Ypres

[142] AN JJ66, fo. 136^{v}, no. 350.

[143] *CUP* i, no. 426, 481–2.

[144] The papacy, notably Gregory IX in 1231, tried repeatedly to restrict the summer vacation to four weeks, but failed. Cf. L. Moulin, *La Vie des étudiants* (Paris, 1991), 76; also sermon by Jean de Montlhéri, BN 14955, fo. 139^{v}, ed. in *Histoire Littéraire de la France,* xxvi. 434–6.

[145] A. Budinszky, *Die Universität Paris und die Fremden an derselben im Mittelalter* (Berlin, 1876), 61; A. Gabriel, *Skara House at the University of Paris* (Notre Dame, Ind., 1960).

students' confraternity was typical in providing support for the students both while in Paris and in Ypres.[146]

The famous 'nations' at the University of Paris provided students with a framework in which to engage with this cosmopolitanism and to challenge the label that they were apolitical.[147] They constituted solidarities wherein students could explore their status and place in society by exploiting 'national' pride and 'inter-national' conflict.[148] There were four nations at the University of Paris: the French, the Norman, the Picard, and the English, with each of these titles referring to very broad geographical remits. Their principal purpose was to defend their rights, and to elect officers who would effect this task: while the University as a corporate body engaged in relations with the town magistrates, the nation was more concerned with relations within the University itself.[149] The nations emerged and gained official recognition in the early thirteenth century as masters' associations within the faculty of arts: the first official mention occurred in 1222, and each nation formed its own distinct corporation with the necessary administrative elected officers.[150] Whilst electoral participation in the nations was limited to members of the faculty, that is, qualified masters, the symbolic solidarities and loyalties fostered by the nations filtered down to occupy an important role in broader student consciousness, their potency fostered by the secrecy of nations' congregations, and their frequent extravagant celebrations.

Rivalries between nations were extremely common. Again the repeated statutes of the University prohibiting such violence constructed stereotypes which in turn empowered and provided a hermeneutic framework for such gestures, but they also drew on observation, reacting in an attempt to limit such behaviour. In 1222, Pope Honorius III issued a decree in direct response to repeated student violence, forbidding nations to attempt to avenge their injuries against one another.[151] Certain issues were acknowledged as particularly inflammatory, and provoked legislation built on bitter experience: in 1249, the University issued a decree about

146 P. Trio, 'A Medieval Students' Confraternity at Ypres: The Notre Dame Confraternity of Paris Students', *History of Universities*, 5 (1985), 14–40.

147 See Budinszky, *Die Universität,* 29–58. See also, on the cosmopolitanism of the university, and the ethnic stereotypes this generated, C. Weeda, 'Ethnic Stereotyping in Twelfth-Century Paris', in M. Cohen and J. Firnhaber-Baker (eds.), *Difference and Identity in Medieval Francia* (Farnham, 2010), 115–35.

148 I use these words advisedly, with no reference to the modern concept of the nation. Cf. Kibre, *Nations*, 18–19.

149 H. Rashdall, *Medieval Universities*, ed. F. Powicke and A. Emden, 3 vols. (Oxford, 1936), i. 318.

150 Kibre, *Nations*, 3–21.

151 *CUP* i, no. 45, 102–4.

the need for peaceful cooperation between nations concerning the election of a rector, responding to armed outbreaks caused by a previous election, and in 1266, the papal legate decreed a further ordinance to the same effect, demonstrating that the problem continued unabated.[152] Such violence between nations enabled both the concretization and the exploration of identities; the structure of the nations and the stereotypes associating them with outbursts of violence suggested modes of behaviour to eager minds. The nations also provided structure and impetus to the tendency to create distinct stereotypical identities to go with each geographical group: according to Jacques de Vitry, the English were regularly denigrated as drunkards, the French as proud and effeminate, the Burgundians as brutish and stupid, the Bretons as frivolous and undecided, the Lombards as greedy and warlike, the Romans as seditious and violent, the Flemish as prodigal, and so on.[153] These clichés could be explored and rendered more potent through conflict, both for the macho qualities which could be demonstrated through violence, and for the possibilities they offered for denigrating other groups to one's own advantage: such was the case in violent conflicts between the Picards and the English in 1277 and 1281.[154]

The fear reflected in and induced by the process of stereotyping focused attention on acts of violence between nations, ensuring the audience needed to render the students' gestures more powerful in terms of identity formation.[155] Concomitantly, students could counter the alternative model which posited them as disinterested and apolitical members of the universal Church, unaffected by narrow geographical loyalties. At the climax of tensions between Flanders and the French crown in the 1290s and 1300s, the presence of Flemish students at Paris provided others with an opportunity to show themselves to be politically engaged, masculine, and belligerent, but strategic in their use of violence. Such was the scale and publicity of the violence that in 1297 Philip IV had to issue a

[152] Ibid., no. 187, 215–16; no. 409, 449–58.

[153] Jacques de Vitry, *Historia Occidentalis*, 92. A similar set of stereotypes is to be found in the 13th-cent. list of proverbs, *Li dit de l'apostoile*: 'li plus sage homme sont en Lombardie'; 'li plus trahitre en Hongrie'; 'li plus ireux sont en Alemaingne'; 'li plus apert home en France'; 'li plus sot en Bretaingne'; 'li plus enquérant en Normandie'; 'li plus grant en Danemarche'; 'li mieldre buveor en Engleterre': G. Crapelet (ed.), *Proverbes et dictons populaires aux XIIIe et XIVe siècles* (Paris, 1831), respectively 70, 72, 74, 75, 76, 78. Weeda points out that these labels did not correspond precisely to the groups designated by the nations: 'Ethnic Stereotyping', 115–35.

[154] Respectively, Boutaric, *Actes*, i, no. 291, 345 (1277); *Chronique anonyme française* in *RHGF* xx. 131. See also the explanation given by an anonymous Parisian preacher, ed. in Langlois, 'Sermons parisiens', 554.

[155] The timing is significant, as a sense of 'French' identity was developing in this period: cf. J. Strayer, *The Reign of Philip the Fair* (Princeton, 1980), 314–79.

decree ordering the cessation of hostile action towards Flemish students.[156]

Debates about which nation a particular student should belong to crystallized much of the hostility between nations at the university. In 1266, a lengthy quarrel broke out concerning the inception of a resident of the diocese of Beauvais: the diocese fell clearly within the geographical remit of the Picard nation, but the student himself, one Jean de Ulliaco, declared a preference for the French nation.[157] The dispute foregrounded various other tense issues concerning elections, with the papal legate finally intervening to impose a settlement between the two nations and an end to the violence.[158] It is clear from the language of this settlement and the recurrence of terms such as 'contemptus' and 'prejudicius' that issues of pride were at stake. Violence took place in the form of spontaneous hand-to-hand fights between individuals, as well as premeditated and organized pitched battles. This brutality was spectacular, and served to exacerbate rivalries and promote proud identities by exploiting the publicity of such stunts. The legate's settlement repeatedly described the 'injuria' done to French nation by the Picards as 'manifesta', and he used the term 'dissensio', borrowing vocabulary from Augustinian distinctions between the just and the unjust war. The legate condemned student behaviour, but his pontifications demonstrated that students' attempts to publicize their xenophobic engagement had been successful. The same text also shows how the nations accused each other of subverting and disturbing each other's ceremonies, particularly in this case the inception ceremony of Jean de Ulliaco. Ceremonial display and celebration was an important feature of the nations, and such disruptive attempts were frequent: in 1275, the faculty of arts was obliged to decree that its members were not to intrude upon the festivities of nations other than their own.[159] A letter of 1276 by the papal legate Simon de Brie described a particular set of circumstances wherein one group of students had disrespectfully intruded upon the festivities of a particular nation, carrying out violence on religious objects important to the ceremony, shouting blasphemous terms, and bearing arms.[160] The bravado evident in this episode, and the accompaniment of verbal expressions of disrespect, points to the rivalries at stake.

[156] *CUP* ii, no. 601, 75 (this is a proscription on violence against students because of the Flemish rebellion, whether by other students or laypeople).

[157] R. Poupardin, 'Documents relatifs au conflit universitaire de 1266', *Bulletin de la Société de l'Histoire de Paris*, 36 (1909), 57–64.

[158] Cf. Kibre, *Nations*, 21; *CUP* i, no. 409, 449–58; Budinszky, *Die Universität*, 33.

[159] *CUP* i, 461, 530–2.

[160] Ibid., 470, 540–1.

Disputes between nations could take the form of pitched battles, wherein students demonstrated their ability to take part in highly organized violence, contesting stereotypes of either apolitical seekers of knowledge or of irrational brutes. They proclaimed their integral role in society and imitated full-scale war. In 1281, the Picards and the English became embroiled in a vast dispute of doubtful origin, but most probably connected to insults proferred by both sides, and exacerbated by the contiguity of the housing of both nations. According to the chronicle of Guillaume de Nangis, the violence was so severe that many feared a cessation of the university; many Picards were killed in the fighting, and many others were forced to flee.[161] The scale of the fighting evoked (allowing for the doubtless exaggeration of the chronicler) implies the self-consciously strategic nature of the violence. According to de Nangis, the English even tore down the houses of their Picard enemies.[162]

2.4. Students as students

But it was not only in opposition to each other that students sought violently to explore and expose a sense of identity. Their place in society was also conceived in relation to other groups within that society, most notably in the famous town/gown dichotomy, and in the tense relationships established with the friars within the University; noticeably there is no concrete evidence of the fiery relations between teachers and students so feared by moralists and legislators. The stereotyping process, as the characteristics of 'students' as a category were generalized and set apart, suggested that identity was to be sought in conflictual terms, and whether deviant or not, still in contrastive relation to the rest of society.[163]

Violent town versus gown disputes became increasingly common over the course of the thirteenth century, promoting a vicious spiralling of mutual tension and mistrust.[164] Although a particular area of the city was dominated by the university, interaction between townspeople and students on a day-to-day basis was inevitable, and promoted by the coterminous nature of their accommodation, commercial transactions, religious ceremonies, and so on; the potential for tension, and for attempting to

[161] Guillaume de Nangis, *Chronique*, i. 256; *CUP* i, no. 479, 564; *Gesta Philippi III Francorum regis* in *RHGF* xx. 521; *Chronique anonyme*, *RHGF* xxi. 131.

[162] Guillaume de Nangis, *Chronique*, i. 256.

[163] On students as a social group, see A. Seifert, 'Studium als soziales System', in J. Fried (ed.), *Schulen und Studium im Sozialen Wandel des Hohen und Späten Mittelalters* (Sigmaringen, 1986), 601–19; Frank Rexroth (ed.), *Beiträge zur Kulturgeschichte der Gelehrten im Späten Mittelalter* (Ostfildern, 2010).

[164] See Cabanès, *Mœurs intimes*.

mould identities in relation to other people, was enormous.[165] Students were keen to assert their superiority and played on the fears of their cohabitants by bearing arms despite repeated prohibitions, setting their more brutal image against the more mundane one of the ordinary Parisian; the papal ordinance of 1261 specifically emphasized the publicity of this gesture, and lamented the armed parades of students through the streets of Paris.[166] Their claimed superiority had a social aspect, as students commonly carried swords, playing on their chivalric connotations. Friars also suffered, to the extent that Innocent IV was reduced to begging the masters of the University in 1253 to desist from violently molesting members of the preaching orders, referring most particularly to disruptions of their liturgical celebrations at the feast of the Assumption.[167]

Chroniclers, who often ignored student misbehaviour since denigrating the university compromised their usual strategy of monarchical glorification, were much more concerned about outbreaks of violence between town and university because of their wider political ramifications: such accounts were usually favourable to students, and stressed how they had been pushed into violent action. The origins of such disputes were often located in the tavern, a common point of contact between the two groups: the playful nature of such gestures could swiftly escalate into something much more alarming as it overflowed onto the street. The violence of 1229 was described by Matthew Paris as a contestation by a group of students over the price of some wine, and the escalation of the incident into a lengthy and costly battle between local inhabitants and students, culminating in the dispersion of the entire university. The townspeople apparently began the violence by beating the students with their bare hands and with sticks; the students then returned the following day, armed with swords, and brutalized their enemies as well as objects such as the contested barrels of wine. The choice of swords by the students was a deliberate attempt to set themselves apart from most of the townspeople, and contrastingly to portray the latter as barbarous and engaging in spontaneous and irrational violence.[168] The *Grandes Chroniques* recount the same incidents, describing the 'grant contens' and 'grant hayne' between the two parties. The account concludes with the charged remark about contemporary Paris: 'Jadiz, en ancien temps, clergie demoura à Athenes et chevalerie en Grece . . . Et tant comme . . . demorront en

[165] H. Koller, 'Stadt und Universität im Spätmittelalter', in E. Maschke and J. Sidow (eds.), *Stadt und Universität im Mittelalter und in der früheren Neuzeit* (Berlin, 1974), 9–27.

[166] *CUP* i, no. 425, 479–81; no. 163, 193.

[167] Ibid., no. 225, 249–50; no. 275, 314–15; no. 250, 287–8; no. 272, 308–9.

[168] Matthew Paris, *Chronica Majora*, iv. 167.

France, e foy, clergié et chevalerie, le renome de France sera fort et ferme et plain de richece et d'onneur'.[169] This comment is part of a strategy of royal support and suggests a distinction between the clergy and the chivalric classes, but it asserts an elevating association. Actions such as the 1229 violent gestures of the students against the townspeople could be construed as attempts to associate themselves with the positive rhetoric and social cachet of chivalry.

However, perhaps the most notable feature regarding student misbehaviour in relation to their cohabitants in Paris is their portrayal of themselves as innocent victims, and indeed their real suffering at the hands of angry townspeople and brutal monks. Students consciously debated the stereotypes assigned to them in this respect, rejecting the label of instigators of illegitimate violence by claiming that they had behaved passively or at least in self-defence. On one level, this was in deliberate defence of their privileges, threatened by the assumption that they abused them, and threatened in the most concrete terms by violent action by the municipality of Paris against students.[170] For example, in 1267, the official of the bishop of Paris and his retainers attacked some students who had congregated before the gate of Notre Dame; the official was punished severely as it was claimed that not only had he contravened university privileges, but that the students had remained passive.[171] Very dramatically, in 1304, a student was tortured and humiliatingly hanged by the Provost of Paris in blatant contravention of university privileges: this was the culmination of a series of cases where students were abused by secular justice despite their jurisdictional exemption.[172] The resulting cessation was accompanied by outpourings of rhetoric from the University defending the privileges of its masters, and claiming martyred innocence; these themes formed the preoccupations of the numerous chroniclers who chose to record the incident.[173] Jurisdictional privileges were to be defended by emphasizing that students did not conform in any straight-

[169] 'Once, in ancient times, learning resided in Athens, and chivalry in Greece. And as long as faith, learning and chivalry remain in France, France's reputation will be strong and firm and full of wealth and honour': *Grandes Chroniques*, vii. 61. Almost the same phrase is repeated in Guillaume de Nangis, after the account of the Great Dispersion, as explanation of the urgency of encouraging the students to return to Paris, i. 182. On this incident, cf. *Chronicon Giradi ab Arvernia*, 214; *E Chronico Alberici Monachi Trium Fontium*, 599; *Majus Chronicon Lemovicense a Petro Coral et Aliis conscriptum*, 764; Ralph of Coggeshall, *Chronicon Anglicanum*, 192.

[170] Cf. Kibre, *Privileges*, e.g. 134.

[171] *CUP* i, no. 415, 463–7.

[172] *CUP* ii, no. 619, 91–2. This took place in the context of the conflict between Philip IV and Boniface VIII. Also e.g. *CUP* i, no. 475, 560–1 (1277); no. 504, 589–90 (1281).

[173] e.g. *Chroniques de Saint Denis*, 677; Girardus de Fracheto, *Chronique*, 23; *Chronique Anonyme*, *RHGF* xxi. 139; *Excerpta e Memoriali Historiarum Johannis a Sancto Victore*, 642.

forward manner to the stereotypes imputed to them. Indeed, a chivalric identity could even be claimed, as in an educational treatise by an anonymous German student at Paris in 1347, not through violence but through the status engendered by these very privileges.[174]

Students were quick to portray themselves as acting in self-defence both within and outside Paris, in order to counter the image of anarchic and brutal youths. The records of the Paris Parlement contain many examples of students accusing lay people or monks of submitting them to unprovoked brutality. In 1314, a Parisian student named Guillaume de Jehannes accused the Abbess of Notre Dame of Soissons and the local mayor of unjustly seizing his belongings and injuring him.[175] In 1317, Nicholas de Crones, a guard, was accused by his student victim of wounding and insulting him.[176] In 1310, a certain Salomon le Breton claimed that he had been stripped and robbed on his way to University, and violently abused.[177] A student named Jean de Noys accused Jean d'Ambaville and various inhabitants of Dieppe in 1329 of breaking down the doors of his lodgings, and stealing his books.[178] What is particularly interesting about these cases is that the students did not fear to press charges, suggesting that they believed in their ability to portray their own innocence. In such cases, student accusations used the same rhetoric so often employed to castigate student misbehaviour in order to characterize their attackers as engaging in aberrant violence.[179] A rare surviving letter from 1300 refers us to an ongoing dispute between the University of Paris and the Abbot and monastery of Bec concerning the allegation that a monk of the monastery had inflicted unprovoked violence upon a young student.[180] The crime is colourfully characterized as 'sceleratissimum', and the victim referred to as 'puerum innocentem'. The story is, of course, likely to have been far more complicated, but its presentation thus by the masters of the University draws attention to attempts to project the violent stereotype away from students and onto their enemies.

Perhaps the most dramatic clash between students and those with whom they came into daily contact in Paris occurred in 1278, as the monks of Saint-Germain-des-Près took up weapons, and set out armed

[174] See Cobban, *Medieval Universities*, 232.

[175] Boutaric, *Actes*, ii, no. 4312, 126 (1313); *CUP* ii, no. 713, 171.

[176] *CUP* ii, no. 740, 200.

[177] Boutaric, *Actes*, ii, no. 3808, 77 (1310); no. 3255, 27 (1304).

[178] Furgeot and Dillay, *Actes*, i, no. 297, 31 (1329).

[179] e.g. *CUP* ii, no. 745, 204, about an attack on Pierre de Vinacis by two men from the diocese of Amiens.

[180] G. Post, 'Three Letters Relating to the University of Paris *c.*1284–1289', *Speculum*, 14 (1939), 478–82.

and *en masse* to punish students violently for decades of irritations.[181] Principally at stake was the popular area known as the Pré-aux-clercs, a popular recreational space for students, but one over which the monks claimed unique territorial rights. Space and its uses was then the issue which served to crystallize tensions, and to render visible the perceived intrusion of the students upon the life of the city. This was a planned attack, as the highly detailed judicial proceedings following it made clear; most shockingly for its judges, the abbot himself helped to organize it, and he, as well as monks, their servants and the men of Saint-Germain participated. Although documents emanating from the abbey suggest that the students had behaved provocatively, the scale of the violence by the abbey is striking. The attack was deliberately public: musical instruments and bells enhanced the spectacle. The monks apparently called out 'ad mortem clericorum', inviting other townspeople to join in the general bloodshed and extending the battle-lines to marginalize students by pitting them against everyone else. The violence, as portrayed in the University's calls for justice, corresponded in character to the stereotype usually imposed upon students: Gerardus de Dola was wounded fatally in the head, many others were run through with swords, a certain Jordanus was wounded with arrows and sticks, Adam de Pontisara lost an eye, and so on. The violence was accompanied by insults and threats which embodied the rising tension between the groups. The repercussions for the abbey of Saint-Germain were long-lasting and the episode occupied a prominent place in social memory, disrupting familiar stereotypes and dichotomies.[182]

3. CONCLUSION

Students were continuously subject to powerful processes of stereotyping: two distinct models focused respectively either on their violent behaviour, or on their lack of worldliness and attachment to higher intellectual ideals. Both labels were developed in response to observed behaviour, but both

[181] The fullest account is given in *CUP* i, no. 480, 564–6. Cf. F. Lehoux, *Le Bourg Saint Germain des Près* (Paris, 1898). There were many other instances of violence against students, notably the so-called 'pastoureaux' movement of the 1251: *CUP* i, no. 198, 224–5; Matthew Paris, *Chronica Majora*, v. 246; *Grandes Chroniques*, vii. 162–6; Kibre, *Privileges*, 101. There were also major clashes between students and the cathedral chapter: ibid. 124.

[182] A. Destemberg, 'Morts violentes et lieux de mémoire: Les Réparations faites à l'université de Paris à la fin du Moyen Age', *Traverse: Zeitschrift für Geschichte, Revue d'Histoire*, 2 (2008), 37–48.

likewise affected student behaviour, most particularly, the perpetration of violence by students. At a transitional stage in their lives, students engaged with such generalizations in order to explore their own social and gendered identities. Both for historians, and for contemporaries for whom the University was a focal point of attention, student misbehaviour was highly significant: it crystallized the intertwined relationships between observers' attitudes towards violence, prescriptive frameworks concerning its perpetration, and how the culprits motivated and characterized their own actions. In contrast to violence carried out on the street by established members of society, students acted playfully to manipulate stereotypical constructions of their behaviour: and they were usually explicitly having fun. But in contrast to their fellow tavern-goers left with their drinks, when students emerged into the open, they engaged with society, both as individuals and as a group. Many students surely left their violent pasts firmly in the realm of youthful follies, and went on to lead respectable lives; but the experiences of all were formative in constructing attitudes towards, and understandings of, the role of violence.

5

Urban Uprisings

The angry crowd, irrational and swept along by its own accumulating fury: such was the portrait by chroniclers of a phenomenon perceived as immensely more threatening for society and authority than the mischief of students, the brawling of drunken revellers, or the everyday conflicts of the medieval street. In contrast to many other forms of violence encountered by contemporaries on a daily basis, urban uprisings were quintessentially collective in form, origins, and repercussions. Whereas other forms of illegitimate violence, even those of the vilified students, were deemed to involve considered choices by individuals, urban rebellions evoked fears of individual morality subsumed in the amorphous mass of an unthinking but brutal herd. The geography of uprisings corroborated such fears: whereas street violence, tavern violence, student violence, and domestic violence all took place in spaces associated with interactions between individuals, urban uprisings self-consciously emerged from the dim squalor of the alleyways into the vast open public squares of the towns.[1]

[1] The historiography of revolts is vast. Naturally, the main line of debate has been between those who perceive uprisings as essentially reactionary—G. Fourquin, *Les Soulèvements populaires au Moyen Age* (Paris, 1972), 1—and those who argue that more radical agendas were at stake: J. Dumolyn, '"Criers and Shouters": The Discourse on Radical Urban Rebels in Late Medieval Flanders', *Journal of Social History*, 42/1 (2008), 111–35. There has been focus on the contestation of corruption: S. Reynolds, 'Medieval Urban History and the History of Political Thought', *Journal of Urban History*, 9 (1982), 14–23. More recent work has attempted to correlate urban unrest with structural changes engendered by the Black Death: S. Cohn, *Lust for Liberty: The Politics of Social Revolt in Medieval Europe, 1200–1425* (Cambridge, Mass., 2006). The pre-Black Death revolts have been analysed in economic terms: E. Lalou, 'Les Révoltes contre le pouvoir', in *Violence et Contestation au Moyen Age: Actes du 114ᵉ Congrès National des Sociétés Savantes, Paris, 1989* (Paris, 1990), 159–83; G. Mollat and P. Wolff, *Ongles bleus et Ciompi: Les Révolutions populaires en Europe au XIVᵉ et XVᵉ siècles* (Paris, 1970), 11–38. In this area of France, they were aggravated by the Franco-Flemish conflict: Lalou, 'Les Révoltes', 171. On the kinds of solidarities involved, see B. Chevalier, 'Corporations, conflits politiques et paix sociale en France aux XIVᵉ et XVᵉ siècles', *Revue Historique*, 258 (1982), 17–44. Conflict has also been seen as a way of renewing discussion and creating its own sense of community: G. Rosser, 'Conflict and Political Community in the Medieval Town: Disputes between Clergy and Laity in Hereford', in G. Rosser and T. Slater (eds.), *The Church in the Medieval Town* (Aldershot, 1998), 20–43. The most recent approach sees these uprisings in terms of

The period 1260 to 1315 was coloured by a flurry of urban unrest.[2] The prosperous towns of north-east France were located ideologically between the centralizing tendencies of the royal power-base in Paris, often conflicting seigneurial and episcopal authorities, and the militant urban autonomy enjoyed by the Flemish towns.[3] They experienced an extraordinary density of protests: for example at Saint-Riquier in 1264, Arras in 1285, Laon in 1295, Beauvais in 1305, Saint Omer 1306, Paris in 1306, Péronne in 1308, Poix in 1310, Saint Quentin, and Abbeville in 1311.[4]

Crowd violence is a phenomenon which continues to puzzle theorists of violence. From early psychoanalytical notions of the 'ideal ego', the subjective representation of the leader with whom the members of a crowd exclusively identify themselves, to modern sociological debates, the transformation of a peaceful individual into a violent member of a mob still bewilders and frightens.[5] Sociologists and criminologists now negotiate their way between the twin poles of contagion theory, where the crowd itself apparently inspires people to behave in a certain way, and convergence theory, where people who wish to act in a certain way gather together to form a crowd.[6] The crowd phenomenon is more complex than either of these models would suggest: people are drawn together by similar concerns, but the very fact of gathering together itself promotes certain behavioural modes.[7] Action is undertaken by the collectivity, but individuals have distinct roles to play; while certain pre-established rules are

responses to governmental growth: J. Watts, *The Making of Polities: Europe, 1300–1500* (Cambridge, 2009), particularly 263–82. I would like to acknowledge the extremely stimulating work of Patrick Lantschner, and to thank him for very interesting discussions.

[2] See Cohn, *Lust for Liberty*; Lalou, 'Les Révoltes', 159–83.

[3] See J. Strayer (ed.), *Studies in Early French Taxation* (Harvard, 1939), 26.

[4] These examples have been selected in order to illustrate certain striking forms of behaviour: for a list of revolts, see Lalou, 'Les Révoltes', 161–3. Precise references for the revolts will be given as they are analysed in more detail.

[5] S. Freud, *Civilization and its Discontents*, tr. J. Riviere (London, 1930). Freud was responding to the concept of the 'collective soul' in G. Le Bon, *The Crowd: A Study of the Popular Mind* (London, 1896). Freud objected that crowds do not have a soul of their own; Jung, on the other hand, coined the notion of the 'collective unconscious': C. Jung, *Selected Writings*, ed. A. Storr (London, 1983).

[6] Contagion theory was developed by Le Bon, *The Crowd*. For convergence theory, see e.g. H. Cantril, *The Psychology of Social Movements* (New York, 1941).

[7] This is 'emergent-norm' theory. Social behaviour is not entirely predictable, but neither are crowds entirely irrational; people come together with similar interests, but the crowd itself suggests certain patterns of behaviour: R. Turner and L. Killian, *Collective Behaviour* (Princeton, new edn. 1972); C. Tilly, *The Contentious French: Four Centuries of Popular Struggle* (Cambridge, Mass., 1986): 'The existing repertoire constrains collective action: far from the image we sometimes hold of mindless crowds, people tend to act within known limits, to innovate at the margins of existing forms, and to miss many opportunities available to them in principle. That constraint results in part from the advantages of familiarity, partly from the investment of second and third parties in the establishment of

followed, the process is organic and rules are made up as the protest progresses.[8]

Contemporary sources, despite often acknowledging the involvement of the 'commune' in uprisings, typically characterized collective action as that of cruel and randomly composed mobs, describing them as 'grant plenté de gens', or 'innumerosa populi multitudine congregata'.[9] According to these sources, uprisings were perpetrated by large, amorphous bodies of people, with no structuring principles and no moral framework: they were outside the law, destroying the bonds which held communities together. Evidence emanates almost entirely from those hostile to the uprisings: chroniclers writing in the interests of royal, seigneurial, or ecclesiastical authorities, the Paris Parlement and the Pope eager to discredit and repress such potentially threatening displays. Although legal and ecclesiastical responses to violence engaged with Roman law corporatism and the paradigm of corporate delict, frequently punishing or excommunicating the entire community, such discourse minimized the sense of a rational and strategic body, evoking instead irrational mobs perpetrating acts of aberrant violence. Repressive polemic sought to disconnect uprisings from the flow of civic life by drawing attention to their lawlessness. In Laon, the rebels were stigmatized as having no more credible political agenda than that of common criminals, and outbreaks of violence explained 'propter multitudinem delinquencium congregatum'.[10] The uprising of 1285 in the flourishing city of Arras provoked an anxious royal reaction, and the Paris Parlement was swift to prosecute the offending parties and to categorize their actions as criminal.[11] The list of crimes rhetorically accumulates: 'raptum, multrum, incendium', even forging coins.[12] A contemporary Artesian chronicle explored the motivation of the rebels, and suggested that they were

forms of collective action', 390. See also Y.-M. Bercé, *Fête et révolte: Des mentalités populaires du XVIe au XVIIe siècle* (Paris, 1976), 13–15.

[8] 'These varieties of action constitute a repertoire in something like the theatrical or musical sense of the word; but the repertoire in question resembles that of *commedia dell'arte* or jazz more than that of a strictly classical ensemble: people know the general rules of performance more or less well and vary the performance to meet the purpose at hand': Tilly, *Contentious French*, 390.

[9] Respectively: 'a great crowd of people' (report by Saint Omer *échevins*: ADPC, A928/7); 'an innumerable crowd of people gathered': Laon repressive Act of Parlement (in A. Giry (ed.), *Documents sur les relations de la royauté avec les villes* (Paris, 1885), no. LIII, 146–7). Similar stereotypes can be found in visual representations: C. Raynaud, *La Violence au Moyen Age, XIIIe au XVe siècle* (Paris, 1990), 25–7.

[10] 'On account of the congregated mob of delinquents': Bishop Roger's letter to the Pope in P. Varin (ed.), *Archives Législatives de la ville de Reims*, 2 vols. (Paris, 1840), i. 289–91.

[11] *Olim*, ii. 245–6.

[12] 'Pillaging, murder, arson'.

inspired by the devil to such scandal and tumult, setting them outside the bounds of all moral frameworks.[13] Such accounts pandered to common contemporary fears by describing collective violence as motivated only by the nebulous impulse of the crowd. Rebels in Saint Omer were described by the outraged *échevins* as mad and enraged like an uncontrolled animal; a large crowd apparently gathered in 1305 and 's'émurent follement'.[14] In Paris, when rebels ransacked the houses of the hated Provost in 1306, royalist chronicles described their behaviour as 'oultrages' and 'damnosa', and used a virtuosic accumulation of semantics of destruction: 'destruire', 'dégaster', 'froisser', 'briser', and 'corrompre'.[15] Moreover, the revolt as a whole was described in this and other chronicles as 'dissencion', 'seditio', or 'commocion'.[16] Such terms relegated the violence to the realm of non-communication, sinful disorder, and chaos.

However, there is a large gap between the reality of urban politics and the denunciations of the chroniclers. This chapter will demonstrate that the violent gestures of urban protestors were actually highly strategic and carefully considered: they were also considerably milder than our stereotype of the Middle Ages would lead us to expect, with little obvious physical injury or loss of life. And, whilst accusations of violence were certainly used to discredit rebels, a detailed analysis reveals much of this violence actually to have been deliberate play-acting, drawing attention to its own theatricality. Urban uprisings, then, tell us as much about violence as a discursive label, and violence as something to be playfully mimicked, as they do about collective brutality in its crudest form. But this is not to say that urban uprisings were just about having fun, and this chapter will explore the logic behind these events.

Chroniclers portrayed those involved in urban uprisings as lawless and destructive of community narrowly conceived as a single aggregate entity. But the reality was one of multiple overlapping communities, embodied in a multiplicity of competing and overlapping jurisdictional authorities and moral or religious frameworks, which might be termed violence-ordering

[13] F. de Locres (ed.), *Chronicon Belgicum*, 3 vols. (Arras, 1616), i. 431–2.

[14] 'Became madly agitated': ADPC, A928/7.

[15] 'Outrages', 'damned', 'destoy', 'lay waste', 'break up', 'smash', 'destroy': *Chronique anonyme, RHGF* xxi. 127; Guillaume de Nangis, *Chronique et continuation de sa chronique*, ed. H. Géraud, 2 vols. (Paris, 1843), i. 355–6; J.-M. Viard (ed.), *Grandes Chroniques* (Paris, 1934), viii. 250–2.

[16] 'Dissension', 'sedition', 'disturbance': *Grandes Chroniques*, viii. 250; Nangis, *Chronique*, i. 355; *Chronique anonyme*, *RHGF* xxi. 127.

institutions.[17] Most of the communes were granted formal independence in the twelfth century,[18] but the tensions between different groups created by inconclusive definitions of relative power structures, and exacerbated by a period of extremely swift economic growth in this region, engendered increasing unrest. Unease tended to focus on jurisdictional boundaries and questions of moral, religious, or political authority in regulating behaviour. Production and exchange intensified, and with it grew the gap between rich and poor, both in material terms, and in structures of power, as wealthy urban patriciates developed into local oligarchies.[19] Increasingly corrupt, these oligarchies frequently engendered intra-civic strife, as the ordinary townspeople sought to defend their prerogatives and to stand up against blatant corruption and abuse.[20] Accompanying the growth of urban power was that of the power of the crown. In the late thirteenth century, the French crown was increasingly concerned to project its power into the provinces, and its most powerful means of doing so was jurisdictional, both via the elaboration of law codes which were not geographically restricted and via appellate jurisdictions.[21] Moreover, powerful ecclesiastical establishments vied with municipal councils concerning jurisdictional and fiscal powers: to compound matters, the cathedral chapters in these towns in the late thirteenth century were increasingly dominated by foreigners, excluding prominent townspeople from these important regulatory positions, and awakening not so latent feelings of xenophobia.[22] The violent action of urban uprisings, whether real or feigned, contested the hegemony of those regulatory frameworks, and to do so, drew upon the kinds of physical gestures associated with those same frameworks or communities.

[17] This breaks down the tripartite Aristotelian scheme of individual, household, and polis: see G. Rosser, *Medieval Westminster* (Oxford, 1989), e.g. 247.

[18] e.g. Abbeville, 1130: F.-C. Louandre, *Histoire d'Abbeville* (Abbeville, 1883), 149; Arras, 1191: P. Bougard, *Histoire d'Arras* (Paris, 1988), 53; Beauvais, 1122: J. Ganiage, *Histoire de Beauvais et du Beauvaisis* (Toulouse, 1987), 304; Laon, 1128: J. Denton, 'The Second Uprising at Laon and its Aftermath, 1295–98', *Bulletin of the John Rylands Library*, 72/3 (1990), 79; Péronne, 1209: P. Decagny, *Histoire de l'arrondissement de Péronne* (Péronne, 1844), 64; Saint Quentin, 1151: A. Giry and E. Lemaire (eds.), *Archives anciennes de la ville de Saint Quentin, précédées d'une étude sur les origines de la commune de Saint-Quentin*, 2 vols. (Saint Quentin, 1888), ii, pp. ix–xxx; Saint Omer, 1127: A. Derville, *Histoire de Saint Omer* (Lille, 1981), 46; Saint Riquier, *c.*1126: A. Thierry, *Recueil des monuments inédits de l'histoire du Tiers Etat*, 4 vols. (Paris, 1850–70), iv. 578–9.

[19] D. Nicholas, *The Growth of the Medieval City: From Late Antiquity to the Early Fourteenth Century* (London, 1997).

[20] Mollat and Wolff, *Ongles bleus*, 32–7.

[21] J. Strayer, *The Reign of Philip the Fair* (Princeton, 1980), 196–7.

[22] The case of Laon was particularly extreme: H. Millet, *Les Chanoines du chapitre cathédral de Laon: 1272–1412* (Rome, 1982), 60–3.

1. THEATRE

It is 1264 in Saint-Riquier, north-east France. We have emerged from the dingy and labyrinthine alleyways to stand in the magnificent central square. The elaborate and flamboyant Gothic façade of the newly built abbey church majestically dominates one side of the square and sets the scene for the sense of spectacle which imbues events here: religious processions, civic ceremonial, violent judicial punishment, and theatrical performances, and of course, rebellions. In 1264, the men of the town constructed a reliquary resembling that which housed the relics of St Riquier, the patron saint of the town, and placed in it a dead cat, which they claimed was St Riquier (though the papal bull suggests that this 'relic' was made of wood).[23] In another custom-made reliquary they placed a horse-bone, and claimed that it was that of St Vigor, another local saint.[24] Two remaining accounts survive in a bull of Urban IV, exhorting the bishop of Arras to impose penitence on the culprits,[25] and in a fifteenth-century cartulary of the abbey of Saint-Riquier which gives a summary account of the event.[26] Both accounts seem to be based upon a letter of complaint sent by the monks to Urban IV, though some of the details differ. According to the accounts, the culprits dressed up in robes of animal skins, and processed around the town bearing the 'relics' and water over which they had performed a mock blessing. Two men then staged a pre-prepared and brutal fight in front of the relics. The bearers of the relics cried out to St Riquier to reconcile the two men, who stopped fighting immediately, embraced, and kissed one another. The perpetrators then constructed a small oratory with a mock altar surrounded by expensive curtains, on which they placed the 'relics'. Pilgrims came to visit the relics, apparently unaware of the deception, and for two days and two nights the townspeople performed vigils and lewd dances, with the consent and even

[23] St Riquier was a 7th-cent. pagan from Amiens who protected two Irish missionaries and subsequently became an abbot. His relics were kept in the monastery at Saint-Riquier, and had recently been displayed by the monks in order to raise funds for the building of the abbey church: D. Farmer, *Oxford Dictionary of Saints* (Oxford, 1978), 455. Note the chronological coincidence of this revolt with the institution of the feast of Corpus Christi 1264: M. Rubin, *Corpus Christi* (Cambridge, 1999), 176–7.

[24] Vigor was the 6th-cent. bishop of Bayeux, born in Artois and educated at Amiens. He founded a monastery in the town which then adopted his name: Saint-Vigueur-le-Grand: Farmer, *Saints*, 524.

[25] The papal bull was described, and mistakenly placed in Viterbo, in the Cartulaire A de Saint-Riquier, AMA, fo. 34^v. The whole bull is edited in J. Guiraud (ed.), *Les Registres d'Urbain IV*, 4 vols. (Paris, 1900), ii, no. 654, 314.

[26] AMA, *Inventaire des titres de l'abbaye de Saint-Riquier*, fo. 33. Extracts of this can be seen in Thierry, *Monuments*, iv. 582–3.

participation of the mayor and town council. Violence was involved, but it was mock brutality, deliberately fictional: the fight between townsmen was a game, which could be stopped at any moment.

This extraordinary series of events draws striking attention to the theatricality of urban uprisings in this period. It is no coincidence that such uprisings were particularly prominent at the time and in the region in which vernacular theatre was born. Arras, the central town in the Picardy region, is widely acknowledged to be the birthplace of vernacular drama: both theatre and uprisings were integral to an intensely dramatic and performed contemporary urban culture.[27] Over the course of the thirteenth century, Arras witnessed the creation of five masterly plays: *Le Jeu de Saint Nicholas* by Jean Bodel, *Courtois d'Arras, Le Garçon et l'Aveugle, Le Jeu de la Feuillée, Le Jeu de Robin et Marion*.[28] These plays displayed a highly developed and sophisticated sense of humour, and were politically engaged via satire and the inclusion of well-known contemporary figures in the action. Fiction and reality were blurred as the plays were performed in the public arena of the town square, and the audience invited to vociferous interaction with the actors. The subject matter was both playful and political, and often involved scenes of simultaneously ludic and cruel violence. By exploiting such theatrical forms, uprisings not only engaged with the various urban solidarities which expressed themselves through vernacular drama, but were also able to draw upon models established in the theatre for groups to act as aggregates of individuals. Indeed, it was the collective nature of theatrical productions which distinguished them from other forms of thirteenth-century literature rather than their performed quality, since the vast majority of literature in this period was performed.[29] The theatre involved a series of characters interacting in accordance with predetermined roles which they could then embellish and personalize, embodying tensions between premeditated and spontaneous behaviour.

Theatre in Arras lay at the very heart of civic identity and at the intersection of a variety of urban solidarities, solidarities which were vividly expressed and explored in the subject matter of the plays. The

[27] C. Mazouer, *Le Théâtre français du Moyen Age* (Paris, 1998), 21; C. Symes, *A Common Stage: Theater and Public Life in Medieval Arras* (Ithaca, NY, 2007), 1–20.

[28] Jean Bodel, *Le Jeu de Saint Nicholas*, ed. J. Dufournet (Paris, 2005); *Le Courtois d'Arras*, ed. E. Faral (Paris, 1958); *Le Garçon et l'Aveugle: Jeu du XIIIe siècle*, ed. J. Dufournet, (Paris, 1989); Adam de la Halle, *Le Jeu de la Feuillée*, ed. J. Dufournet (Ghent, 1977); Adam de la Halle, *Le Jeu de Robin et Marion*, ed. J. Dufournet (Paris, 1989).

[29] P. Zumthor, 'Pour une poétique de la voix', *Poétique*, 40 (1979), 514–24. The distinction between 'plays' and other kinds of texts was not always clear: e.g. the text of *Courtois d'Arras* is found in four manuscripts described as a 'lai': Symes, *Common Stage*, 72–3. Although it is tempting to link the Saint-Riquier uprising to Corpus Christi plays, there is no evidence for this particular form of theatre in France at this date.

Jeu de Saint Nicholas on one level thematizes the relationship between the Cathedral and the town of Arras in its structural opposition of the King of Saracens and the very recognizable townspeople.[30] The town's most famous relic was inherently theatrical: a candle apparently blessed by the Virgin, it was housed in a small chapel in the magnificent central square of the town. This candle was linked to a foundation myth of Arras, involving two itinerant minstrels who were guided to it by the Blessed Virgin Mary in order to heal the ergotism then afflicting the inhabitants.[31] The symbol of the confraternity of *jongleurs* or minstrels, the candle became the miraculous object which placed theatrical performance at the centre of Artesian identity and which legitimated cultural performance as a valid expression of communal anxieties and solidarities.[32]

Many uprisings, with their mock and real violence, took place in the same spaces as theatrical performances, promoting a sense of spectacle and assuring the presence of an audience. In 1285, a group of disaffected artisans in Arras violently seized the relic which had been lent temporarily by the Cathedral to the *échevins* to process through the central square of the town known as the 'Petite Place'. The rebels hijacked the procession and redirected it, returning the item to its original home.[33] The town square upon which their protest was focused was a vast open space, some 7,000 metres square, and the scene of numerous vernacular productions beside the small chapel housing the candle of the *confrérie des jongleurs*. The rebels thus physically located themselves in a space in which collective identities were manipulated, and boundaries between present reality, representation, fiction, and wishes for the future were blurred. Focusing the uprising around the relic was also an implicit engagement with the themes exercising contemporary playwrights: for example, the contemporaneous *Jeu de la Feuillée* by Adam de la Halle devotes a long scene to a cutting satire upon the cult of relics, and its lucrative monopoly by religious authorities (ll. 331–6). Engaging with a well-known theatrical theme, in the space in which such drama was staged, situated the rebellion in a

[30] For a detailed exposition of this reading of the play, see Symes, *A Common Stage*, 32–7.

[31] Cf. R. Berger, *Le Nécrologe de la confrérie des jongleurs et des bourgeois d'Arras (1194–1361)* (Arras, 1970), 41–6; P. Chevallot (ed.), *Notre-Dame des ardents d'Arras: Faits et documents* (Abbeville, 1918), 330–1.

[32] Relics could embody communal identity: R. Trexler, *Public Life in Renaissance Florence* (Ithaca, NY, 1991), 57–8.

[33] *Olim*, ii. 245–6; Boutaric, *Actes*, i, no. 2544, 241 (1285); letter of the canons of Arras, in de Locres, *Chronicon Belgicum*, 448; judgment of the count regarding failure of châtelain to execute his judicial duties in ADPC, A901; extract from later copy of cartulary of Artois in ADN, B1463. See also A. Guesnon, 'Adam de la Halle et le *Jeu de la Feuillée*', *Moyen Age*, 28 (1915), 173–233.

landscape of cultural performances which expressed contemporary tensions and sought to debate the frameworks which regulated everyday life.

In Saint-Riquier, the rebels were engaging in a long-standing dispute with the local abbey concerning jurisdictional rights and the authority to condemn violent behaviour.[34] Although there was no clear provocation for their actions in 1264, by engaging with theatrical forms they were able to challenge ecclesiastical prerogatives in judging deviant behaviour, and to exploit theatrical models of acting as part of a troupe. The papal account defined the participants as a 'universitas hominum', evoking a group bound by a sworn oath, and showing each participant with a particular role.[35] The term 'role-play' originates in the use of medieval actors' 'roles', small fragments of text which provided the actors only with their cues and their own lines, and which encouraged improvisation.[36] While the concept of 'roles' evokes the preparedness and repetition of a set of lines or actions, it also evokes a sense of spontaneity, and embodies the tension between the nostalgic referencing of a golden past and the progress of divergence, the backward/forward-looking oscillation of uprisings. The participants in the Saint-Riquier uprising played predetermined roles, from the costumed bearers of the 'relics', mock fighters and the invoker of St Riquier, to the assembled crowd which cried out 'miracle'. As in medieval theatre, the participants had distinct parts to play, and yet depended upon each other for their cues and for the context which would give sense to their own actions. The roles provided the thread which bound together the participants as a group, and which still allowed for dramatic spontaneity.

The Saint-Riquier rebels, in their careful planning, prepared elaborate props and drew upon techniques which were used in the theatre. The reliquaries were built both to mimic and to mock the true reliquaries of St Riquier and St Vigor: 'relics' were acquired and disguised, costumes were carefully prepared, and even an elaborate mock-chapel was built.[37] The props provided a framework around which the protesters could perform their planned display, and improvise further upon the chosen themes. Much was carefully choreographed, drawing upon theatrical techniques for ensuring dramatically effective interactions between performers: the lewd dancing, which, according to the papal bull, even

34 These disputes can be traced in Boutaric, *Actes*, i, nos. 548, 49 (1260); 619, 56 (1261); 861, 78 (1264); etc.

35 *Registre d'Urbain*, ii. 314.

36 G. Runnalls, 'An Actor's Rôle in a French Morality Play', *French Studies*, 42 (1988), 398–407.

37 On disguise, see A. Hawkins and L. Merricks, '"Wee be black as Hell": Ritual, Disguise and Rebellion', *Rural History*, 4/1 (1993), 41–53.

involved the *échevins* and mayor of the town, was discussed in advance, though its precise form responded spontaneously to the prevalent mood. Moreover, the dancing invited the participation of those who had been, until that moment, mere spectators. The type of collective behaviour undertaken in the theatre involved not only the actors in a given play, but the audience too, as boundaries between representation and reality, stage and world, became blurred: often actors would wander amongst the crowd, and shouting and verbal engagement with the characters was conventional.[38] The actual actors in the pre-prepared combat in Saint-Riquier were the two fighters and the bearers of the 'relics' who called on them to stop fighting, but the sense of the scene depended upon the large crowd gathered behind the bearers of the relics, participating in the joke, and acting out their mock incredulity: the 'miracle' depended upon being seen in order to be meaningful. Of course, the scene gained even more potency from the disparity between the different roles of the various members of the crowd: some deliberately assumed the role of pretending to believe in the miracle and raising a parodic cheer, but those further off, unaware of the deception, must have entertained a genuine belief in the authenticity of what they saw before them. Far from being an irrational mass, this crowd was of shifting composition, and challenged ecclesiastical frameworks through dramatic collective behaviour.

The growing crowd, gradually coalescing around a group of individuals with a planned programme of action, was a frequent phenomenon: collectivities were both planned in advance and spontaneously aggregated. In Péronne in 1308, a violent uprising was initiated by a small group of local notables who attacked the *prévôt* of the town and *doyen* on account of their investigation into the levying of the tax known as the *maltôte*: as concentric circles of spectators joined in, 3,000 townspeople apparently gathered together.[39] The *prévôt* was acting on the orders of the royal deputy, the *bailli* of Vermandois, and according to the 'arrêt', the mayor, *jurés,* and entire commune were culpable in this instance. This was not a protest about levels of taxation, but rather about who had the right to levy taxes. According to the repressive edict imposed by the Paris Parlement after the event, the rebels shouted out battle cries and called for the death of their opponents. While the attribution of such shouts form part of the stereotypical characterization of the uprising by the authorities as irrationally violent, they also reveal a repertoire of theatrical lines to be spoken and elaborated. The prevalence of theatre in urban cultures which were, in any case, profoundly performative provided models of

[38] J. Enders, *Death by Drama and Other Medieval Urban Legends* (Chicago, 2002), 10.
[39] Boutaric, *Actes*, ii, no. 3517, 51 (1308).

cooperative action which were drawn upon in uprisings carried out not by uncontrollable and spontaneous mobs, but by groups of people with interdependent roles, combining planned strategies and dangerous improvisation. These techniques were also used for the expression of the moral, religious, and political frameworks which regulated urban life and provided 'grammars' of violence: the very frameworks which uprisings contested and negotiated.

2. FORMS OF LEGITIMATE VIOLENCE

Violent punishment was theatre, a gruesome performance in which executioner and condemned enacted scripted roles, where the crowd watched and sometimes became involved, and where there was always room for improvisation. Such punishments were the most explicit manifestation of jurisdictional authority in a range of practices which concretized civic relationships and demonstrated the authority of one community over another by claiming the right to regulate behaviour. These 'grammars of violence' represented more than just interpretative frameworks for assessing the harmful import of individual or collective violence; they represented ideas of community, and were vehemently and violently debated by groups who drew on the same punitive gestures to assert their own legitimacy.[40] The choice of the Petite Place in Arras as the site of the violence in the 1285 uprising drew also upon the jurisdictional connotations of the space: this was the arena in which judicial violence was publicly dispensed. Far from being aberrant and disconnected, the protestors' violence claimed a function akin to that played by hegemonic violence, and the rebels thus challenged the monopoly of a single group over jurisdiction.

The violence in Laon in 1295 replayed gestures from a variety of discourses of legitimate violence, and far from embodying only the irrational and cruel impulses of the crowd as suggested by repressive reactions, communicated their reluctance to accept the regulatory frameworks imposed by rival groups in civic life.[41] In order to refute two disrespectful

[40] Marc Boone makes a similar point in characterizing violence by the *métiers* in Flanders as an assertion of their own integral role in the power structures of the towns and a claim to the legitimate use of force: '*Armes, coursses, assemblees et commocions*: Les Gens de métiers et l'usage de la violence dans la société urbaine flamande à la fin du Moyen Age', *Revue du Nord*, 359 (2005), 7–33.

[41] This revolt has been discussed in detail by Denton, 'The Second Revolt', 79–92. Denton identifies the six main sources regarding the revolt: the dean of Laon's account for the king (BN, Pic. 284, no. 23); two letters by the bishop of Laon (BN, Lat. 4042, fo. 128^{v}, and in a formulary edited in Varin, *Archives de Reims*, i. 289–91); a letter to the pope from the cathedral churches of the province (BN, Pic. 284, no. 23); three copies of a papal letter

knights' apparent belief in their superiority to the commune, the townspeople used swords to strike their victims, reproducing the chivalric forms of violence which the noblemen were apt to attribute exclusively to their own group. Particularly striking is the reproduction, and subversion, of forms of judicial punishment, as the crowd contested the two noblemen's jurisdictional immunity. The two men were pelted with stones by the angry crowd, lapidation being a punitive judicial motif at least since biblical times.[42] Humiliating discourse, 'diversis injuriis, dampnis, gravaminibus et pressuris' apparently accompanied the physical blows, intensifying their rhetorical impact.[43] The victims were dragged from the Cathedral by their feet and their hair, a humiliating inversion, and perhaps even a form of dehumanization, since this was a method by which animals would be dragged. There is an irony to this process of dehumanization, given that the polemic of chroniclers and legal authorities often attempted to discredit rebels in the same way, describing them as 'bestiales' and their behaviour as 'inhumaniter'. Repeated characterization of rebels in the sources as animals, hungry for violence and slaughter, fundamentally challenged the meaningfulness of rebellious gestures as beasts were not thought to communicate; and yet the rebels themselves engaged with such rhetoric by attempting to dehumanize *their* rivals, demonstrating their clear belief that *they* were acting in the interests of the common good and civilized order, and revealing the whole process of uprising and repression to be interactive and reciprocal.

While dragging their victims along, the crowd also whipped them, evoking atonement and penance, and obliging the victims to suffer for their earlier transgressions: whipping had particular resonance in the late thirteenth century, given the notoriety of flagellant processions, but it had a much longer history, and was often evoked in hagiographical texts whether as self-inflicted penance or as penance imposed by spiritual masters in the interests of ever greater spiritual purity.[44] When the victims reached their destination, they were forced to stand up, a gesture which

sent to the king, archbishop of Reims, and bishops and chapters of the province, and to the papal executors, and replicated in a papal bull (BN, Pic. 284, nos. 25, 24; AN, J701, no. 108; see also G. Digard (ed.), *Les Registres de Boniface VIII*, 4 vols. (Rome, 1907–39), i, no. 1533, 561); the decree of the Parlement of Paris (Giry, *Documents*, no. LIII, 147–8).

42 Pope Boniface VIII's letter from Anagni, 30 Aug. 1295, to the archbishop of Reims regarding the revolt: *Registres de Boniface*, i, no. 356, 126–7; e.g. 2 Cor. 11: 25.

43 'Various insults, damages, troubles and oppressions': *Registres de Boniface*, iii, no. 4010.

44 e.g. Elisabeth of Hungary: Jacobus de Voragine, *The Golden Legend: Readings on the Saints*, tr. W. Granger Ryan, 2 vols. (Princeton, 1991), ii, no. 168, 302–18. For a discussion of the flagellants, see C. Lawrence, *The Friars: The Impact of the Early Mendicant Movement on Western Society* (London, 1994), 117–21.

gave a judicial air to proceedings, as victims of judicial violence were usually also expected to raise themselves to face their punishment.[45] One of the victims was thrown into jail: there, after lengthy torture, his tendons were cut, and he died a few days later.

Contesting judicial frameworks and their jurisdictional embodiment in communities meant that boundaries were all-important. Prison bounds were renegotiated during the Saint Quentin revolt, when, instead of allowing members of the commune to be imprisoned by the monks of the abbey, the townspeople established new limits by imprisoning the abbey cook and a servant. Before leaving the abbey, the burghers destroyed the garden gate, indicating their anger with the way in which the chapter claimed exclusive jurisdictional rights over areas of land.[46] The protestors preceded their physical gestures with a volley of verbal abuse, in order to reinforce the sense of the 'otherness' of their target.

The participants in the Abbeville revolt of 1311 similarly drew upon structures of civic solidarity, led by the mayor and the *échevins*, whilst expressing a collective jurisdictional identity by chasing and stoning a cleric named Raoul Coullart, who had been acquitted by the local ecclesiastical court of the murder of a certain Jean Lefèvre.[47] The protesters visibly and performatively rejected the immunity of ecclesiastical space, forcibly removing their victim from a place of sanctuary to a location of legal accountability. This violence was part of a long chain of outbreaks of tension between communal and ecclesiastical authority; a 1281 Act of the Parlement heavily fined the inhabitants of Abbeville for attacks upon the abbey itself.[48]

Debates concerning jurisdiction were centred on more complex disputes about the right to regulate everyday life which were more complex than polarized struggles between abbey and town, or even spiritual and temporal powers. The uprising at Abbeville involved more fluid combinations of shifting solidarities: this was no mere mob, but a shifting coalition of interests. Abbeville was a town beset by feuding, and in the midst of this jurisdictional quarrel, deep-set rivalries between powerful families were being played out: the abbey refused to arrest one of its own whom the town held responsible for a murder. The mayor during the uprising of 1311 was named Jean L'Orfèvre, the name of the original murder victim.[49] While he cannot have been the murdered man, as

[45] M. Merback, *The Thief, the Cross and the Wheel: Pain and the Spectacle of Punishment in Medieval and Renaissance Europe* (London, 1999), 132, 138.

[46] *Archives de Saint Quentin*, i, no. 234, 213.

[47] Boutaric, *Actes*, i, no. 3807, 77 (1310).

[48] Ibid., no. 2317, 222 (1281).

[49] AMA, MS 115, fo. 51^{v}.

another documented incident of 1314 apparently occurred 'en la seconde mairie Jehan l'Orfèvre',[50] the L'Orfèvre family must have been an important one within the town oligarchy. Likewise, although Raoul Coullart, who was accused of the murder and victimized by the protest, was apparently a cleric, the documents reveal a number of mayors and local notables with the surname Coullart in this period: indeed, only in 1306, the mayor was Fremin Coullart, and again in 1371, Esteule Coullart was mayor.[51] This evidence, though only circumstantial, implies the status of both the L'Orfèvres and the Coullarts as important families in the Abbeville oligarchy. In turn, this challenges the assumption that disputes between the municipal and the ecclesiastical authorities point to two polarized worlds; rather, the two spheres were interconnected by kinship ties (the Coullart family penetrating both contexts), and interfamilial rivalries intensified disputes, allowing issues of civic pride and identity potently to coincide with urban faction and rivalries.[52] Whereas feuding was categorized as a crime of *lèse-commune*, and heavily punishable, the dichotomy between commune and family could be softened and manipulated.[53] The Abbeville uprising demonstrates that interfamilial rivalries and communal interest, unlawful violence and jurisdictional 'grammars', were not necessarily seen in contrasting terms: feuding relations overlapped with struggles about the structure of the commune and its various jurisdictional authorities.

The crown reaction to the revolt itself had the conflictual context of rising tension between the kings of France and England, again placing the Abbeville uprising on a broader canvas of overlapping jurisdiction and personal hostilities.[54] Earlier in 1307, the mayor and two *échevins* had been accused of corrupt administration by the other *échevins* and many members of the commune. The *seneschal* of the count of Ponthieu, an

[50] Ibid., fo. 52^r. A striking further example of the overlap between clan rivalries, jurisdictional tensions, and socio-economic concerns is provided by the inter-urban war between Lille and Douai in this period: E. Lecuppre-Desjardin, 'De l'invective à la prise de conscience identitaire: La Guerre entre Douai et Lille (1284–1285)', *Civilisation Médiévale*, 18 (2007), 415–33.

[51] AMA, MS 115, fo. 55^v; Fremin Coullart was also mayor in 1276, cf. ibid., fo. 18^r; MS 114, fo. 36^r.

[52] A comparison may be drawn with the feuding of the famous Van Artevelde family in Ghent: D. Nicholas, *The Van Arteveldes of Ghent: The Varieties of Vendetta and the Hero in History* (Ithaca, NY, 1988).

[53] e.g. AMA, MS 115, fo. 22^v: a feud of 1232 between the families of Clément le Charbonnier and Jacquement de Sénarmont, which even involved the parties renouncing their loyalty to the commune in order to pursue their enmity, was punished by fines and the destruction of the parties' houses.

[54] Cf. M. Vale, *The Origins of the Hundred Years War* (Oxford, 1996), 71–2; M. Prestwich, *Edward I* (London, 1988), 71–3.

officer of the king of England, had taken control of the commune in place of the accused men. The mayor and *échevins,* however, appealed to the king of France, who used his officer, the *prévôt* of Saint-Riquier to support their case. Philip IV thus became involved in the affair in 1308, and instigated an investigation which finally decided in favour of the English *sénéchal.* The matter was reopened in 1311, when the former mayor and *échevins* demanded a retrial.[55] Against this background of tension, the king of France claimed to investigate the 1311 uprising himself and ratified the local ecclesiastical verdict, instructing the local *bailli* to enforce the obedience of the commune.[56]

Engaging with other forms of legitimate violence which punctuated the urban landscape provided rebellious actions with rhetorical force, and transformed angry mobs into strategic bodies acting upon models of carefully structured judicial bodies. Judicial violence was underwritten by a discourse characterizing the common good as the practical well-being of the community, a discourse which placed law and its apparently necessary violence as the essential component of a rightly ordered community.[57] Indeed, Augustine's definition of just war proposed that peace and the common good were only to be assured via the rightful use of force within a legal framework; the virtuous soldier was characterized as judge.[58] The judicial forms of violence used by rebels firmly asserted the motivation of their uprising within the paradigm of the practical common good of the community.

3. CIVIC CEREMONIAL

The competing authority of the various communities within towns could likewise be expressed through civic ceremonial, visualizing power and the right to condemn particular forms of violent behaviour. Through multiple layers of civic symbolism, the large open town squares were ideal sites for both manifestations and violent contestations of power and identity by the civic community.[59] In this setting, frameworks of desirable civic

[55] Thierry, *Monuments*, 76–8.

[56] *Olim*, iii. 542.

[57] M. Kempshall, *The Common Good in Late Medieval Political Thought* (Oxford, 1999), 13–14.

[58] See Augustine, *De Civitate Dei,* ed. M. Dods (London, 2000), 19.13.

[59] Control of such squares operated both on a symbolic and a strategic level: M. Boone, 'Urban Space and Political Conflict in Late Medieval Flanders', *Journal of Interdisciplinary History*, 32/4 (2002), 621–40.

behaviour were visualized through performances by clearly articulated corporate bodies.[60]

The town square in Arras, site of the 1285 uprisings, was the symbolic centre of civic life. War and peace were announced in this square, and changes of government and law, while the town hall magisterially dominated proceedings. A monument known as the 'pierron' provided a symbol of civic identity and oligarchical rule and its column, supported by four lions, was used by *échevins* to swear oaths upon. The 'bretèque' was the balcony used for official communal announcements, and surveyed the square imperiously.[61] In an adjacent square, the 'Grand' Place', another famous form of spectacular violence regularly took place: that of jousting tournaments, odd to imagine in the centre of a thriving town. The square was also the hub of the commercial life of the city, and markets regularly took place in both the Petite and the Grand' Place.

However, the very connotations of civic success also marked the sources of tension in this apparently flourishing town.[62] The city's dependence on commerce meant that it was particularly susceptible to the shifts taking place at the end of the twelfth and beginning of the thirteenth centuries, as the Italian merchants increasingly bought directly from the producers towards the end of the 1260s, and as luxury cloth became more and more popular. At the same time, the town became overwhelmed by enormous debts, which were further exacerbated by external pressures, such as the requirement of 6,000 livres to pay for the army in the Languedoc in 1272. Heavy taxation was required, and those most affected by it became increasingly resentful of the corrupt oligarchy, their great wealth, and opulent lifestyles; a large *assise* in 1287 provoked much discontent.[63] Fiscal abuse was the subject of satire amongst the famous poets of Arras, and engendered anger amongst the populace, who in 1282 petitioned the count of Artois to investigate the corrupt behaviour of the

[60] D. Nicholas, *Urban Europe 1100–1700* (London, 2003), 167–73. The role of urban processions and their representation of the body of citizens is discussed by M. James, 'Ritual, Drama and the Social Body', *Past and Present*, 98 (1983), 6–29; K. Lilley, *City and Cosmos: The Medieval World in Urban Form* (London, 2009), 158. But processions also embodied hierarchies and, as well as negotiating conflict, could also provoke it: K. Ashley and W. Hüskin, *Moving Subjects: Processional Performances in the Middle Ages and the Renaissance* (Amsterdam, 2001), 17.

[61] M. Ungureanu, *La Bourgeoisie naissante: Société et littérature bourgeoises d'Arras aux XIIe et XIIIe siècles* (Arras, 1955), 68–70; E. Van der Neste, *Tournois, joûtes, pas d'armes dans les villes de Flandre à la fin du Moyen Age* (Paris, 1996).

[62] 'Powerful, an ancient city, full of riches, revelling in wealth and rejoicing in prosperity': quoted in R. Berger, *Littérature et société arrageoise: Les Chansons et dits artésiens* (Arras, 1982), 104–5.

[63] Bougard, *Arras*, 62–6.

échevinage.[64] In 1302, the count created a body of twenty-four men which would represent the populace more fairly and stem the abuse, though this created so much tension amongst the *échevins* that another investigation had to follow in 1305, revealing corruption, fraud, violence, and murder. The case of Jean Cabos, unfairly imprisoned and tortured for having spoken out about their tax abuse, is indicative of the general atmosphere.[65] The *échevinage* was inflexible in its composition, into which ordinary members of the commune had no hope of penetrating, and from its first mention in 1111, into the late thirteenth century, the same family names reappear: Pouchin, Crespin, Louchart, and Cosset, for example.[66] Yet many of the strongest critics of the *échevinage*'s conduct were themselves from notable families.[67] So the term 'commun' in accounts of unrest referred to a wide variety of social groups, including rich merchants, rich drapers such as Thomas de Bourriane, and those of patrician extraction such as Robert Nazart: they were drawn together by their opposition to the current regulatory body.[68] Just as the corrupt *échevins* expressed their collective identity in the square via sworn oaths, announcements made from the balcony of the town hall, and the famous procession which was disrupted in 1285, so the rebels mimicked these rites in order to challenge the way in which the community was currently administered. They mocked the procession of the *échevins* with the relics by violently disrupting it in the very space of civic ceremonial. The uprising was described in the decree of the Parlement as 'conspiracionis seu taquenhanis': the latter term implies a ludic outburst, but the former, while intended to vilify the rebels as wily and frightening, draws attention to their own constructed collective identity.[69]

In any case, despite the *échevins*' best attempts, civic identity never was the monopoly of a single group, but was constantly contested, notably by craft groups. The 1285 revolt had an added social dimension, as most of the rebels were artisans and contested not only the current administration of the town council, but also the current composition of the official craft solidarities, as well as the attempted exclusion of such communities from the political life of the town. The *métiers* had long represented a powerful and vociferous series of groups, and mentions of associations forming

[64] e.g. *Jeu de la Feuillée*, ll. 223–4; also Berger, *Littérature*, nos. 2 and 13, which lampoon civic corruption in the 1260s.

[65] ADPC, A1009. See J. Lestocquoy, *Les Dynasties bourgeoises d'Arras* (Arras, 1945), 62.

[66] Ungureanu, *Bourgeoisie*, 38.

[67] Berger, *Nécrologe*, 49.

[68] Ibid. 41.

[69] *Olim*, ii. 245.

amongst these professions date from 1111.[70] In 1253, all associations were (unsuccessfully) banned by the *échevinage*, as they were perceived as hotbeds of sedition, in recognition of their potential for aggressively affirming collective identities.[71] After returning the reliquary to the Cathedral, the 1285 rebels apparently rushed to the houses of the most prominent members of the *gueudes*, and seized their banners. The banners were an expression of militant identity for craft groups, evoking both symbolic notions of community and profession, and chivalric military connotations.[72] The protestors engaged with a clearly delineated form of collective action, in order to challenge the very nature of the collectivities involved. They then paraded the banners around the town, shouting threats to the councillors. According to the count, they also seized the keys of the town gates, challenging ownership of the boundaries of the town.[73]

The rebellion was announced by the sounding of the town bell or *tocsin*. Many of these communes were granted bells at the same time as their administrative independence, and the bell became a tangible symbol of a glorious civic identity.[74] Moreover, when communes were dissolved because of rebellious behaviour, the bell was often confiscated as a focal point of sedition. In Arras, the belfry housed three crucial bells: the 'cloque des ouvriers' which regulated working hours, the 'bancloque' which marked ceremonies of the *échevins*, and the 'cloche des effrois' which was sounded to warn of fires, invasions, or other great dangers.[75] Sounding the 'bancloque' located the uprising within a framework of civic time, regulating the municipal and commercial life of the town.[76] The resounding toll of the huge bell in the town of Laon set apart the time of an uprising in 1295, marking it as distinct and profoundly meaningful for the community.[77] Violence was provoked when two noblemen struck the submayor of the city on the jaw; harsh and insulting words apparently preceded the physical violence. The noblemen, realizing the potential implications of their action, fled to the Cathedral where they were sheltered by a clerical relative. But the citizens of Laon rang the *tocsin* announcing the start of a bloody expression of their dissatisfaction with the situation, and deliber-

[70] For a more nuanced evaluation of the appearance of a 'régime corporatif', see Chevalier, 'Corporations', 18.

[71] See Berger, *Littérature*, 83–4.

[72] Carrying an unfurled banner carried signified a state of open war: M. Keen, *The Laws of War in the Late Middle Ages* (London, 1965), 105.

[73] ADPC, A901.

[74] e.g. C. Patart, *Les Cloches civiles de Namur, Fosses et Tournai* (Brussels, 1976), 190–4.

[75] Ungureanu, *Bourgeoisie*, 66.

[76] J. Le Goff, 'Le Temps du travail dans la "crise" du XIVe siècle: Du temps médiéval au temps moderne', in *Pour un autre Moyen Age* (Paris, 1977), 66–80.

[77] Giry, *Documents*, no. LII, 145; *Registres de Boniface*, i, no. 355, 125.

ately setting this time apart. Some of the sworn councillors, other potentates, and a large number of armed men stormed the Cathedral and dragged out the two noblemen and the clerk from their putative sanctuary. The crowd then displayed all its brutality, kicking, wounding, and pelting their three victims with stones, knives, and swords. They dragged them back to the house of the submayor, and one of the noblemen was then thrown into the municipal prison. The noblemen had challenged civic pride and identity. Moreover, the Cathedral had offended the jurisdictional autonomy of the commune by sheltering the men, and by positing its superior immunity. The townspeople progressed through symbolically laden spaces, from the Cathedral, to the town square, to the town prison, geographically representing their collective identity in relation to the challenge presented to it, and dramatically closing the town gates.

The right to punish this revolt provoked a lengthy struggle between king and pope, and the uprising itself was only one amongst a cascade of events as various communities debated their rights and relations towards one another. A notarial act recorded the dean of Laon's version of events presented to the king in early March 1296.[78] Two letters from the bishop of Laon, Robert de Trote, to the Pope and the priests of Laon respectively, subsequently repeated the same sequence of events, urging the pope to take action in place of the king.[79] In May 1296, the cathedral churches of the province of Reims also wrote to the Pope, describing the events, and pleading for assistance.[80] This latter account formed the basis of the three papal letters of August 1296 on the subject, addressed to the king, the archbishop of Reims, and other ecclesiastical dignitaries of the province, and to the archdeacons of Orléans and Troyes, the papal executors.[81] A papal bull issued later reiterated the same story, and claimed jurisdiction.[82] After an altercation lasting over a year, and situated at the heart of broader debates between king and pope over clerical taxation and the relationship between spiritual and temporal power, the king eventually established his sole right to take punitive action.[83] The decree of the Parlement of Paris confiscated many of the symbols of the commune, and imposed a large fine.[84] The commune was ordered to undertake a

[78] BN, Pic. 284, no. 22, quoted in Denton, 'Second Uprising', 80–2.
[79] In Varin, *Archives de Reims*, i, 289–91.
[80] BN, Pic. 284, no. 23, quoted in Denton, 'Second Uprising', 80–3.
[81] *Registres de Boniface*, i, respectively nos. 356, 355, and 363 (126, 125, 129).
[82] Ibid., no. 1533, 560–7.
[83] The whole affair is described in detail in Denton, 'Second Uprising', particularly the debate between king and pope, 79–90.
[84] Giry, *Documents*, no. LIII, 148; *Olim*, ii. 384–5; Boutaric, *Actes*, i, no. 2895, 289 (1295).

quasi-liturgical procession to the Cathedral, the site of the original offence, and to carry wax effigies of their three murdered victims, identical in weight to the corpses. The procession involved the entire community, and obliged them to assume moral responsibility for what had happened through an act of collective penance. The king's response focused upon his temporal jurisdictional rights, whilst drawing upon the rhetoric of spiritual jurisdiction. The punishment provided a spectacle which denigrated the jurisdictional pretensions of both townspeople and pope.

Many accounts of revolts referred more specifically to the corporate constitution of rebellious groups. The revolt of 1311 in Saint Quentin, essentially a conflict of jurisdiction between the municipality and the local abbey, was described in the punitive sentence of the Paris Parlement as led by 'majore[. . .] et jurat[ibus] ville Sancti Quentini . . . cum magna multitudine armatorum'; the inhabitants were condemned to a huge fine and to pay damages to the abbey.[85] The tension had been long-standing, fuelled partly by the specific question of jurisdiction in the *faubourg d'Isle*, and partly by economic considerations of rights of pasture.[86] Amidst vilifications of all the participants, the Parlement recognized the corporate and civic nature of the groups involved: rather than an irrational angry crowd, the revolt was undertaken by a carefully structured solidarity which was modelled upon, and thus engaged with the interests of, the municipality. While the involvement of the mayors and *échevins* was recounted in such sources primarily in order to shock, it nevertheless indicates the logical and differentiated structure of collective behaviour. These theatrical uprisings drew on civic structures and models of corporate behaviour in order to defend or contest the ways in which those same structures claimed to regulate municipal life, and, more particularly, to regulate violence.

4. LITURGICAL PROCESSIONS

But secular law and power were not the only types of authority shaping urban life, and they overlapped with religious paradigms which attempted to establish moral authority. The collective violence of urban uprisings challenged the exclusivity of ecclesiastical dominance over communal morality again by appropriating religious and liturgical models of collective behaviour. Essentially protestors were still contesting claims to regulate and define behaviour (including violence), and often did so by mimicking liturgical elements in their own violent actions. As ecclesiastical bodies

[85] Edited in *Archives de Saint Quentin*, i, no. 234, 213.

[86] Ibid., p. cxxxviii. Lalou, 'Les Révoltes', 169.

sought to express a spiritual framework for the community through religious processions encompassing a number of different spaces within the town, rebels disrupted such processions and reconfigured such claims to moral authority.[87]

For the annual Pentecostal festivities in Arras, the cathedral canons would process the relic to the town square to hand it over temporarily to the *échevins*, who would then advance ceremonially through the town in a display of symbolic legitimation.[88] In 1285, the procession was disrupted: the protestors carried the relic back to the Cathedral, damaged it on the way, and violently challenged the solemn form of the procession, reversing its implications for the public spaces through which it passed. Whereas the spaces of the official route had indicated the sacrality of the relics, and were in turn sacralized by their presence, the rebels reconfigured these connotations and rewrote the symbolism of various spaces. By depriving the *échevins* of the relic with its blessed connotations, the protestors implicitly rejected the councillors' role in establishing moral and spiritual frameworks for the day-to-day life of the town. Moreover, this message was achieved by assuming the interdependent roles suggested by the constitution of the ecclesiastical procession itself which visibly reproduced the hierarchical structures of the Cathedral and of the municipal council.

These mock-liturgical roles were even more explicit in an earlier uprising in the nearby town of Saint Valéry in 1232 where the townspeople furthered their long-standing hatred of the monks of the local abbey with a series of violent and blasphemous actions, including processing around the church, explicitly assuming the roles of the various members of the abbatial hierarchy, shouting and sprinkling cursed water on the ground, and then setting fire to the abbey and passing an image of the Virgin Mary and of John the Baptist through the flames while chanting the *miserere*.[89] The sole surviving account in a papal bull is evidently exaggerated to highlight the diabolical and blasphemous character of the protestors. It nevertheless indicates the profound desire of the townspeople to contest ecclesiastical dominance over the moral life of the town. Likewise, in the Saint-Riquier uprising, the various participants assumed the roles of different figures within the liturgical hierarchy and municipality, in order both to draw upon the structures of those collectivities, and to contest their moral and regulatory authority: men clothed in animal skins played the role of monks processing the relic; two more played the

[87] See B. Hanawalt and K. Reyerson (eds.), *City and Spectacle in Medieval Europe* (Minneapolis, 1994), pp. ix–xviii.

[88] De Locres, *Chronicon Belgicum*, 432.

[89] Thierry, *Monuments*, 705–8.

role of uncontrollable townspeople; another played the role of an ecclesiastical dignitary calling for peace in the name of the saint. Physical violence here was never more than ludic, but teasingly subverted the moral authority of the abbey. Those involved not only challenged the abbey's hierarchical sway, but also appropriated its right to work miracles, and, in the process, claimed those miracles to be as fictional as the Church's right to stem interpersonal violence as staged by the two actors.

It is particularly striking that so many of these disturbances focused upon relics which were integral to the identity, often to the foundation myth, of the town. By mimicking the relics of St Riquier, the local saint who was said to have welcomed two Irish monks to the area in 590, converted to Christianity, and founded the town's abbey, the protestors contested not only ownership of these relics, but their very relevance to the thirteenth-century life of the town.[90] They parodically subverted the liturgical devotional practices and respectful adoration surrounding the relics, and, on one level, contested the monopolization by the monks of the moral authority embodied in this foundation myth. On another level, the challenge was more profound, as protestors challenged the centrality of a sixth-century saint to their contemporary sense of municipal identity and moral economy. The monks of Saint-Riquier controversially and regularly attempted to impose a general truce during the festive periods and claimed unique jurisdiction over any violent misbehaviour taking place during such times: they argued that, as representatives of St Riquier himself, they were the legitimate protectors of the town's well-being. The claim had engendered a number of violent quarrels, notably in the October celebrations of 1263, when the townspeople (mayor and *échevins*) were condemned for using swords and other arms for the purpose of imposing justice themselves.[91] As the mocking protestors in May 1264 cried out that St Riquier had miraculously resolved their staged fight, they contested the relevance of intervention by a spiritual power in the regulation of interpersonal violence.

The embodiment of spiritual authority in liturgical practices was contested in Beauvais in 1305 by deliberate and pointed disruption of devotional forms. Conflicts here between the commune and the ecclesiastical authorities were common, frequently spilling over into violence. The 1305 rebellion, recorded in a number of chronicles and repressive royal and episcopal edicts, was provoked specifically by the bishop's

[90] Whether this indicates religious scepticism on the part of the protesters remains a vexed question; clearly, though, they contested the implications of the relics for their community.

[91] Boutaric, *Actes*, i, no. 862, 79 (1264); *Olim*, i. 604.

attempt to oblige everyone to use the episcopally owned mills along the river, and to pay for the privilege.[92] The magistrates of the town proclaimed the abolition of this due, and officially announced that everyone had the right to build bridges across the river. In retaliation, the bishop's men destroyed the houses of a number of townspeople, who reacted by building barricades and attacking significant places such as the bishop's palace, two chapels, and the tower. The bishop had to flee the town, and promptly began besieging it with a large armed force. Following royal intervention, he was able to re-enter Beauvais, only to be greeted by renewed violence. The fighting continued for several months until, eventually, the royal power was able to impose a settlement: the commune was obliged to pay for restitution for damaged goods and a huge fine of 10,000 livres to the king; but the bishop was also obliged to pay a composition of 6,000 livres; arbitrators imposed further penances and a fine of 8,000 livres on the townspeople.[93] Economically motivated, the uprising once again embodied clashing notions of community and struggles for the right to impose moral or judicial authority. The canvas was one of long-standing and shifting rivalries: in 1149, the bishop, chapter, and commune memorably allied against the domineering nobles, and a quarrel in 1199 between the bishop and the commune ended in a shared hatred and contestation of the royal power.[94] A rebellion in 1233 began with a vertically divided 'dissensio inter burgenses, minoribus insurgentibus contra majores'; the royal power intervened in order to support the former group, but the bishop contested royal intervention, placing the diocese under an interdict himself, and calling upon papal support.[95] The 1305 rebellion was described in most of the sources as a 'dissensio', following the model of the destructive crowd. Nevertheless, even while keen to

[92] Letters from Philip IV: Giry, *Documents*, no. LXII, 162–4; no. LXV, 168 (from P. Louvet, *Histoire du diocese de Beauvais*, 2 vols. (Paris, 1631–5), ii. 495, 508); letter from the bishop to the clergy of Beauvais: this entire document is published as a footnote to Giry, *Documents*, no. LXII, 163–4, from Louvet, *Histoire*, ii. 492; settlement issued by royal commissioners: Giry, *Documents*, no. LXVI, 169–73, from Louvet, *Histoire*, ii. 515; decree of Paris Parlement: Giry, *Documents*, no. LXIII, 164. Likewise, chronicle accounts: Guillaume de Nangis, *Chronique*, 592; Girardus de Fracheto, *Chronique, RHGF* xxi. 26; *Excerpta e Memoriali Historiarum Johannis a Sancto Victore, RHGF* xxi. 645. See also Lalou, 'Les Révoltes', 165–60.

[93] Respectively: Giry, *Documents*, no. LXIV, 166; no. LXV, 168; LXVI, 170–3. Also Louvet, *Histoire*, ii. 501, 508, 515. See Ganiage, *Histoire de Beauvais*, 52–3.

[94] See L.-H. Labande, *Histoire de Beauvais et de ses institutions communales jusqu'au commencement du XV siècle* (Paris, 1892), 63–5.

[95] 'Dissension between the great and the lesser burghers of the town': Guillaume de Nangis, *Chronique*, i. 185; *Alberici monachi Trium Fontium chronicon, RHGF* xxi. 607; Philippe Mousket, *Chronique rimée, RHGF* xxii. 58; Vincent de Beauvais, *Speculum historiale*, ed. M. Taraye (Paris, 1999), bk 30.

discredit the rebels as an irrational rabble, the sources evoked a more complex model of collective action: the 'congregata communia' was traced back to a meeting of the ringleaders, and the phrase 'per conspirationem' both vilified the rebels, and evoked the interplay of carefully planned stage-direction and spontaneous improvisation by the angry crowd.[96]

New boundaries were established and old ones broken during the course of this revolt, physically and visibly altering the relative position of the ecclesiastical community within the town. Shutting the gates had a strategic purpose, as it served to exclude the bishop and physically to mark the townspeople's rejection of his jurisdictional and economic dominance. As the rebels invaded the bishop's palace, they negated his authority and rejected the boundaries imposed by this hated figure. They freed those incarcerated in the bishop's prison, breaking down its doors 'violenter'.[97] The weapons used by the rebels mainly had military connotations, with stones also spontaneously thrown: the townspeople appeared 'arbalistis, telis, jaculis, clypeis, lapidibus, gladiis et fustibus'.[98] Though the rhetorical accumulation matches the polemical purpose of the bishop in producing this account, the rhetoric of the violence itself is also clear; the rebels were self-consciously combating the bishop on his own terms as he attacked with a militarily structured corps of armed men. Violence was focused on the bishop's palace. Large portions of the building were burnt, evoking religious connotations of total annihilation and purification with biblical precedent.[99] Particular emphasis was placed upon the shattering of doors and windows, even within the palace, demonstrating again the symbolic importance of breaking old boundaries and establishing new ones. Strikingly, the rebels seized all the wine and food they could find, but, instead of consuming it, they poured it all away, as if they were now themselves liturgically washing clean a corrupt place.[100] The crowd was not carried away by the sight of riches to pillage and plunder, but symbolically visualized its disdain for the bishop and his way of life, and a refusal to honour him in the manner he expected: reproducing liturgical forms, the crowd likewise drew upon ecclesiastical models of acting as a body. More

[96] The arbitrators' settlement: Giry, *Documents*, no. LXVI, 169; Louvet, *Histoire*, ii. 515.

[97] Bishop's letter to the clergy of Beauvais: footnote to Giry, no. LXII, 163; Louvet, *Histoire*, ii. 488.

[98] 'Bows, darts, javelins, shields, stones, swords and clubs', ibid.

[99] Cf. Gen. 9: 24.

[100] Bishop's letter to the clergy of Beauvais: footnote to Giry, *Documents*, no. LXII, 163; Parlement's decree edited ibid., no. LXIV, 166; Louvet, *Histoire*, ii. 481, 501.

obviously symbolic was the desecration of holy places.[101] The two chapels, according to the records of the Paris Parlement, were ransacked by the rebels, who focused upon the books, chalices, and other rich ornamentation: they destroyed it in the manner of Christ overturning the tables of the moneylenders.[102] The bishop's moral authority and even his spiritual calling were questioned as attention was drawn to his luxurious way of life, and by engaging with devotional forms of expression themselves, protestors spectacularly appropriated that authority.

Even in their most violent moments, these crowds did not act as unthinking mobs, but carried out distinct roles, acting strategically and collectively to contest the moral and jurisdictional authority of secular and religious collectivities. They could engage with forms of behaviour and structures of solidarity associated with spiritual authority in the medieval town. The right to regulate town life, particularly through the interpretation of violence, was debated. It was by theatrically reproducing the collective behaviours by which such regulatory frameworks were embedded in communities that those involved in uprisings rhetorically asserted their own authority and integral place on the urban landscape.

5. CARNIVALS AND CONTESTATIONS

Most strikingly for contemporaries, it was the timing of many uprisings which connected them intrinsically to religious ceremonial and spectacular performances of spiritual authority. Violence in Arras broke out in 1285 during the Pentecostal fair, a time one looked forward to, and a time one could look back on: it was, moreover, a time when normal social constraints were relaxed, performances of various kinds produced, and shifting roles assumed. The timing of the uprising moreover had different implications for different groups, embedding the uprising at the intersection of a number of different local solidarities: Pentecost was a religious festival during which the Cathedral canons publicly demonstrated their spiritual primacy in the town; it was a time of municipal celebration, during which the *échevins* sought ceremonially to evoke their central role; it was a holiday from work, but with economic implications as it was shortly followed by the commercial fair.

[101] Arbitrators' settlement: Giry, *Documents*, no. LXVI, 170 and Louvet, *Histoire*, ii. 515; bishop's account: footnote to Giry, *Documents*, no. LXVII, 163, and Louvet, *Histoire*, ii. 492.

[102] John 2: 15.

Festivals and feast days were an integral part of the urban calendar. They were part of urban cultures which recognized their own need for reflexivity and spaces in which to question the order of things the better to live harmoniously day by day. It is perhaps unsurprising that, in the same vein as their use of theatrical forms, uprisings should have drawn upon the moments, spaces, and gestures of carnival. Those in authority were afraid of the seditious potential of such events because they knew their hegemony over moral and legal regulation would be challenged, but these events were nevertheless fundamentally part of urban life.[103] The permissive and fluid atmosphere of carnival was particularly potently illustrated in the small town of Poix in 1310.[104] The annual celebration lasted several days, involving the temporary inversion of the hierarchy, with the crowning of a commoner king: in 1310 the celebration erupted into violence provoked by long-standing tensions between the local seigneurial Tyrel family and the commune. This hostility was multi-faceted: the military obligations of the town were one source of hostility between lord and commune, and in 1268 the commune was fined by the Paris Parlement for having failed to fulfil its military duty to their *seigneur*.[105] Taxation was another problematic issue, and several accounts describe daring rescues by the townspeople of animals confiscated by the *seigneur* because they had failed to pay their dues.[106] The Paris Parlement frequently had to intervene in order to settle jurisdictional disputes between the Tyrels and the people of Poix. The original charter had stipulated that such disputes be regulated by any one of the communes of Amiens, Abbeville, or Saint Quentin; the Parlement itself only intervened when disputes had reached a degree of intensity with which the neighbouring communes were ill-equipped to deal.[107] The *seigneur* Tirel responded violently and forcefully, and even tried to abolish the commune in 1281, only to be reprimanded by the Parlement.[108] A climax was reached in 1306, when the Parlement revoked all jurisdiction from the *seigneur* during his lifetime, on account of illegal and brutal violence committed by him towards members of the commune; indeed

[103] See Bercé, *Fête*, 7–13; M. Aston, 'Corpus Christi and Corpus Regni: Heresy and the Peasants' Revolt', *Past and Present*, 143 (1994), 3–47.

[104] Boutaric, *Actes*, ii, no. 3710, 67 (1309); *Olim*, iii. 495–6.

[105] Boutaric, *Actes*, i, no. 1247, 113 (1268); *Olim*, i. 717–18.

[106] Boutaric, *Actes*, i, no. 2441, 233 (1282); *Olim*, ii. 208–9.

[107] 'If the parties concerned demanded to be judged by the mayor and the *échevins*, or if the mayor and the *échevins* claimed the case before it could be carried before the lord, the judgment should be given by the mayor and the *échevins*': Boutaric, *Actes*, i, no. 896, 82 (1264).

[108] Boutaric, *Actes*, i, no. 2322, 223 (1281); *Olim*, ii. 173.

every one of his victims was to be entitled to an annual pension from the *seigneur*'s own funds.[109]

In 1310 a certain Guérard Pellicier was chosen as 'king' for the day, and his companions became 'king-makers'. The festival time of the carnival provided a space for mimesis, parody, and the renegotiation of identities. The hierarchies within these communities were not delineated with sufficient clarity to fit a Bakhtinian model of carnivalesque inversion serving ultimately to bolster the status quo, but rather, these rebels drew upon the strange subversions of the carnival to explore the boundaries between reality and fiction.[110] Pellicier and his companions initially played fictional roles, but their actions shifted from an imagined world to the real world of physical pain when the *seigneur* tried to arrest Pellicier for having stolen a goblet. The community rallied to negate his jurisdictional authority, and asserted the illegitimacy of his brutality by engaging in judicial forms of violence themselves; they rescued the prisoner and lapidated the *seigneur* and his men. The goblet is described as a 'ciphus', an ornate and status-signifying object, and was probably an element of the carnival game. The playfulness of the incident was highlighted by the Parlement decree which described the participants as 'ludentes'. It is the placing of the uprising at the nebulous boundary between representation and reality which gives it its peculiar expressive force, and locates it systemically as another means of expression in a broadly performative society.

Significantly, the Parisian revolt of 1306, provoked by the re-establishment of 'good money' and the consequent real increase in rents, did not immediately follow Philip IV's ordinance to revalue the coinage, but simmered ominously and finally erupted three months later near Christmas, when the more permissive and fluid atmosphere of celebration proved conducive to the role-play of revolt. These rebels were primarily motivated by economic concerns, but the timing and form of their protest suggests a deeper questioning of the regulatory rights and authority of the various collectivities within the city. The *Grandes Chroniques* describe the composition of the rebels as artisans with a commonalty of interests in protesting against the rise in rents: 'foulons et tisserans, taverniers et pluseurs autres ouvriers d'autres mestiers, et firent aliance ensemble'.[111]

[109] Boutaric, *Actes*, ii, no. 3339, 34; *Olim*, iii. 176.

[110] M. Bakhtin, *L'Œuvre de François Rabelais et la culture populaire au Moyen Age et sous la Renaissance*, tr. A. Robel (Paris, 1970), 13–21.

[111] 'Fullers and weavers, tavern-keepers and several other workers from different trades, and they made an alliance together': *Grandes Chroniques*, viii. 250–2. Other accounts in *Chronique anonyme*, *RHGF* xxi. 139; *Chronique anonyme*, *RHGF* xxi. 127; Guillaume de Nangis, *Chronique*, i. 355–6; Gerardus Fracheto, *Chronicus*, 27; *Excepta Johannis a Sancto Victore*, 647.

According to the chronicles, the alliance was hostile both to the king and to the ruling burghers of the city, most particularly the provost, Barbette, who was popularly held responsible for the situation.[112]

The uprising was spectacularly theatrical and rhetorical. Medieval dramatic spectacle did not rely upon a single backdrop, but famously used the system of *décor simultané* whereby a series of painted backdrops would be juxtaposed on a single stage, allowing the actors to move between them to represent geographical movement.[113] In the Parisian uprising, attention was so focused on its various tableaux, and the areas between them became so indistinct, that the chroniclers gave different orderings of the places visited by the rebellion: some writers recorded that the rebels began by pillaging the town house of the provost of the merchants, Étienne Barbette, then proceeded to the Temple to harangue the king;[114] others asserted that the story began at the Temple and that the rebels subsequently moved on to Barbette's town house, a scenario which seems more likely in that the rebels would first have tried non-punishable means and only proceeded on their dangerous journey of destruction after encountering the king's obstinate silence.[115] Movement from here to the house of Barbette is not documented, because it was apparently uneventful: action was entirely focused upon this key location, the symbol of the affluence of the man the rebels held responsible for their economic repression. They destroyed the trees in his garden and demolished much of the building, but without stealing anything. They then proceeded to Barbette's out-of-town house, where they pillaged, cut up feather pillows, and watched the clouds of feathers descend anarchically onto the street; they emptied barrels of wine into the gutter, smashed all breakable items, and trampled gold and silver objects in the mud, potently juxtaposing the precious nature of these objects with the filth of the street. The rhetorical intention of these actions is clear. The rebels did not attempt to steal any of the silver or gold: they destroyed rather than appropriated the luxurious comfort of the feather pillows. Not only were these locations of immense significance, as visible embodiments of the inequity of Barbette's policy, but the actions of the rebels upon them served to endow them with renewed significance

[112] Barbette was *échevin* from 1293 to 1296, *prévôt* of the merchants twice, as well as a successful businessman: R. Cazelles, *Nouvelle Histoire de Paris* (Paris, 1972), 98.

[113] See G. Runnalls, '*Mansion* and *lieu*: Two Technical Terms in Medieval French Staging?', *French Studies*, 35 (1981), 385–93.

[114] *Grandes Chroniques*, viii. 250–2: this ordering vilified the rebels further by suggesting that the pillaging was spontaneous and totally unprovoked by the king's refusal of their demands.

[115] Guillaume de Nangis, *Chronique*, i. 355–6; Gerardus Fracheto, *Chronique*, 27; *Chronique Excerpta Johannis a Sancto Victore*, 647; *Chronique anonyme*, *RHGF* xxi. 127; *Chronique rimée de Saint-Magloire*, *RHGF* xxii. 85.

as the site of their refusal to submit voicelessly to such oppression, and their claim to moral authority.

The mutable boundaries and unconventional behaviour which characterized festive periods could be extended into violent attacks on regulatory hegemony. And just as festive periods were both repetitive and remembered, urban uprisings took place, not as chroniclers suggested, as isolated aberrant moments, but self-consciously within a historical continuum, gaining meaning and potency from such connections. Grand narratives of struggle for civic liberties were constructed, whose moral authority was juxtaposed with the grammars of law and spiritual prescriptions about civic behaviour. Collective violence engaged not only with the civic and religious regulation of town life, but also with traditions of urban uprisings; they replayed and expanded roles from past events.

The ennobling value of history is one of the central features and motivations of collective memory: shared historical knowledge selected because of its meaning for the group which remembers it.[116] Collective memory in this case is the framework from which the roles of the urban revolts sprang, and it provided them with a sense of their place in civic history: it informed participants and observers that this had happened before, and that it was all the more meaningful for that. Very often collective memory has a tendency to focus on victimhood, and concentrates on the definition of present identity by the evocation of a persecuting other. Verbal reminiscences of previous revolts connected the revolt of 1295 in Laon to historic civic privileges. The revolt was notoriously characterized by shouts of 'Communia! Communia!' accompanying the initial infraction into the church, and the subsequent leading of the victims to the house of the submayor.[117] These shouts evoked the famous 1112 rebellion, which had ultimately led to the granting of the communal charters.[118] Such a reference could be used to terrify adversaries: it amplified witnesses' perception of the importance of the events unfolding before their eyes, and alarmed the ecclesiastical authorities who remembered only too well, 150 years later, the murder of Bishop Gaudry. But in the eyes of the participants, this collective memory helped to legitimize the present by virtue of a noble past, a past in which the people of the commune had defined legitimate and illegitimate violence, and had authoritatively punished the main offender. By evoking the original quarrel with the arch-enemy of the people, it defined these roles in terms of a

[116] J. Fentress and C. Wickham, *Social Memory* (Oxford, 1992), 6–7.

[117] *Registres Boniface,* i, no. 355, 125–6.

[118] See the account in Guibert de Nogent, ed. in J. Benton, *Self and Society in Medieval France* (Toronto, 1984), 145–90.

distinctive other. The roles were given meaning, and a predetermined hermeneutics presented to spectators whereby the violence of the revolt was to be understood as the historically validated assumption of judicial authority by the crowd.

Collective memory could inform the actions of rebels by suggesting particular forms of violence to be used. Abbeville, for instance, was beset by jurisdictional tension between the local ecclesiastical court and the commune, which gained its charter in 1130:[119] a series of violent clashes occurred throughout the thirteenth century, with attacks by the townspeople on the abbey and on abbey property.[120] For the notables of the town in the revolt of 1311 to behave quite so violently would be surprising, were it not for the fact that extreme violence against the abbey and its men had become a local tradition.[121]

Orality played a crucial role in the transmission of collective memories of revolts, asserting and continually reaffirming their moral authority and their right to distinguish legitimate from illegitimate violence. In Saint Quentin, violent tension between the chapter and the commune fuelled numerous brutal revolts in 1213, 1247, and 1296, and most memorably in 1311; further protests against royal fiscal and military demands took place in 1240, 1293 and 1295, and against the archbishop of Reims in 1299.[122] Almost certainly stories about the successive revolts would have been passed down between the generations, particularly since they all revolved around the same issue of the relationship between chapter and commune. Each successive revolt could gain greater potency from common knowledge of its precedents, and from the awareness that it could be inscribed in a long history of hostility. This in turn influenced the way in which rebels behaved, knowing that they were continuing a tradition of violent authority, that their actions could be thus glorified, and that they already had examples of collective and meaningful behaviour to follow.

Urban violence situated itself, moreover, not only in relation to historical violence, but also in relation to other outbreaks of violence in neighbouring towns; drawing on models from elsewhere of collective protest, the north-eastern French revolts could thus associate themselves with the civic rhetoric of other areas. Evidence of cross-influence between the Flemish revolts and the revolt in Saint Omer is extremely persuasive.

[119] Thierry, *Monuments*, iv. 6–14.

[120] Boutaric, *Actes*, i, no. 2317, 222 (1281); *Olim*, ii. 172.

[121] On traditions of violent protest, see Mollat and Wolff, *Ongles bleus*, 10.

[122] Giry, *Archives de Saint Quentin*, pp. xcvi–xcvii; no. 234, 213; e.g. Boutaric, *Actes*, i, no. 2912, 290 (1296); *Olim*, ii. 398; ADPC, A728. Lalou, 'Les Révoltes', 169.

In the 1300s, a shifting coalition of interests in Saint Omer contested the corruption and exclusivity of the contemporary oligarchy. The situation was rendered more complex by the proximity of the town to Flanders: Audomarois remained intensely aware of their 'Frenchness' due to involvement in the Flemish war in 1297 to 1304, and after the *Matins* of Bruges in 1302 the town found itself a refuge for Flemish supporters of the French crown. However, not all Audomarois felt patriotic, and in 1302, one Simon Hannebaert was put on the wheel, drawn, hanged, and his ashes flung to the winds, for having vociferously wished that his town might fall into the hands of the count of Flanders.[123] Nevertheless, in 1306, the Flemish hero, Peter Coninck, sent a letter of advice to the rebels in Saint Omer to encourage them in their dispute with the local oligarchy. The content of the letter is only recorded in an account by the hostile *échevinage*, according to which Peter exhorted the leaders of the weavers and the fullers to follow the successful example of the people of Bruges, and advised them to bind together with the humbler *métiers*.[124] The inclusion of the letter was a shock tactic by the *échevins*, for Peter was a fearful figure, but the transcription nevertheless seems to be genuine. Shortly afterwards, the *métiers* carried out an armed attack on the hall where the *échevins* were accustomed to meet and, on 'mauvais mercredi', liberated the so-called Five Valets, representatives of the *métiers*, who had been imprisoned by the oligarchy. Much of this was inspired by events at Bruges, which had become notorious, but the roles assumed by the participants responded also to the specific circumstances of the incarcerated Five Valets. Again, following the model of Bruges, an intense street fight ensued: the *métiers* wounded many of the 'bonnes gens' of the town, and ransacked their houses. A new riot followed on 'mauvais vendredi', with another armed attack on the hall, personal verbal threats, and a further appeal by the *métiers* to the countess. Events gathered their own momentum: as the violence intensified, the behaviour of the participants no longer depended upon direct reference to what happened at Bruges, because the violent actions had by then gained their own meaning, and their own frame of reference. By drawing upon contemporaneous modes of collective action, and moulding them to suit specific local solidarities and shifting coalitions, the rebels rhetorically claimed for themselves the right to regulate the community.

[123] Derville, *Saint Omer*, 64.

[124] This account is reproduced ibid. 274–6; individual complaints were brought against the Mainabourse brothers and various other individuals for their actions during the hostilities in ADPC, A928/1, A928/5, A928/7, A928/8. A full account of the revolt can be found in Derville, *Saint Omer*, 64–9.

Coninck's letter specifically focused upon the careful composition of the crowds involved in the uprising: rather than an amorphous mass, it was a strategically constructed body of individuals. Moreover, these loyalties were constantly shifting, as individuals changed allegiance and coordinated their personal interests with that of the group. The working classes had been marginalized economically by statutes of 1210, and were further threatened by legislation from the ruling *échevins* in 1280, which brutally repressed any expressions of solidarity by the *métiers* with threats of burying them alive.[125] The 1305 revolt then began as a socially motivated uprising, but even the first outbursts of violence overlapped with more factional solidarities, as the *métiers* (including both employers and employees) were led by a group of rich ousted oligarchs, headed by one Gérart Mainabourse. What is more, at this point in the revolt, the power of the rebels was such as to persuade Countess Mahaut of Artois to support their cause, apparently convinced of the unacceptable corruption of the *échevins*. When this rebellion succeeded in bringing down the municipal government, and a new oligarchy was installed by the countess, the 'teams' shifted, and the *métiers* split, as the employees found themselves excluded from government by their now politically successful employers: a new coalition of crafts organized itself to attack the newly powerful party. Both of these newly formed sides constantly suspected each other of forming an alliance with the banished former *échevins*. When Mahaut of Artois cynically promised a satisfactory solution for all parties, but actually excluded all but the old councillors, her betrayal engendered the reunification of the *métiers*: they besieged her château with the help of the Flemish, and engineered a full-scale social war targeting the rich and the property of the noblemen in the surrounding countryside. The rebellion had social, geographical, and political dimensions which continually shifted and intersected. Personal interests were mingled with collective ones, sides shifted, but never was crowd fever so intense that the individuals who constituted it forgot themselves.

6. CONCLUSION

An early thirteenth-century satirical poem from Arras describes a violent bid for civic power led by Flemish weavers in Arras in the 1220s.[126] The details remain entirely mysterious, but the nature of the humour is telling.

[125] This text is transcribed in Derville, *Saint Omer*, 272–3. Another account of the revolt is provided in Nicholas, *Growth*, 298–300.

[126] Berger, *Littérature*, no. XXIII.

The weavers assume knightly attire, though they simply do not have the requisite skill and must tie their feet to the stirrups to avoid being unhorsed. The poet plays on these knightly pretensions by evoking the conventions of *chansons de geste*: one wife begs her husband not to go because of a dream she had the previous night; another combatant promises his beloved that he will marry her come the spring; and God works a thunderous miracle on their behalf.[127] The text is even written in epic assonant *laisses*. The poem has no denouement, and it remains unclear whether the minstrel is mocking the ambitious schemes of the craftsmen, or affectionately condoning them whilst decrying the hypocrisy of the nobility. Strikingly though, the text rests upon the deliberate paralleling of different forms of violent action, and the assumption that collective uprisings were not simply aberrant, but situated on a wider stage of cultural expression.

All the uprisings of this period were followed by costly reprisals.[128] Nevertheless, the very severity of the response of the authorities draws attention to their perceived importance as a means of expressively negotiating the fraught relationships between the various collectivities which constituted medieval towns. Whereas urban uprisings were frequently characterized by hostile chroniclers and repressive authorities as disconnected and meaningless, in practice the rebels situated themselves meaningfully within towns characterized by spectacular displays. Far from involving the inchoate and bestial crowds evoked by chroniclers, the uprisings were undertaken by groups self-consciously functioning corporately: organized groups of individuals with structured and interdependent roles to play. Much of the behaviour of the crowds during these uprisings was spontaneous, and motivated by the momentum of the angry collectivity. But spontaneous gestures gained rhetorical impetus and strategic meaning from the planned and constructed nature of the uprisings. Shifting coalitions were drawn together by convergent interests, and engaged in violence which sought to address particular concerns. These were struggles about the validity of frameworks for interpreting, regulating, and punishing violent behaviour. These 'grammars' had developed

[127] Respectively, ll. 81–91; 95–103; 133–40; 166–71.

[128] e.g. in Laon, all activities associated with the commune were forbidden, and, as well as hefty fines payable to the dean and chapter, it was ordained that one hundred members of the commune, 'en cotes sans ceintures, les chies nus, sans chaperons et sans coiffes' should process to the Cathedral, bearing 'trois figures de cire . . . et illeques les offerront en signe de faire restitucion a leglise de trois hommes qui contre limmunite et la franchise de leglise dessus dite par force et par violence furent de cele eglise hors trait': decree of Philip IV, 1298, AN L733, no. 82 (A) and AD Aisne G2 fol. 90^{v}–91^{r}, ed. in Denton, 'Second Uprising', 90–2.

out of the multiplicity of medieval communities within a single town and, while each claimed to regulate misbehaviour often by spectacular displays of legitimate violence, they inevitably clashed. The collective violence of uprisings, in debating the legal or spiritual authority claimed by the various communities, drew on the same models, often highly theatrical, of collective behaviour and violent gestures in order to exploit the rhetoric of legitimate violence. In doing so, urban uprisings were not aberrant irregularities, but phenomena at the heart of urban life.

6

Domestic Violence in Paris and Artois[1]

> Celui qui d'amor fine/Amer me soloit et chierir/Sovent me fais batre et ferir.[2]

The idyll of courtly love, or the nightmare of domestic abuse: so the heroine of one of Gautier de Coinci's miracle tales juxtaposes our wildly polarized clichés of medieval marriage. We travel now from the busy town squares and quintessentially collective uprisings, to the intimate setting of the home and spousal relations.[3] It is here, in medieval marriage, that the fundamental medieval ambivalence about interpreting and assessing violence is crystallized.

Several *jeux partis*, debate poems from the Puy of thirteenth-century Arras, pose the problem in particularly stark (and knowingly humorous) terms as they take the acceptability of domestic violence as their central theme: is one justified in beating one's lover to ensure the continuation of the relationship? Can a lover beat a proud woman to induce respect? Given the choice between being beaten by one's wife on account of one's mistress, or seeing one's mistress being beaten by her husband, what should be done? These dilemmas provoke discussions about reputation, which could be both damaged and shored up by the communal awareness of wife-beating; the relationship between affection and brutality, seen to be complex and shifting; and the usefulness of domestic discipline versus anxiety about penalties in the ecclesiastical courts.[4] By comparison with the other debate poems and their lyrical concerns, these seem at first sight

[1] An earlier version of this appeared as 'Violent Discipline or Disciplining Violence? Domestic Violence in Late Thirteenth- and Early Fourteenth-Century France', *Cultural and Social History*, 6/1 (2009), 9–27. I am grateful to the editors for permission to reuse some of this material.

[2] 'He who used to love and cherish me so courteously, now beats me and strikes me all the time': *De Deuz fammes que Nostre Dame converti*, in Gautier de Coinci, *Miracles de Nostre Dame*, ed. F. Koenig, 4 vols. (Geneva, 1955), i, no. 33, ll. 64–6.

[3] Whilst discipline of children is a fascinating topic, I simply do not have the evidence to sustain a discussion here. See J. Swanson, 'Childhood and Childrearing in *ad status* Sermons by Later Thirteenth-Century Friars', *Journal of Medieval History*, 16/4 (1990), 309–31.

[4] A. Jeanroy (ed.), *Recueil général des Jeux Partis français* (Paris, 1926), respectively, nos. 19, ll. 23–7, 44–5; 80, ll. 37–40, 41–50, 51–64; 134, ll. 18–21, 72–4, 926–8, 134–7.

to be more frivolous, deliberate attempts to undermine courtly ethics by juxtaposing them with the harsher realities of everyday life. But a more fundamental ambivalence is at stake: 'Que dame fust laidengie,/ . . . c'est trop grant vilounie', and yet after the beating, 'mieus l'ameroit/Et li menroit meilleur vie/Que s'il ne l'eüst touchie'.[5]

As we have seen in the ways in which different forms of violence were represented, the stated purpose of interpersonal or collective violence often claimed to mimic that of the law, but still provoked ambivalent and troubled reactions. We must continue to ask how far violence aligned itself with the ordering functions of legal mechanisms, and at what point it diverged and disordered. This was a very fluid line, and one which reveals widespread uncertainty regarding the proper functions both of law and of violence. Such hesitancy about the nature of violence more broadly was epitomized in complex and adaptive contemporary understandings of the nature of domestic violence. Some acts of domestic physical brutality were defined as reprehensible and deviant 'violence', while others were lauded as normal patriarchal discipline of a deviant victim: some domestic violence was considered justifiable, even legalistic, discipline, while some was itself disciplined as unacceptable.[6] It was, of course, a highly gendered construction. Perpetrating violence was an effective way of asserting a particular form of masculinity, and attributing violent behaviour to others helped to construct gendered identities.

Moreover, the history of domestic violence operates at the interface of the public and the private, revealing the subtle perceived differences and reciprocal influences between collective and intimate spaces; the interpretation of domestic violence embodied contemporary anxiety about the

[5] 'It's very disgraceful to beat a woman'; 'she would love him more and behave better than if he hadn't touched her': no. 134, ll. 63–4 and 58–60 (134–7).

[6] Work on medieval domestic violence in other areas of Europe has tended to focus on this distinction: little work has been done on northern France in this period. B. Hanawalt, 'Violence in the Domestic Milieu of Late Medieval England', in R. Kaeuper (ed.), *Violence in Medieval Society* (Woodbridge, 2000), 197–214; S. Butler, *The Language of Abuse: Marital Violence in Later Medieval England* (Leiden, 2007), 2–28; R. Helmholz, *Marriage Litigation in Medieval England* (Cambridge, 1974); T. Dean, 'Domestic Violence in Late-Medieval Bologna', *Renaissance Studies*, 18/4 (2004), 527–43; A. Finch, '*Repulsa uxore sua*: Marital Difficulties and Separation in the Later Middle Ages', *Continuity and Change*, 8/1 (1993), 11–38; S. Bednarski, 'Keeping it in the Family? Domestic Violence in the Later Middle Ages: Examples from a Provençal Town', in I. Davis, M. Müller, and S. Rees Jones (eds.), *Love, Marriage, and Family Ties in the Later Middle Ages* (Turnhout, 2003), 277–99; M. Brozyna, 'Not Just a Family Affair: Domestic Violence and the Ecclesiastical Courts in Late Medieval Poland', ibid. 299–311; D. Nicholas, *The Domestic Life of a Medieval City: Women, Children and the Family in Fourteenth-Century Ghent* (Lincoln, Neb., 1985), 33–52.

primarily communal or interpersonal implications of violence.[7] Marriage was at once an intimate institution and one sanctioned by public law and ceremony, perceived as a microcosm of the state from Aristotle onwards.[8] Domestic discipline was perceived as a crucial element in a rightly ordered society, ensuring the preservation of rightful hierarchies and correcting any threat to social harmony; domestic violence, on the other hand, had disrupting, destabilizing implications not only for individual marriages, but for society as a whole.[9] A fine line was drawn between the two phenomena, but the scale was a sliding one and criteria nebulous and vague. These were societies increasingly characterized by nuclear families, but where wider kinship loyalties continued to be important.[10] Boundaries between private and public spaces were highly significant, saturated with social and legal implications, but flexible and open to negotiation.[11] Sociologists today have highlighted both the frequency and the danger of relegating understandings of domestic violence to the private sphere, but the dichotomy was more subtly and ambivalently drawn in the late thirteenth and early fourteenth centuries.[12] The experience and reception of domestic violence demonstrated a high degree of sensitivity to such nuances, and the very definition of gestures as violent rather than disciplinary was dependent upon the implications of the public and the private.

[7] This has been the focus of much historiography of early modern domestic violence, e.g.: L. Roper, *The Holy Household: Women and Morals in Reformation Augsburg* (Oxford, 1989), 165–205; S. Amussen, '"Being Stirred to Much Unquietness": Violence and Domestic Violence in Early Modern England', *Journal of Women's History*, 6 (1994), 70–89; J. Ferraro, 'The Power to Decide: Battered Wives in Early Modern Venice', *Renaissance Quarterly*, 48/3 (1995), 492–512.

[8] Cf. C. Jorgensen Itnyre (ed.), *Medieval Family Roles: A Book of Essays* (New York, 1996), p. xii.

[9] 'La brutalité évidente des comportements domestiques n'indique donc pas une absence de solidarité, loin s'en faut, car il faut distinguer la violence licite et habituelle du dérapage agressif entraînant la mort d'un individu, dans des cas plus exceptionnels': R. Muchembled, *La Violence au village: Sociabilité et comportements populaires en Artois du XVe au XVIIe siècle* (Turnhout, 1989), 195.

[10] The mixture of conjugal nuclear ties, and wider loyalties are discussed in: D. Frappier-Bigras, 'La Famille dans l'artisanat parisien du treizième siècle', *Le Moyen Age*, 95 (1980), 47–74; J. Heers, *Family Clans in the Middle Ages: A Study of Political and Social Structures in Urban Areas*, tr. B. Herbert (Amsterdam, 1977), 247–52; D. Herlihy, 'Family Solidarity in Medieval Italian History', in D. Herlihy, R. Lopez, and V. Slessarev (eds.), *Economy, Society and Government in Medieval Italy* (Kent, Ohio, 1969), 173–85; Nicholas, *Domestic Life*, 1–12. On extended definitions of family, see D. Herlihy, 'Family', *American Historical Review*, 96/1 (1991), 1–16.

[11] Cf. E. Salisbury *et al.* (eds.), *Domestic Violence in Medieval Texts* (Gainesville, Fla., 2002), 4.

[12] Cf. M. Albertson Fineman and R. Mykitiuk (eds.), *The Public Nature of Private Violence* (New York, 1994), pp. xiii–xv.

Intimate violence within marriage also had collective social implications in a broader sense, both for contemporaries and for the historian of violence. It is widely accepted amongst sociologists, and was likewise a staple of medieval thought on the subject, that individuals from violent homes were more likely to be involved in violent incidents outside the home: whether true or not, such determinism shaped expectations.[13] The connection can rarely be documented in the Middle Ages, though occasional cases are telling: a young man convicted of murder in Saint Omer in 1307 was the son of a man who had been prosecuted for excessive violence towards another young boy of his household.[14] Violence is often a learnt form of behaviour, and growing up in a household where physical brutality is frequent, even normative, may teach that this is a natural response to certain situations; both children and spouses, quite logically, can begin to consider violence as a normal reaction.[15] If violence within the household influenced and lay at the heart of other manifestations of violence in a more public arena, the study of domestic violence becomes central to an understanding of thirteenth- and fourteenth-century society. Violence as a form of communication was, in many cases, ingrained from an early age, certain gestures were familiarized from childhood, and distinctions between discipline and violence deeply culturally rooted.

Ambivalence about the precise distinction between domestic discipline and domestic abuse, and hesitation about the primarily private or public implications of such behaviour, is contained in the interplay of the practice of domestic violence, canon and secular law discussions of the role of violence in marriage, and contemporary legal proceedings: this was a symbiotic three-way relationship. Canon and secular lawyers constructed a fluid system whereby the acceptability of violence depended on the degree of brutality, and actual prosecutions intertwined this logic with attitudes of the local community, status of the actors, and physical placing of the violence. Though it is difficult to disentangle violence from the legal reactions it entailed, the law and the practice of violence exerted powerful reciprocal influences in establishing patterns of deviance, and in problematizing and nuancing the notion of domestic violence. These three distinct

[13] 'One public function of the household was to provide a place where individuals were socialized for their role in the wider community': C. Beattie *et al.* (eds.), *The Medieval Household in Christian Europe c. 850–1550: Managing Power, Wealth, and the Body* (Turnhout, 2003), 3.

[14] ADPC, A225/4, A268/1.

[15] 'The family, more than any other social institution, is the primary mechanism for teaching norms, values, and techniques of violence': R. Gelles, *The Violent Home: A Study of Physical Aggression Between Husbands and Wives* (Beverly Hills, Calif., 1972), 169. This is, nevertheless, a problematic stance, given its deterministic implications.

levels of discourse will be examined one by one, in order the more clearly to illuminate their interconnections. Domestic violence was such a pervasive element in medieval society that it provided a common trope for contemporary popular literature, such as the *fabliaux* and popular miracle tales, an analysis of which will be intertwined with commentary of law, prosecution, and practice. Such texts drew on the experience of their diverse audiences to engage them through bawdy laughter with the problems presented by the interpretation of domestic violence; they questioned and undermined even the fluid lines between discipline and abuse established in prescriptive legal and moral discourse. Both abusive husbands and their victims were made into figures of fun for audiences with whom these inconclusive themes would have resonated uncomfortably.

1. LEGAL PRESCRIPTION

Domestic violence most often fell within the purview of canon law. The sacramentalization of marriage and increasing formalization of its legitimacy and content in the Fourth Lateran council of 1215 focused canonical attention upon it as an institution. While secular legislation rarely mentioned marriage, canon law was profoundly concerned with its regulation.[16] The international reach and theoretical universalism of canon law corresponded to the internationalism and cross-class compass of the moral economy of marriage: theoretically at least, everyone was affected by canon law and marriage, whatever their geographical provenance or social status.[17] Moreover, canon law's concern with the moral well-being of the individual pushed it to transgress boundaries of the public and the private. Unlike secular law, canon law was concerned with the individual, not just with society, and thus the private became intensely significant.

The importance of legislation and the practice of law as a site of contesting values makes canon law an important frame for thirteenth-century ambivalence about the practice of domestic violence, and the relationship between the public and the private. On the one hand, physical discipline within marriage was presented as crucial to the har-

[16] There are a few exceptions from this period, notably Philippe de Beaumanoir's *Coutumes de Beauvaisis*, ed. A. Salmon (Paris, 1899); A. Esmein, *Le Mariage en droit canonique*, 2 vols. (Paris, 1929), i. 67–98; C. Donahue, jun., *Law, Marriage and Society in the Later Middle Ages* (Cambridge, 2007), 7–12.

[17] Church teachings 'helped to make households similar and commensurable': D. Herlihy, *Medieval Households* (Camridge, Mass., 1985), 134; 'While most legal systems were confined to a particular region or locality, canon law emerged as a working and often quite effective international law': J. Brundage, *Medieval Canon Law* (London, 1995), 3.

mony and order of the institution: on the other hand, the original Roman law concept of *maritalis affectio* was increasingly stressed to condemn excessive abuse or mistreatment between partners.[18] Moreover, canon law stressed the public implications of private violence, protecting or disrupting public order.

The fundamental hierarchy in marriage promoted by canon law derived from biblical texts, notably St Paul: 'Wives, submit yourselves to your own husbands as you do to the Lord. For the husband is the head of the wife as Christ is the head of the church, his body, of which he is the Saviour' (Ephesians 5: 22–4). Drawing on Augustine, Ambrose, and Jerome, Gratian, 'the father of the science of canon law', in his *Decretum,* reiterated this fundamental order, stressing its centrality in an ordered society.[19] Husbands were head of a divinely ordained, *natural* order, and anything which disrupted this was not only dangerous, but unnatural:[20] their superiority was apparently owing to the fact that they were fashioned in God's image, whereas women originated only from Adam's rib.[21] Gratian therefore explicitly gave husbands a legal right to maintain order in the household, by force if necessary. The moral obligation of the husband to preserve this order was a social duty, and an important element of his masculine role. Following Augustine, marriage was compared to other hierarchical relationships between teacher and pupils, master and servants, king and subjects, abbot and monks: all such relationships were essential for social harmony, and were to be preserved by physical correction of deviants.[22] Women who threatened social harmony by assuming a dominant position within a marriage were to be forcibly corrected. The vocabulary used to describe such discipline is 'coactio' (force), 'pena' or 'punitio' (punishment), 'correctio' (correction), 'castigatio' (chastisement): it was normative, expressly carried out in the interests of harmony and order.[23] Uxoricide was, unsurprisingly, outlawed by Gratian, and described as an act 'concitatus a diabolo', savage, and bestial, illustrating the perception that excessive domestic violence undermined the notion of a civilized society.[24] Nevertheless, even when condemning uxoricide most

[18] Cf. M. Sheehan, *Marriage, Family and Law in Medieval Europe* (Cardiff, 1996), 266–7.

[19] All references to Gratian are cited in standard format, and are from Gratian, *Decretum,* ed. E. Friedberg, 2 vols. (Leipzig, 1879; repr. Graz, 1959). I am very much indebted in this section to J. Brundage, 'Domestic Violence in Classical Canon Law', in Kaeuper, *Violence,* 183–94. Gratian, C. 33, q. 5, cc. 12–19.

[20] Gratian, C. 33, q. 5, c. 12.

[21] Ibid., cc. 12, 18, 19.

[22] Ibid., c. 14.

[23] Ibid., q. 2, d.p.c. 9 and c. 10.

[24] 'Inspired by the devil': Gratian, C. 33, q. 2, c. 8.

whole-heartedly, Gratian still mitigated the penance owed by those husbands who killed their wives in a fit of passion arising from the discovery of the spouse's adultery.[25] The most extreme forms of domestic violence were condemned, but domestic discipline was given a broad and relatively unproblematic interpretation. Gratian stressed husbands' responsibility for the good behaviour of their wives; while allowing that only non-deadly force should be used, he nevertheless advocated the imprisonment of errant wives in the house and punitive restrictions on their diet.[26]

The problems with this relatively straightforward distinction became increasingly clear over the course of the thirteenth century. The gruesome *fabliau*, *La Mégère Emasculée*, from mid-thirteenth-century Picardy, though reusing an earlier motif, presents the trope of the unsubmissive wife painfully and violently disciplined.[27] The male protagonist largely adheres to the precepts of Gratian regarding domestic discipline but, despite the *fabliau*'s comic pretence at didacticism and tongue-in-cheek epilogue, it engages with its diverse audience via a more complex and troubling presentation. A shrewish mother advises her newly wed daughter to follow her example, and to keep her husband submissive by contradicting him as much as possible. The count overhears this, and determines to force his wife into submission. When she deliberately contradicts his orders to the cook, he mutilates and banishes the cook, and then beats his wife so severely that she is incapacitated for three months. When his mother-in-law comes to stay, he decides to teach her a lesson too, and, making two excruciating incisions in her buttocks, pretends to remove the testicles of a bull, claiming that these are responsible for her domineering behaviour.

Structurally and superficially, the story stresses the importance of physical discipline for misbehaving wives. The plot depends upon a straightforward structure of cause and effect, one which the wife in her turn must learn: the count teaches her that each act of unsubmission on her part will be the cause of violent discipline on his part. When his wife and mother-in-law finally understand and realize the implacability of this structure, they reform their behaviour, and submit. The rationale

[25] Ibid., c. 5. [26] Ibid., c. 10.

[27] *NRCF* viii/83. This motif was popularized over the course of the 13th cent.: J. Brunvard, 'The Folktale Origin of *The Taming of the Shrew*', *Shakespeare Quarterly*, 17/4 (1966), 345–59. My reading of these texts is partly inspired by Kaeuper's reading of chivalric texts where he suggests that ambivalence about the justifiability of knightly violence is 'better explained by the pressing force of societal issues, rather than any Derridean indeterminacy in a conflicted text': R. Kaeuper, 'Chivalry and the "Civilizing Process"', in Kaeuper, *Violence*, 26.

of this violent discipline is clear, as each gesture responds to an explicit provocation. Both the wife and her mother promise to change their behaviour definitively; the sense of closure is reinforced by the pithy aphorism which underlines the ordering function of the violence in the tale:

> Tele est ce cest romanç la some:
> Dehait feme qui despit home.[28]

However, there is a clash between the stylistic characteristics of the tale and its straightforward structure, a clash which engages with ambivalence about the justifiability and acceptability of domestic violence. Even the masculinity of the count, apparently reinforced through powerful displays of violence, is compromised. The sheer extent of the violence carried out by the count is troubling not merely for a modern reader, but also for medieval contemporaries, as indicated by the reactions of the intra-textual characters: the wife (before she herself becomes a victim) is horrified by the way her new husband treats his dogs and horse. The text dwells with insistence on the grotesqueness of the violence carried out by this man, and on his brutality. The inappropriateness of the violence perpetrated on the cook is highlighted by the use of judicial motifs of cutting off an ear and gouging out the eye: the ubiquity of their use for the punishment of thieves render the lack of correlation between such a punishment and the cook's crime (preparing all the sauces with garlic) much more evident.[29] While the count's punishment may respond logically in a structural sense, the punishment is irrationally excessive.

Canon lawyers also became more aware of the potentially disruptive implications of domestic abuse, and the texts of the decretists, while accepting a basic need for discipline, focused increasingly on defining the limits of acceptable physical correction of wives; they were keen to distinguish between the right of the husband to punish his wife, and explicitly legal prerogatives. Specific types of violence were enumerated, in order to ensure rational correlation between the misdemeanour of the victim and the imposed punishment: certain physical gestures were now to be defined as rational correction upholding the law, others as unacceptable violence. According to Laurentius Hispanus (d. 1248) and others, husbands were only authorized to mete out light discipline, and only the punishment

[28] 'This is the conclusion of this story: cursed is the woman who despises men', ll. 667–8.

[29] ll. 411–412. Perhaps the teller of the *fabliau* was also responding to a growing anxiety about the excessive violence of noblemen, and their ongoing attempts to usurp legal prerogatives with extreme cruelty.

of minor offences was within their remit: graver misdemeanours on the part of the wife were to be referred to the legal authorities.[30] A husband was explicitly not permitted to beat heavily or to scourge his wife, as such serious punishments required the authority of a judge. Hispanus moreover restricted discipline to beatings with the hands and strict words: no sticks or other weapons were to be used. Such canonists again recommended the imprisonment of the wife in the house, and the restriction of her diet: such discipline was perceived as a rational and proportionate response to the perceived wrongdoing, re-establishing correct order in the household, rather than a chaotic atmosphere of violence.[31] Distinctions were made between different forms of violence, but remained fluid and nebulous: if the threat of force was sufficiently great to have frightened a 'constant man' or a 'constant woman', the gestures were deemed to be violent and excessive and the marriage could even be invalidated.[32]

The legitimacy of the discipline also increasingly hinged upon the status of the victim.[33] Whereas Gratian had readily accepted the analogy between servants and wives, the decretists refined and nuanced this. The *Ordinary Gloss* of Johannus Teutonicus on Gratian's *Decretum*, which by the late thirteenth century had assumed the status of the standard teaching on the subject in the Paris schools, defined more closely the boundaries of the husband's authority, and drew a distinction between the marital hierarchy and other social relationships. Teutonicus justified his claim that husbands should chastise their wives only moderately by explaining that wives were quite different from maidservants, that they enjoyed a higher status, and were thus more deserving of respect and should be the subject of less intense authority.[34] While forms of violence and status of the victim were increasingly closely defined, the misdemeanours for which wives might be chastised were to be limited to those specified by the law whose role increasingly eclipsed that of the husband himself in maintaining order: canonists claimed that a husband would be justified in objecting to generally insubmissive or insulting behaviour, or adultery.

[30] Laurentius Hispanus, *Glossa Palatina* to C. 7, q. 1, c. 39, quoted in Brundage, 'Domestic Violence', 186n., and in H. Ansgar Kelly, 'Rule of Thumb and the Folklaw of the Husband's Stick', *Journal of Legal Education*, 44 (1994), 341–65.

[31] Cf. William Durand, *Speculum Iudicale* (Basel, 1574; repr. Aalen, 1975), 2.443; cited in Brundage, 'Domestic Violence', 186n.

[32] Helmholz, *Marriage*, 90–1.

[33] The rank of the victim was particularly important in such determinations in an early modern context: J. Hardwick, 'Early Modern Perspectives on the Long History of Domestic Violence: The Case of Seventeenth-Century France', *Journal of Modern History*, 78 (2006), 1–36.

[34] Johannes Teutonicus, *Glossa Ordinaria* to C. 7 q. 1, c. 39, cited in Brundage, 'Domestic Violence', 186n.

Such correlations between misdemeanour and punishment shifted the focus to the motive of the husband in administering physical violence to his wife, reflecting a more widespread emphasis on intention amongst moral thinkers.[35] Husbands were warned not to let anger dominate them and drive them to irrational acts. Anger was an integral feature of much interpersonal violence, but generally served as a mitigating factor since it suggested a loss of moral control by the perpetrator and a diminished effect on the community as a whole. The case of domestic violence provided an opportunity for a much more nuanced exposition of different types of anger. Husbands were to chastise their wives with expressions of controlled and functional indignation, commonly construed as typically male in its measure and authority. Were they to let anger get the better of them, its connotations would become quite different: indicative of a loss of control, the relinquishing of moral authority, and, more fundamentally, loss of the male prerogative and even feminization, as rash anger was characterized as peculiarly female. Discipline more explicitly served a closely defined order, and any violence whose function remained tangential to that order was unacceptable and liable itself to be disciplined.

This was the main concern of secular legislation, though evidence is limited because marital issues were not theoretically a concern of such courts. A rare exception is presented by Philippe de Beaumanoir's *Coutumes du Beauvaisis* which explicitly addressed the issue of domestic violence and attempted to draw distinctions between discipline and abuse. Beaumanoir explained that, while such cases of marital anger and conflict, 'des mautalens qui meuvent en mariage', really lay within the purview of the ecclesiastical courts, secular courts were sometimes obliged to deal with complaints by women about the division of common property and the lack of a separated spouse's contribution to living expenses.[36] His choice of the term 'mautalens' is indicative, etymologically suggesting anger's propensity negatively to undermine goodwill and aspiration ('talens').

Like the canonists, Beaumanoir placed heavy emphasis on the importance of the husband's intention in beating his wife: his anger was to be restrained and strategic. A husband who throws his wife out of the marital home for no reason was described as cruel, and should be ordered to take her back: such an action was only to be justified when an obvious cause could be cited.[37] Likewise, of course, women were not allowed to leave their husbands without a most extreme cause.[38] Again and again, Beau-

[35] e.g. P. Abelard, *Ethics*, ed. and tr. D. Luscombe (Oxford, 1935), 29.
[36] 'The disagreements which arise in marriage': Beaumanoir, ii, no. 1626, 331.
[37] Ibid., no. 1627, 332. [38] Ibid.

manoir used the term 'resnablement' to evoke the importance of rational correlation between the misdemeanour of the woman and the violent punishment by her husband: a husband should give 'resnables commandements', and correct his wife 'resnablement'.[39] Drawing on the vocabulary used by the canonists, husbands were cast here in the role of preservers of order, and should 'chastier' their wives, evoking the idea of moral correction; moreover they were to 'reprendre' the faults of their wives, again drawing attention to the *re*-establishment of moral harmony and balance.[40]

In order to elucidate what precisely constituted reasonable cause for domestic discipline, Beaumanoir listed various vices for which wives could and should be disciplined in the interest of society as a whole. Wives could be beaten for insulting or inappropriately spoken words: 'aucune folie qu'ele dist'.[41] More specifically, words spoken to contradict the husband and challenge his authority, by criticizing his judgement or disrespectfully cursing him, were evoked as just cause for punishment. But actions were also included: a wife could be beaten 'pour aucun mesfet qu'ele fist'.[42] Disobeying her husband, and disregarding his orders was construed as a crime worthy of discipline, jeopardizing the rightful marital hierarchy. Graver still were those cases of wives guilty of adultery or 'folie de son cors', and such wives should be severely chastised.[43] Even when 'preudefames de leurs cors', Beaumanoir pointed out that women were prone to a whole gamut of other vices, for which the husband must always be vigilant and ready to cure the evil. Lexical choices repeatedly evoked the moral necessity and social desirability of disciplining an errant wife: 'il loit bien a l'homme a batre sa fame', 'est il bien mestiers que li maris soit chastieres de sa fame resnablement', 'bon sera pour li oster de cel vice'.[44] Nevertheless, the very precision of Beaumanoir's specification of the function of domestic discipline and when it could be used underlines that it was not always considered to be an appropriate response.

But reasonable anger was not in itself a sufficient category. The violent husband in *La Mégère émasculée* remains calm and emotionally controlled throughout the tale. Yet this does not render his actions any less cruel. When punishing his wife for her contradictory instructions to the cook, he beats her so severely that he leaves her for dead. The grotesqueness of his

[39] Ibid., no. 1629, 333. [40] Ibid., no.1631, 334.
[41] 'Any foolishness she might say': ibid., nos. 1628, 1631, 333–4.
[42] 'Any misdemeanour she might do': ibid., no. 1628, 332.
[43] 'Bodily foolishness': ibid., no. 1630, 334.
[44] 'It is appropriate for a man to beat his wife'; 'It is right that a man should reasonably punish his wife'; 'it is good to distance her from this vice': ibid., no. 1631, 334.

character undermines his actions, even if his anger appears collected; the *affectio maritalis* evoked in the line 'Son segnor ama et servi' just seems ironic and risible after his behaviour. The 'castration' of his mother-in-law is dwelt on with such horrific detail as to thoroughly destabilize the notion of domestic order preserved through force. He humiliates her in front of the servants, disrupting social hierarchy, and disregards all notions of courtly behaviour by shaming her sexually:

> Uns des sergans le rasoir prant,
> Le nage demi pié li fent,
> Son poing i met o ot enclos
> Un des collons au tor mout gros.[45]

In a sense, this extreme reassertion of the distinction between her femininity and his masculinity even undermines his own position.

It is the count's gestures which render him so grotesque, and secular legal thought tried to characterize such cases by categorizing physical gestures of domestic violence: those which served a corrective purpose, and those which should themselves be treated as unacceptable and disciplined in their turn. First, Beaumanoir underlined the importance of the frequency of domestic violence: a wife who was only occasionally beaten had, apparently, no reason to complain of her husband's treatment of her.[46] Women who wished to leave the marital home on account of an abusive husband were admonished to bear in mind that 'mout doit preudefame soufrir et endurer avant qu'ele se mete hors de la compaignie de son mari'.[47] Beatings involving only the hands, and not resulting in the death or severe bloodshed of the victim, were acceptable and to be left as intimate matters in which the court should not interfere: the vocabulary used here was the common 'battre'. However, discipline should not exceed certain boundaries, and 'mort ou mehaing' were specified as the point at which that boundary was transgressed.[48] But while 'mort' was a very straightforward category, the severe wounding implied by 'mehaing' was a more fluid and ambivalent one: at what point did a severe beating become 'mehaing'? Beaumanoir excluded death threats and 'afolement' from the types of acceptable chastisement, but again, the difference between 'afolement' and the permitted 'battement' was only one of degree, and there was no absolute scale allowing distinction of the two.[49]

[45] 'One of the servants takes a blade, makes a slit half a foot deep, and plunges his fist into it, holding one of the large testicles of a bull', ll. 565–8.

[46] Beaumanoir, ii, no. 1628, 332.

[47] 'An honest woman must suffer and endure a great deal before she withdraws from the company of her husband': ibid., no. 1629, 333.

[48] 'Death or wounding'. [49] 'Mutilation'.

Another legal text, the *Summa de legibus Normannie* contained a brief excursus on domestic violence: it evoked similar distinctions in claiming that, as long as the husband only struck his wife, this was justifiable correction.[50] Domestic violence, according to this text, must involve the worst excesses before it was to be considered unacceptable. Moreover, the text again stresses the importance of the husband's intention and the nature of his anger, stating that it was only *unreasonable* beatings which did not respond to any specific provocation which were to be themselves disciplined.

Some of the forms of correction advocated by the decretists, such as restriction of the wife's diet and diminution of her budget for clothing, were challenged by Beaumanoir who warned that a wife who felt her husband was trying to starve her was justified in leaving the marital home: restrictions on diet were open to widely differing interpretations. Women were permitted to leave husbands who beat them excessively, such men being placed in the same category as adulterers, thieves, and other criminals. On the other hand, men who beat their wives within reasonable limits were placed in the same bracket as husbands who were engaged in violent private disputes with their wives' relatives: the behaviour of such men was deemed acceptable, and their wives were obliged to continue to support them.[51]

The types of canonically prescribed discipline likely to be incurred by misdirected domestic violence included heavy fines: ecclesiastical courts could fine the husband up to one-third of the property he had contributed to the marriage, and could even impose separation on grounds of cruelty. Research from the remaining records of the ecclesiastical courts, most notably that of Helmholz for England, shows that *saevitia* (savagery) was the most frequent complaint in almost all divorce suits (even where other more financially motivated complaints were also being lodged):[52] *saevitia* again evokes animal-like behaviour, threatening the harmony and very framework of ordered and civilized society. It was relatively rare that divorce would be granted because of marital cruelty: of the two types of medieval divorce, simple separation (*divortium a mense*) and the cancelling of mutual sexual obligations (*divortium a mense et thoro*), only the former seems to have been granted for marital cruelty in the northern French case.[53]

[50] Cf. E.-J. Tardif (ed.), *Summa de legibus Normanniae* in his *Coutumiers de Normandie*, 2 vols. (Paris, 1896), ii, ch. 85, no. 8, 204.

[51] Beaumanoir, ii, no. 1629, 333.

[52] Helmholz, *Marriage*, 105; Brundage, 'Domestic Violence', 187.

[53] Ibid. 187–92: this is in contrast to the English case. See also Donahue, *Law*, 523–4.

Nevertheless, distinguishing 'discipline' or 'chastisement' from *saevitia* remained problematic. It was an indistinct line between the so-called rational, civilizing tendencies of corrective punishment, strategically reinforcing domestic order and harmony, and the irrational, animal-like, chaotic implications of *saevitia* and cruelty. Although all domestic violence is nowadays criminalized, it is interesting to find sociologists and their subjects still using similar categories of 'expressive' or 'dysfunctional', and 'instrumental' or 'functional' gestures to explain the phenomenon of violence within marital partnerships.[54] The canonists provided no straightforward answers to such problems: their attempts to delimit boundaries remained fluid, their definitions imprecise, and their scale of physical gestures descending into violence a sliding one. Sweeping statements about the importance of 'moderation' or 'reasonableness' in chastising one's wife failed to impose any precise categories. Medieval ambivalence about what sorts of physical gestures constituted legitimate use of force in the interests of social order and harmony, and which gestures were to be defined as 'violence', chaotic and irrational, corrupting and destabilizing the social order, was embodied in the canonical legislative position regarding domestic violence.

Beaumanoir was drawing on customary law rooted in communities, organically arising from collectively established norms. Whilst in many ways a far more prescriptive discourse, canon law nevertheless also intersected with the needs and norms established by communities. Via the practice of confession, its frameworks filtered down to actual couples on a day-to-day basis, and churchmen became more aware of the marital practices and assumptions of their flocks. The rise of confession, imposed as an annual obligation on all Christians by the Fourth Lateran council of 1215, meant that the relationship between Church law and the everyday lives of Christians was tightened and more closely regulated.[55] Both confessors and confessants attempted to distinguish between acceptable and unacceptable household violence. Again the very need for such distinctions demonstrates a deep-rooted ambivalence, and the categories established were nebulous and fluid. Moreover, confession and its associ-

[54] Such distinctions and terminology correspond to a broader sociological trend to distinguish between 'rational' and 'irrational' violence: E. Marx, 'Some Social Context of Personal Violence', in M. Gluckman (ed.), *The Allocation of Responsibility* (Manchester, 1972), 281–321; or 'realistic' versus 'unrealistic' violence: L. Coser, *The Functions of Social Conflict* (repr. London, 1998), 49.

[55] Cf. L. Boyle, 'The Fourth Lateran Council and Manuals of Popular Theology', in T. Hefferman (ed.), *The Popular Literature of Medieval England* (Knoxville, Tenn., 1985), 30–44; P. Biller, 'Introduction', in P. Biller and A. Minnis (eds.), *Handling Sin: Confession in the Middle Ages* (York, 1998), 1–35.

ated literature confronted the hesitant dichotomy of the public and the private, enabling it to engage with both the public and private implications of marriage and to understand the complexities involved in separating the intimate from the communal. Confession was essentially to be a private and intimate affair, but it took place not only for the salvation of the individual, but explicitly for the moral well-being of Christendom in its collective sense. Whereas penances were increasingly (after Lateran IV) to be carried out privately in the sinner's own home as an individual matter, many of the penances imposed, such as fasting, could be readily observed and interpreted by the wider community, and explicitly public penance did persist.[56] Although penitential literature rarely treats domestic violence as a self-contained type of sin, various illuminating comments were made upon the subject in more general sections on marriage, violence, and anger.

The rules upon which confession rested were expounded in penitentials and confessors' manuals, the tools of the trade for those guiding their penitent flock. The expansion of confession engendered a need for literature guiding the confessors, and the thirteenth century witnessed a profusion of manuals of confession, *Summae*, encyclopediae of vices and virtues, sermons, and manuals of pastoral care. The *Summae* for confessors were the most intellectually high-brow genre within this literature, designed for an audience of educated clerics.[57] Likewise, compendia of vices and virtues were popular and widespread, but intended for use on a more intellectual level. Manuals of confession on the other hand were adapted to a more basic and practical level.[58]

These texts showed that the canonical concern with the importance of intention and reasonable anger in the practice of domestic violence was an important element in confession: writers on confession, the confessors, and the penitents were all attuned to the effect of motivation on the categorization of their actions. Uxoricide was the most frequently addressed form of domestic violence and, although it was never condoned, its degree of sinfulness was shown to be dependent upon its intention. The issue was addressed in Robert of Flamborough's *Liber Poenitentialis* written between 1208 and 1213; Flamborough studied in Paris and by 1213 was sub-prior of Saint-Victor. His text took the form of a dialogue between a priest and a penitent, and the entire second book was devoted

[56] 'Every step of private penance, from confession to satisfaction, might threaten the privacy of the penitent': M. Mansfield, *The Humiliation of Sinners: Public Penance in Thirteenth-Century France* (Ithaca, NY, 1995), 78, 90–1; T. Tentler, *Sin and Confession on the Eve of the Reformation* (Princeton, 1977), 13.

[57] Boyle, 'Fourth Lateran Council', 33.

[58] Tentler, 'Sin and Confession', 48–9.

to the subject of marriage, with teaching mainly derived from the *Summa decretorum* of Huguccio.[59] He explained that matricide was a greater sin than uxoricide, implicitly because killing one's mother was more unnatural and less understandable than killing one's wife.[60] John of Freiburg, the Dominican writer of the enormously successful *Summa Confessorum* of 1298, stated that the penalty for uxoricide must be higher than that for matricide in order to discourage what is a much more common and easily entered into sin.[61] Likewise, Alain de Lille, famous Parisian master and author of the *Liber Poenitentialis*, assigned penances to all cases of uxoricide, but emphasized that uxoricides perpetrated 'sine causa' were more sinful than those responding to provocation or misbehaviour by the victim.[62]

These texts implicitly admitted the acceptability of any domestic 'discipline' which did not cause permanent damage or death to the woman. Indeed, some went so far as to state that such discipline formed part of the husband's social duties, and that failure to discipline an errant wife was in itself sinful and damaging to society. Alain de Lille specified that a husband who failed to punish and prevent his wife from sleeping with another man became an effective accomplice in her sin and should do penance accordingly.[63] John of Freiburg explained that a husband had a social duty not to hide any crime of his wife, but to punish it and prevent its recurrence for the collective good: a husband who deliberately concealed the misdemeanours of his wife became complicit in her sin.[64] In contrast, violence perpetrated by an inferior on a superior, whether a child against its parent, or a wife against her husband, was in no circumstances to be interpreted as disciplinary, but was immediately to be punished and atoned for as sinful, disruptive of order, and utterly unacceptable.[65]

Confessional material reiterated the importance of the evacuation of irrational emotion from the perpetration of rightful discipline, although

[59] F. Firth, 'Introduction', in Robert of Flamborough, *Liber Poenitentialis*, ed. F. Firth (Toronto, 1971), 5–14.

[60] Flamborough, ii. 59, 91.

[61] John of Freiburg, *Summa Confessorum* (Paris, 1519), 9, q. 4, fo. 230. The Dominican order had been commissioned by the papacy as 'Confessors-at-large', and John of Freiburg saw himself as providing an up-to-date and clear version of earlier thought on the subject, most notably that of Pennafort: L. Boyle, 'Summae Confessorum', in *Les Genres littéraires dans les sources théologiques et philosophiques médiévales: Définition, critique et exploitation. Actes du Colloque international de Louvain-la-Neuve, 25–27 mai 1981* (Louvain-la-Neuve, 1982), 233–6.

[62] Forty copies of the *Liber Poenitentialis* alone survive. 'Absque lege, vel sine causa': Alain de Lille, *Liber Poenitentialis*, ed. J. Longère (Louvain, 1965), 2. 66, 81.

[63] Alain de Lille, 2. 115, 105.

[64] John of Freiburg, 2, q. 48, fo. 221.

[65] Alain de Lille, 2. 28, 62–3; 2. 36, 66.

once again, the definition of anger was problematic, rendering the boundary between acceptable and unacceptable violence fluid. Anger was repeatedly defined as an irrational force, diabolically inspired, and leading to all kinds of marital problems: according to Flamborough, anger engenders impatience, indignation, insults, fights, shameful words, blasphemy, arguments, and grief, and causes those in positions of authority to forget their dignity and to shout and beat people beneath them.[66] It featured as a vice in Peraldus' compendium of vices and virtues, where the devil figured introducing marital discord (referred to here as 'inimicitia') into a couple's relationship through the medium of anger.[67]

Rightful intention was embodied in the actual gestures of domestic violence, and confessors' literature drew on canonistic distinctions for practical situations, as well as the cultural norms of their own flocks. Blood was the crucial element distinguishing an acceptable beating from an outbreak of excessive violence and, as in canon law, the death or permanent disablement of the victim was condemned.[68] The brief *Summa Parisiensis*, a summa on Gratian's *Decretum* preserved in a single manuscript from Bamberg, but originating in thirteenth-century Paris for the use of confessors, stated that marital discipline was acceptable as long as it stopped short of murder, and was perpetrated 'juste et rationabiliter': broad legitimacy was given to abusive husbands, and no precise assessment of what constituted just and rational behaviour was provided.[69] Such literature was acutely aware of the problematic nature of domestic violence, the negotiability of the line between violence and discipline, but only established nebulous criteria which could be interpreted in vastly differing ways. Moreover, this ambivalence clearly responded to an overall reluctance to condemn what was widely perceived as an important ordering force in a fundamental social unit. And what was the place of Christian forgiveness in a system which advocated violence in response to transgressions? The count in *La Mégère Emasculée*, despite his self-righteousness, expressly ignores his wife's pleas for Christian forgiveness, stating his preference for physical violence. If domestic discipline is supposed to operate through the reasonable use of force, and to impose a hierarchy with the husband in a position of authority because he is inherently more reasonable, then *La Mégère Emasculée* questions that

[66] Flamborough, iv. 201, 181–2.
[67] Peraldus, *Summa virtutum et vitiorum* (Paris, 1519), iii/1, fo. cci.
[68] Alain de Lille, 2. 66, 81; John of Freiburg, 9, q. 1, fo. 229.
[69] T. McLaughlin (ed.), *The Summa Parisiensis on the Decretum Gratiani* (Toronto, 1952), C. 17, q. 4, c. 33.

notion of reason, showing that it can be used to justify what is clearly repulsive and excessive brutality.

La Mégère Emasculée does not stand alone amongst the *fabliaux* in its depiction of domestic violence re-establishing or reinforcing a domestic hierarchy: it is only the most extreme in a series of similar tales. Some depict the struggle for ascendancy in the household being enacted physically in a fight between husband and wife, and again a conflict is established between the structural and the stylistic import of the tale. In the short tale of *Sire Hain et Dame Anieuse*, the conjugal couple reach such a state of discord that they decide the only way to resolve their problems is with a fight.[70] In a comic episode, husband and wife are pitched against each other and tear at each others' hair and clothes in a frantic bid for victory. Of course, Hain wins—though only just—and Anieuse is obliged henceforth to behave more respectfully towards him. However, this straightforward structural advocation of the function of domestic violence is undermined by the fact that it was Anieuse who suggested the resort to violence in the first place: it is no longer straightforwardly the rational and functional tool of the husband, but one brought into play by the apparently unreasonable wife. While again a short epilogue closes the tale and evokes the functionality of domestic violence, the glaring contrast between its pithiness and the long-drawn out nature of the fight slyly suggests that the maxim masks a genuine and troubled questioning of the resort to violence: 'fetes aussi fetement/Comme Hains fist de sa moillier'.[71]

2. THE PRACTICE OF DOMESTIC VIOLENCE

These inconclusive prescriptive discourses on domestic abuse shaped and were shaped by the practice of spousal violence. Of course, this layer of reality is largely screened from the grasp of the historian, filtered by legislation, prosecution, and imaginative literature. However, a bridge between the legalistic nuances of canon and customary law and the physical acts of abuse is provided by thirteenth-century exempla which often drew on real life to provide illustrative anecdotes for preachers.[72] Many exempla also furnished the subject matter for *fabliaux* which would subtly undercut the original moral point. While the function of exempla

70 'Sire Hain et Dame Anieuse', *NRCF* ii/5.

71 'Act in the same way that Hain did with his wife': ll. 408–9.

72 Cf. F. Tubach, *Index exemplorum: A Handbook of Medieval Religious Tales* (Helsinki, 1969); *Thesaurus Exemplorum Medii Aevii* at http://gahom.ehess.fr/thema (accessed Sept. 2010), henceforth THEMA.

was primarily hortatory, encouraging obedience to and awareness of scriptural precepts and canon law prescriptions, they were effective because the situations they depicted were quotidian and recognizable; they explained the prescriptions of the Church regarding marriage, whilst evoking practical responses to such prescriptions. Preachers rarely completely invented the stories; rather many drew on their significant experience as confessors to recount the sins of their subjects in the complex and nuanced way in which such misdemeanours were perpetrated and interpreted in everyday life. Thomas of Cantimpré, for example, was active as a confessor and explicitly drew on his own experience with penitents.[73] Preacher-confessors drew on stories heard in confession (in turn constructed by the confessant along the lines suggested by the confessor's questioning), and reconstructed them for hortatory purposes as exempla. The practice of domestic violence mediated via these tales from the confessional clearly *was* profoundly affected by the moral system propagated by canon law and sermons, and was coloured by the same ambivalence about the fine line between discipline and abuse.

Superficially, the exempla reiterated an understanding of the need for domestic discipline in order to preserve rightful order and social harmony. Jacques de Voragine's exempla emphasize again and again the primary function of domestic discipline to preserve the rightful hierarchy. According to his scheme, men embody reason, while women only embody fleshly thoughts, and it is therefore imperative that the husband be the head of the household, by force if necessary.[74] Beatings and verbal threats are recommended in order to keep the household in order, with the cautionary tale, apparently drawn from the preacher's own experience, of a man who failed to chastise his wife sufficiently, and consequently lost a large part of his property.[75] Women are characterized as wasteful and unreasonable, deliberately provoking the husband, and contradicting him for the sake only of contradiction—witness the case of the young wife who apparently put her fingers in a hole where her husband had fixed sharp nails and ordered her not to touch.[76]

However, while such easy justifications for domestic abuse were frequently cited, most probably by the perpetrators themselves, the exempla suggest that understandings were more complex, and that those confessing

[73] A. Murray, 'Confession as a Historical Source in the Thirteenth-Century', in Ralph Davis *et al.* (eds.), *The Writing of History in the Middle Ages: Essays Presented to Richard Southern* (Oxford, 1981), 275–322. Of course, not all exempla originated in this way.

[74] Jacobus de Voragine, *Sermones aurei* (Paris, 1760), 151, cited in THEMA.

[75] Galand de Reigny, *Parabolaire*, ed. C. Friedlander (Paris, 1992), no. 28, cited in THEMA.

[76] Tubach, *Index*, no. 5278; cf. also 5284, 5285.

acts of domestic violence were not so comfortable with their actions; certainly the anecdotes suggest that victims of such actions were uncertain how to respond and interpret the gestures from which they suffered. Jacques de Voragine tells of a widow who refused to remarry because, she implied, having a good authoritative husband one lives in fear of his death, having a bad husband one lives in fear of unprovoked violence: while the widow accepted the forceful domination of a husband, she was equally aware of how easily boundaries of acceptability could be transgressed.[77]

The exempla show that a profound uneasiness was felt by all concerned regarding the causes of domestic violence. Just as confessors' manuals and penitentials such as that of Alain de Lille underlined the importance of a just cause and right intention for domestic discipline,[78] so the exempla showed how easily causes of violence could be unjust, how often misunderstandings occurred, and how many reactions were excessive responses, and understood as such by their perpetrators. Numerous exempla present the devil introducing marital discord into harmonious partnerships, by tempting the husband to punish his wife irrationally for an imagined crime: thus, the motif of spousal misunderstandings is introduced. A typical tale explains how the devil tricked a man into believing his wife was having an affair with the local priest, when in fact she went to church so often only because of her devotion: the duped husband killed his innocent wife, and explained his actions by his belief in a diabolically inspired misunderstanding.[79] In another tale, it is a meddlesome old lady who insinuates to both the husband and the wife independently that each is planning to kill the other, thus inspiring marital discord and misdirected violence as the husband beats his innocent wife in the belief that she is trying to kill him.[80] The preacher here highlights the fragility of the notion of reasonableness of cause in domestic violence, and draws on his confessants' awareness that the justifiability of domestic discipline is extremely problematic and easily undermined: moreover, the role of the surrounding community is evoked, as the husband seems to be acutely aware of the influence malicious gossip may have on his behaviour.

The canonists' emphasis on rightful intention and emotion certainly coloured the self-perception of the perpetrators of domestic violence. The exempla refer repeatedly to the role of anger in acts of excessive domestic

[77] Jacobus de Voragine, *Sermones aurei*, 111, cited in THEMA.

[78] Alain de Lille, ii. 25, 61.

[79] *Dits de Jehan de Saint Quentin*, ed. B. Munk Olsen (Paris, 1978), 93–8, cited in THEMA. Cf. also Tubach, *Index*, no. 2707.

[80] Adolphe de Vienne, *Doligamus*, ed. P. Casali (Florence, 1997), no. 9, cited in THEMA.

violence: both preachers and confessants were aware that emotion was a distinguishing element in such acts. Anger and the importance of discipline were weighed up against one another in various contexts—marital, parental, and monastic—with one exemplum showing St Anselm warning an abbot not to beat children too much as anger may then dominate.[81] Another even suggests that the sin of anger represents such a serious risk to the person in authority that sometimes it is better to forego discipline in order to avoid falling into this snare.[82]

Likewise the surviving legal material attests to an awareness of the role of anger in acts of discipline which exceeded their own authority, instituting chaos rather than order. In a case of 1303 from Fampoux in Artois, a man beat his daughter much harder than he intended in a fit of anger; according to the account, it was his awareness of his anger which caused him to realize that his gestures had exceeded mere discipline, and to flee.[83] A much later case of 1353 from Saint-Martin-des-Champs describes the murder by Symonnet de Bennes of his wife Nicole—his ready confession suggesting a degree of regret at an emotional outburst, rather than attempted justification of legitimate discipline.[84] A distinction is thus made, even by the perpetrators, between normative and aberrant violence. The most horrific acts of domestic violence come from families with a record of violent behaviour in other spheres, pointing to a perception that most families could carry out moderate discipline, but that excessive violence correlated to an abnormally violent atmosphere.[85] For example, in the 1300s, the Parisian parish of Saint-Maur-des-Fossés witnessed multiple tragedies in the household of an English artisan called Richardus: he murdered his mother-in-law, and his wife was then found guilty of infanticide.[86] The figure of the mother-in-law was a rather common trope in accounts of domestic violence, often blamed for pushing an otherwise reasonable husband into unreasonable behaviour. The framing of a case of 1338, initially brought by the mother-in-law against her son-in-law and another man (presumably his master or associate), suggests that the son-in-law, Guillaume Johan, was forced to behave brutally by her meddlesome behaviour; the record implies that she increased levels of

[81] Tubach, *Index*, no. 261. [82] Ibid., no. 670.
[83] ADN, B13596/58. [84] Tanon, 552.
[85] NB: Herlihy notes that there was less community sympathy for men who were well known for violence, drinking, and regular abuse: *Medieval Households*, 12. Again, this corresponds to modern sociological theory where domestic violence is often interpreted as occurring in contexts where violence has become a learned behavioural response: e.g. Gelles, *Violent Home*, 172.
[86] Tanon, 334.

familial tension by making public her claim that she had been woefully misled in marrying her only daughter to a man she believed to be a wealthy merchant. In this case, Guillaume's violence was apparently an assertion of his authority in the household.[87]

If the perpetrators of domestic abuse were acutely aware of the importance of rightful intention, they seem also to have been influenced by canon law distinctions between different types of gestures within domestic abuse. The exempla reveal a clear awareness amongst confessants that the type of violence carried out categorizes it as sinful or dutiful: men who murder their wives are condemned and condemn themselves, men who beat their wives with hands or sticks are lauded, and present their own actions with pride.[88] Popular sources such as the *fabliaux* would suggest that the common 'legitimate' disciplining of wives involved 'mere' beatings with the hands.[89] Whilst the few cases which came to the courts usually involved weaponry, this only further corroborates the idea that beating with the hands was considered acceptable, and most probably common. Later evidence from the episcopal court of Paris at the end of the fourteenth century, concerning marital separations, most often includes accusations of marital abuse: a distinction was made in such cases between 'saevitia', implying cruelty and use of weapons by the husband, and 'rancor', where beatings do not seem to have involved weapons and both parties admitted to mutual dislike.[90] The message that beating with the hands was acceptable, beating with weapons, savage, seemed to have struck a chord amongst the perpetrators of domestic violence.[91]

Moreover, the attitude of the victims to domestic abuse was also shaped by the rather hesitant moral system propounded by canonists. Whilst very few exempla present the victim's point-of-view, other sources demonstrate that, while women were demoralized and harmed by domestic so-called discipline, they seem, at least superficially, to have accepted the role of the virtuous suffering wife. This is indicated primarily by the minimal legal redress sought by victims, compared to the widespread practice indicated by contemporary literature. The legal sources from the late thirteenth and

[87] Furgeot and Dillay, *Actes*, i, no. 2235, 215.

[88] e.g. Tubach, *Index*, no. 5282; Galand de Reigny, no. 28, cited in THEMA.

[89] Cf. H. Wheeler, 'Les Représentations de la violence dans les fabliaux et *le Roman de Renart*', (DEA thesis, Paris III—Nouvelle Sorbonne 2001), appendix 3.

[90] J. Petit (ed.), *Registre des causes civiles de l'officialite de Paris, 1384–1387* (Paris, 1919): e.g. see for *saevitia*, cols. 21–2, 93; for *rancor* or *odio*, cols. 64, 91. On the other hand, sometimes accusations of financial mismanagement were a helpful way of getting spousal cruelty heard in court.

[91] Similar distinctions have been found in the Provençal and Polish cases: cf. respectively Bednarski, 'Keeping it in the Family', 277–99; Brozyna, 'Not Just a Family Affair', 299–311.

early fourteenth centuries contain no cases where the complainant was the victim: most often women accepted domestic abuse until they died from it, at which point the local legal official or friends of the victim might take action. In thirteenth- and fourteenth-century France, a positive spin was given to victimhood by a widespread discourse associating victims of violence with Christian virtue, even with Christ-like suffering: women could be active and collaborative agents in their own passion. Modern sociological research shows that the 'I deserved it' reaction is common today as well.[92] The personal piety of women in this period is said to have been much influenced by themes of asceticism and devotion to the figure of the suffering Christ, and the experience of domestic violence could feed into this gender-specific religious sensitivity.[93] Such preoccupations are particularly vivid in contemporary hagiography, with a multitude of female saints experiencing domestic abuse, and rejoicing in this opportunity for painful *imitatio Christi.* Many female saints used the metaphor of the family and suffering wives to evoke their mystical experiences, and figures such as Angela of Foligno in Italy (d. 1309), Yvette of Huys in Flanders (d. 1229), and Dorothea of Montau (d. 1394) apparently intensified their mystical experience through the pain they suffered at the hands of their husbands.[94] Such figures bear important witness to victims' reactions, because they provided models and inspiration for contemporary suffering women. Literature produced by men was, unsurprisingly, quick to embody this attitude typified in the story of Griselda, told first by Boccaccio and Petrarch, but probably originating in an earlier folk tale. But the theme was also enthusiastically taken up by female saints and writers, including no less a figure than Christine de Pizan.[95]

Yet the implication that men and even women straightforwardly accepted justifications of high levels of domestic violence should not be taken at face value. The disjunction between the assumed prevalence of domestic violence and its minimal reporting must also reflect the enormous obstacles for women wishing to seek redress. Imaginative literature provided a rare forum for the effect on ordinary women to be considered. The motif of the patiently suffering wife was frequently evoked in miracle literature, but engaged with unease about such martyrdom. Such figures are common in Gautier de Coinci's thirteenth-century popular collection of Marian miracles, well-known in both Chartres (where they were

[92] Gelles, *Violent Home*, 179.

[93] Cf. C. Walker-Bynum, *Fragmentation and Redemption: Essays on Gender and the Human Body in Medieval Religion* (New York, 1991), 181–238.

[94] Herlihy, *Medieval Households*, 112–16.

[95] Cf. Salisbury, *Domestic Violence*, 12.

produced) and Paris. The tale *De deuz fammes que Nostre Dame converti* tells of two women who hate each other, because one is having an affair with the other's husband.[96] The betrayed wife longs for vengeance, most particularly because her amorous husband now treats her violently and contemptuously. She does not dare to harm her rival, because she knows her husband would punish her brutally for such an offence, so she prays to the Virgin for revenge. Mary appears to the woman, and explains that she cannot harm the rival, as this other woman is one of her most devoted servants. The wife, in despair, reveals the whole story to her rival, who is so touched by the Virgin's refusal to harm her that she abandons her lover and dedicates her life to Mary.

This story bears witness to uneasiness with the motif of the patiently suffering wife: whilst at several removes from the practice of violence, the tale claims verisimilitude and sets itself up as a socially engaged response to the unrealistic ideals of theological and hagiographical texts. In her textual capacity as a historical figure, this wife's acceptance of whatever 'discipline' her husband should choose is tempered by the murderous thoughts which occupy her concerning his lover: her suffering is far from that of a Christian saintly martyr. Her acceptance of domestic violence is problematized by her resort to the perversion of religion in her vengeful prayers to the Virgin.

Moreover, the order of the household which is preserved through her reluctance to challenge her husband's behaviour is not a comfortable one, but rather further complicated by the story's condemnation of the husband's behaviour. He is an adulterer whose behaviour cannot be justified, and should not be passively accepted. His righteousness and the harmony of their household is shown to be nothing more than a hypocritical façade; his violent behaviour is unacceptable and excessive, lacking reasonable cause, and inspired only by his sexual desire for another woman. The wife graphically describes the abuse in her tirade to her rival, and explains that she does nothing to provoke it:

> Sovent me fais batre et ferir . . .
> Il ne m'aimme ne ne me prise,
> Ains me froisse tote et debrise
> Quant un seul mot en os tentir.[97]

Her language reflects the lexical choices of the legal records ('battre', 'ferir', 'froisser'), further underlining its excessiveness.

[96] Gautier de Coinci, *Miracles*, i. 33.

[97] 'He often beats and strikes me . . . He does not love or respect me. Now he beats me all over, and thrashes me when I dare even to say a single word': ll. 66–70.

The complaint evokes sympathy, distress, and indignation on the part of the audience, and, of course, this is the point: it is, after all, a miracle story. Its function was to present the Virgin Mary responding to concerns which would resonate with her followers. The intervention of the Virgin indicates the intransigency of the situation: the husband's behaviour is unacceptable, yet cannot be challenged without jeopardizing the stability of traditional hierarchies. A miracle is the only solution, and it is followed by an agreement on a course of action between the two women, so that the spouses can live happily ever after without any need for explicit criticism of the husband.

When the Virgin was unavailable to respond to such crises, the legal process of remission provided an opportunity for husbands to explain themselves. The various aspects of the problematization of domestic violence in practice can be effectively illustrated by a case from Saint-Germain-en-Laye in 1325.[98] The case is recounted in one of the earliest letters of remission, and the detailed account of the crime by the perpetrator himself required for the appeals procedure provides a glimpse into both the initial motivation of the husband, and the way in which he thought it appropriate, *post facto*, to describe his action. On 25 February 1325, Colin le Barbier killed his wife Eustache La Barbière semi-accidentally with a billiard stick. His attempt at extenuation demonstrates an understanding and awareness of the distinctions and ambivalences of canon law and contemporary Christian morality of violent disciplining. In his defence, he first explained very precisely the misdemeanour of his wife, in order to elucidate the justification for the beating: she had insulted him repeatedly with 'paroles mout vilaines et injurieuses', behaviour widely taken to justify physical discipline.[99] Colin tried to escape from his wife's unreasonable behaviour by going to play billiards with his friends, but she followed him and continued to insult him in public: Colin's embarrassment in front of his companions is palpable, and it was his friends who apparently then urged him to discipline his wife, with even an edge of criticism for his patience implied by the 'merveillement' of his friends that he could tolerate so much. If her nagging was stereotypically feminine, he needed publicly to assert his masculinity through controlled anger and discipline. The role of the surrounding community in the perpetration of domestic discipline was evoked, together with the sense

[98] AN, JJ24, fo. 430, no. 733.

[99] I have found no mention of insults by the wife in canon law, but Hardwick notes a long-standing tendency for 'husbands, wives, neighbours and courts [to concur] that women's inappropriate speech could be cause for conjugal discipline': Hardwick, 'Early Modern Perspectives', 1–36.

that the husband had a social duty to maintain the marital hierarchy. Colin further explained that he did not become angry, but that his actions remained functional and rational, contrasting his behaviour with that of his wife, apparently 'meue de mauvaiz esperit'. When describing the blow that finally killed her, he was careful to stress that his intention was not to kill, but merely to frighten her into silence and submission. The weapon used was the stick with which he was playing, and it is specified that the instrument was not pointed, as this would recategorize his physical gesture as unacceptable violence. Most compelling for the court was the reputation of Colin: since he apparently had no previous history of domestic abuse, his behaviour was categorized as that of a rational and righteous man, provoked, even necessitated, by the unacceptable and disruptive behaviour of his wife. Colin was evidently uncertain in the first place about the acceptability of physically attacking his wife, hence his hesitancy to beat her at all; when he did so, he was careful to avoid evincing unrestrained anger, to express an acceptable and clear intention, and to avoid the use of a normally fatal weapon. Canonical ambivalence about domestic violence affected the way in which it was carried out and narrated by its perpetrators and victims.

3. THE PROSECUTION OF DOMESTIC VIOLENCE

This letter of remission demonstrates how canon law prescriptions concerning domestic violence influenced its actual perpetration. Colin le Barbier acted in a way influenced by the ambiguities of legal regulations. But his appeal also shows his knowledge of the nature of the prosecution of domestic violence and the influence of this knowledge on the way he presented that behaviour to the court. Prosecution is the most obvious point of contact at which the community became involved in 'reading' acts of violence.

While one of the most useful sources for legal reactions to domestic violence is, naturally, marriage litigation contained in the records of the ecclesiastical courts, no such records survive for the period and regions under investigation here.[100] Turning to the surviving secular law records of Artois and Paris reveals a surprising amount of litigation occasioned by the practice of domestic violence. These records again both draw upon and

[100] With the exception of the register of accounts of the keeper of the Arras episcopal seal for 1328: fines in this document focus upon adultery and usury, and do not mention domestic violence. For a slightly later period, cf. Petit, *Registre des causes civiles.*

shape the fine line between normative correction and deviant violence in contemporary perceptions, as the interaction of canon law, the practice of violence, and prosecution constructed sliding scales of acceptability.

The nature of these legal records points to the collective social implications of domestic violence. About 90 per cent of cases were initiated *ex officio*—that is, the legal system took it upon itself to gather evidence and present a case for the prosecution. Such a process demonstrates that excessive domestic violence was not perceived as affecting merely the individuals concerned, but as an assault on the common good. Discipline, though private, was perceived, like law, to be a crucial pillar of an ordered society, as demonstrated by the canonical prescriptions, but excessive abuse was seen to threaten the entire social order, trangressing the fine line between the public and the private.

Behaviour within marriage clearly had implications beyond the intimate boundaries of the home, and the prosecution of domestic violence reveals complex networks of support.[101] Moreover, the nature of prosecutions of domestic violence also reveals, more cynically, who, apart from the actual victim, felt threatened by a husband's abuse of his wife. The family of the victim seems rarely to have intervened (at least legally), whereas friends and neighbours played a much more prominent role: such was the case when Marie le Gasset was beaten to death by her husband in 1317.[102] In 1338 in Saint-Martin-des-Champs, Jehan le Saulnier engaged in excessive and noisy beating of his pregnant wife, and was reported by their neighbour, Perrin de la Chapelle.[103] In 1275 in Saint-Maur-des-Fossés, Jehannot, son of Gautier de Broche, viciously beat his wife: her friends later reported his excessive abuse, and agreed his banishment with the court.[104] Again, the line between normative correction and chaotic abuse had been crossed, and the harmony of society as a whole was at risk. A few cases provoked a hue and cry, witness the public reaction to Jehan Duquesne's stabbing of his ex-wife where a large section of the community responded to the crime; having found him with the bloody knife in his hand, the crowd ensured the capture of the perpetrator, and defended social harmony.[105]

However, collective reactions to domestic violence were also coloured by ambivalence, revealed by the communal reluctance to assume the

[101]'No household was an island': C. Dyer, 'Public and Private Lives in the Medieval Household', in Davis *et al.*, *Love, Marriage*, 237.

[102] Boutaric, *Actes*, ii, no. 4980, 196 (1316). This was not always the case as e.g. Bednarski finds that families were very supportive in the Provençal case: 'Keeping it in the Family', 292.

[103] Tanon, 515. [104] Ibid. 325. [105] Ibid. 485.

husband guilty. Such reluctance illustrates not only a hesitant respect for the boundaries of the home, but also a sense that domestic hierarchies should only be criticized in the most extreme circumstances. In 1327, it was the friends of the convicted Macy de Molembes, one of the king's cooks, who appealed on his behalf, demonstrating their concern for what they perceived to be an unjust condemnation of his justifiable disciplining of his wife, Jeanne.[106] Likewise, one Gilles de Vitry was acquitted in 1301 of an accusation that he had murdered his wife.[107] Many recorded cases noted the refusal of the community to report the violence of the husband, on account of the consequent risk of social disruption: for example, Jehan de Sausuelle beat his pregnant wife, Alice, to death in 1332, but was finally acquitted when none of his friends or neighbours was prepared to provide any incriminating evidence.[108] But this was not indifference: feelings ran high in such cases. In 1341, a secular clerk from Amiens named Nicholas was accused of beating his wife: when the case came to the Paris Parlement, he was acquitted, and the mayor and *échevins* of Amiens were punished severely for their actions, indicating a reluctance at the highest level to condemn violent husbands. What had been the actions of the Amiens *échevins*? They had stripped Nicholas until he was half-naked, tied him to a horse by his neck, left him to freeze on a cold winter's night, and thrown all his possessions into the street: hardly the behaviour of those agnostic about his misdemeanours. The Parlement's interpretation of the case suggested that the accusation of domestic violence had been merely a pretext for a deeper grudge, but it could only have been an effective pretext if domestic violence was an emotive issue.[109] It was also one which was remembered for years to come, rather than accepted as a normal part of life, witness the description in 1269 of a domestic murder twenty-four years previously.[110]

Increasing attention was paid in secular legal records to the precise gestures used by the perpetrator: the very definition of the act as violence hinged on the precise actions and weapons used. Generally speaking, domestic violence needed to engender very serious consequences, principally the death of the victim, before any legal intervention could be expected: about half of the cases explicitly treating violence done to a wife by her husband in the records examined resulted in the death of the victim. Weapons are always indicated, most often knives, as these came quickly to hand, and clearly placed the action in the category of illicit

[106] AN, JJ64, fo. 344ᵛ.
[107] Boutaric, *Actes*, ii, no. 3130, 15 (1301).
[108] AN, JJ66, fo. 263ᵛ.
[109] Furgeot and Dillay, *Actes*, i, no. 3713, 374 (1341).
[110] ADPC, A18/2.

violence.[111] In one particularly gruesome case, a man from Saint Omer was said to have poured quick-silver down his wife's throat—perhaps in response to the stress of being also suspected of forging coins.[112] When verbal abuse could be shown to have accompanied the physical blows, the excessive nature of the brutality and the husband's irrational anger was apparently revealed, as in the case of a husband in Aire, who insulted and beat his wife so that she died of her injuries.[113]

The vocabulary used in the records is telling, and indicates the need for precision concerning the interpretation of the violence: lexical nuances were crucial in the categorization of the act as unacceptable violence or as laudable discipline. 'Navrer' served to signify the wounding rather than the mere beating of the victim, and the spilling of blood, a sign that the violence had transgressed the boundaries of legitimacy.[114] Often the affected part of the body was specified, as in 'navrer en la teste', as the precise bodily location of the wound was cardinal in the assessment of its severity.[115] Substantives were used to evoke the disruptive, non-corrective, damage done to the victim's body: 'injures', 'sévices', 'coups orbes'.[116] Such terms were intended to refer to the unacceptability of the gravity of the wounds caused to the woman. The courts were interested, however, not merely in the physical gestures used by aggressors, but also in the accompanying verbal violence, the 'vilains mots', which implied excessive humiliation and anger. When Guillaume Renaud beat his pregnant wife in Saint-Maur-des-Fossés in 1270, he apparently allowed anger to get the better of him as he repeatedly insulted her.[117] Many of the female victims in the records were recorded as pregnant at the time of the attack. One victim in Saint-Maur-des-Fossés in the 1260s was beaten so severely by her husband that her child was born dead: the legal prosecution seized on any decisive factor which would help it to categorize the husband's actions as illegitimate and violent, rather than corrective and disciplinary.[118] Miscarriages caused by domestic abuse were decisive

[111] Dean notes that knives were the most frequent weapons used in assaults in Bologna: Dean, 'Domestic Violence', 527–43.

[112] ADPC, A149/3. 'Vif argent' figures in the *Dit d'un mercier*, ll. 22–5, where the speaker boasts that he has excellent mercury in a little pouch of fish skin for sale: BN, MS fr. 19152, fos. 42^{v}–43^{r}, ed. Philippe Ménard in *Mélanges de langue et de littérature du Moyen Age et de la Renaissance offerts à Jean Frappier*, 2 vols. (Geneva, 1970), ii. 797–808. It was sometimes used for skin complaints, or for venereal diseases, but this usage may have been later. Mercury was also used in metallurgy, and the money-forging activities of this man may account for his possession of the poison.

[113] ADN, B13597, fo. 102^{v}.

[114] e.g. ADPC, A140/1.

[115] 'To wound in the head': e.g. Tanon, 469.

[116] 'Wounds', 'brutalities', 'dirty blows': e.g. ADPC, A46/9; Tanon, 462.

[117] Tanon, 338. [118] Ibid. 337–8.

factors in the court's interpretation of the legitimacy of an act of violence.[119] On the other hand, if the unborn child of the victim was apparently unharmed by the attack, this could contribute to the acquittal of the abuser, whose actions could thus be construed as remaining within legitimate bounds: for example, the reported miscarriage of Colete de Soissons in 1336, was later discovered to be fabricated and her unborn child safe, so her abuser was acquitted.[120]

Doctors were frequently employed to help the court in its hesitancy regarding the categorization of domestic abuse; they testified to the gravity of the woman's wounds and, on the sliding scale of acceptable and unacceptable physical brutality, their assessment of the state of the victim was crucial. Doctors were, essentially, reading the victim's body for signs which would indicate the type of gestures from which the victim had suffered: the body became a crucial hermeneutic tool for the understanding of the violence.[121] If the victim died of her wounds, as in cases of murder or manslaughter more generally, doctors were called upon to bear witness to the length of time which it took the victim to die, and whether the death could be attributed to the violence beyond reasonable doubt. In 1304 in Lens, Jaquemon le Vasseur of Verquigneul beat his wife so severely that she died within forty days: he was fined 12 livres, a more lenient penalty than that for straightforward murder, but much heavier than what he would have had to pay if his wife had survived or taken longer to die.[122] The eagerness of the legal record to note such detail demonstrates how such nuances could entirely alter the categorization of a case. Some cases revealed an astonishing lack of compassion in this respect. Colin le Barbier's wife, who died of the wound received when he threw a billiard stick at her, is said to have died principally because she failed to take proper care of the wound, 'plus par son mauvaiz gouvernement que outrement': thus, the letter of remission implies, her death was primarily her own fault, and Colin did not necessarily inflict a fatal blow.[123]

Legal records were likewise attuned to the spatial configuration of acts of violence, crucial in the attempt to distinguish between forceful

[119] AN, JJ66, fo. 263^{v}.

[120] Tanon, 482. In this case she was not beaten by her husband, but by one Jehannot Lebidant.

[121] Hardwick notes in 17th-cent. accounts the importance of signs on the body such as bleeding, disrupted pregnancy, dishevelled hair, and torn clothing: Hardwick, 'Early Modern Perspectives', 16.

[122] ADN, B13596/2621.

[123] 'More because of the poor care she took, than for any other reason': AN, JJ64, fo. 430, no. 733.

correction and turbulent violence. The public and the private was an essential distinction, and different types of power and authority were exercised in each.[124] Such legal frameworks were superimposed on a general sense that what went on in the home was characterized by intimacy and was to a certain extent distinct from collective social processes. Domestic violence which emerged from the context of the home provided a clear indication that a boundary between discipline and disruptive violence had been crossed. In 1302 in Avesnes, Aliaume le Kieutepointier, beat his wife in her brother's house: the legal records draw attention to the physical placing of this violence, as it served to place the gestures firmly in the category of unacceptable violence.[125] Likewise, the best way in which a victim could defend herself was to run outside to make the event public; thus the boundary between private and public would be transgressed, and the community authorized, indeed provoked, to seek redressive action.[126] The motif of the hue and cry served to make a private complaint public, and to evoke the communal interest in a case of private violence.[127] When Jehanne, the ex-wife of Jehan Duqeusne, was found by neighbours bleeding and dying, a hue and cry by candlelight was immediately convoked: crucially, the incident took place in the street.[128] On the other hand, if the wife's misdemeanour happened in public, as in the case of Colin le Barbier, the need for domestic discipline was apparently even stronger, as the public ramifications of an intimate disagreement were more potentially damaging.[129] As long as discipline or violence ran parallel to the law, its role was a public one; when it transgressed legal prerogatives, its place in the public sphere was more problematic.

But thirteenth- and fourteenth-century ambivalence about normative and deviant violence could not rely on an absolute dichotomy between the public and the private spheres to resolve its hesitancy: as the hesitancy of the canon law position showed, the private had public implications and vice versa. Many prosecuted cases of domestic violence specified that the act took place in the home of the victim: such cases, though spatially conforming to a model of private discipline, had broader implications as society in general was destabilized by the undermining of one of its

124 Cf. G. Duby, 'Private Power, Public Power', in Duby (ed.), *Revelations of the Medieval World: A History of Private Life* (Cambridge, Mass., 1988), 7–14. However, the contrast must not be exaggerated: Dyer, 'Public and Private', 237–41.

125 ADPC, A117/2.

126 Cf. Hardwick, 'Early Modern Perspectives', 19: 'early modern working women employed a repertoire of publicizing actions as a central part of their strategy to secure help'.

127 Duby, 'Private Power', 14.

128 Tanon, 485.

129 AN, JJ66, fo. 263^{v}, no. 626.

foundational units. For example, in the 1320s, Jean de Sausuelle killed his wife and unborn child in his home; he was eventually remitted because no one had seen the act take place, but this privacy clearly did not imply that it was acceptable.[130] The legal record confronts its own ambivalence while making the point that perpetrators should not believe they can hide behind private boundaries.

Hesitancy concerning the assessment of domestic violence shaped the punishments meted out to the guilty. Courts were relieved when the perpetrator fled—a common occurrence—as this saved them the bother of trying to evaluate the criminality of the case. In 1306, in the jurisdiction of Saint-Germain-des-Près, Philippe Moreau beat his wife very severely and, when he realized that he had killed her, fled; a half-hearted hue and cry failed to catch him, and the court contented itself with confiscating his property.[131] The community was thus rid of an unstable and disruptive individual, without having to make any clear statements about the acceptability of domestic violence: the perpetrator effectively punished himself, and the jurisdictional authorities even benefited financially from the outcome.

Occasionally, the court banished the perpetrator, forbidding him to return to the area under pain of death. Such measures were only applied in cases of indisputably deliberate uxoricide: legal officials were unwilling to pass such unconditional sentences in any but the most obviously unacceptable incidents. Jehan de Broche, who deliberately murdered his wife in Saint-Maur-des-Fossés in 1275, was banished overseas after a lengthy negotiation and agreement between the court, his dead wife's friends, and himself: clearly he was a disruptive member of society, but one who could not be corporally punished without destabilizing the fundamental hierarchy of marriage.[132] Many perpetrators were imprisoned pending trial, which was then implicitly construed as sufficient punishment in itself, although there is no mention of imprisonment being originally intended as penal. This was another effective method of avoiding outright condemnation of marital physical aggression whilst still imposing some disciplinary action over a disruptive member of society. For example, Guillot Depont of Saint-Martin-des-Champs was imprisoned for several months pending and during his trial for the excessive beating of a woman, but released after the trial, despite being caught in the act by one Guiot de Florville.[133]

[130] Ibid. [131] Tanon, 440. [132] Ibid. 325.

[133] Ibid. 482. Cf. J. Dunbabin, *Captivity and Imprisonment in Medieval Europe (1100–1300)* (Basingstoke, 2002), 98–113.

Comparing fines for domestic violence as opposed to punishments for violence between men is revealing. Where non-domestic murderers were not capitally punished or banished, fines tended to be extremely high, ranging from 60 to 100 livres; where peace was made with the family of the victim, the composition was usually 32 livres.[134] These payments were only lowered in cases of self-defence or other extenuating circumstances.[135] In contrast, men who murdered their wives were typically fined less, witness the case of Jaquemon le Vasseur of Verquigneul who murdered his wife in Lens in 1304, and paid a fine of only 12 livres; or the case of Jehan from Delettes who killed his wife in Aire in 1308, and was fined only 10 livres.[136] Some of the payments made by the perpetrators were not fines, but compositions made in order to ward off the threat of more severe punishment: this form of resolution was a common response to all forms of violence in this period and was an implicit acknowledgement that the representative of the common good did not necessarily have the right to interfere in interpersonal violence. In the case of domestic violence, compositions were a way of avoiding categorical condemnation of the offence. In Arras in 1294, the favour of the corrupt *bailli*, Jehan Beauquesne, was bought by the mother of Pierre de Savie, when the latter was accused of the murder of his wife: Pierre de Savie was released with no further punishment.[137] A twist in the story was revealed during a later investigation into charges of corruption against Jehan de Beauquesne: the mother of de Savie had been unwilling to bribe Beauquesne in this way, but he had threatened that 'il feroit celui Pierot pourrir en prison' until she capitulated and made a financial offer to the *bailli* which she then failed to honour until threatened further.[138] Beauquesne was not particularly interested in the charge of domestic violence, merely in the possibility of financial gain, but the fact that he was able to release a man publicly known to have murdered his wife testifies to a widespread ambivalence,

[134] e.g. Jehan de Goisnai de le Buveriere was obliged to pay a fine of 60 livres for the murder of the son of Pieron des Wastines in Lens in 1303 (ADN, B13596, ed. in B. Delmaire, *Le Compte General d'Artois pour 1303–1304* (Brussels, 1977), no. 1240); in 1304 in Calais, Jehan le Maistre paid a fine of 130 livres for the murder of Willaume Mictre (ADN, B13596, ed. Delmaire, no. 4003); composition of 32 livres in the case of Baudien Estieven de Hellefaut who killed Danel le Prevost de Biekenes in 1304 in Saint Omer (ADN, B13596, ed. Delmaire, no. 1931); see also cases ADPC, A205/4; ADN, B13596, fo. 87^{v}; ADN, B13596, fo. 107^{r}; B13597, fo. 11^{v}.

[135] e.g. a case of self-defence in Hesdin in 1302: ADPC, A188/3; or an accident in Arras in 1304: ADN, B13596, ed. Delmaire, no. 2279; an accident in Saint Omer in 1304, ADN, B13596, fo. 87^{v}; ADPC, A205/4.

[136] Respectively, ADN, B13596, ed. Delmaire, no. 2621; ADN, B13597, fo. 102^{v}.

[137] ADPC, A41/28.

[138] 'He would make Pierot rot in prison'.

both about the justifiability of such violence in the first place, and about its implications for the community.

More substantial fines do appear in the records, but they tended to punish crimes where domestic violence was only part of the story. The man who poured quick-silver down his wife's throat was fined a crippling 60 livres, but he was also suspected of forgery and was clearly viewed as a criminal character.[139] Gallon de Fins was fined 60 livres in Bapaume in 1304, but he had not only beaten his wife, but carried out a vengeful armed robbery on his mother-in-law, breaking into her house and allegedly spitefully stealing all her jewels.[140] Capital punishment for wife murderers was extremely rare: courts were unwilling to sanction the unambivalent condemnation of domestic violence, even in its most extreme form, preferring to attribute death to an accident. Moreover, the few letters of remission available for this early period bear witness to the reluctance of legal authorities to remain faithful to an outright condemnation of domestic abuse. Colin le Barbier was released because of his apparent good character, the court being unwilling to allow one act against his wife to outweigh his reputation as an upright member of the community.[141] Other cases were repealed with no such straightforward explanation, merely a general unwillingness to allow men who had been 'provoked' by their wives to be unambivalently punished: Macy de Molembes's appeal against his sentence was successful, but the record does not deem it necessary to state why.[142]

In the attempt to distinguish between acceptable or deviant physical gestures, the legal records also paid close attention to the status of the various actors. Numerous cases of beatings of other people's wives—likewise, beatings by masters of other masters' apprentices, or beatings by parents of other parents' children—testify to the importance of the ordering function of domestic discipline.[143] Beating someone else's wife was categorically deemed unacceptable, for such a beating did not serve the domestic hierarchy, but represented the encroachment of one authority on another in an anarchic manner totally opposed to the apparently ordering function of rightly executed domestic violence. In 1340, Girart Congnart beat his neighbour's wife: the complainant was the husband, who must have realized that his own domestic hierarchy

[139] ADPC, A149/3. [140] ADN, B13596, fo. 85v.

[141] AN, JJ64, fo. 430.

[142] Ibid., fo. 344^{v}; see also JJ66, fo. 263^{v}.

[143] e.g. respectively ADN, B13596, fo. 99^{v}; ADN, B13596, ed. Delmaire, no. 760—this might include stepchildren.

was thus jeopardized.[144] Moreover, in this case, the aggressor repeatedly insulted his victim, thus making the slight on the honour of her husband yet more obvious. Family relations were even more strained in a case from Normandy in 1321, when Colin Clarel confessed in the Church court that he had beaten his brother's wife.[145] Nor was it acceptable to strike one's mother-in-law, though in the case of Guillaume Johan, it was decided that such a beating was merited since *she* was the one who had attempted to interfere in his domestic hierarchy by trying to shield her daughter from his blows.[146] Status could shift with marital circumstances. The case of Jehan Duquesne, prosecuted for the wounding of his ex-wife, was surely influenced by the fact that he no longer had legal authority over her, rendering his action violent rather than legitimately disciplinary.[147] The social status of the victim could also be brought into play to assess the categorization of the husband's action: in 1299, the husband of the Dame de Beauval was ordered to leave her alone, and to pay her and her children a pension of 300 pounds per annum, for it was deemed inappropriate to treat such a socially elevated person with humiliating abuse.[148]

The rare cases of women who carried out violence on their husbands were punished unambivalently; here there was no doubt that a fundamental hierarchy had been unforgivably transgressed. Although there is little surviving evidence for communal carnivalesque beatings of husbands who were abused by their wives in this period, the trope of battered husbands was a common one in images and literature: one satirical poem from Arras even advised husbands how to avoid the blows of their spouses by being thoroughly domesticated.[149] In the contemporary English case, murdering one's husband was construed as a form of treason since the disrespect for authority and the disordering effect on society were deemed so severe.[150] Husband murderers were invariably executed, usually burnt, witness the cases of Hauline de Sernin of Hesdin in 1306 and Emmelot le Marsain of Bourchuel in 1299.[151] The dominant assumption that the

[144] Tanon, 528.

[145] *Registre de l'officialité de l'abbaye de Cérisy*, ed. M. Dupont (Caen, 1880), 345.

[146] Furgeot and Dillay, *Actes*, i, no. 2235, 215 (1338).

[147] Tanon, 485.

[148] *Olim*, iii. 31; Boutaric, *Actes*, ii, no. 3040, 6 (1299). The repercussions of this case rumbled on: in 1311, the proceedings of the first case were questioned; Boutaric, *Actes*, ii, no. 3925, 88. In 1317, her son and his accomplices were accused of riding armed into the village of Beauval, and shouting threats of 'Tuez! Tuez!' in front of the house of the dame de Beauval, by then widowed: Boutaric, *Actes*, ii, no. 4871, 184.

[149] R. Berger, *Littérature et société arrageoise: Les Chansons et dits artésiens* (Arras, 1982), no. XVII.

[150] Hanawalt, 'Violence', 197.

[151] ADN, B13596, fo. 45^v, and ADPC, A2, fo. 31^v.

controlled anger of domestic discipline was more masculine than the unrestrained rage of domestic violence nicely corroborated the idea that women were prey to uncontrolled emotion which they could unleash on their husbands.[152] Some such women were even accused of witchcraft, a trope of extreme demonically inspired emotion otherwise unusual in this early period: in 1318, an investigation was conducted into accusations that several widows had been using enchanted wax to cast a spell on their husbands and to poison them.[153] Infanticide was a more common crime attributed to women, and often was treated leniently owing to the assumption that women were unable to control their emotions and could easily slip into insanity.[154]

There was a tendency to resort to clichés in the prosecution of domestic violence committed by women, as a means of articulating the assumptions about gender raised by such cases.[155] Indeed, modern sociological studies also highlight the tendency of courts to opt out of straightforward confrontation of domestic crimes.[156] This worked both ways. The problematic nature of violence by men was explained away by clichés such as the husband who aberrantly loses his temper when provoked by his wife and crimes of passion.[157] Frequently, husbands resorted to the excuse that their wife was trying to harm them, picking up on a trope used in literature and in the exempla. Conversely, a favourite motif of the courts was that of the jealous wife—citing sexual jealousy between women as a cause of violence by the women themselves and a provocation to the men—which provided a model into which to fit violence which was otherwise hard to classify. Such was the interpretation of events in 1338, when Nicole, wife of Guillaume Damour, was caught beating one Eudelot, whom she apparently accused of sleeping with her husband.[158]

[152] See e.g. the case of a woman who murdered her husband in Laon, 1281 (Boutaric, *Actes*, i, no. 2353, p. 225); or the case of Gilonne 'la Cordelete', accused of poisoning her husband with the help of Guiot Ansel and one Guérard in 1311 (Boutaric, *Actes*, ii, no. 3964, 92). Women were stereotypically suspected of killing their husbands by poisoning: see Dean, 'Domestic Violence', 527–43.

[153] Boutaric, *Actes*, ii, no. 5200, 220 (1317).

[154] e.g. P. Viollet (ed.) , *Les Etablissements de Saint Louis*, 2 vols. (Paris, 1881–6), i, no. 39, 55. Nevertheless, infanticide did not always meet with leniency: e.g. a woman was buried alive for this crime in the 1300s in Ozouer-la-Ferrière, a parish of Saint-Maur-des-Fossés, Tanon, 334; this was a particularly tragic case, as her husband was accused of murdering his mother-in-law.

[155] Use of stereotypes has also been noted in Bologna: Dean, 'Domestic Violence', 533; also Helmholz, *Marriage*, 105.

[156] Cf. J. Meier, 'Feminist Theory and Legal Norms', in *The Public Nature of Private Violence*, 121–30.

[157] AN, JJ64, fo. 430; the 'crime of passion' was particularly frequent in the Polish case: Brozyna, 'Not Just a Family Affair', 299–311.

[158] Tanon, 508.

Whilst often constructed to draw an interpretive line under an issue, stereotypes in fact serve only to raise more questions. Legal prosecutions may have relied on stereotypical constructions in order to dodge more troubling questions about gender, law, and discipline, but such glosses were deconstructed in the social commentary of imaginative literature. The husband-beating wife is frequently taken to be the most straightforwardly carnivalesque literary treatment of domestic violence, critiquing but reinforcing violent patriarchy with a comic inversion of the usual hierarchy. Yet close reading reveals story-tellers and their audiences subverting stereotypes of wicked wives and dignified husbands and questioning the authority of violence in the home. In the popular *fabliau La Bourgeoise d'Orléans*, the eponymous heroine wants to have an affair, but is faced with the difficulty of an excessively jealous husband.[159] He decides to pretend to go on a business trip, in order to trick her into letting her lover into the house. She understands what he is up to, secretly lets the lover in, then, when her husband returns in disguise, she tells the servants that her husband is an importunate lover who needs a good beating. The servants happily oblige, while she enjoys herself in another room with her lover: her bruised husband rejoices in the loyalty of his wife apparently manifested through such a display of violence.

Here, domestic violence is questioned both structurally *and* stylistically. Whilst it is structurally shown to reinforce a domestic order, and to support the victorious party in a marital dispute, the victorious party here is not the husband, but the wife. Most straightforwardly, the tale undermines the notion of marital hierarchy, since the husband is patently so much stupider than his wife. The audience is left with the sense that he deserved the bruises, and that such a dim person is not an appropriate figure of authority: excessively jealous husbands are invariably mocked in the *fabliaux*, drawing on a more widespread condemnation, epitomized in *Le Roman de la Rose*.[160] His use of deception to try to ensnare his wife is taken as unmanly, his ready acceptance of violence without a struggle exhibiting a feminine passivity, de-essentializing more common gender categories. A social dimension is added in the *fabliau Bérengier au long cul*, where a high-born wife shames her low-born husband by threatening him with knightly violence and causing him to run away. The stereotype of the husband-beating wife is far more complex here, as her social station is used to underscore her husband's inadequacy: moreover, he *is* violent, but his

[159] *NRCF* iii/19.

[160] Guillaume de Lorris and Jean de Meun, *Le Roman de la Rose*, ed. Armand Strubel (Paris, 1992), ll. 8459–9444.

violence towards his wife at the start of the story is brutal and shores up a form of masculinity which the tale unmasks as a sham.[161]

More subtly, these stories complicate the notion of intention. In *La Bourgeoise*, an attack is made on the common legal trope of a crime of passion, where violent behaviour by the husband or wife would be partially justified, at least explained, by their sense of anger and betrayal, and need to re-establish a moral order. Whilst penitentials attempted to demonstrate that uxoricides provoked by the adulterous behaviour of the spouse could be leniently interpreted, *La Bourgeoise* breaks down the straightforward dichotomy of wronged husband and suffering but guilty victim, by portraying the moral weakness and ready resort to violence of both parties. By criticizing the husband's premeditated entrapment of his wife, the tale invites the observation that a respectable and courageous husband would simply confront his wife about the issue, and the tale ends with the tart comment that 'Son mari, qui la vot deçoivre:/Il meïmes brasça son boivre!'[162] Another *fabliau*, *Les Tresses*, tells of a jealous husband (in this case justifiably so) who brutally beats and cuts the hair off a woman whom he mistakenly believes to be his wife. He is eventually humiliated, and the message is a confusing and destabilizing one, for the brutality of his violence compromises his rightful intention, and his brute force is defeated by the wit of his wife.[163]

Although the violence in *La Bourgeoise* structurally supports an order of sorts, it is also excessive and the husband suffers far more than would be functionally necessary. It provides an apparently comic spectacle both for the servants and for the audience of the *fabliau*, and the violence quickly acquires a momentum of its own. Yet, the *fabliau* clearly makes the point that, granted the gender inversion here, such violence does not exceed legitimate bounds, as the wife orders the servants 'Mes gardez bien, ne le tuez!'[164] If the violence results in the death of the husband, she realizes that it will be deemed socially unacceptable, and yet the *fabliau* questions the validity of this boundary given that what actually takes place is so obviously socially disruptive.

These challenging tales reveal grotesque delight combined with deep uneasiness about domestic violence. It is shown up as a problematic solution, the cowardly option, which moreover can so easily support the wrong order. The easy and risible satisfaction of the husband of the

161 *NRCF* iv/34.
162 'Her husband, who tried to deceive her, brewed his drink himself': ll. 324–5.
163 *NRCF* vi/69.
164 'But, be careful not to kill him!': l. 240.

Bourgeoise with the situation leaves the audience asking itself whether society's acceptance of marital violence is not itself ridiculous.

4. CONCLUSION

Definitional problems concerning the implications of medieval violence and its relationship to law are crystallized in thirteenth- and fourteenth-century ambivalence about domestic violence. Thirteenth-century legal and canonical thinkers struggled to delimit illegitimate and disruptive 'violence', as opposed to legitimate and ordering force, and juxtaposed the interpersonal and collective implications of individual acts of brutality. On the one hand, measured physical force by husbands was corrective discipline, in the service of social order, both within the home, and in society as a whole. As such, it was enacted in a spirit of righteous anger and was deemed effectively 'manly'. On the other hand, it could easily become anarchic violence, disrupting social orders in a vicious display of bloodshed, and this was described as savage, unruly, even typically feminine anger. The difficulty of distinguishing between these types and the failure to establish anything but nebulous and negotiable boundaries was intensified by the fluidity of the dichotomy between the public and the private: domestic violence crossed the threshold between the intimate and the collective, and reluctance to interfere in private hierarchies was mingled with anxiety about their public implications. Canon law grappled with these issues and, together with the practice of physical force in marriage and its legal prosecution, formed part of a tripartite discourse on violence. Such concerns resonated in contemporary imaginations via the literature which dramatized these questions and anxieties.

Conclusion

1. VIOLENCE AS COMMUNICATION

Thirteenth- and early fourteenth-century practices and understandings of domestic brutality draw stark attention to widespread and profound contemporary concern regarding the broader functions and legitimacy of violence. At the same time, the lauded function of physical force within marriage apparently lay at the very heart of the ordering and communicative role of violence more generally. Husbands were to use physical gestures in order to communicate punitive messages of authority to their errant wives, and to impose rightful order in the household, as a prerequisite for a harmonious society.

Violence was, in this period, integral to negotiations of identity, and a powerful acknowledged means of exploring and crystallizing social relationships. Brutal physical gestures embodied notions of honour, both personal and familial, with kinship groups frequently engaging together in vengeance strategies: forms of such violence varied according to degree of urbanization and demographic nature of the town in question, revealing socio-economic contingency. Violence was likewise perceived as a key means of impressing one's friends, and the prominence of young men as perpetrators suggests that such actions had peculiar potency in transitional life phases. It was particularly in this context that violence was intimately connected to questions of gender. Groups of young men, particularly students, sought to assert a particular kind of masculinity in relation to the women they raped, but also in rivalrous relation to each other. Such actions assured membership of a group, and reveal the motivating force of peer pressure. Students in particular negotiated their way between membership of a variety of groups by engaging in ludic but deeply strategic violence—from membership of a 'macho' group of friends, to membership of a university 'nation', to membership of the student body in opposition to the body of the townspeople. Likewise the civic identities of the burgeoning towns were articulated through collective violent action, which, through its own careful composition, expressed the corporate nature of the community. This period and region witnessed the birth of vernacular drama, another form of performance in what were profoundly theatrical urban landscapes: in these cultures of performance—from judicial to literary to civic—violence played its own central role. Even in the tavern, violent gestures subversively commented upon the state of society, dramatically recreating and playfully exaggerating the role-play of everyday life.

It was the recognized meaningfulness of violent gestures which made such strategic acts of physical communication possible. The Aristotelian paradigm for the relationship between body and soul suggested that states of the soul could be manifested in the body. Physical marks on the body were endowed with the status of signs, which could indicate something beyond their own presence. Such bodily semiotics were further explored and disseminated in a variety of discourses which meant that they became deeply embedded in cultural attitudes towards violence. Medical practitioners read physical marks on the body as symptoms, rendering the invisible visible; sermon exempla and popular hagiographical texts recounted tales of spiritual states physically manifested upon the bodies of the subjects; accumulated legal texts attempted to regulate the interpretation of acts of illegitimate violence. In a culture where violence and signs on the body were 'read', 'readers' and observers of violence themselves empowered the perpetrators, who knew that, while their intended messages might be contested, they *would* be observed and interpreted.

Space was used strategically by perpetrators of violence, and the frequent use of public spaces meant that violent messages could be made meaningful by the presence of multiple spectators. The street provided an arena in which honour could be defended publicly, and social relations memorably negotiated. Protesters in urban uprisings emerged from these narrow, dingy alley-ways into the magnificent public squares, in order to assert the legitimacy of their actions, and their centrality to civic life and pride: there, they could engage with the interpretative frameworks of geographically coterminous civic performances in order to ensure that their actions would be observed, remembered, and read in a particular way. It was the relationships *between* spaces which were particularly exploited by students, as they contested on the one hand their relegation to a particular quarter and, on the other hand, the stereotype of brawling students aimlessly roaming the city. The notion of space was even thematized in the long-standing and brutal quarrel between the students and the abbey of Saint-Germain-des-Près concerning the contested area known as the 'Pré-aux-clercs'. Legal readings of violence were filtered through the framework of spatial configurations, as, in a period of multiple and conflicting jurisdictions, the particular location of a given act of violence was crucial to its legitimacy, its sense, and the legal response.

However, differing legal responses complicated the triangular communicative relationship of perpetrator, victim, and spectator: violent messages invited multi-layered levels of reading, from those of casual observers, to family members, to legal reactions. Moreover, the interpretation of violent events was an ongoing process involving the personal and collective remembering of incidents, and their narrativization by perpetrators, victims, and observers to fit structures demanded by communal memories and appeals procedures. Much of the interpretation of violence was informed by pre-existing stereotypes, imposing a particular hermeneutic framework upon given configurations of events. The process was nevertheless a reciprocal one, and the example of student violence demonstrates that miscreants were acutely aware of the labels imputed to them, and attempted to manipulate them to their advantage as they strove to assert their desired identity.

2. INDETERMINACIES

Perpetrators, victims, and spectators were multifarious and, although there were shared grammars of violence, their readings of acts of brutality were not always neatly aligned. The reading of violence was coloured by many layers of ambivalence and indeterminacy, and these hesitations were intensified by the transitional nature of the period in a legal, political, and ideological sense. Whether violence, even exercised illicitly, was nevertheless an ordering force, or whether it inevitably generated only disorder and destruction, remained a matter of debate; the line between ordering and disordering violence was fluid, as reactions to domestic violence potently demonstrate. Vengeance killings on the street provide another example, as contemporary responses understood the element of social negotiation in such gestures, whilst condemning their potentially destructive effect on the community. From a different angle, disorder could be contained, as in the case of tavern violence, apparently ensuring the harmony of everyday life by providing an outlet for anarchic brutality. A similar attitude was frequently expressed regarding students, but contemporaries were well aware that violence could not so straightforwardly be canalized, and continued to worry that allowing misbehaviour in specific spaces or contexts would not restrain, but rather fuel, further chaos.

One way of approaching the problem of distinguishing ordering and disordering violence was via the question of emotion, a theme which has thus far only been implicit owing to the nature of the sources. Much violence, then as now, was perpetrated in a spirit of anger or over-excitement, and the motivation of the aggressor was obscured in a flurry of emotion. Readings of such violence could be constructed *post hoc*, witness cases of domestic violence where perpetrators sought to justify their appeals by representing their motivation and the reasons for particular forms of violence. But the emotion itself was also the subject of intense ambivalence. The distinction was between violence carried out in a spirit of rational communication and violence provoked by an outburst of excessive emotion, a distinction which broadly corresponds to the modern sociological distinction between instrumental and expressive violence.[1] Even if excessive emotion represented dangerous disorder and controlled anger was fulfilled through disciplining violence, it was not always straightforward to distinguish between the two. Moreover, the dichotomy in question was far from sharp: anger itself was clearly not just an innate response, but a social construction which was instrumentalized and used strategically in acts of violence to negotiate social relations.[2]

Discussions of violence in the moralizing contexts of canon law, preaching, and confessional material focused particular condemnation upon expressive violence, and brutal outbursts of excessive emotion: Prudentius's *Psychomachia* placed the patient and non-violent Job alongside the figure of *Ira* tearing her clothes in uncontrollable fury, and Albertanus of Brescia warned that excessive emotion could lead to madness and violence.[3] Yet anger *per se* was not always considered to be wicked: 'In our ethics, we do not so much inquire into whether a pious soul is angry as to why he is angry . . . I am not aware that any right thinking person would find fault with anger at a wrongdoer who seeks his amendment'.[4] On the other hand, moralists were unwilling entirely to relinquish and reject instrumental violence as a mechanism whereby social relations might be regulated. Thus, moralists considered that the greatest threat to moral well-being lay, not in controlled violence which could in some cases serve the cause of order and virtue, but in uncontrolled anger,

[1] Cf. E. Marx, 'Some Social Context of Personal Violence', in M. Gluckman (ed.), *The Allocation of Responsibility* (Manchester, 1972), 281–321.

[2] D. L. Smail has discussed the instrumentalization of emotions, though without the element of physical violence: 'Common Violence: Vengeance and Inquisition in Fourteenth-Century Marseille', *Past and Present*, 151 (1996), 28–59. On the issue of whether anger is innate or a social construction, cf. B. Rosenwein, 'Controlling Paradigms', in Rosenwein (ed.), *Anger's Past: The Social Uses of an Emotion in the Middle Ages* (Ithaca, NY, 1998), 233–48.

[3] L. Little, 'Anger in Monastic Curses', in Rosenwein, *Anger's Past*, 14. Also, NB Martin of Braga: 'One need not be angry to correct wrongdoers. Since anger is a sin of the soul, one must not correct a sinner with a sin', ibid. 12.

[4] Augustine, *City of God*, quoted in Little, 'Anger', in Rosenwein, 9–35. A similar distinction is to be found between impatient anger and zealous anger in Gregory the Great's *Moralia*: ibid. 12.

one of the seven deadly sins. The vast array of confessional material from the thirteenth century concurred in condemning the sin of anger. The early thirteenth-century Robert of Flamborough condemned those succumbing to fits of rage, and Guillaume Peraldus's popular compendium of vices and virtues from the mid-thirteenth century highlighted the evil connotations of anger, and drew attention to its close links with the most sinful forms of violence.[5]

Yet they also described the importance of violence imposed to establish order, most frequently through discipline. Alain de Lille, *c.*1200, distinguished between acts of violence perpetrated 'iratus', and those carried out 'propter disciplinam', roundly condemning the former, but admitting that the latter could, on occasion, be more acceptable even if punishable by law.[6] This condemnation of violence provoked by excessive emotion, alongside a persisting attachment to a functional economy of violence, was reiterated in the exempla stories used in sermons. Numerous exempla described the malicious effects of anger upon the soul of the sinner, and a few contrasted it directly with the use of rightly ordered violence. This tension was pithily expressed in the story of Fabius Cunctator, describing how he first conquered his rage, and then was able to direct his violence successfully to conquer Hannibal.[7] Many stories describe the importance of mastering anger before inflicting violent discipline.[8]

The question of emotion responded to a second layer of ambivalence in medieval readings of violence, namely its collective or interpersonal implications. Debates simmered concerning the respective implications of emotional and strategic violence, whether the one should be read as primarily concerning the individual and the other as threatening the well-being of the community, or vice versa. Whilst moral theologians were primarily concerned about the fate of the individual, secular legislation focused increasingly on the community and the common good, and this led to rather different conclusions about emotion. In contrast to the focus on rage of moral discourse, secular legislation increasingly considered that excessive emotion rendered an act of violence less threatening; that an act perpetrated because of spontaneous anger lacked the clear communicative strategy with collective implications which would oblige legal mechanisms to intervene. In contrast to the readings of the moralists,

[5] Robert of Flamborough, *Liber Poenitentialis*, ed. F. Firth (Toronto, 1971), bk iv, no. 201, 181–2; Peraldus, *Summa virtutum et vitiorum* (Paris, 1519), pars iii, cap. I, fo. cci.

[6] Alain de Lille, *Liber Poenitentialis*, ed. J. Longère (Louvain, 1965), 2. 25, 61–2.

[7] *Castigos*, ed. P. de Gayangos (Madrid, 1860), 118, cited in http://gahom.ehess.fr/thema (accessed Feb. 2012), henceforth THEMA.

[8] Ibid. 148, cit. in THEMA; Roberto Caracciolo, *Quaresimale in volgare*, ed. E. Esposito (Rome, 1993), 42, cit. in THEMA.

strategic violence was read as a threat to the community as a whole which needed to be repressed, whereas expressive violence, whether drunken or angry, was relegated to the interpersonal sphere and provoked less anxiety. Accidental death was not to be punished as severely as premeditated murder, partly because the intention violently to resolve a conflict was absent: the authorities were not confronted with a rival.[9] Likewise, anger was often considered to be a mitigating factor: if an assailant acted under the influence of excessive emotion or alcohol, his acts were, of course, unacceptable, but they were nevertheless seen to be less threatening to the legal authorities and were relegated to the sphere of interpersonal quarrels.

There is a second major difference in preoccupation between secular legislation and moral discourse, and that is, obviously, the concern of the former with the role of law. Boundaries between law and violence were blurred, and this is the third layer of indeterminacy: the law itself was physically violent, and interpersonal violence often claimed quasi-legal authority. Attempts were made to assert the distinction and to posit law as a grammar of violence. Secular legislation was therefore ever more anxious to clamp down on interpersonal violence which tried to align itself with the function of the law, in other words, violence which presented itself as instrumental and strategic, exercised in a spirit of righteous anger. The reason lies in the transitional nature of this period. As legislative attempts were increasingly made to codify and to systematize the interpretation of violence, legal theorists were concerned to transfer the legitimate practice of functional violence to the authorities, promoting the idea of an ordered society where violent ordering was conducted only by those in an official position. Instrumental violence carried out by private individuals was increasingly conceived of as a threat to this function of the authorities, and to the public good. Repeated attempts to ban private war in 1245, 1257, 1270, 1302, 1306, 1311, and 1314 (repeated because so unsuccessful) and prohibitions on carrying arms, expressed both in local custumals such as that of Beaumanoir, and in royal ordinances such as that of 1288, underlined the notion that premeditated violence to defend honour or reputation was unacceptable.[10] The concept of vengeance was questioned, and refined, since it apparently usurped a right which should belong to the law: Beaumanoir explicitly described the function of law as 'la venjance des mefès'—vengeance for misdeeds.[11] The distinction is potently demon-

[9] Beaumanoir, i, no. 934, 473.

[10] Cf. e.g. ibid., no. 996, 504. And respectively *Ordonnances des Rois de France*, ed. E. de Laurières, 22 vols. (Paris, 1849), i. 56, 84, 111, 344, 435, 493, 538. These primarily concerned nobles.

[11] Beaumanoir, i, no. 936, 474–5.

strated by legal thinking surrounding crimes of passion. Beaumanoir clarified that if a cuckolded husband were to take violent action immediately upon discovering his humiliation in a spirit of extreme anger, then his violence was, to some extent, excused. However, if the husband were to wait before responding to the affront, then his violence should be condemned; such an offender should be dragged and hanged as a threat to a rightly ordered society who tried to take the law into his own hands.[12]

Developing legal mechanisms *did* increasingly attempt to restrict the instrumental perpetration of violence, but moral discourses contested the accompanying exculpation of excessive emotional displays. In a sense, the distinction was between moral and civic virtue, the one more profoundly threatened by uncontrolled anger, the other by strategic contestations of social relations. But the dichotomy was not so clear in practice, and moral and legal readings were held in tension generating a great deal of ambivalence in assessing the harmfulness of violence. Sometimes the contrasting reactions of legal and moral discourses broke down, as in the case of domestic violence. Here, secular law continued to follow the moralists' lead in accepting that violence perpetrated in a spirit of anger represented the greatest threat, perhaps because domestic violence still primarily lay within the remit of the ecclesiastical courts.[13] Expressive and instrumental, spontaneous and rational violence were not distinct phenomena. Moreover, excessive emotion had collective connotations, and instrumental violence had implications for the spiritual health of the individual. Attempts to separate the exercise of violence and the role of law were inconclusive, and the period remained one of transition and hesitation.

3. EMOTIONAL REACTIONS

Although it is hard to trace interpersonal violence through the fourteenth century, owing to the upheavals of the Hundred Years' War which affected both the exercise of justice and record-keeping, these concerns continued to exercise contemporaries.[14]

Let us conclude by visiting the annual celebrations of the Confrérie de Saint Eloi of the Parisian guild of goldsmiths. Every year between 1339

[12] Ibid., no. 934, 473.
[13] e.g. ibid. ii, no. 1629, 333.
[14] C. Gauvard, *De grace especial* (Paris, 1991), 232–5 and 686–8, 765–6; E. Cohen, *The Crossroads of Justice: Law and Culture in Late Medieval France* (Leiden, 1993), 27–53; Y. Lanhers, 'Crimes et criminels au quatorzième siècle', *Revue Historique*, 240 (1968), 325–37.

and 1382, the guild undertook the major expense of staging a miracle play, and the plays survive in a lavish manuscript copy known as the *Les Miracles de Notre Dame par personnages.*[15] Aside from the obligatory glorification of the Blessed Virgin Mary, the plays took the concerns of a broad and varied audience, and posed difficult and challenging questions concerning the implications of physical violence. Emotion and strategy intricately overlap in the plays, and consequently ordering and disordering violence becomes difficult to distinguish, the collective or interpersonal implications of physical gestures open to negotiation, and the relationship between violence and the law troubled. There are no easy or comforting answers in these plays, which work to generate a series of impossible dilemmas entangling the protagonists and, indeed, the spectators, resolvable only by the miraculous and cathartic intervention of the Virgin.[16]

Many of the plays represented socially embedded thirteenth-century narratives. For example, the *L'Enfant donné au diable* was recounted by the early thirteenth-century Gautier de Coinci,[17] and circulated also in Latin versions, most notably that of Gautier's contemporary, Vincent de Beauvais.[18] *Une Femme que Nostre Dame garda d'estre arse* likewise drew upon Gautier de Coinci, whose own account was based upon earlier Latin texts.[19] *La Femme du roy de Portugal* reworked a narrative from the *Vie des Pères*, a popular collection of miracle stories from the mid-thirteenth century, surviving in over thirty manuscripts.[20] In each of these three tales, the heroine commits a violent crime in a moment of despair or anger: the first reacts to an intra-marital rape by vowing to give any resultant offspring to the devil,[21] the second murders her son-in-law in response to a rumour circulating that she is having an affair with him, and the third

[15] *Les Miracles de Nostre Dame par personnages*, ed. Gaston Paris and Ulysse Robert, 7 vols. (Paris, 1876–93), i. 3–59; i. 149–204; iv. 178–238 respectively. Cf. R. Glutz, *Miracles de Nostre Dame par personnages: Bibliographie und neue Studien zum Text, Entstehunsgszeit und Herkunft* (Berlin, 1954); G. Runnalls, 'The Manuscript of the *Miracles de Nostre Dame par personnages*', *Romance Philology*, 22 (1968), 15–22.

[16] D. Maddox and S. Sturm-Maddox, 'French Drama of the Fourteenth Century: *The Miracles de Nostre Dame par personnages*', in their *Parisian Confraternity Drama of the Fourteenth Century: The Miracles de Nostre Dame par personnages* (Turnhout, 2008).

[17] Gautier de Coinci, *Miracles de Nostre Dame*, i, no. 22.

[18] Vincent de Beauvais, *La Vierge et le miracle: Le 'Speculum historiale'*, ed. M. Taraye (Paris, 1999), 137–41. Cf. Adolfo Mussafia, *Über die von Gautier de Coincy benützten Quellen* (Vienna, 1894).

[19] The story originates in a real incident of 1096: there are twelve extant Latin versions from the 12th cent.: V. Väänänen, *D'une fame de Laon qui estoit jugie a ardoir que Nostre Dame delivra: Miracle versifié par Gautier de Coinci* (Helsinki, 1951), 9–11. Väänänen provides edns. of the Latin text of the monk Hermann, and the vernacular version of Gautier de Coinci.

[20] *La Vie des Peres*, ed. F. Lecoy, 3 vols. (Paris, 1987–99), ii. 84–109.

[21] Admittedly a curse is a form of verbal not physical violence, but it raises similar issues.

murders both her rapist and a woman who attempts to usurp her place as queen. In each tale, the woman's excessive emotion is condemned by both moralists and legalists for provoking actions which are perceived as catastrophic both for the soul of the subject, and for the well-being of the community. But, at the end of each, the Blessed Virgin Mary descends to save the woman from the consequences of her actions and so problematizes earthly readings of the violence perpetrated by the women. In earlier versions of these tales, the women are presented as the victims of diabolical temptation, their anger equated with loss of control; in these later versions, their anger is treated more ambivalently, as an instrumental reaction to their own situation as victims of violence.

Anger dramatically encapsulates the multiple layers of ambivalence surrounding the reading of violence. It engages the audience through shared sentiment, and it becomes clear that there is no obvious distinction between instrumental and expressive emotion, even as physically manifested. Anger is the cipher through which the audience is drawn into the disturbing problem of violence.

In *Une Femme que Nostre Dame garda d'estre arse,* the audience, through shared indignation, recognizes the strategic nature of the woman's act. Her violence is cast as disordering by the law, and yet, through emotional engagement, the audience becomes aware of its functional nature and of her deep need to protect herself. Likewise, the violence of the eponymous *Femme au roy de Portugal* seems, to an empathetically indignant audience, strategically to defend her place in the marriage bed of her king and to assert hierarchical order, and yet concomitantly provokes horror at the sheer degree of bloodshed, the cruelty, and the innocence of the woman who is, in fact, her victim. It remains unclear whether the unbending response of the law is opposed to, or merely sublimated by, the mercifulness of the Virgin Mary's intervention: whether violence provoked by a prior act of brutality is therefore mitigated and should be met with a compassionate response.[22] The role of the women's anger is problematized, and the straightforward dichotomy between excessively emotional and rational violence undermined by the clearly strategic nature of their responses: their anger is structurally portrayed as a response to perceived wrongs, and no alternative to their instrumental violence is posited.

Whether ordering or disordering, the reach, interpersonal or collective, of a given act of violence remains deeply problematic in the plays. *Une Femme que Nostre Dame garda d'estre arse* questions the collective

[22] The Virgin Mary was not always merciful: she is equally to be found punishing sinners who believed they would escape with impunity.

implications of the excessive response of the heroine, Guibour. The *bailli* attempts to burn her with the explicit intent of purifying the community, and yet the play makes clear that it was that community itself which slandered Guibour and provoked the violence in the first place (ll. 48–9). When Mary comes to save the condemned woman, she does not justify the murder, but stresses that any threat to the common good was more deep-rooted than Guibour's actions, and emphasizes the sense of entrapment perpetrated by the community upon Guibour (ll. 1128–32). In *La Femme du roy de Portugal*, the queen's crime is even recast in the name of the common good, as Mary reveals the crimes perpetrated by the *seneschal* (who raped the queen) and the chaplain (who revealed her secret) and thus re-reads the implications of the murders. Moreover, the role of the Church is problematized by the figure of the chaplain who claimed to have reported the angry crime of the queen in the interests of the community, but in doing so neglected the spiritual welfare of a member of his flock. Likewise, the inadequacy and venality of the Church is revealed in *L'Enfant donné au diable* as the child promised to the devil is only able to secure papal help upon payment of a hefty fee (ll. 839–40). A rape, which would seem to be intensely personal in its reach, is shown to engender a mother's curse with both communal implications (in the social exclusion of the young boy) and individual consequences (as the ownership of his soul is threatened).

In this last case, the law is that of contract, but the broader question of the relationship between violence and the law is raised. In the final dramatic trial before God, where Mary and the devil contest ownership of the child, a legal contract itself provoked by an act of sexual violence is contested through colourful verbal violence and the threat of physical brutality.[23] The dichotomy between law and violence is broken down further in *La Femme que Nostre Dame garda d'estre arse*, where the audience is made to feel that the cruelty of the *bailli* is in no way diminished by having the law on his side. The emotional responses of shock provoked by Guibour's illicit violence are paralleled in the horror at the *bailli*'s legal violence, undermining the discursive boundaries between the two. Law itself becomes a subject of conflict, only to be resolved by Mary's intervention, which can rise above it in these cases. In *La Femme au Roy de Portugal*, those who exercise the law are shown to be corrupt and self-serving, motivated by their own interpersonal conflicts. Solid boundaries between violence and law have not yet been established, nor has the reach of the consequences of violence as interpersonal or affecting the

[23] This is also a comic moment, as the devils point out that Mary will of course win the trial because God would never dare to contradict his mother: ll. 1380–5.

community as a whole been delineated; violence remains both ordering and disordering, subject to contradictory readings. Hesitation was engendered in these plays through their presentation of emotions at once strategic and expressive. The gendering of the subject matter is striking, and shows how the complexities of the use of violence were intensified in the case of the disenfranchised, and those in a socially subordinate position.

4. AMBIVALENCE

It is ambivalence, then, which stands out as the salient feature of medieval understandings of violence more generally. Whether violence could function effectively as communication to order and harmonize society, or whether it inevitably degenerated into chaotic disorder where meaning was multivalent and incomprehensible, remained a matter of ongoing debate. This deeply rooted and eloquently expressed ambivalence constitutes an important corrective to teleological accounts of the history of violence. Norbert Elias's famous 'Civilising Process' provides a paradigm whereby not only state repression, but shifting social and psychological structures, particularly those of a nascent 'court society', are said to have imposed taboos upon the impulsive medieval resort to violence.[24] The Foucauldian model of insidious entrapment of the individual in a web of state-based hegemony suggests a developing monopolization of the interpretation of violence by the powerful.[25] But the reality was subtler and more sophisticated: the Middle Ages do not deserve to be so swiftly dismissed. Social and psychological structures shaped the perpetration and understanding of violence, but the result was not a single shift or overarching paradigm, rather the instilling of ambivalence about the very definition of violent behaviour. What constituted 'violence' in its medieval sense, destructive of order, illicit, aberrant, remained an open and complex question.

At the heart of much of this ambivalence lay the issue of community. Should acts of violence be read in individual or collective terms? Who was implicated by the various kinds of violence? Readings of violence on the street, whether by perpetrators, observers, or legal authorities, hesitated concerning the essentially private or public implications of such events. At the historical moment in which notions of the common good were given increasing prominence, the question was a pressing one. Street violence was perpetrated in the space where the individual qua individual took his

[24] N. Elias, *The Civilizing Process*, tr. E. Jephcott (Oxford, 1978), 3–8.

[25] M. Foucault, *Surveiller et punir* (Paris, 1975), e.g. 75–7, 291–5. Foucault's interest lies in a later period, and his characterization of the Middle Ages rests on little evidence.

or her place in the community, and therefore presented profound problems of interpretation: should such acts be seen as negotiations of relationships between individuals, or matters with far-reaching and dangerous public implications? Revellers in the tavern exploited their apparently detached position from the rest of society; they engaged with more or less impunity in violence which appeared to operate in a sphere entirely distinct from that of the common good. Such violence was portrayed as self-consciously subverting established patterns of violent communication through a deliberate sense of excess and disequilibrium between provocation and response. And yet, even here, violence was commenting upon the nature of society as a whole; even in the most drunken moments, violent offenders implicitly used the self-conscious excess of their own actions to critique the perceived imbalance of rapidly shifting socio-economic circumstances. Students were notorious frequenters of the tavern and, through exploitation of the stereotypes so often imputed to them, they subverted and manipulated still further established paradigms of violent communication. Moreover, their violence was explicitly conceived of in terms of identity formation and adherence to a particular group, whether a peer group, a gender group, a so-called university 'nation', or a more generic student group visualized in opposition to the townspeople. While contemporary observers were acutely aware of the primarily ludic nature of student violence, legal and university authorities, preachers, and chroniclers were anxious about the wider repercussions of student misbehaviour on a European level.

In the case of urban uprisings, the collective dimension of violence was uncontested. Yet here too, ambiguity centred on the ordering or disordering nature of such violence. Participants claimed to be carrying out legitimate political protest in the interests of urban order, and to this end presented their actions as fully engaged performances amidst a variety of performative practices in everyday urban life. Established authorities nevertheless read these acts as indicative of terrifying disorder. The definition of violence was bound to be contested, and is shaped by the relationship between violence and the law, fluid categories themselves. This was a transitional period in which the lines had yet effectively to be drawn.

The study of domestic violence encapsulates all these anxieties and contradictions, shaped by a multitude of different prescriptive discourses, moral, political, and legal. Physical violence in marriage was perceived at once as an ordering and legitimate force, and as a potentially dangerous and excessive response to wifely misdemeanours. Rightly ordered marriage was posited as the cornerstone of society as a whole, but reluctance to interfere in what was seen to be an essentially intimate matter undermined such readings of physical brutality.

It was, perhaps, these indeterminacies which ensured that violence, and legal responses to it, would be remembered for years afterwards. Violence was not so ubiquitous that contemporaries failed to notice or to care. And violence hurt. No matter how common it may have been, how high-faluting the discussion it engendered, it hurt physically and psychically. Real individuals suffered, and it is to them, and to all those who grow up believing violence to be acceptable or inevitable, that this book is dedicated.

Select Bibliography

SELECT MANUSCRIPT AND ARCHIVAL SOURCES

Abbeville: Archives Municipales

Livre Rouge de l'Echevinage: MS 115.

Inventaire des titres de l'abbaye de Saint-Riquier.

Arras: Archives Départementales du Pas-de-Calais

(Series A: Trésor des chartes des comtes d'Artois)

General accounts of the *bailli* of Artois: A123, A124, A126, A127, A128, A815/1.

General account of the *maître* of the count of Artois: A815/2.

Accounts of the *bailli* of Arras: A124, A140/1, A166/2, A188/1, A200/2, A206/2, A208/1, A223/2, A259/1, A282/1, A289/1, A294/2.

Accounts of the *bailli* of Aubigny and Avesnes: A1014/18, A141/1, A144/2, A156/1, A163/2, A177/2, A198/2, A205/1, A208/2, A211/2, A221/2, A221/2, A236/1, A253/2, A259/2, A304/3, A308/1, A314/1, A317/2.

Accounts of the *bailli* of Bapaume: A130/2, 166/3, A169/1, A176/2, A177/3, A196/2, A205/2, A206/3, A211/3, A211/3, A215/1, A221/3, A223/3, A249/2, A259/3, A262/1, A267/1, A276/1, A282/2, A305/1, A320/1.

Accounts of the *bailli* of Hesdin: A129/1, A155/9, A166/5, A168/1, A188/3, A190/4, A196/3, A198/3, A213/1, A221/4, A234/3, A237/1, A239/2, A246/2, A249/4, A260/1, A267/3, A291/2, A294/5, A304/5.

Accounts of the *bailli* of Saint Omer: A149/3, A155/5, A156/5, A166/9, A169/2, A176/7, A188/5, A198/5, A201/2, A205/4, A208/4, A215/4, A221/6, A225/4, A239/5, A253/5, A260/4, A268/1, A289/1, A291/3, A308/6, A314/3, A318/4.

Records of expenses of the court of Artois: A1015.

Miscellaneous charters with relation to violent events: A2, A46, A49/14, A52/6, A54/15, A56/21, A240/3, A928/1, A928/5, A928/7, A298/8, A959/4.

Conflicts of jurisdiction: A18, A35/2, A49/2, A906, A909, A918, A921, A934/1, A938, A955.

Investigations and trials: A35, A903, A904, A930, A933, A939, A941, A956, A958.

Complaints about corrupt justice: A41, A48, A56/6, A57/28, A57/29, A924, A929, A931/2, A935/2.

Punishments of rebellious towns: A52/7, A52/16, A905.

Lille: Archives du Nord (Series B: Trésor des chartes des comtes d'Artois)

General accounts of the *bailli* of Artois: B13595.

General accounts of the *receveur* of Artois: B13596, B13597.

Conflicts of jurisdiction: B922, B923, B946, B955, B965, B1164, B1471, B1489.

Paris: Archives Nationales

Series JJ: Royal acts and letters of remission: JJ42a, JJ48, JJ49, JJ61, JJ64, JJ66, JJ72, JJ78.

Series L: Ecclesiastical records with relevance to the University of Paris: L421, L427.

Series LL: Ecclesiastical cartularies of the diocese of Paris: LL7, LL8, LL9, LL10.

Series M: Royal bulls relevant to the University of Paris: M67a, M74.

Series S: Early records of the Picard nation: S6201, S6202.

Paris: Bibliothèque Nationale

Fonds latin: Sermons: MSS lat. 962, 15971, 14955.

Fonds français: Dits: MSS fr. 837, 24432.

PRINTED PRIMARY SOURCES

Abelard, Peter, *Ethics*, ed. and tr. D. Luscombe (Oxford: Blackwell, 1935).

Adam de la Halle, *Le Jeu de la Feuillée*, ed. J. Dufournet (Ghent: Éditions Scientifiques, 1977).

——*Le Jeu de Robin et Marion*, ed. J. Dufournet (Paris: Flammarion, 1989).

Adolphe de Vienne, *Doligamus*, ed. P. Casali (Florence: Sismel, 1997).

Akehurst, F. (ed. and tr.), *Etablissements de Saint Louis* (Philadelphia: University of Pennsylvania Press, 1996).

Alain de Lille, *Liber Poenitentialis*, ed. J. Longère (Louvain: Éditions Nauwelaerts, 1965).

——*The Plaint of Nature*, tr. J. Sheridan (Toronto: Pontifical Institute of Mediaeval Studies, 1980).

Alexandre de Paris, *Le Roman d'Alexandre*, ed. E. Armstrong and L. Harf-Lancner (Paris: Lettres Gothiques, 1994).

Aquinas, Thomas, *Summa Theologica*, in *Opera Omnia* (Rome: Leonine edn., 1882–).

Aristotle, *De Anima*, tr. W. Hett (Cambridge, Mass.: Loeb, 1957).

Auduoin, E. (ed.), *Recueil de documents concernant la commune et la ville de Poitiers*, 2 vols. (Poitiers: Imprimerie Moderne, Nicolas, 1923).

Augustine, *De Civitate Dei*, ed. M. Dods (London: Modern Library Edition, 2000).

Barbazan, E. (ed.), *Fabliaux et contes des poètes françois des xii, xiii, xiv, et xve siècles*, 3 vols. (Paris: Crapelet, 1766).

Berger, R. (ed.), *Littérature et société arrageoises au XIIIe siècle: Les Chansons et dits artésiens* (Arras: Commission départementale des monuments historiques du Pas-de-Calais, 1988).

——(ed.), *Le Nécrologe de la confrérie des jongleurs et des bourgeois d'Arras (1194–1361)* (Arras: Mémoires de la Commission Départementale des Monuments historiques du Pas-de-Calais, 13, 1970).

Béroul, *Tristan et Iseut*, ed. A. Ewert (Oxford: Blackwell, 1939).

Beugnot, A. (ed.), *Les Olim*, 4 vols. (Paris: Imprimerie Royale, 1839–1848).

Blangez, G. (ed.), *Ci nous dit: Recueil d'exemples moraux,* 2 vols. (Paris: Société des anciens textes français, 1979–86).

Boogaard, V. Van den, and Noomen, W. (eds.), *Nouveau recueil complet des fabliaux,* 10 vols. (Assen: Van Gorcum, 1983–96).

Boulay, F. du, *Historia Universitatis Parisiensis,* 6 vols. (Paris: Mason, 1665–73).

Boutaric, E. (ed.), *Actes du parlement de Paris: Première série, 1254–1328*, 2 vols. (Paris: H. Plon, 1863–7).

Breul, K. (ed.), 'Le Dit de Robert le diable', in *Abhandlungen Herrn Prof. Dr. Adolf Tobler* (Halle: Niemeyer, 1895), 464–509.

Brooke, R., *Writing of the First Companions: Scripta Leonis, Rufini et Angeli Sociorum S. Francisci* (Oxford: Clarendon Press, 1970).

Caesar of Heisterbach, *Dialogus miraculorum*, ed. J. Strange (Cologne: Lempertz, 1851).

Chrétien de Troyes, *Le Chevalier au Lion*, ed. D. Hult (Paris: Lettres Gothiques, 1994).

Crapelet, G. (ed.), *Proverbes et dictons populaires avec les dits du mercier et des marchands et les crieries de Paris aux XIIIe et XIVe siècles* (Paris: Crapelet, 1831).

Dante Alighieri, *Commedia*, ed. and tr. J. Sinclair, 3 vols. (Oxford: Oxford University Press, new edn.1981).

Delaborde, H.-F. (ed.), *Œuvres de Rigord et Guillaume le Breton* (Paris: Librairie Renouard 1882), ll. 97 and 94–5.

Delmaire, B., *Le Compte General d'Artois pour 1303–1304* (Brussels: Académie Royale de Belgique, 1977).

Denifle, H., and Châtelain, E. (eds.), *Chartularium Universitatis Parisiensis,* 4 vols. (Paris: University of Paris, 1889–97).

Digard, G. (ed.), *Les Registres de Boniface VIII,* 4 vols. (Rome: École française de Rome, 1907–39).

Dufournet, J. (ed.), *Le Garçon et l'aveugle: Jeu du XIIIe siècle* (Paris: Champion, 1989).

Duplès-Agier, H. (ed.), *Registre criminel du Châtelet de Paris du 6 septembre 1389 au 18 mai 1392,* 2 vols. (Paris: Société des Bibliophiles, 1861–4).

Dupont, M. (ed.), *Registre de l'officialité de l'abbaye de Cérisy* (Caen: Société des antiquaires de Normandie, 1880).

Espinas, G., *Recueil de documents relatifs à l'histoire du droit municipal,* 3 vols. (Paris: Collection de documents inédits, 1934–43).

Étienne Boileau, *Les Métiers et corporations de la ville de Paris*, ed. R. de Lespinasse and F. Bonnardot (Paris: Imprimerie nationale, 1879).

Étienne de Bourbon, *Anécdotes historiques, légendes et apologues tirés du recueil inédit d'Étienne de Bourbon, Dominicain du XIIIe siècle*, ed. E. Lecoy de la Marche (Paris: Société de l'Histoire de France, 1877).

——*Tractatus de diversis materiis praedicabilibus*, ed. J. Berlioz and J. L. Eichenlaub, 3 vols. (Turnhout: Brepols, 2002–).

Faral, E. (ed.), *Le Courtois d'Arras* (Paris: Champion, 1958).

Finot, J., *Inventaire sommaire des archives du nord* (Lille: Presses universitaires de Lille, 1885).

Fossier, R., *Chartes de coutume en Picardie: XIe–XIIIe siècle* (Paris: Bibliothèque Nationale, 1974).

Fournier, M., *Les Statuts et privilèges des universités françaises depuis leur fondation jusqu'en 1789*, 4 vols. (Paris: Bouillon, 1970).

Furgeot, H., and Dillay, M. (eds.), *Actes du Parlement de Paris: Deuxième série de l'an 1328 à l'an 1350. Jugés (lettres, arrêts, jugés)*, 3 vols. (Paris: Imprimerie Nationale, 1920–75).

Galand de Reigny, *Parabolaire*, ed. C. Friedlander, J. Leclercq, and G. Raciti (Paris: Cerf, 1992).

Gautier de Coinci, *D'une fame de Laon qui estoit jugie a ardoir que Nostre Dame delivra*, ed. V. Väänänen (Helsinki: Academia Scientiarum Fennica, 1951).

——*Miracles de Nostre Dame*, ed. Frederic Koenig, 4 vols. (Geneva: Droz, 1955).

Gayangos, P. de (ed.), *Castigos* (Madrid: Biblioteca des autores espagnoles, 1860).

Géraud, P., *Paris sous Philippe-le-Bel d'après des documents originaux* (Paris: Crapelet, 1837).

Gilles li Muisis, *Poésies*, ed. J.-M. Kervyn de Lettenhove, 2 vols. (Louvain: Imprimerie de J. Lefever, 1882).

Giry, A. (ed.), *Documents sur les relations de la royauté avec les villes* (Paris: Picard, 1885).

——and Lemaire, E. (eds.), *Archives anciennes de la ville de Saint Quentin, précédées d'une étude sur les origines de la commune de Saint-Quentin*, 2 vols. (Saint Quentin: Poette, 1888).

Glénisson, J., and Guerout, J., *Registres du trésor des chartes: Inventaire analytique*, i. *Règne de Philippe le Bel* (Paris: Archives Nationales, 1958).

Grandes Chroniques de France, ed. J. Viard, 10 vols. (Paris: Société de l'histoire de France, 1920–53).

Gratian, *Decretum*, ed. E. Friedberg, 2 vols. (Leipzig: B. Tachnitz, 1879).

Guillaume du Breuil, *Stilus curie parlamenti*, ed. F. Aubert (Paris: Picard, 1909).

Guillaume de Lorris and Meun, Jean de, *Le Roman de la Rose*, ed. A. Strubel (Paris: Lettres Gothiques, 1992).

Guillaume de Nangis, *Chronique et continuation de sa chronique*, ed. H. Géraud, 2 vols. (Paris: Société de l'histoire de France, 1843).

Guillaume de Saint-Pathus, *Les Miracles de Saint Louis*, ed. P. Fay (Paris: Champion, 1931).

——*La Vie de Saint Louis*, ed. H.-F. Delaborde (Paris: Picard, 1899).

Guillaume Peraldus, *Summae vitiae et vitiorum* (Paris, 1519).

Guiraud, J., and Dorez, L. (eds.), *Les Registres d'Urbain IV*, 4 vols. (Paris: École française de Rome, 1900).

Hauréau, B., *Notices et extraits de quelques manuscrits latins de la Bibliothèque Nationale: Histoire Littéraire de la France*, xxvi (Paris: Firmin Didot, 1873).

Hugh of Saint Victor, *Didascalion*, ed. C. Buttimer, 2 vols. (Washington DC: Catholic University Press, 1939).

Hugo von Trimberg, *Der Renner*, ed. G. Ehrismann, 4 vols. (Berlin: Walter de Gruyter, 1970).

Huguccio da Pisa, *Liber Derivationum*, ed. E. Cecchini and G. Arbizzoni (Florence: Sismel, 2004).
Isidore of Seville, *Etymologiae*, ed. W. Lindsay (Oxford: Oxford University Press, 1911).
Jacquemart Giélée, *Renart le nouvel*, ed. H. Roussel (Paris: Picard, 1961).
Jacobus de Voragine, *The Golden Legend: Readings on the Saints*, tr. W. Granger Ryan, 2 vols. (Princeton: Princeton University Press, 1991).
——*Sermones aurei*, ed. R. Clutius (Augsburg and Cracow: Apud Christophorum Bartl, 1760).
Jacques de Vitry, *The Historia Occidentalis of Jacques de Vitry: A Critical Edition*, ed. J. F. Hinnebusch (Fribourg: Fribourg University Press, 1972).
——*Sermons*, ed. J. Crane (London: Folklore Society, 1898).
Jean de Joinville, 'Vie de Saint Louis', tr. C. Smith, in *Joinville and Villehardouin: Chronicles of the Crusades* (London: Penguin, 2008).
Jeanroy, A. (ed.), *Recueil général des Jeux Partis français*, ed. A. Långfors and L. Brandin (Paris: Champion, 1926).
——and Guy, H. (eds.), *Chansons et Dits artésiens du XIIIe siècle* (Bordeaux: Bibliothèque des Universités du Midi, 1898).
Jehan Bodel, *Le Jeu de Saint Nicholas*, ed. J. Dufournet (Paris: Garnier Flammarion, 2005).
Jehan de Saint Quentin, *Dits de Jehan de Saint Quentin*, ed. B. Munk Olsen (Paris: Société des anciens textes français, 1978).
Johannes de Friburgo, *Summa Confessorum* (Paris: Jehan Petit, 1519).
John of Salisbury, *Policraticus*, ed. C. Nederman (Cambridge: Cambridge University Press, 1991).
Jubinal, A., *Jongleurs et trouvères ou choix de saluts, épitres, rêveries et autre pièces légères des XIIIe et XIVe siècles* (Paris: Merklein, 1835).
Kervyn de Lettenhove, J.-M. (ed.), *Collection de Chroniques Belges inédites: Codex Dunensis sive diplomatum et chartarum medii aevi* (Brussels: Académie Royale de Belgique, 1875).
Langlois, M., and Langers, Y. (eds.), *Confessions et jugements de criminels au Parlement de Paris (1319–50)* (Paris: Archives Nationales, 1971).
Laurière, E. de, Secousse, D.-F., Vilebault, M. de, Bréquigny, M. de, and Pardessus, J.-M. de (eds.), *Ordonnances des rois de France de la troisième race*, 22 vols. (Paris: Imprimerie Royale, 1723–1849).
Lecoy, F. (ed.), *La Vie des Pères*, 3 vols. (Paris: Société des anciens textes français, 1987).
Lecoy de la Marche, F., ed., *La Chaire française au Moyen Age* (Paris: Renouard, 1886).
Little, A. (ed.), *Liber exemplorum ad usum praedicantium* (Farnborough: Gregg, 1966).
Locres, F. de (ed.), *Chronicon Belgicum* (Arras, 1616).
Löseth, E. (ed.), *Robert le diable, roman d'aventures* (Paris: Firmin Didot, 1903).
Luard, H. (ed.), *Annales Prioratus de Dunstaplia (AD 1–1297)*, 3 vols. (London: Rolls Series, 1866).

Mansi, G. *et al.* (eds.), *Sacrorum conciliorum nova et amplissima collectio*, 29 vols. (Florence: Graz, 1960–1).

Marnier, M. (ed.), *Ancien coutumier inédit de Picardie (1300–1323) contenant les coutumes notoires, arrets et ordonnances des cours, assises et autres jurisdictions de Picardie au commencement du quatorzième siècle* (Paris: Techner, 1840).

Paetow, L. (ed.), *Two Medieval Satires: La Bataille des xii de Henri d'Andeli and the Morale Scholarium of John of Garland* (Berkeley, Calif.: University of California Press, 1914).

Paris, G., and Robert, U. (eds.), *Miracles de Nostre Dame par personnages*, 6 vols. (Paris: Société des anciens textes français, 1876–93).

Paris, Matthew, *Chronica Majora*, ed. H. Luard, 7 vols. (London: Longman, 1866).

Peraldus, *Summae virtutum et vitiorum* (Paris, 1519).

Petit, J. (ed.), *Registre des causes civiles de l'officialité de Paris, 1384–1387* (Paris: Imprimerie Nationale, 1919).

Philippe de Beaumanoir, *Coutumes du Beauvaisis*, ed. A. Salmon, 2 vols. (Paris: Collection de textes pour servir à l'étude, 1899).

——*The Coutumes of Philippe of Beaumanoir*, ed. F. Akehurst (Philadelphia: University of Pennsylvania Press, 1992).

Post, G., 'Three Letters Relating to the University of Paris c.1284–1289', *Speculum*, 14 (1939), 478–82.

Poupardin, R., 'Documents relatifs au conflit universitaire de 1266', *Société de l'histoire de Paris: Bulletin*, 36 (1909), 57–64.

Pseudo Boethius, *De Disciplina Scholarium*, ed. O. Weijers (Leiden: Brill, 1976).

Ralph of Coggeshall, *Chronicon Anglicanum*, ed. J. Stevenson (London: Rolls Series, 66, 1875).

Rapetti, P., and Chabaille, F. (eds.), *Li livres de jostice et de plet* (Paris: Firmin Didot, 1850).

Recueil des historiens des Gaules et de la France, 24 vols. (Paris, 1738–1904).

Richard, A. (ed.), *Inventaire-sommaire des Archives départementales antérieures à 1790: Pas-de-Calais. Archives Civiles—Série A*, 2 vols. (Arras: Imprimerie de la Société du Pas-de-Calais, 1878–87).

Robert of Flamborough, *Liber Poenitentialis*, ed. F. Firth (Toronto: Pontifical Institute of Medieval Studies, 1971).

Roberto Caracciolo, *Quaresimale in volgare*, ed. E. Esposito (Rome: Galatina, 1993).

Roger of Hoveden, *Chronica*, ed. W. Stubbs, 4 vols. (London: Rolls Series, 51, 1871).

Rosenfeld, H.-F. (ed.), *Mittelhochdeutsche Novellenstudien* (Leipzig: Mayer & Müller, 1927).

Ruelle, Pierre, *Les Dits du Clerc de Vaudoy* (Brussels: Presses universitaires de Bruxelles, 1969).

Rutebeuf, *Œuvres complètes de Rutebeuf*, ed. M. Zink (Paris: Bordas, 1989).

——*Poèmes concernant l'université de Paris*, ed. H. Lucas (Paris: Nizet, 1952).

Stehmann, W. (ed.), *Die Mittelhochdeutsche Novelle vom Studentenabenteuer* (Berlin: Mayer & Müller, 1909).
Strubel, A., Bellon, R., Lefèvre, S., and Boutet, D. (eds.), *Le Roman de Renart* (Paris: Gallimard, 1998).
The Summa Parisiensis on the Decretum Gratiani, ed. T. McLaughlin (Toronto: Pontifical Institute of Medieval Studies, 1952).
Symonds, J., *Wine, Women and Song: Medieval Latin Students' Songs* (London: Chatto & Windus, 1884).
Tanon, L., *Histoire des justices des anciennes églises et communautés monastiques de Paris* (Paris: Picard, 1883).
Tardif, A. (ed.), *Coutumier d'Artois: Publié d'après les manuscrits 5248 et 5249 fonds français de la Bibliothèque nationale* (Paris: Picard, 1883).
——(ed.), *Summa de legibus Normanniae* (Paris: Picard, 1896).
Teulet, A., *et al.* (eds.), *Layettes du Trésor des chartes: Inventaire analytique suivant l'ordre chronologique*, 4 vols. (Paris: Archives nationales, 1863–1902).
Thesaurus Exemplorum Medii Aevii at http://gahom.ehess.fr/thema/index.php.
Thierry, A., *Recueil des monuments inédits de l'histoire du Tiers Etat* (Paris: Firmin Didot, 1850–70).
Thomas de Cantimpré, *Bonum universale de apibus* (Douai: Belleri, 1627).
Thomas de Kent, *Le Roman d'Alexandre*, ed. B. Foster and I. Short (Paris: Champion, 2003).
Tubach, F., *Index exemplorum: A Handbook of Medieval Religious Tales* (Helsinki: Suomalainen Tiedeakatemia, 1969).
Väänänen, V. (ed.), '*Des fames, des dez et de la taverne*', *Neuphilologische Mitteilungen*, 47 (1946), 104–13.
Vallée, A., Jassemin, H., and Viard, J. (eds.), *Les Registres du Trésor des Chartes: Inventaire analytique*, ii and iii (Paris: Archives Nationales, 1999).
Vincent de Beauvais, *Le Speculum Historiale de Vincent de Beauvais*, ed. M. Taraye (Paris: Champion, 1999).
Viollet, P. (ed.), *Etablissements de Saint Louis*, 2 vols. (Paris: Collection de documents inédits, 1881–6).
Walter Map, *Latin Poems*, ed. T. Wright (London: Camden Society, 1841).
Welter, J., *Tabula Exemplorum* (Paris: Occitania, 1926).
William Durand, *Speculum Iudicale* (Basel: Apud Ambroisium et Aurelium Frobenios fratres, 1574; repr. Aalen: Scientia, 1975).
William of Tournai, *De instructione puerorum*, ed. J. Corbett (Indianopolis: Medieval Institute University of Notre Dame, 1955).

PRINTED SECONDARY WORKS

Akehurst, F. 'Good Name, Reputation and Notoriety in French Customary Law', in T. Fenster and D. Smail (eds.), *Fama: The Politics of Talk and Reputation in Medieval Europe* (Ithaca, NY: Cornell University Press, 2003), 75–94.
Akers, R., *Criminological Theory: Introduction and Evaluation* (Chicago: Roxbury Publishing Co., 1999).

Allen, C., *Law in the Making* (Oxford: Oxford University Press, new edn. 1964).

Althoff, G., 'Schranken der Gewalt: Wie gewalttätig war das "fristere Mittelalter?"', in H. Brunner (ed.), *Der Krieg im Mittelalter und in der frühen Neuzeit* (Wiesbaden: Reichert, 1999), 1–23.

Amussen, S. '"Being Stirred to Much Unquietness": Violence and Domestic Violence in Early Modern England', *Journal of Women's History*, 6 (1994), 70–89.

Ansgar Kelly, H., 'Rule of Thumb and the Folklaw of the Husband's Stick', *Journal of Legal Education*, 44 (1994), 341–65.

Arendt, H., *On Violence* (New York: Harcourt, 1970).

Armstrong, N., and Tennenhouse, L. (eds.), *The Violence of Representation: Literature and the History of Violence* (New York: Routledge, 1989).

Arnade, P., Howell, M., and Simons, W., 'Fertile Spaces: The Productivity of Urban Space in Northern Europe', *Journal of Interdisciplinary History*, 32/4 (2002), 515–48.

Arnold, J., 'Religion and Popular Rebellions from the Capuciati to Niklashausen', *Journal of Cultural and Social History*, 6/2 (2009), 149–61.

Ashley, K., and Hüskin, W., *Moving Subjects: Processional Performances in the Middle Ages and the Renaissance* (Amsterdam: Rodopi, 2001).

Aston, M., 'Corpus Christi and Corpus Regni: Heresy and the Peasants' Revolt', *Past and Present*, 143 (1994), 3–47.

Aubert, F., *Le Parlement de Paris de Philippe le Bel à Charles VII* (Paris: Picard, 1887–90).

Bachrach, B., and Nicholas, D. (eds.), *Law, Custom and the Social Fabric in Medieval Europe* (Kalamazoo, Mich.: Medieval Institute Publications, 1990).

Baranski, Z., 'Dante's Signs: An Introduction to Medieval Semiotics and Dante', in J. Barnes and C. O'Cuilleanain (eds.), *Dante and the Middle Ages* (Dublin: Irish Academic Press, 1995), 139–81.

Baraz, D., *Medieval Cruelty: Changing Perceptions, Late Antiquity to the Modern Period* (Ithaca, NY: Cornell University Press, 1993).

Barthes, R., 'Histoire et sociologie du vêtement', *Annales ESC*, 12/3 (1957), 430–41.

Bartlett, R., *Trial by Fire and Water: The Medieval Judicial Ordeal* (Oxford: Clarendon Press, 1986).

Bataillon, L.-J., 'Approaches to the Study of Medieval Sermons', *Leeds Studies in English*, 11 (1980), 19–35.

——'Bulletin d'histoire des doctrines médiévales: Le Treizième Siècle', *Revue des sciences philosophiques et théologiques*, 64 (1980), 101–31.

——'Les Crises de l'université de Paris d'après les sermons universitaires', in A. Zimmermann (ed.), *Die Auseinandersetzungen an der Pariser Universität im xiii Jahrhundert* (Berlin and New York: Miscellanea Mediaevalia, Veröffentlichungen des Thomas-Instituts des Universität zu Köln, 10, 1976), 155–69.

——*La Prédication au XIIIe siècle en France et Italie* (Aldershot: Variorum, 1993).

——'Sermons rédigés, sermons reportés (XIIIe siècle)', *Medioevo e Rinascimento*, 3 (1989), 69–86.

Batany, J., 'Punitions, impunités et fonctions sociales, théories morales et récits', *La Justice au Moyen Age, Senefiance, CUERMA,* 46 (1986), 43–63.

Battifol, L., 'Le Châtelet de Paris vers 1400', *Revue Historique,* 63 (1897), 42–55, 266–83.

Beattie, C., Maslakivic, A., and Rees Jones, S. (eds.), *The Medieval Household in Christian Europe c.850–c.1550: Managing Power, Wealth and the Body* (Turnhout: Brepols, 2003).

Becker, H., *Outsiders* (New York: Free Press, 1963).

Bédier, J., *Les Fabliaux: Études de littérature populaire et d'histoire littéraire du Moyen Age* (Paris: Champion, 1893).

Beik, W., 'The Violence of the French Crowd from Charivari to Revolution', *Past and Present,* 197 (2007), 75–111.

Bell, C., *Ritual Theory, Ritual Practice* (Oxford: Oxford University Press, 1992).

Benjamin, W., 'Zur Kritik der Gewalt', *Archiv für Sozialwissenschaft und Sozialpolitik,* 47 (1920/21), 809–32.

Benton, J., *Self and Society in Medieval France* (Toronto: Toronto University Press, 1984).

Benveniste, H., 'Le Système des amendes pénales en France au Moyen Age: Une première mise en perspective', *Revue d'histoire du droit français et étranger,* 70 (1992), 1–28.

Bercé, Y.-M., *Fête et révolte: Des mentalités populaires du XVIe au XVIIIe siècle* (Paris: Hachette, 1976).

Bériou, N., *L'Avènement des maîtres de la Parole: la prédication à Paris au XIIIe siècle* (Paris: Institut d'études augustiniennes, 1998).

——'La Reportation des sermons parisiens à la fin du XIIIe siècle', *Medioevo e Rinascimento,* 3 (1989), 87–123.

——*La Prédication de Ranulphe de la Houblonnière: Sermons aux clercs et aux simples gens à Paris au XIIIe siècle* (Paris: Études Augustiniennes, 1987).

Berlioz, J., *Saints et damnés: La Bourgogne du Moyen Age dans les récits d'Etienne de Bourbon, inquisiteur (1190–1261)* (Dijon: Les Éditions du bien public, 1989).

Berlow, R. K., 'The Development of Business Techniques Used at the Fairs of Champagne from the End of the Twelfth Century to the Middle of the Thirteenth Century', *Studies in Medieval and Renaissance History,* 8 (1971), 28–35.

Bernstein, A. E., 'Teaching and Preaching Confession in Thirteenth-Century Paris', in A. Ferreiro (ed.), *The Devil, Heresy and Witchcraft in the Middle Ages: Essays in Honor of Jeffrey B. Russell* (Leiden: Brill, 1998), 111–30.

Bildhauer, B., *Medieval Blood* (Cardiff: University of Wales Press, 2006).

Biller, P., and Minnis, A. (eds.), *Handling Sin: Confession in the Middle Ages* (York: York Medieval Press, 1998).

——'John of Naples: Quodlibets and Medieval Theological Concern with the Body', in P. Biller and A. Minnis (eds.), *Medieval Theology and the Natural Body* (York: York Medieval Press, 1997), 3–8.

Black-Michaud, J., *Cohesive Force: Feud in the Mediterranean and the Middle East* (Oxford: Blackwell, 1975).

——*Feuding Societies* (Oxford: Blackwell, 1975).

Blanc, O., 'Historiographie du vetement: Un bilan', in *Le Vêtement: Histoire, archéologie et symbolique vestimentaires au Moyen Age* (Paris: Léopard d'Or, 1989), 7–28.

Blok, A., *Honour and Violence* (Cambridge: Polity Press, 2001).

Boca, L., *La Justice criminelle et l'échevinage d'Abbeville au Moyen-Age* (Lille: Daniel, 1930).

Bodenheimer, M.-O., 'La Représentation théâtrale de la violence dans quelques *Miracles de Nostre Dame par personnages*', in *La Violence dans le monde médiéval, Senefiance,* 36 (1994), 55–67.

——'Le Rôle de la mère dans les *Miracles de Nostre Dame par personnages*', in *Bien Dire et Bien Aprandre: Revue de médiévistique*, 6 (1998), 490–8.

Bois, G., *The Crisis of Feudalism: Economy and Society in Eastern Normandy, c.1300–1500* (Cambridge: Cambridge University Press, 1984).

Boockmann, H., 'Das grausame Mittelalter: über ein Stereotyp in Geschichte', *Wissenschaft und Unterricht*, 38 (1987), 1–9.

Boone, M., '*Armes, coursses, assemblees et commocions:* Les Gens de métiers et l'usage de la violence dans la société urbaine flamande à la fin du Moyen Age', *Revue du Nord,* 359 (2005), 7–33.

——'Urban Space and Political Conflicts in Late Medieval Flanders', *Journal of Interdisciplinary History*, 32/4 (2002), 621–40.

Bordua, D., 'Recent Trends: Deviant Behavior and Social Control', *Annals*, 369 (1967), 149–63.

Bossy, J. (ed.), *Disputes and Settlements: Law and Human Relations in the West* (Cambridge: Cambridge University Press, 1983).

Bougard, P., Jacquer, A., Hilaire, Y., and Nolibos, A. (eds.), *Histoire d'Arras* (Dunkerque: Éditions des Beffrois, 1988).

Bourdieu, P., 'La Force du droit: éléments pour une sociologie du champ juridique', *Actes de la recherche en sciences sociales,* 64 (1986), 3–19.

——*Language and Symbolic Power*, tr. G. Raymond (Cambridge: Polity Press, 1991).

Boutet, D., and Strubel, A., *Littérature, politique et société dans la France du Moyen Age* (Paris: Presses Universitaires de France, 1979).

Bowsky, W., 'The Medieval Commune and Internal Violence: Police Power and Public Safety in Siena, 1287–1355', *American Historical Review*, 73 (1967), 1–17.

Boyce, G., *The English-German Nation in the University of Paris during the Middle Ages* (Bruges: St Catherine Press, 1927).

Boyle, L., 'The Fourth Lateran Council and Manuals of Popular Theology', in T. Hefferman (ed.), *The Popular Literature of Medieval England* (Knoxville, Tenn.: University of Tennessee Press, 1985), 30–44.

——'Summae Confessorum', in *Les Genres Littéraires dans les sources théologiques et philosophique médiévales: définition, critique et exploitation: Actes du Colloque international de Louvain-la-Neuve, 25–27 mai 1981* (Louvain-la-Neuve: Louvain University Press, 1982), 227–37.

Braithwaite, J., *Crime, Shame and Reintegration* (Cambridge: Cambridge University Press, 1989).

Braun, M., and Herbereichs, C. (eds.), *Gewalt im Mittelalter: Realitäten, Imaginationen* (Munich: Wilhelm Fink Verlag, 2005).
Brémond, C., Le Goff, J., and Schmitt, J.-C., *L'"Exemplum', Typologie des Sources du Moyen Age Occidental,* 40 (Turnhout: Brepols, 1982).
Brissaut, Y., 'L'Infanticide à la fin du Moyen Age', *Revue historique de droit français et étranger,* 50 (1972), 229–56.
Brooke, C., *The Medieval Idea of Marriage* (Oxford: Clarendon Press, 1989).
Brooke, R., *The Coming of the Friars* (London: Allen & Unwin, 1975).
Brookman, F., *Understanding Homicide* (London: Sage, 2005).
Brown, W., *Violence in Medieval Europe* (Harlow: Longman, 2011).
——and Gorécki, P. (eds.), *Conflict in Medieval Europe: Changing Perspectives on Society and Culture* (Aldershot: Ashgate, 2003).
Brundage, J., 'Domestic Violence in Classical Canon Law', in R. Kaeuper (ed.), *Violence in Medieval Society,* (Rochester: Boydell Press, 2000), 183–95.
——*Law, Sex and Christian Society in Medieval Europe* (Chicago: University of Chicago Press, 1987).
——*Medieval Canon Law* (London: Longman, 1995).
Brunvard, J. 'The Folktale Origin of *The Taming of the Shrew*', *Shakespeare Quarterly,* 17/4 (1966), 345–59.
Budinszky, A., *Die Universität Paris und die Fremden an derselben im Mittelalter* (Berlin: Hertz, 1876).
Bur, M., *Histoire de Laon et du Laonnais* (Toulouse: Privat, 1987).
Burkert, W., *Homo Necans,* tr. P. Bing (Berkeley, Calif.: University of California Press, 1983).
Butler, J., *Gender Trouble: Feminism and the Subversion of Identity* (New York: Routledge, 1990).
Butler, S., *The Language of Abuse: Marital Violence in Later Medieval England* (Leiden: Brill, 2007).
Butterworth, A., *Poetry and Music in Medieval France: From Jean Renart to Guillaume de Machaut* (Cambridge: Cambridge University Press, 2002).
Bynum, C. W., *Fragmentation and Redemption: Essays on Gender and the Human Body in Medieval Religion* (New York: Zone Books, 1991).
Cabanes, D., *Mœurs intimes du passé: La Vie d'étudiant* (Paris: Albin Michel, 1949).
Camille, M., *Image on the Edge: The Margins of Medieval Art* (London: Reaktion Books, 1992).
Camporesi, P., *The Incorruptible Flesh: Bodily Mutilation and Mortification in Religion and Folklore,* tr. T. Croft-Murray (Cambridge: Cambridge University Press, 1988).
Canning, J., Lehmann, H., and Winter, J. (eds.), *Power, Violence and Mass Death in Pre-Modern and Modern Times* (Aldershot: Ashgate, 2004).
Cantril, H., *The Psychology of Social Movements* (New York: Wiley, 1941).
Carabine, D., *John Scot Eriugena* (Oxford: Oxford University Press, 2000).
Carbasse, J.-M., *Histoire du droit pénal et de la justice criminelle* (Paris: Presses Universitaires de France, 2000).

——'Ne homines interficiantur: Quelques remarques sur la sanction médiévale de l'homicide', in S. Dauchy, J. Monballyu, and A. Wijffels (eds.), *Auctoritates: Xenia RC van Caenegem Oblata* (Brussels: Paleis der Academiën, 1997), 165–85.
Carbonnières, L. de, *La Procédure devant la chambre criminelle du Parlement de Paris au quatorzième siècle* (Paris: Champion, 2004).
Carolus-Barré, L., 'La Grande Ordonnance de 1254 sur la réforme de l'administration et la police du royaume', in *Septième centenaire de la mort de Saint Louis: Actes des colloques de Royaumont et de Paris (21–27 mai 1970)* (Paris: Belles Lettres, 1976), 85–96.
Carroll, S. (ed.), *Cultures of Violence: Interpersonal Violence in Historical Perspective* (London: Palgrave Macmillan, 2007).
Castan, Y., *Honnêté et relations sociales en Languedoc* (Paris: Plon, 1974).
Castells, M., *Luttes urbaines* (Paris: François Maspero, 1973).
Cazelles, R., *Nouvelle histoire de Paris* (Paris: Hachette, 1972).
——'Quelques réflexions à propos des mutations de la monnaie royale française', *Le Moyen Age*, 72 (1966), 83–105.
Chabas, M., *Le Duel judiciaire en France XIIIe–XVe siècles* (Paris: Jean Favard, 1978).
Champion, P., 'Liste des tavernes de Paris d'après les documents du XVe siècle', *Bulletin de la société de l'histoire de Paris,* 39 (1912), 259–67.
——*La Vie de Paris au Moyen Age* (Paris: Calmann-Lévy, 1933).
Charbonnier, P., 'L'Entrée dans la vie au XVe siècle, d'après les lettres de rémission', in *Entrées dans la vie: Initiations et apprentissages. XIIe congrès de la société des historiens médiévistes de l'enseignement supérieur public, Nancy 1981* (Nancy: Presses Universitaires de Nancy, 1982), 71–103.
Châtelain, P., 'Notes sur quelques tavernes fréquentées par l'université de Paris aux XIVe et XVe siècles', *Bulletin de la Société de l'histoire de Paris,* 14 (1898), 87–109.
Chesnais, J., *Histoire de la violence* (Paris: Laffont, 1981).
Chevalier, B., 'Corporations, conflits politiques et paix sociale en France aux XIVe et XVe siècles', *Revue Historique,* 258 (1982), 17–44.
Chevallot, P. (ed.), *Notre-Dame des ardents d'Arras: Faits et documents* (Abbeville: F. Paillart, 1918).
Cheyette, F., 'Suum cuique tribuere', *French Historical Studies,* 6 (1969), 287–99.
Chiffoleau, J., *Les Justices du pape: Délinquance et criminalité dans la région d'Avignon au XIVe siècle* (Paris: Publications de la Sorbonne, 1984).
Cobban, A., 'Medieval Student Power', *Past and Present,* 53 (1971), 28–66.
——*The Medieval Universities: Their Development and Organisation* (London: Methuen, 1975).
Cockburn, J., 'Patterns of Violence in English Society: Homicide in Kent, 1560–1986', *Past and Present,* 130 (1991), 70–106.
Cohen, E., 'The Animated Pain of the Body', *American Historical Review*, 105 (2000), 36–68.
——*The Crossroads of Justice: Law and Culture in Late Medieval France* (Leiden: Brill, 1993).

——'The Expression of Pain in the Later Middle Ages: Deliverance, Acceptance and Infamy', in F. Egmond and R. Zwijnenberg (eds.), *Bodily Extremities: Preoccupations with the Human Body in Early Modern European Culture* (Aldershot: Ashgate, 2003), 195–221.

——'The Hundred Years' War and Crime in Paris, 1332–1488', in E. Johnson and E. Monkkonen (eds.), *The Civilization of Crime: Violence in Town and Country since the Middle Ages* (Urbana, Ill.: University of Illinois Press, 1996), 109–24.

——'Patterns of Crime in Fourteenth-Century Paris', *French Historical Studies,* 11 (1980), 307–27.

——*Peaceable Domain, Certain Justice: Crime and Society in Fifteenth-Century Paris* (Hilversum: Verloren, 1996).

——Cohen, M., and Firnhaber-Baker, J. (eds.), *Difference and Identity in Medieval Francia* (Farnham: Ashgate, 2010).

Cohn, N., *The Pursuit of the Millennium: Revolutionary Millenarians and Mystical Anarchists of the Middle Ages* (London: Temple Smith, 1970).

Cohn, S., *Lust for Liberty: The Politics of Social Revolt in Medieval Europe, 1200–1425: Italy, France, and Flanders* (Cambridge, Mass.: Harvard University Press, 2006).

——'Popular Insurrection and the Black Death: A Comparative View', in *Rodney Hilton's Middle Ages*, ed. C. Dyer *et al.* (Oxford: Oxford University Press, 2007).

——*Popular Protest in Medieval Europe* (Manchester: Manchester University Press, 2004).

Coleman, C., and Moynihan, J., *Understanding Crime Data: Haunted by the Dark Figure* (Buckingham: Open University Press, 1996).

Collins, R., 'Three Faces of Cruelty: Towards a Comparative Sociology of Violence', *Theory and Society,* 1 (1974), 415–40.

Contamine, P., and Guyotjeannin, O. (eds.), *La Guerre, la violence et les gens au Moyen Age* (Paris: Éditions du CTHS, 1996).

Copeland, R. (ed.), *Criticism and Dissent in the Middle Ages* (Cambridge: Cambridge University Press, 1996).

Coser, L., *The Functions of Social Conflict* (London: Routledge, repr. 1998).

Counson, A., *Dante en France* (Paris: Fontemoing, 1906).

Courtenay, W., 'The Parisian Franciscan Community in 1303', *Franciscan Studies,* 53 (1993), 155–73.

——*Parisian Scholars in the Early Fourteenth-Century: A Social Portrait* (Cambridge: Cambridge University Press, 1999).

——*Teaching Careers at the University of Paris in the Thirteenth and Fourteenth Centuries* (Notre Dame, Ind.: University of Notre Dame Press, 1988).

——and Miethke, J. (eds.), *Universities and Schooling in Medieval Society* (Leiden: Brill, 2000).

Cowell, A., *At Play in the Tavern: Signs, Coins, and Bodies in the Middle Ages* (Ann Arbor: University of Michigan Press, 1999).

Crowther, N., 'Water and Wine as Symbols of Inspiration', *Mnemosyne*, 32/4 (1979), 1–11.
Davies, B., *The Thought of Thomas Aquinas* (Oxford: Oxford University Press, 1992).
Davis, I., Müller M., and Rees Jones, S. (eds.), *Love, Marriage, and Family Ties in the Later Middle Ages* (Turnhout: Brepols, 2003).
D'Avray, D., *Medieval Marriage: Symbolism and Society* (Oxford: Oxford University Press, 2005).
——*The Preaching of the Friars: Sermons Diffused from Paris before 1300* (Oxford: Clarendon Press, 1985).
——'Sermons to the Upper Bourgeoisie by a Thirteenth-Century Franciscan', in D. Baker (ed.), *The Church in Town and Countryside* (Studies in Church History, 16; Oxford: Oxford University Press, 1979), 187–99.
——'Some Franciscan Ideas about the Body', *Archivum Franciscanum Historicum*, 84 (1991), 343–63.
——and Bériou, N. (eds.), *Modern Questions about Medieval Sermons: Essays on Marriage, Death, History and Sexuality* (Spoleto: Centro italiano di studi sull'Alto medioevo, 1994).
——and Tausche, M., 'Marriage Sermons in *Ad status* Collections of the Central Middle Ages', *Archives d'histoire doctrinale et littéraire du Moyen Age,* 47 (1980), 71–119.
Davy, M., *Les Sermons universitaires parisiens de 1230–1231* (Paris: Vrin, 1931).
——'La Situation juridique des étudiants à l'université de Paris au XIIIe siècle', *Revue de l'histoire de l'église de France,* 17 (1931), 297–311.
Dean, T., *Crime in Medieval Europe* (Harlow: Longman, 2001).
——'Domestic Violence in Late Medieval Bologna', *Renaissance Studies*, 18 (2004), 527–43.
Decagny, P., *Histoire de l'arrondissement de Péronne* (Péronne: J. Quentin, 1844).
Delehaye, H., *The Legends of the Saints,* tr. D. Attwater (London: Chapman, 1962).
Delisle, L., 'Sur deux documents relatifs à Paris, insérés dans un ms. de l'abbaye des Dunes', *Bulletin de la Société de l'Histoire de Paris,* 3 (1876), 76–111.
——'Sur un passage des poésies de Gilles li Muisis relatif à l'Université de Paris', *Bulletin de la Société de l'Histoire de Paris,* 9 (1882), 95–100.
Delmaire, B., *Le Diocèse d'Arras de 1093 au milieu de XIVe siècle: Recherches sur la vie religieuse dans le nord de la France au Moyen Age* (Arras: Mémoires de la commission départementale d'histoire et archéologie du Pas-de-Calais, 1994).
Denifle, H., *Die Universitäten des Mittelalters bis 1400* (Berlin: Verlag, 1885).
Denton, J., 'The Second Uprising at Laon and its Aftermath, 1295–98', *Bulletin of the John Rylands Library,* 72 (1990), 79–92.
Derrida, J., Force de loi: Le '*Fondement mystique de l'autorité*' (Paris: Galilée, 1994).
Derville, A., 'Arras au 13e siècle: à propos de la thèse de Roger Berger', *Revue du Nord,* 64 (1982), 193–200.
——*Histoire de Saint Omer* (Lille: Presses Universitaires de Lille, 1981).

——*Les Villes de Flandre et d'Artois, 900–1500* (Villeneuve d'Ascq: Presses Universitaires du Septentrion, 2002).

Desmaze, C., *Le Châtelet de Paris* (Paris: de Cosse, 1854).

Destemberg, A., 'Morts violentes et lieux de mémoire: Les réparations faites à l'université de Paris à la fin du Moyen Age', *Traverse: Zeitschrift für Geschichte, Revue d'histoire,* 2 (2008), 37–48.

Dieulafroy, M., 'Le Miracle de la femme que Nostre Dame garda d'estre arse', *Bulletin de la Société de l'Histoire du Théâtre,* 2 (1906), 100–10.

Doelle, H., (ed.), *Die Behandlung der Trunkenheit im Strafrecht* (Frankfurt: Metzner, 1960).

Donahue, C., Jr, *Law, Marriage and Society in the Later Middle Ages* (Cambridge: Cambridge University Press, 2007).

Dragonetti, R., 'Le *Jeu de Saint Nicholas de Jean Bodel*', in L. Arrathoon (ed.), *The Craft of Fiction: Essays in Medieval Poetics* (Rochester, Mich.: Solaris Press, 1984), 369–91.

Dubois, D. J., and Lemaître, J.-L., *Sources et méthodes de l'hagiographie médiévale* (Paris: CERF, 1993).

Duby, G., *A History of Private Life: Revelations of the Medieval World* (Cambridge, Mass.: Harvard University Press, 1988).

Ducoudray, G., *Les Origines du Parlement de Paris et la justice aux XIIIe et XIVe siècles* (Paris: Hachette, 1902).

Duerr, H., *Nacktheit und Scham: Der Mythos vom Zivilisationsprozess* (Frankfurt: Suhrkamp, 1988).

Dufournet, J., 'Variations sur un motif: La Taverne dans le théâtre arrageois du XIIIe siècle', in J. Backès (ed.), *Farai chansoneta novele: Hommage à Jean-Charles Payen* (Caen: Centre de Publications de l'Université de Caen, 1989), 161–74.

Dumolyn, J., '"Criers and Shouters": The Discourse on Radical Urban Rebels in Late Medieval Flanders', *Journal of Social History,* 42/1 (2008), 111–35.

Dunbabin, J., *Captivity and Imprisonment in Medieval Europe (1100–1300)* (Houndmills: Palgrave, 2002).

——'Meeting the Costs of University Education in Northern France, c.1240–c.1340', *History of Universities,* 10 (1991), 1–27.

Dutton, P., 'Illustre Civitatis et Populi Exemplum: Plato's *Timaeus* and the Transmission from Calcidius to the End of the Twelfth Century of a Tripartite Scheme of Society', *Mediaeval Studies,* 45 (1983), 108–12.

Edgerton, S., *Pictures of Punishment* (Ithaca, NY: Cornell University Press, 1985).

Egbert, V., *On the Bridges of Medieval Paris: A Record of Early Fourteenth-Century Life* (Princeton: Princeton University Press, 1974).

Eisner, M., 'Long-Term Historical Trends in Violent Crime', *Crime and Justice,* 30 (2003), 83–142.

Elias, N., *Uber den Prozess der Zivilisation* (Basel: Haus zum Falken, 1939).

Elliott, D., *Spiritual Marriage and Sexual Abstinence in Medieval Wedlock* (Princeton: Princeton University Press, 1993).

Enders, J., *Death by Drama and Other Medieval Urban Legends* (Chicago: University of Chicago Press, 2003).

——*The Medieval Theater of Cruelty: Rhetoric, Memory, Violence* (Ithaca, NY: Cornell University Press, 1999).

Entrées dans la vie: Initiations et apprentissages. XIIe congrès de la société des historiens médiévistes de l'enseignement supérieur public, Nancy 1981 (Nancy: Presses Universitaires de Nancy, 1982).

Esmein, A., *Histoire de la procédure criminelle en France* (Paris: Picard, 1882).

——*Le Mariage en droit canonique,* 2 vols. (Paris: Sirey, 1929).

Espinas, G., 'Les Guerres familiales dans la commune de Douai aux XIe et XIIIe siècles: Les Trêves et les paix', *Nouvelle revue historique de droit français et étranger*, 23 (1899), 415–73.

——*La Vie urbaine de Douai au Moyen Age*, 4 vols. (Paris: Picard, 1913).

Fabre, A., *Études historiques sur les clercs de la Bazoche* (Paris: Potier, 1856).

Farmer, S., 'Down and Out and Female in Thirteenth-Century Paris', *American Historical Review,* 103 (1998), 344–70.

——*Surviving Poverty in Medieval Paris: Gender, Ideology, and the Daily Lives of the Poor* (Ithaca, NY: Cornell University Press, 2001).

La Faute, la répression et le pardon: Actes du 107e congrès national des sociétés savantes, Brest 1982 (Paris: CTHS, 1984).

Fawtier, R., *The Capetian Kings of France: Monarchy and Nation 987–1328* (London: Macmillan, 1960).

——*Histoire des institutions françaises au Moyen Age,* 3 vols. (Paris: Presses Universitaires de France, 1957–62).

Fentress, J., and Wickham, C., *Social Memory* (Oxford: Blackwell, 1992).

Ferruolo, S., *The Origins of the University: The Schools of Paris and their Critics 1100–1215* (Stanford, Calif.: Stanford University Press, 1985).

——'Parisius—Paradisus: The City, its Schools and the Origins of the University of Paris', in T. Bender (ed.), *The University and the City: From Medieval Origins to the Present* (Oxford: Oxford University Press, 1988), 22–38.

Feuchère, P., *Les Châtelains d'Arras: De l'épée à la plume* (Arras: Commission départementale d'histoire et d'archéologie du Pas-de-Calais, 1948).

Finch, A., 'The Nature of Violence in the Middle Ages: An Alternative Perspective', *Historical Research,* 70/173 (1997), 249–68.

——'*Repulsa uxores sua*: Marital Difficulties and Separation in the Later Middle Ages', *Continuity and Change,* 8/1 (1993), 11–38.

——'Women and Violence in the Later Middle Ages: The Evidence of the Officiality of Cerisy', *Continuity and Change*, 7/1 (1992), 23–45.

Fineman, M., and Mykitiuk, R. (eds.), *The Public Nature of Private Violence: The Discovery of Domestic Abuse* (New York: Routledge, 1994).

Firnhaber-Baker, J., 'From God's Peace to the King's Order: Late Medieval Limitations on Non-Royal Warfare', *Essays in Medieval Studies,* 23 (2006), 19–30.

——'Seigneurial War and Royal Power in Later Medieval Southern France', *Past and Present*, 208 (2010), 37–76.

Fossier, R, *La Terre et les hommes en Picardie jusqu'à la fin du XIIIe siècle*, 2 vols. (Paris: Béatrice-Nauwelaerts, 1968).

Foucault, M., *Surveiller et punir* (Paris: Gallimard, 1975).
Foulon, C., *L'Œuvre de Jehan Bodel* (Paris: Presses Universitaires de France, 1958).
——and Foulet, L., 'Les Scènes de taverne et les comptes du tavernier dans le *Jeu de Saint Nicholas* de Jean Bodel', *Romania*, 68 (1944), 422–44.
Fouret, C., 'La Violence en fête: La Course à l'Epinette à Lille à la fin du Moyen Age', *Revue du Nord*, 249 (1981), 377–90.
Fourquin, G., *Les Campagnes de la région parisienne à la fin du Moyen Age* (Paris: Presses Universitaires de France, 1964).
——*Les Soulèvements populaires au Moyen Age* (Paris: Hachette, 1972).
François, M., 'Notice sur les lettres de rémission transcrites dans les registres du Trésor des Chartes', *Bibliothèque de l'École des Chartes*, 103 (1942), 317–24, and 104 (1943), 310–25.
Frappier-Bigras, D., 'La Famille dans l'artisanat parisien du treizième siècle', *Le Moyen Age*, 95 (1980), 56–62.
Freud, S., *Civilisation and its Discontents*, tr. J. Riviere (London: Hogarth Press, 1930).
Gabriel, A., *Garlandia: Studies in the History of the Medieval University* (Frankfurt: Knecht, 1969).
——*Skara House at the Medieval University of Paris* (Notre Dame, Ind.: Medieval Institute, 1960).
——*Student Life in Ave Maria College, Medieval Paris* (Notre Dame, Ind.: Medieval Institute, 1955).
Ganiage, J. (ed.), *Histoire de Beauvais et du Beauvaisis* (Toulouse: Privat, 1987).
Gauvard, C., *De grace especial: Crime, état et société en France à la fin du Moyen Age* (Paris: Publications de la Sorbonne, 1991).
——*Une question d'état et de société: Violence et criminalité en France à la fin du Moyen Age* (Lille: Presses Universitaires de Lille, 1989).
——'Violence citadine et réseaux de solidarité: L'exemple français aux XIVe et XVe siècles', *Annales ESC* 48/5 (1993), 1113–26.
——*Violence et ordre publique au Moyen Age* (Paris: Picard, 2005).
Geertz, C., *The Interpretation of Cultures: Selected Essays* (London: Hutchinson, 1973).
Gelles, R., *The Violent Home: A Study of Physical Aggression between Husbands and Wives* (Beverly Hills, Calif.: Sage, 1974).
Geltner, G., 'Mendicants as Victims: Scale, Scope, and the Idiom of Violence', *Journal of Medieval History*, 36/2 (2010), 126–41.
Geremek, B., *The Margins of Society in Late Medieval Paris*, tr. J. Birrell (Cambridge: Cambridge University Press, 1987).
Gibbon, E., *The Decline and Fall of the Roman Empire*, 5 vols. (London: Allen Lane, new edn. 1994).
Gillingham, B., *The Social Background to Secular Medieval Latin Song* (Ottawa: Institute of Medieval Music, 1998).
——'Turtles, Helmets, Parasites and Goliards', *Music Review*, 95 (1994), 249–74.

Gillingham, J., and Holt, J. (eds.), *War and Government in the Middle Ages* (Cambridge: Cambridge University Press, 1984).
Girard, R., *La Violence et le sacré* (Paris: Grasset, 1972).
Given, J., *Society and Homicide in Thirteenth-Century England* (Stanford, Calif.: Stanford University Press, 1977).
Glorieux, P., 'Sermons universitaires parisiens de 1267–1268', *Recherches de théologie ancienne et médiévale,* 16 (1949), 40–71.
Gluckmann, M., *Essays on the Ritual of Social Relations* (Manchester: Manchester University Press, 1962).
Glutz, R., *Miracles de Nostre Dame par personnages: Bibliographie und neue Studien zu Text, Entstehungszeit und Herkunft* (Berlin: Akademie-Verlag, 1954).
Gonthier, N., *Cris de haine et rites d'unité: La Violence dans les villes, XIIIe au XVIe siècles* (Turnhout: Brepols, 1992).
Goodich, M., *Violence and Miracle in the Fourteenth Century* (Chicago: University of Chicago Press, 1995).
——(ed.), *Voices from the Bench: The Narratives of Lesser Folk in Medieval Trials* (London: Palgrave Macmillan, 2006).
Gorochov, N., *Le Collège de Navarre de sa fondation (1305) au début du XVe siècle (1418)* (Paris: Champion, 1997).
Graff, H., 'A Reply', *Journal of Interdisciplinary History*, 9/3 (1979), 465–71.
Grand, R., 'Justice criminelle, procédure et peines dans les villes aux XIIIe et XIVe siècles', *Bibliothèque de l'École des Chartes,* 101 (1941), 70–80.
Gravdal, K., *Ravishing Maidens: Writing Rape in Medieval French Literature and Law* (Philadelphia: University of Pennsylvania Press, 1991).
Green, T., 'Societal Concepts of Criminal Liability for Homicide in Mediaeval England', *Speculum,* 47/4 (1972), 669–94.
Greenshields, M., *An Economy of Violence in Early Modern France: Crime and Justice in the Haute Auvergne, 1587–1664* (University Park, Pa.: Pennsylvania State University Press, 1994).
Groebner, V., *Defaced: The Visual Culture of Violence in the Late Middle Ages*, tr. P. Selwyn (New York: Zone Books, 2004).
Grossel, M., 'Le Monde d'ici-bas, un royaume de violence: Le Siècle dans les *Miracles de Nostre Dame* de Gautier de Coinci', *La Violence dans le monde médiéval: Senefiance,* 36 (1994), 265–83.
Grundy, R., *Soma in Biblical Theology* (Cambridge: Cambridge University Press, 1976).
Guesnon, A., 'Adam de la Halle et le *Jeu de la Feuillée*', *Moyen Age*, 28 (1915), 173–233.
——*La Satire à Arras au XIIIe siècle* (Paris: Hachette, 1900).
Gurevich, A., *Medieval Popular Culture* (Cambridge: Cambridge University Press, 1990).
Gurr, T., 'Historical Trends in Violent Crime: A Critical Review of the Evidence', *Crime and Justice: An Annual Review of Research*, 3 (1981), 295–350.

Guyon, G., 'La Justice pénale dans le théâtre religieux du XIVe siècle: *Les Miracles de Nostre Dame par personnages*', *Revue historique de droit français et étranger*, 30 (1991) 465–86.

Habermas, J., *The Structural Transformation of the Public Sphere: An Inquiry into a Category of Bourgeois Society* (Cambridge, Mass.: Harvard University Press, 1991).

——and Lennox, S. and F.,'The Public Sphere: An Encyclopedia Article', *New German Critique*, 3 (1974), 49–55.

Hahn, C., *Portrayed on the Heart: Narrative Effect in Pictorial Lives of Saints from the Tenth through the Thirteenth Century* (Berkeley, Calif.: University of California Press, 2001).

Halbwachs, M., *On Collective Memory*, ed. and tr. L. Coser (Chicago: Chicago University Press, 1992).

Hallam, E., and Everard, J. (eds.), *Capetian France, 987–1328* (London: Longman, 2001).

Halphen, L. (ed.), *Aspects de l'université de Paris* (Paris: Albin Michel, 1949).

Halsall, G., *Violence and Society in the Early Medieval West* (Woodbridge: Boydell Press, 1998).

Hamel, S., *La Justice dans une ville du nord de la royaume de France au Moyen Age: Étude sur la pratique judiciaire à Saint Quentin (fin XIe–début XVe siècle)* (Turnhout: Brepols, 2012).

Hammer, C., 'Homicide in Fourteenth-Century Oxford', *Past and Present*, 78 (1978), 4–23.

Hanawalt, B., *Crime and Conflict in English Communities, 1300–1348* (Cambridge, Mass.: Harvard University Press, 1979).

——'The Female Felon in Fourteenth-Century England', *Viator*, 5 (1974), 253–68.

——*'Of Good and Ill Repute': Gender and Social Control in Medieval England* (Oxford: Oxford University Press, 1998).

——'Violence in the Domestic Milieu of Late Medieval England', in R. Kaeuper (ed.), *Violence in Medieval Society* (Woodbridge: Boydell Press, 2000), 197–214.

——and Kobialka, M. (eds.), *Medieval Practices of Space* (Minneapolis: University of Minnesota Press, 2000).

——and Reyerson, K. (eds.), *City and Spectacle in Medieval Europe* (Minneapolis: University of Minnesota Press, 1994).

——and Wallace, D., *Medieval Crime and Social Control* (Minneapolis: University of Minnesota Press, 1999).

Hanford, J., 'The Medieval Debate between Wine and Water', *Proceedings of the Modern Language Association*, 28/3 (1913), 315–67.

Hardwick, J., 'Early Modern Perspectives on the Long History of Domestic Violence: The Case of Seventeenth-Century France', *Journal of Modern History*, 78 (2006), 1–36.

Harold-Riggins, S., *The Socialness of Things: Essays on the Socio-Semiotics of Objects* (Berlin: Mouter de Gruyter, 1994).

Harvey, H., *Theatre of the Basoche: The Contribution of the Law Societies to French Mediaeval Comedy* (Cambridge, Mass.: Harvard University Press, 1941).
Haskins, C., *The Rise of the Universities* (New York: Holt, 1923).
——*Studies in Mediaeval Culture* (Oxford, Clarendon Press, 1929).
Hawkins, A., and Merricks, L., '"Wee be Black as Hell": Ritual, Disguise and Rebellion', *Rural History*, 4/1 (1993), 41–53.
Heers, J., *Le Clan familial au Moyen Age* (Paris: Hachette, 1974).
——*Fêtes, jeux, joutes, dans les sociétés d'Occident à la fin du Moyen Age* (Paris: Vrin, 1971).
Helmholz, R., *Marriage Litigation in Medieval England* (Cambridge: Cambridge University Press, 1974).
Héricourt, A. d', and Godin, A., *Les Rues d'Arras* (Brussels: Éditions Culture et Civilisation, 1976).
Herlihy, D., 'Family', *American Historical Review*, 96/1 (1991), 1–16.
——'Family Solidarity in Medieval Italian History', in D. Herlihy, R. Lopez, and V. Slessarev (eds.), *Economy, Society and Government in Medieval Italy* (Kent, Ohio: Kent State University Press, 1969), 173–85.
——*Medieval Households* (Cambridge, Mass.: Harvard University Press, 1985).
Hilton, R., *Bondsmen Made Free: Medieval Peasant Movements and the English Rising of 1381* (London: Temple Smith, 1973).
Hindley, A., '*L'Escole au deable*: Tavern Scenes in the Old French Moralité', *Comparative Drama*, 33 (2000), 454–73.
Ho, C., 'Corpus Delicti: The Edifying Dead in the *Exempla* of Jacques de Vitry', in J. Hammesse, B. Kienzle, A. Thayer, and D. Stoudt (eds.), *Medieval Sermons and Society: Cloister, City, University* (Louvain-la-Neuve: Brepols, 1998), 203–18.
Holmes, G., *Dante* (New York: Hill & Wang, 1980).
Holmes, J., *An Introduction to Sociolinguistics* (Harlow: Longman, 1992).
Howard Bloch, R., *Medieval French Literature and Law* (Berkeley, Calif.: University of California Press, 1977).
——*Medieval Misogyny and the Invention of Western Romantic Love* (Chicago: Chicago University Press, 1991).
Hunt, T., 'A Note on the Ideology of Bodel's *Jeu de Saint Nicolas*', *Studi Francesi*, 58 (1976), 67–72.
James, M., 'Ritual, Drama and the Social Body in the Late Medieval English Town', *Past and Present*, 98 (1983), 3–29.
Jaritz, G. (ed.), *Die Strasse: Zur Funktion und Perzeption öffentlichen Raums im Späten Mittelalter* (Vienna: Verlag der Österreichischen Akademie der Wissenschaften, 2001).
Jauss, H., *Towards an Aesthetic of Reception*, tr. T. Bahti (Minneapolis: University of Minnesota Press, 1982).
Jehel, G., and Racinet, P., *Education et cultures dans l'Occident chrétien du XIIe au XVe siècle* (Paris: Éditions du Temps, 1998).
Johnson, E., and Monkkonen, E., *The Civilization of Crime: Violence in Town and Country since the Middle Ages* (Urbana, Ill.: University of Illinois Press, 1996).

Jordan, W. C., 'Anti-Corruption Campaigns in Thirteenth-Century Europe', *Journal of Medieval History*, 35/2 (2009), 204–19.

—— *The French Monarchy and the Jews: From Philip Augustus to the Last Capetians* (Philadelphia: University of Pennsylvania Press, 1989).

Jorgensen Itynre, C. (ed.), *Medieval Family Roles: A Book of Essays* (New York and London: Garland Publishing, 1996).

Kagay, D., *The Final Argument: The Imprint of Violence on Society in Medieval and Early Modern Europe* (Woodbridge: Boydell & Brewer, 1998).

Kaiser, R., *Trunkenheit und Gewalt im Mittelalter* (Vienna: Böhlau, 2002).

Kaueper, R., *Chivalry and Violence in Medieval Europe* (Oxford: Oxford University Press, 1999).

——(ed.), *Violence in Medieval Society* (Woodbridge: Boydell, 2000).

—— *War, Justice and Public Order: England and France in the Later Middle Ages* (Oxford: Oxford University Press, 1988).

Keller, H.-E., 'Pour une réhabilitation des *Miracles de Nostre Dame par personnages*: A propos du *Miracle d'une Femme que Nostre Dame garda d'estre arse*', *French Forum*, 12 (1987), 133–45.

Kempshall, M., *The Common Good in Late Medieval Political Thought* (Oxford: Clarendon Press, 1999).

Kibre, P., *The Nations in the Medieval Universities* (Cambridge, Mass.: Medieval Academy of America, 1948).

——*Scholarly Privileges in the Middle Ages: The Rights, Privileges and Immunities of Scholars at the Universities of Bologna, Padua, Paris, and Oxford* (Cambridge, Mass.: Medieval Academy of America, 1962).

Kieckhefer, R., *Unquiet Souls: Fourteenth-Century Saints and their Religious Milieu* (Chicago: Chicago University Press, 1984).

Koller, H., 'Stadt und Universität im Spätmittelalter', in E. Maschke and J. Sidow (eds.), *Stadt und Universität im Mittelalter und in der früheren Neuzeit* (Berlin: Thorbecke, 1974), 9–27.

Kümin, B., 'Friede, Gewalt und öffentliche Räume: Grenzziehungen im alteuropäischen Wirtshaus', in C. Ulbrich, C. Jarzebowski, and M. Hohkamp (eds.), *Gewalt in der Frühen Neuzeit* (Berlin: Dunkler & Humblot, 2005), 130–9.

——and Tlusty, B. (eds.), *The World of the Tavern: Public Houses in Early Modern Europe* (Aldershot: Ashgate, 2002).

Labande, L., *Histoire de Beauvais et de ses institutions communales jusqu'au commencement du XVe siècle* (Paris: Imprimerie nationale, 1892).

Lalou, E., 'Les Révoltes contre le pouvoir', in *Violence et Contestation au Moyen Age: Actes du 114e Congrès National des Sociétés Savantes, Paris, 1989* (Paris: Éditions du Comité des travaux historiques et scientifiques, 1990), 159–83.

Langlois, C.-V., 'Sermons parisiens de la première moitié du XIIIe siècle, contenus dans le manuscrit 691 de la Bibliothèque d'Arras', *Journal des Savants*, 9 (1916), 488–98, 548–59.

Langlois, E., *Adam le bossu, trouvère artésien du XIIIe siècle* (Paris: Hachette, 1951).

Langmuir, G., 'Community and Legal Change in Capetian France', *French Historical Studies*, 6 (1969) 277–86.

Lanhers, Y., 'Crimes et criminels au XIVe siècle', *Revue Historique,* 240 (1969), 325–37.

Laurence, A., 'Les Comptes du bailli d'Arras au XIVe siècle: Source de droit criminel et pénal' (unpublished thesis, École des Chartes, 1967).

Lavoie, R., 'Justice, criminalité et la peine de mort en France au Moyen Age', in *Actes du Ve Colloque de l'institut d'études médiévales de l'université de Montréal* (Montreal: L'Aurore, 1979), 31–55.

Lawrence, C., *The Friars: The Impact of the Early Mendicant Movement on Western Society* (London: Longman, 1994).

Le Bon, G., *The Crowd: A Study of the Popular Mind* (London: Benn, 1896).

Lecuppre-Desjardin, E., 'De l'invective à la prise de conscience identitaire: La Guerre entre Douai et Lille (1284–1285)', in M. Aurell (ed.), *Convaincre et persuader: Communication et propagande aux XIIe et XIIIe siècles* (Poitiers: Centre d'études supérieures de civilisation médiévale, 2007).

——and Van Bruaene, A.-L. (eds.), *Emotions in the Heart of the City (14th–16th century): Studies in European Urban History 5 (1100–1800)* (Turnhout: Brepols, 2005).

——and ——(eds.), *De Bono communi: The Discourse and Practice of the Common Good in the European City (13th to 16th Centuries)/Discours et pratique du Bien Commun dans les villes d'Europe (XIIIe–XVIe siècle)* (Turnhout: Brepols, 2010).

Lees, C. (ed.), *Medieval Masculinities: Regarding Men in the Middle Ages* (Minneapolis: University of Minnesota Press, 1994).

Lefèbvre, H., *Writings on Cities*, tr. and ed. E. Kofman and E. Lebas (Oxford: Blackwells, 1996).

Leff, G., *Paris and Oxford Universities in the Thirteenth and Fourteenth Centuries* (New York: Wiley, 1968).

Le Goff, J., *Les Intellectuels au Moyen Age* (Paris: Seuil, 1985).

——'Quelle conscience l'Université médiévale a-t-elle eue d'elle-même', in J. Le Goff (ed.), *Pour un autre Moyen Age* (Paris: Gallimard, 1999), 181–98.

——'Le Temps du travail dans la "crise" du XIVe siècle: Du temps médiéval au temps moderne', in J. Le Goff, *Pour un autre Moyen Age* (Paris: Gallimard, 1977), 66–80.

——and Schmitt, J.-C. (eds.), *Le Charivari* (Paris: EHESS, 1995).

Leguay, A., 'Les Troubles urbains dans le nord de la France à la fin du XIIIe siècle et au début du XIVe siècle', *Revue d'histoire, économique et sociale,* 3 (1976), 281–303.

Leguay, J.-P., *La Rue au Moyen Age* (Rennes: Ouest France, 1984).

Lehoux, F., *Le Bourg Saint Germain des Près* (Paris, 1898).

Lemercier, P., 'Une Curiosité judiciaire au Moyen Age: La Grâce par mariage subséquent', *Revue d'Histoire du Droit Français et Étranger*, 33 (1955), 464–74.

Le Roux de Lincy, A., and Tisserand, L. (eds.), *Paris et ses historiens au XIVe et XVe siècles* (Paris: Imprimerie impériale, 1867).

Lestocquoy, J., *Patriciens du Moyen Age: Les Dynasties bourgeoises d'Arras du XIe au XVe siècle* (Arras: Mémoires de la commission départementale du Pas-de-Calais, 1945).

——*La Vie sociale et économique à Arras du XIIe au XVe siècle* (Arras: Mémoires de la commission départementale du Pas-de-Calais, 1941).

Lewis, A., *Royal Succession in Capetian France* (Cambridge, Mass.: Harvard University Press, 1981).

Lewis, E., *Medieval Political Ideas* (London: Routledge, 1954).

Lewis, P., *Later Medieval France* (London: Macmillan, 1968).

Lieblein, L., 'Flexible Iconography: The Experience of the Spectator of Medieval Religious Drama', *Le Moyen Age*, 19 (1988), 135–48.

Lilley, K., 'Cities of God? Medieval Urban Forms and their Christian Symbolism', *Transactions of the Institute of British Geographers*, 29 (2004), 296–313.

——*City and Cosmos: The Medieval World in Urban Form* (London: Reaktion, 2009)

——*Urban Life in the Middle Ages: 1000–1400* (London: Palgrave, 2002).

Little, L., *Religious Poverty and the Profit Economy in Medieval Europe* (London: Longman, 1978).

——'Les Techniques de la confession et la confession comme technique', in G. Barone *et al.* (eds.), *Faire croire: Modalités de la diffusion et de la réception des messages religieux du XIIe au XVe siècle* (Rome: École française de Rome, 1981), 87–99.

Longère, J., *La Prédication Médiévale* (Paris: Études Augustiniennes, 1983).

Lorenz, K., *On Aggression*, tr. M. Kerr Wilson (New York: Wiley, 1971).

Louandre, F.-C., *Histoire d'Abbeville* (Abbeville: A. Boulanger, 1883).

Louvet, P., *Histoire et antiquités du diocese de Beauvais*, 2 vols. (Paris: Valet, 1631–5).

Luchaire, A., *Les Communes françaises* (Paris: Hachette, 1890).

Lyon, E., 'Un manuscript inédit de Beaumanoir', in *Mélanges Paul Fournier* (Paris: Sirey, 1929), 479–86.

McVaugh, M., *The Rational Surgery of the Middle Ages* (Florence: SISMEL, 2006).

Maddern, P., *Violence and Social Order: East Anglia, 1422–1442* (Oxford: Oxford University Press, 1992).

Maddox, D., and Sturm-Maddox, S. (eds.), *Parisian Confraternity Drama of the Fourteenth Century: The Miracles de Nostre Dame par personnages* (Turnhout: Brepols, 2008).

Mandressi, R., *Le Regard de l'anatomiste: Dissections et invention du corps en Occident* (Paris: Seuil, 2003).

Mansfield, M., *The Humiliation of Sinners: Public Penance in Thirteenth-Century France* (Ithaca, NY: Cornell University Press, 1995).

Marsh, P., and Campbell, A. (eds.), *Aggression and Violence* (Oxford: Oxford University Press, 1982).

Martin, L., *Alcohol, Sex and Gender* (Basingstoke: Palgrave, 2001).

Martines, L. (ed.), *Violence and Civil Disorder in Italian Cities 1200–1500* (Berkeley, Calif.: University of California Press, 1972).

Marx, E. 'Some Social Context of Personal Violence', in M. Gluckman (ed.), *The Allocation of Responsibility* (Manchester: Manchester Uinversity Press, 1972), 281–321.

Maschke, E., and Sydow, J. (eds.), *Stadt und Universität im Mittelalter und in der früheren Neuzeit* (Berlin: Verlag Sigmaringen, 1977).

Mazo Karras, R., *From Boys to Men: Formations of Masculinity in Late Medieval Europe* (Philadelphia: University of Pennsylvania Press, 2003).

Mazouer, C., *Le Théâtre Français du Moyen Age* (Paris: SEDES, 1998).

Merback, M., *The Thief, the Cross and the Wheel: Pain and the Spectacle of Punishment in Medieval and Renaissance Europe* (London: Reaktion, 1999).

Meyerson, M., Thiery, D., and Falk, O., *'A Great Effusion of Blood?': Interpreting Medieval Violence* (Toronto: Toronto University Press, 2004).

Michaud-Quantin, P., *Sommes de casuistique et manuels de confession* (Louvain: Béatrice Nauwalaerts, 1962).

Miller, W., *Bloodtakings and Peacemakings: Feud, Law and Society in Saga Iceland* (Chicago: University of Chicago Press, 1990).

Millet, H., *Les Chanoines du chapitre cathédral de Laon: 1272–1412* (Rome: École française de Rome, 1982).

Misraki, J., 'Criminalité et pauvreté en France à l'époque de la guerre de cent ans', in M. Mollat (ed.), *Les Pauvres au Moyen Age: Étude sociale* (Paris: Hachette, 1978), 530–45.

Mollat, M., and Wolff, P., *Ongles bleus et Ciompi; Les Révolutions populaires en Europe au XIVe et XVe siècles* (Paris: Hachette, 1970).

Monier, F., 'L'Administration et la condition juridique des habitants de la ville d'Arras au douzième siècle', in *Mélanges Paul Fournier* (Paris: Sirey, 1929), 551–64.

Monkkonen, E.,'Systematic Criminal Justice History: Some Suggestions', *Journal of Interdisciplinary History*, 9/3 (1979), 451–64.

Moore, R., *The Formation of a Persecuting Society* (Oxford: Oxford University Press, 1987).

Moulin, L., *La Vie des étudiants au Moyen Age* (Paris: Albin Michel, 1991).

Muchembled, R., *La Violence au village: Sociabilité et comportements populaires en Artois du XVe au XVIIe siècle* (Turnhout: Brepols, 1989).

Muir, E., *Mad Blood Stirring: Vendetta in Renaissance Italy* (Baltimore: Johns Hopkins University Press, 1993).

Muir, L., 'European Communities and Medieval Drama', in A. Hindley (ed.), *Drama and Community: People and Plays in Medieval Europe* (Turnhout: Brepols, 1999), 1–17.

Murray, A., 'Confession as a Historical Source in the Thirteenth-Century', in R. H. C. Davis, and J. Wallace-Hadrill (eds.), *The Writing of History in the Middle Ages: Essays Presented to Richard William Southern* (Oxford: Clarendon Press, 1981), 275–322.

——*Reason and Society in the Middle Ages* (Oxford: Clarendon Press, 1978).

——*Suicide in the Middle Ages*, 2 vols. (Oxford: Oxford University Press, 1998).

Muscatine, C., *The Old French Fabliaux* (New Haven: Yale University Press, 1986).
Mussafia, A., *Über die von Gautier de Coincy benützten Quellen* (Vienna: C. Gerold's Sohn, 1894).
Neel, C. (ed.), *Medieval Families: Perspectives on Marriage, Household, and Children* (Toronto: University of Toronto Press, 2004).
Neste, E. Van der, *Tournois, joûtes, pas d'armes dans les villes de Flandre à la fin du Moyen Age* (Paris: École des Chartes, 1996).
Nicholas, D., *The Domestic Life of a Medieval City: Women, Children and the Family in Fourteenth-Century Ghent* (Lincoln, Neb.: University of Nebraska Press, 1985).
—— *The Growth of the Medieval City: From Late Antiquity to the Early Fourteenth Century* (London: Longman, 1997).
—— *The Later Medieval City, 1300–1500* (New York: Longman, 1997).
—— *The Metamorphosis of a Medieval City: Ghent in the Age of the Van Arteveldes, 1302–1390* (Lincoln, Neb.: University of Nebraska Press, 1987).
—— *Urban Europe 1100–1700* (London: Palgrave, 2003).
Nirenberg, D., *Communities of Violence: Persecution of Minorities in the Middle Ages* (Princeton: Princeton University Press, 1996).
Nykrog, P., *Les Fabliaux: Étude d'histoire littéraire et de stylistique médiévale* (Copenhagen: Ejnar Munsksgaard, 1957).
Paoli, G., *Taverne et théâtre au Moyen Age* in *Théâtre et spectacles hier et aujourd'-hui: Moyen Age et Renaissance* (Paris: CTHS, 1991).
Patart, C., *Les Cloches civiles de Namur, Fosses et Tournai* (Brussels: Crédit communal de Belgique, 1976).
Patzer, M., 'The *Miracles de Nostre Dame par personnages*', *Modern Language Notes,* 20 (1905), 44–8.
Payen, J.-Ch., 'Théâtre médiéval et culture urbaine', *Revue d'Histoire du Théâtre,* 35 (1983), 233–50.
Penn, D., *The Staging of the 'Miracles de Nostre Dame par personnages' of manuscrit Cangé* (New York: Columbia University Press, 1933).
Perroy, E., 'Les Crises du XIVe siècle', *Annales ESC,* 4 (1949), 167–81.
——'Une émeute fiscale à Montbrison sous Philippe le Bel', *Mélanges offerts à M. Jean Dufour* (Montbrison: Au siège de la Diana, 1940), 61–70.
Petit-Dutaillis, C., *Les Communes françaises* (Paris: Albin Michel, 1947).
Peyer, H., *Gastfreundschaft, Taverne und Gasthaus im Mittelalte*r (Munich: Oldenbourg, 1983).
Phythian Adams, C., 'Rituals of Personal Confrontation in Late Medieval England', *Bulletin of the John Rylands Library,* 73 (1991), 10–25.
Pirenne, H., *Histoire du Moyen Age: La Civilisation occidentale* (Paris: Hachette, 1941).
Porteau-Bitker, A., 'Criminalité et délinquance féminines dans le droit pénal XIIIe–XIVe siècles', *Revue historique de droit français et étranger,* 58 (1980), 103–14.

——and Talazac-Laurent, A., 'La Renommée dans le droit pénal laïque du treizième au quinzième siècle', *Médiévales*, 24 (1993) 67–81.
Post, G., *Studies in Medieval Legal Thought* (Princeton: Princeton University Press, 1964).
Prestwich, M., *Edward I* (London: Methuen, 1988).
Pullan, B., and Reynolds, S., *Towns and Townspeople in Medieval and Renaissance Europe* (Oxford: Oxford University Press, 1990).
Quinones, R., *Foundation Sacrifice in Dante's Commedia* (University Park, Pa.: Pennsylvania State University Press, 1994).
Rashdall, H., *The Universities of Europe in the Middle Ages*, ed. F. Powicke and A. Emden, 3 vols. (Oxford: Clarendon Press, 1936).
Rau, S., and Schwerhoff, G. (eds.), *Zwischen Gotteshaus und Taverne: Offentliche Räume in Spätmittelalter und Früher Neuzeit* (Vienna: Böhlau, 2004).
Raybin, D., 'The Court and the Tavern: Bourgeois Discourse in *Li Jeus de Saint Nicolai*', *Viator*, 19 (1988), 177–92.
Raynaud, C., *La Violence au Moyen Age: XIII*e*–XV*e *siècle* (Paris: Léopard d'Or, 1990).
Reames, S., *The Legenda Aurea: A Reexamination of its Paradoxical History* (Madison, Wis.: Wisconsin University Press, 1985).
La Rémission des crimes: Communications présentées par l'Institut d'Anthropologie Juridique de Limoges (Limoges: Presses Universitaires de Limoges, 1984).
Rexroth, F., (ed.), *Beiträge zur Kulturgeschichte der Gelehrten im Späten Mittelalter* (Ostfildern: Thorbecke, 2010).
——*Das Milieu der Nacht: Obrigkeit und Randgruppen im Spätmittelalterlichen London* (Göttingen: Vandenhoeck & Ruprecht, 1999).
Rey-Flaud, H., *Le Cercle magique: Essai sur le théâtre en rond à la fin du Moyen Age* (Paris: Presses Universitaires de la France, 1973).
——*Pour une dramaturgie du Moyen Age* (Paris: Presses Universitaires de France, 1980).
Reynolds, S., *Kingdoms and Communities in Western Europe, 937–1300* (Oxford: Oxford University Press, 1984).
——'Medieval Urban History and the History of Political Thought', *Journal of Urban History*, 9 (1982), 14–23.
Ribémont, B., 'Arras, le vin, la taverne et le "capitalisme": Le Théâtre profane du XIIIe siècle et la question d'argent', *Le Moyen Age*, 111 (2005), 59–70.
Riches, D. (ed.), *The Anthropology of Violence* (Oxford: Blackwell, 1986).
Ricoeur, P., *État et violence: Troisième conférence annuelle du foyer John Knox* (Geneva: Association du Foyer John Knox, 1957).
Ridder-Symoens, H. de (ed.), *Universities in the Middle Ages* (Cambridge: Cambridge University Press, 1992).
Rigg, G., 'Golias and Other Pseudonyms', *Studi Medievali*, 18 (1977), 65–109.
Robertson, D., *The Medieval Saints' Lives: Spiritual Renewal and Old French Literature* (Lexington, Ky.: French Forum, 1995).
Romaine, S., *Language in Society: An Introduction to Sociolinguistics* (Oxford: Oxford University Press, 1994).

Rosenwein, B., and Little, L., 'Social Meaning in Monastic and Mendicant Spiritualities', *Past and Present,* 63 (1974), 4–32.

Rosenwein, S. (ed.), *Anger's Past: The Social Uses of an Emotion in the Middle Ages* (Ithaca, NY: Cornell University Press, 1998).

Rosser, G., 'Conflict and Political Community in the Medieval Town: Disputes between Clergy and Laity in Hereford', in G. Rosser and R. Slater (eds.), *The Church in the Medieval Town* (Aldershot: Ashgate, 1998), 20–42.

——*Medieval Westminster, 1200–1540* (Oxford: Clarendon Press, 1989).

——and Holt, R. (eds.), *English Towns: A Reader in English Urban History, 1200–1540* (London: Longman, 1990).

Roux, S., 'Habitat urbain au Moyen Age: Le Quartier de l'université à Paris', *Annales ESC,* 24 (1969), 1196–1219.

——*Paris in the Middle Ages*, tr. J. McNamara (Philadelphia: University of Pennsylvania Press, 2009).

Rubin, M., *Corpus Christi: The Eucharist in Late Medieval Culture* (Cambridge: Cambridge University Press, 1991).

Ruff, J., *Violence in Early Modern Europe* (Cambridge: Cambridge University Press, 1996).

Runnalls, G., 'An Actor's Rôle in a French Morality Play', *French Studies,* 42 (1988), 398–407.

——'Form and Meaning in Medieval Drama', in D. Trotter (ed.), *Littera et Sensus: Essays on Form and Meaning in Medieval French Literature Presented to John Fox* (Exeter: University of Exeter Press, 1989), 95–108.

——'*Mansion* and *lieu*: Two Technical Terms in Medieval French Staging?', *French Studies,* 35 (1981), 385–93.

——'The Manuscript of the *Miracles de Nostre Dame par personnages*', *Romance Philology*, 22 (1968), 15–22.

Russell, F., *The Just War in the Middle Ages* (Cambridge: Cambridge University Press, 1975).

Rychner, J., *Contribution à l'étude des fabliaux*, 2 vols. (Geneva: Neuchâtel/Droz, 1960).

Salisbury, E., Donavin, G., and Llewelyn Price, M. (eds.), *Domestic Violence in Medieval Texts* (Gainesville, Fla: University Press of Florida, 2002).

Salisbury, J. (ed.), *Sex in the Middle Ages: A Book of Essays* (New York: Garland, 1991).

Scheidegger, J., *Le Roman de Renart ou le texte de la dérision* (Geneva: Droz, 1989).

Schmidt, B., and Schröder, I. (eds.), *Anthropology of Violence and Conflict* (London: Routledge, 2001).

Schmitt, J.-C., *La Raison des gestes dans l'Occident médiéval* (Paris: Gallimard, 1990).

——'Recueils franciscains d' "exempla" et perfectionnement des techniques intellectuels du XIIIe au XIVe siècle', *Bibliothèque de l'École des Chartes,* 135 (1977), 5–21.

——'Le Suicide au Moyen Age', *Annales ESC,* 31 (1976), 3–28.

Schnell, R., 'The Discourse on Marriage in the Middle Ages', *Speculum,* 73 (1998), 771–86.

Schneyer, J., *Repertorium der lateinischen Sermones de Mittelalters für die Zeit von 1150–1350*, 9 vols. to date (Münster: Aschendorff, 1969–80).
Schultz, J., *The Knowledge of Childhood in the German Middle Ages 1100–1300* (Philadelphia: University of Pennsylvania Press, 1995).
Schussler, M., 'German Crime in the Later Middle Ages: A Statistical Analysis of the Nuremberg Outlawry Books, 1285–1400', *Criminal Justice History*, 13 (1992), 11–60.
Schwerhoff, G., 'Zivilisationsprozess und Geschichtswissenschaft. Norbert Elias' historischer Sicht', *Historische Zeitschrift*, 266 (1998), 561–607.
Seifert, A., 'Studium als soziales System', in J. Fried (ed.), *Schulen und Studium im Sozialen Wandel des Hohen und Späten Mittelalters* (Sigmaringen: Thorbecke, 1986), 601–19.
Sharpe, J. A., 'The History of Violence in England: Some Observations', *Past and Present*, 108 (1985), 206–15.
Sheehan, M., and Farge, J. (eds.), *Marriage, Family and Law in Medieval Europe: Collected Studies* (Cardiff: University Press of Wales, 1996).
Sivéry, G., *L'Économie du royaume de France au siècle de Saint Louis (vers 1180–vers 1315)* (Lille: Presses universitaires de Lille, 1984).
——'Le Mécontentement dans le royaume de France et les enquêtes de Saint Louis', *Revue Historique*, 545 (1983), 3–24.
Skinner, Q., *The Foundations of Modern Political Thought*, 2 vols. (Cambridge: Cambridge University Press, 1978).
Skoda, H., 'Violent Discipline or Disciplining Violence? Domestic Violence in Late Thirteenth- and Early Fourteenth-Century France', *Cultural and Social History*, 6/1 (2009), 9–27.
Smail, D. L., 'Common Violence: Vengeance and Inquisition in Fourteenth Century Marseille', *Past and Present*, 151 (1996), 28–59.
——'Hatred as a Social Institution in Late Medieval Society', *Speculum*, 76 (2001), 90–126.
——and Fenster, T. (eds.), *Fama: The Politics of Talk and Reputation in Medieval Europe* (Ithaca, NY: Cornell University Press, 2003).
Small, C., 'The Costs of Urban Justice: The Example of Arras, 1300–1329', in M. Miglio and G. Lombardi (eds.), *Simbolo e realtà della vita urbana nel tardo medioevo* (Rome: Vecchiarelli, 1988), 255–68.
——'Prisoners in the Castellany of Artois in the Early Fourteenth Century', *Social History/Histoire sociale*, 26/52 (1993), 345–72.
Sofsky, W., *Violence: Terrorism, Genocide, War*, tr. A. Bell (London: Granta Books, 2003).
Soman, A., 'Deviance and Criminal Justice in Western Europe, 1300–1800: An Essay in Structure', *Criminal Justice History*, 1 (1980), 1–28.
Spierenburg, P., 'Faces of Violence: Homicide Trends and Cultural Meanings: Amsterdam, 1431–1816', *Journal of Social History*, 27/4 (1994), 701–16.
Spufford, P., *Power and Profit: The Merchant in Medieval Europe* (London: Thames & Hudson, 2002).

Stadler-Honnegger, M., *Étude sur les* Miracles de Nostre Dame par personnages (Paris, 1926; Geneva: Slatkine Reprints, 1975).

Stearns Schenck, M.-J., *The Fabliaux: Tales of Wit and Deception* (Amsterdam and Philadelphia: John Benjamins Publishing Co., 1987).

Stefano, G. di, and Bidler, R. (eds.), *La Langue, le texte, le jeu: Perspectives sur le théâtre médiéval. Actes du Colloque de Montréal (1986)* (Montreal: Ceres, 1986).

Stewart, P., and Strathern, A., *Violence: Theory and Ethnography* (London: Continuum, 2002).

Stone, L., 'The History of Violence in England: Some Observations—A Rejoinder', *Past and Present*, 108 (1985), 216–24.

——'Interpersonal Violence in English Society, 1300–1980', *Past and Present*, 101 (1985), 206–15.

Strayer, J. *Medieval Statecraft and the Perspectives of History* (Princeton: Princeton University Press, 1971).

——*The Reign of Philip the Fair* (Princeton: Princeton University Press, 1980).

——(ed.), *Studies in Early French Taxation* (Cambridge, Mass.: Harvard University Press, 1939).

Struve, T., *Die Entwicklung der organologischen Staatsauffassung im Mittelalter* (Stuttgart: Hiersemann, 1978).

Sularik, A., 'The Preaching of William of Luxembourg at the Paris Schools between 1267 and 1285', in *Preaching and Society in the Middle Ages: Ethics, Values and Social Behaviour, Proceedings of the XII Medieval Sermon Studies Symposium* (Padua: Centro Studi Antoniani, 2002), 143–1.

Swanson, J., 'Childhood and Childrearing in *ad status* Sermons by Later Thirteenth-Century Friars', *Journal of Medieval History*, 16/4 (1990), 309–31.

Symes, C., *A Common Stage: Theater and Public Life in Medieval Arras* (Ithaca, NY: Cornell University Press, 2007).

Szövérffy, J., *Secular Latin Lyrics and Minor Poetic Forms of the Middle Ages: A Historical Survey and Literary Repertory from the Tenth to the Late Fifteenth Century*, 4 vols. (London: Classical Folia Editions, 1992–5).

Tannenbaum, F., *Crime and the Community* (New York: Columbia University Press, 1938).

Taverne, locande e stude a Roma nel Rinascimento (Rome: Roma nel Rinascimento, 1999).

Tellier, S. M., 'Quelques nouvelles sources des *Miracles de Nostre Dame par personnages*', *Les Lettres Romanes*, 12 (1957), 127–42.

Tentler, T., *Sin and Confession of the Eve on the Reformation* (Princeton: Princeton University Press, 1977).

——'The *Summa for Confessors* as an Instrument of Social Control', in C. Trinkhaus (ed.), *The Pursuit of Holiness in Late Medieval and Renaissance Religion* (Leiden: Brill, 1974), 103–23.

Texier, P., 'La Rémission au quatorzième siècle: Significations et fonctions', in *La rémission des crimes: Communications présentées par l'Institut Anthropologique et Juridique de Limoges* (Limoges: Institut Anthropologique et Juridique de Limoges, 1984), 193–205.

Thorndike, L., *University Records and Life in the Middle Ages* (New York: Columbia University Press, 1944).

Tilly, C., *The Contentious French: Four Centuries of Popular Struggle* (Cambridge, Mass.: Harvard University Press, 1986).

Tooke, J., *The Just War in Aquinas and Grotius* (London: SPCK, 1965).

Trio, P., 'A Medieval Students' Confraternity at Ypres: The Notre Dame Confraternity of Paris Students', *History of Universities,* 5 (1984), 14–40.

——and Smet, M. De (eds.), *The Use and Abuse of Sacred Places in Late Medieval Towns* (Leuven: Leuven University Press, 2006).

Tuilier, A., *La Vie universitaire parisienne au XIII*[e] *siècle* (Paris: Bibliothèque de la Sorbonne, 1974).

Turner, R., and Killian, L., *Collective Behaviour*, 2nd edn. (Princeton: Princeton University Press, 1972).

Turner, V., *Dramas, Fields and Metaphors: Symbolic Action in Human Society* (Ithaca, NY: Cornell University Press, 1974).

Ullmann, W., *Law and Jurisdiction in the Middle Ages* (London: Variorum, 1988).

Ungureanu, M., *La Bourgeoisie naissante: Société et littérature bourgeoises d'Arras aux XII*[e] *et XIII*[e] *siècles* (Arras: Mémoires de la commission départementale du Pas-de-Calais, 1955).

Vale, M., *The Origins of the Hundred Years War: The Angevin Legacy 1250–1340* (Oxford: Clarendon Press, 1996).

——*The Princely Court: Medieval Courts and Culture in Northern Europe, 1270–1380* (Oxford: Oxford University Press, 2001).

——*War and Chivalry* (London: Duckworth, 1981).

Varty, K., 'Sur le comique du *Roman de Renart*', in J. Dufournet (ed.), *Le Goupil et le paysan* (Paris: Champion, 1990), 167–99.

Vauchez, A., *Sainthood in the Later Middle Ages* (Cambridge: Cambridge University Press, 1997).

Verger, J., *Les Universités au Moyen Age* (Paris: Presses Universitaires de la France, 1973).

La Violence dans le monde médiéval: Senefiance, 36 (Aix-en-Provence: Cuerma, 1994).

Violence et contestation au Moyen Age: Congrès national des sociétés savantes (Paris: CTHS, 1990).

Waddell, H., *The Wandering Scholars* (London: Penguin, 1927).

Watts, J., *The Making of Polities: Europe, 1300–1500* (Cambridge: Cambridge University Press, 2009).

Weber, M., *Economy and Society*, tr. G. Roth and C. Wittich (New York: Bedminster, 1968).

Weinstein, D., and Bell, R., *Saints and Society: The Two Worlds of Western Christendom, 1000–1700* (Chicago: Chicago University Press, 1982).

Wheeler, H., 'Les Représentations de la violence dans les fabliaux et *le Roman de Renart*', (unpublished DEA thesis, Paris III—Nouvelle Sorbonne 2001).

Wickham, C., 'Gossip and Resistance among the Medieval Peasantry', *Past and Present*, 160/1 (1998), 3–24.

Wilkins, N., 'Yet More about the Tavern Bills', *Zeitschrift für romanische Philologie*, 82 (1966), 339–44.
Wolff, P., 'France du nord, France du midi: Les Luttes sociales dans les villes du midi française, XIIIe–XVe siècle', *Annales ESC*, 4 (1947), 443–54.
——'Pouvoir et investissements urbains en Europe occidentale et centrale du XIIIe au XVIIe siècle', *Revue Historique*, 258 (1977), 277–311.
Zink, M., *La Prédication en langue romane avant 1300* (Paris: Nouvelle Bibliothèque du Moyen Age, 1976).
Zorzi, A., 'Giustizia criminale e criminalità nell'Italia del tardo medioevo: Studi e prospettive di ricerca', *Società e storia*, 46 (1989), 942–7.
Zumthor, P., 'Pour une poétique de la voix', *Poétique*, 40 (1979), 514–24.

Index

21793354R00177

Printed in Great Britain
by Amazon